The Heart Has Its Reasons

The Heart Has Its Reasons

Towards a Theological Anthropology of the Heart

Beáta Tóth

CASCADE Books · Eugene, Oregon

THE HEART HAS ITS REASONS
Towards a Theological Anthropology of the Heart

Copyright © 2015 Beáta Tóth. All rights reserved. Except for brief quotations in critical publications or reviews, no part of this book may be reproduced in any manner without prior written permission from the publisher. Write: Permissions, Wipf and Stock Publishers, 199 W. 8th Ave., Suite 3, Eugene, OR 97401.

Cascade Books
An Imprint of Wipf and Stock Publishers
199 W. 8th Ave., Suite 3
Eugene, OR 97401

www.wipfandstock.com

ISBN 13: 978-1-4982-0264-0

Cataloguing-in-Publication Data

Tóth, Beáta
 The heart has its reasons : towards a theological anthropology of the heart / Beáta Tóth

 xiv + 254 p. ; 23 cm. Includes bibliographical references and index.

 ISBN 13: 978-1-4982-0264-0

 1. Theological anthropology. 2. Emotions—Religious aspects—Christianity. 3. Human body—Religious aspects—Christianity. I. Title.

BL256 T784 2015

Manufactured in the U.S.A.   10/22/2015

Beáta Tóth, "Love between Embodiment and Spirituality: Jean-Luc Marion and John Paul II on Erotic Love." *Modern Theology*. Used by permission.

Beáta Tóth, "Our Most Serious Deficiency-Disease": Reason, Faith and the Rediscovery of Sensibility" *New Blackfriars*. Used by permission.

For my husband István and our daughter Júlia, with love

I am two, subject and object;
only death can make me one.

—Sándor Weöres, from "Aphorisms"

Contents

Introduction | ix

1. Reason, Faith, and the Rediscovery of Sensibility | 1
2. The Essential Polarity of the Human Condition | 21
3. Human Likeness to God | 61
4. Human Emotionality and the *Imago Dei* | 101
5. The Unity of Love | 156
6. Between Embodiment and Spirituality | 192
7. Gathering the Threads:
   The Theological Contours of Human Emotionality | 231

Bibliography | 241
Subject Index | 249

Introduction

Dum per quaedam densa et opaca cogor viam carpere.

—Augustinus, *De Trinitate*, 1.3.6

"[A]s I am being forced to pick my way along some dense and obscure path"—these are the words of Augustine at the beginning of his ambitious project to explore the essential unity and the parallel threefold nature of the Trinity.[1] Although the issue I wish to explore is much less complex than classical problems of trinitarian theology, the path I must take in order to approach it is no less dense or obscure. It is a path not easily discernible on the age-old map of theological reflection; it consists of several faint sidetracks and lines ending in what may seem as impasses. In order to verify and update, if necessary, an old map, one has no choice but go to the terrain of first-order reflection and check the original dimensions and particularities of the given theological landscape. Here one must be prepared to leave the beaten track at times or to make one's way through long-untrodden paths where the ground needs to be cleared of the lush undergrowth of accumulated prejudice. One should also be aware of the fact that no country road runs in an absolutely straight line and so some twists and turns are a necessary concomitant of one's intellectual journey.

So what is the path I set out to explore and what corrections do I want to make to the theological map? My main contention is that the theological

1. Augustine, *The Trinity*, 1.3.6.

contours of human affectivity have not yet been adequately indicated on this map and, although it does contain discontinuous lines that eventually add up to a larger network, these lines have rarely been studied on their own and the distinctive shape they outline has hardly been identified yet. While current theology is consciously grappling with the consequences of Enlightenment rationalism and seems to be rather successful in identifying the theological contours of reason, it is much more ignorant of its own tradition concerning human emotionality and is therefore practically unequipped against the dangers of irrational sentimentalism, on the one hand, and an emotionally deficient rationalism, on the other. Such neglect affects the entire shape of the Christian stance towards faith, revelation, and the theology of love. As Michael Paul Gallagher has recently argued, a Christian vision of human affectivity is vital for our understanding of the human predicament and our relationship to God, since "[w]hat is at stake in Christian faith is not any generic openness to the absolute but a zone where incarnate affectivity recognizes and, overwhelmed by wonder, decides about the God whose justice fulfils our hopes. This is the core of Christian experience, as truth, as freedom and as a logic of affectivity."[2] The missing "logic of affectivity" is likewise a major concern for Placide Deseille, who, in commenting on the regrettable disappearance from mainstream theological discourse of the theme of the biblical heart after the Enlightenment, observes that although the theology elaborated by pietism is eminently one based on the heart, it is nonetheless incapable of developing a "Christian logic of affectivity" on the basis of purely affective principles.[3]

And here we touch upon a crucial diagnosis put forward by various proponents of a theory concerning cultural history. They all voice the common conviction that reason and sensibility suffer from an unwholesome dissociation in our world, hence intellect and affectivity are in disharmony. The head and the heart are set in opposition and one usually opts for one at the expense of the other; the two are hardly ever considered as a unified whole and the interaction between them is not conceptualized. True, there are numerous attempts at the exploration of the passional character of reason or the rationality of emotion. However, on the one hand, these accounts are typically written from a philosophical perspective and so they do not reckon in a systematic manner with the particularities of the Christian

---

2. Gallagher here interprets the theology of contemporary Italian theologian Pierangelo Sequeri, whose entire theological quest he sees as directed towards the recuperation of the affective dimension of faith and revelation. Gallagher, "Truth and Trust," 24.

3. Deseille, "Ame-Coeur-Corps," in Lacoste, *Dictionnaire Critique de Théologie*, 30–31.

theological tradition; and, on the other hand, they mostly seek to overcome the dichotomy by leveling out differences between the two sides: either reason is integrated into a concept of emotion, or emotion is made an integral part of reason. The approach I wish to adopt is neither to opt for the heart over against reason, nor to turn the heart into a kind of alternative reason. My search for the traditional logic of Christian affectivity is designed to explore its distinguishing marks and its specific function; it works with the hypothesis of a median zone where affectivity and reason, love and logos coincide and, without losing their distinctive identities, interact in multiple mediations.[4]

Moreover, I am convinced that the issue of human affectivity cannot be addressed on its own and in isolation, but needs to be treated in the wider context of anthropological reflection. Discourse on the emotions has traditionally been scattered throughout various fields of moral and dogmatic theology connected with problems such as the role of the passions in the attainment of virtues (ethics), the passions of Christ's soul (Christology), the role of the emotions in the beatific vision (eschatology), and the human disposition before and after the fall (protology). My account aims to pull together various strands of thought in an effort to outline the anthropological framework in which these seemingly disparate discourses have been embedded. Contrary to many current philosophical treatments, which consider the emotions on their own as isolated entities over against other functions of the mind, traditional theological reflection seems to have neglected the theme of the emotions, failing to devote special attention to it on its own. Such neglect, however, is only apparent since, in traditional accounts, the emotions are treated as part of a larger project, namely, theological anthropology (this is why Aquinas situates his distinctive treatment of the emotions before the discussion of virtues as a preliminary concerning the human constitution). The Christian framework for discourse on the emotions is not to be sought in separate treatises on this topic (as is the case in traditional philosophical accounts), but must be looked for within the context of theological anthropology; the study of the human condition with reference to God and creation, and reflection on the human person viewed in his relation to God, the Creator.

4. In an insightful philosophical study, William J. Wainwright examines the interaction between affectivity and reason and argues for the necessary presence of passional factors in reasoning, on the one hand, and, on the other, the necessary "critique of passional reason" since reason can be both hindered and aided by the emotional element. My approach differs from Wainwright's in that it seeks to explore the theological background to the Christian claim—acknowledged by Wainwright—that reason works well only if one's faculties are rightly disposed and also focuses on the specifically theological portray of human emotionality. Wainwright, *Reason and the Heart*.

The theological logic of affectivity coincides with a larger logic that views the human person as being created in the image of God, recreated through Christ's redemption, and destined to eschatological beatitude in the eternal life of the Triune God. The Christian logic of the emotions is at the same time hierarchical: it revolves around a magnetic centre, the root emotion of love, which organizes every other emotion according to its own logic and towards its own fulfillment. Love is seen as generating a host of positive emotions and, within the Christian framework, it is only these emotions that have a truly ontological status, negative emotions like pain, grief, or distress being regarded as merely deficient forms of unfulfilled love. Consequently, the emotions worthy of the ideal human state of happiness before the fall are thought to be ones connected with love: joy, hope, pleasure, and desire. These are also the ones that, it is hoped, await humans in the blessed state of ultimate beatitude. Finally, the Christian logic of affectivity envisages a polar tension between the sensible and the intellectual, the finite and the infinite, the bodily and the spiritual, internalizing in turn this same tension in a theological vision of love. On this logic, human affectivity is ordered towards likeness to God and eternal beatitude.

Therefore, my inquiry will revolve around three interrelated themes. First, it scrutinizes claims concerning the alleged rupture of intellect and sensibility in the human constitution. Next, it sets out to detect the theological contours of emotionality in the Christian tradition. Third, it approaches the issue of love from the perspective of theological anthropology and in the light of the findings of the two former quests. The first chapter situates the claim concerning the dichotomy of affectivity and reason within the broader context of cultural history, philosophy, and literature. Chapter 2 engages in a constructive dialogue with one specific philosophical anthropological account of the fragile and tensile unity of our human disposition. Paul Ricoeur's *Fallible Man* provides us with the lineaments of a systematic phenomenological framework for the conceptualization of the role of human affectivity and a sophisticated concept of the heart as the site of complex mediation between the vital and the spiritual, the finite and the infinite. The philosophy of *Fallible Man* offers ample food for thought for a theological-anthropological account of the human person who is ideally created in the state of innocence and historically is believed to have fallen and so to have lost such a state.

The conversation started in the philosophical mode is continued in the third and the fourth chapters as a theological quest along the lines of a theology of the image of God. In chapter three, a panoply of patristic authors—together with Thomas Aquinas as a key spokesman for the later tradition—is interrogated on the question of the seat of the image in the human person.⁵ Our dialogue with various voices from the theological tradition ends with a recent distinctive voice: in John Paul II's catecheses on conjugal love, a long process of image-theology receives a completely new expression and entirely renewed emphases with the inclusion of the body in the image of God. The fourth chapter revisits the tradition, enquiring about the place of emotionality with regard to the image within the framework of patristic reflection on the prelapsarian state of original innocence and the human predicament after the fall as it is spelt out along the lines of the biblical creation accounts. The general features of affectivity are gleaned from Thomas Aquinas's account of both human emotions and the specific passions of Christ's humanity. Here, the twofold nature of affectivity receives a forceful expression. This leads us to questions concerning the Christian version of the ancient philosophical ideal of detachment and related aspects of divine impassibility. Finally, the missing dimension of the biblical heart is summoned to enter into dialogue with Ricoeur's idea of mediation in an effort to bridge an ever-growing current gap between reason and affectivity.

The fifth chapter is devoted to the theme of love which emerges as the guiding principle of all Christian talk concerning emotionality. In this chapter the philosophical and the theological voices enter into a closer dialogue and their utterances alternate in a rapid sequence. The love of philosophy and the love of theology appear as identical and yet markedly different doublets. Concepts of love are haunted by the same dichotomy one registers with regard to the twofold nature of affectivity. Accordingly, recent accounts of love are recognized as fighting against a theoretical rupture between *erōs* and *agapē*, embodied love and spiritual charity. The body, which had been long left out of the image of God, had also been dispensed with in the understanding of intellectual love, which was regarded as alone worthy of participation in God's divine charity. What has suffered damage from such a dichotomist approach is the true emotionality of love in the intellectual mode. It is against this background that I turn to two—in many respects parallel—accounts of embodied erotic love in the sixth chapter, in the hope of finding the difference that the inclusion of the body makes for accounts of love and human affectivity. Jean-Luc Marion's embodied erotic phenomenon and John Paul II's theology of embodied love join in a last intriguing dialogue on the nature of unified one-way erotic love. Their differences

---

5. I read Aquinas as a "father of the church," whose position is not unquestionably normative, but whose ideas reveal an original and influential vision. See Otto Hermann Pesch's thoughtful classification of various current stances concerning the theology of Thomas Aquinas. Otto Hermann Pesch, "Thomas Aquinas and Contemporary Theology," in Fergus Kerr, *Contemplating Aquinas*, 185–216.

reveal a basic disparity of vision due to their differing stances, but are also disclosive of the very ruptures inherently present in the philosophical/theological tradition they want to overcome. And this leads us back to the Ricoeurian heart and the symbolic heart of Scripture: love as a curious chimera of age-old reflection might only be adequately grasped through the simultaneously emotional and reasonable prism of the heart. The Christian logic of affectivity should never dispense with a persuasive vision of the tender emotionality of love.

1

Reason, Faith, and the Rediscovery of Sensibility

This is our natural condition and yet most contrary to our inclination.

—B. Pascal, *Thoughts*, fr. 72. "Man's disproportion"

A Curious Diagnosis

Is there something wrong with the modern mind? Does it suffer from a chronic disease? Can one detect symptoms of a potential malaise? There are a few solitary thinkers who, in a bold and curious manner, claim to have diagnosed what they see as a latent and threatening illness: the modern mind has lost its balance, it has become disproportioned and it even shows signs of a fatal disintegration. One such critical voice narrates the following etiology:

> Our anthropological forebears' premature standing up on their hind legs seems to have not only set back our sensory organs but upset the equilibrium of our minds. The one-sided, grotesque triumph of reason stunted the world of our senses and emotions. By understanding our world (an impossible undertaking!) we wanted to master nature, through endless activity, tools, inventions, discoveries and finally even at the cost of murderous

destruction. But reason alone is unable to grasp all of reality. This way, standing on two feet, in an unnatural, forced, dislocated posture, we could only create a tongue that is totally useless even for the faithful description of one of our everydays, incapable for example of putting into words the prevailing (moral) tone. I can say this because I have honestly tried, for five and a half years, to keep making entries every blessed day in the columns of the Logbook entrusted to my care. Yesterday, during breakfast, I gave up.[1]

This is the voice of a Kierkegaardian figure, a veteran sailor named Captain Kirketerp, who, driven ashore after many years of following the sea and no longer having a crew to command, is willy-nilly forced to formulate his own wisdom concerning life and the world. He faithfully continues to record his daily observations in the Logbook entrusted to his care. In a playful but deadly serious conversation with his good old friend Admiral Maandygaard (a no less Kirkegaardian character, we imagine), Kirketerp muses over our deficient human condition and comes up with his own explanation of why the course of events had gone astray. Or rather, his fictitious-scientific narrative may not be meant to explore causes in the first place, but, in an etiological manner, has been invented to interpret the present; it seeks to understand a certain current deficiency in human thought and language.

However, this is a concern rather of the author himself, Géza Ottlik (1912-90), a Hungarian novelist (and former mathematician), who, as one of the finest writers of the twentieth century, struggles to find a kind of meta-language, one that is a more suitable means of grasping reality in its entirety. Written in a complex postmodern prose style, which juggles several intertwining layers of narration in a Borgesian-Joycean manner, Ottlik's short story is a sustained meditation on the possibility of the unattainable: a way to achieve a higher degree of thought despite the fact that, in his words, "we are doomed to failure: our mode of conceptualization is not suitable for this."[2] What we need, says Ottlik's Maandygaard, are multidimensional concepts that are "composites of rational, emotional, volitional, moral and aesthetic elements or units of reality"; unfortunately, however, "of all that we are equipped to understand only the rational component."[3] For what we suffer from is a curious disease, "a pathological hypertrophy of the intellect at the expense of the emotions."

---

1. Ottlik, *Logbook*, 27-28.
2. Ibid., 22.
3. Ibid.

Of course, the very existence of Ottlik's short story is telling proof of literature's magic power to transcend its own limits and realize the impossible: through a real tour de force, Ottlik's *Logbook* manages to convey a sense of such wholesome rationality at work, one that reintegrates into itself the emotional, volitional, moral, and aesthetic element and one that eventually succeeds in faithfully recording, or recreating rather, the multidimensional integrity of human experience and thought. Playful and fictitious, Ottlik's meditation and his own artistic practice invite one to take the import of his (Kirketerp's) pseudo-scientific theory seriously. Modern reason appears to be impoverished in a mysterious manner.

Moreover, Ottlik's narrative reminds us of another distinctive voice of a former student of philosophy, whose entire poetic practice is a constant plea for keeping a wholesome relationship between poetry and philosophy, poetry and religious belief. T. S. Eliot, too, is convinced that there is something wrong with the modern mind; it bears signs of a curious schizophrenia: "the modern world separates the intellect and the emotions, what can be reduced to a science, in its narrow conception of "science," it respects; the rest may be a waste of uncontrolled behavior and immature emotion."[4] In an effort to face such a complex phenomenon, Eliot too formulates a theory that, in his case, is not embedded in the texture of fiction, but is directly put forward as a tentative literary-critical theory in a series of lectures that remained unpublished long after his death.[5]

Interestingly, Eliot, who is often considered to be an intellectual and anti-emotional poet, as a literary critic devoted much of his time to questions of poetic emotion, trying to outline ways in which thought can be captured by way of emotion.[6] In other words, he was seeking to find what he termed "the emotional equivalent of thought" or "thought-feeling" that comes about when philosophical ideas or systems of belief are turned into poetry. Eliot spent years formulating this tentative theory that would explain the occurrence of "metaphysical poetry," which he particularly admired and held as an example for his own poetic practice. What he discovered in the Metaphysical poets was in fact the highest achievement a poet could dream of: the overcoming in certain felicitous moments of what he termed "the dissociation of sensibility," or in other words, "the disintegration of the intellect"; a poet's greatest accomplishment is in rare moments the harmonization of thought and feeling, intellect and sensibility. What Eliot found

---

4. T. S. Eliot, "Catholicism and International Order," in Eliot, *Essays Ancient and Modern*, 117.

5. See Eliot, *The Varieties of Metaphysical Poetry*.

6. See Beáta Tóth, "Imagination, Belief and Abstract Thought within the Orbit of Religious Emotion," in Lemmens and Herck, *Religious Emotions*, 176–82.

was not easy to conceptualize, and we see him constantly struggling to find the right words to establish a suitable conceptual framework capable of expressing his nascent intuitions. In the course of the lectures, he formulates and reformulates in various ways the same stubborn insight: "I take as metaphysical poetry that in which what is ordinarily apprehensible only by thought is brought within the grasp of feeling, or that in which what is ordinarily felt is transformed into thought without ceasing to be feeling."[7] Since the dissociation of sensibility—which in Eliot's view occurred in the seventeenth century—such transforming activity has been the primary task of the best poetry; the poet must always try to contribute to the tantalizing effort of the re-unification of the mind, for no less is at stake than the integrity of modern culture. Thus, Eliot puts forward the following vision:

> Humanity reaches its higher civilization levels not chiefly by improvement of thought or by increase and variety of sensation, but by the extent of cooperation between acute sensation and acute thought. The most awful state of society that could be imagined would be that in which a maximum condition of sensibility was co-existent with a maximum attainment of thought—and no emotions uniting the two. It would probably be a very contented state, and is all the more awful for that.[8]

Such a fissure does not only occur between scientific rationality and sensibility, or philosophy and sensibility, but also affects the relationship between religious belief and religious sensibility. In this respect, Eliot sees the main deficiency of the modern age in the twin problems of the decline of religious belief and the parallel waning of religious sensibility: the modern person is not only unable to believe certain statements about God in the way people in earlier periods could, but he is also unable to feel towards God the way they formerly could. And all this has serious consequences for the attitude towards religion. Because religious feeling is disappearing, expressions of such a feeling become totally meaningless, while intellectual formulations of the same beliefs still retain some intelligibility: "A belief in which you no longer believe is something which to some extent you can still understand, but when religious feeling disappears, the words in which men have struggled to express it become meaningless."[9]

Eliot's curious and admittedly tentative theory has received criticism for being too vague and lacking in scientific rigor; it has been said to be more of a myth than an arguable account of poetic development or cultural

---

7. Eliot, *The Varieties of Metaphysical Poetry*, 220.
8. Ibid., 220–21.
9. T. S. Eliot, "The Social Function of Poetry," in Eliot, *On Poetry and Poets*, 25.

history, and has been dismissed as a strange figment of an eccentric poet's wishful mind.[10] And indeed, Eliot's argumentation in the literary critical essays often implies more than it clearly expresses; his style is often elusive, with sudden shifts of focus, passing remarks, and curious lacunae. Eliot is not a systematic thinker and is not a specialist in the history of mind. He works with vague and undefined concepts and he is unable to give a solid shape to his imaginary theory. Even the key term of his vision, the notion of "sensibility," seems to have become useless for later generations; it has become obsolete and has disappeared almost completely from the language of literary criticism.[11] Younger critics had other important problems to solve, leaving the riddle of sensibility and the intellect unresolved. And yet, what if this half-scientific, half-fictitious, inelegantly and blunderingly put theory contains a grain of truth? Might we not need a new vision, a new narrative that retells the essential unity of the mind: the intellect and sensibility?

The Grandeur of Reason and Pascal's Mysterious Heart

In the prolonged silence a third voice can be heard from afar, from a remote quarter of the seventeenth century. This too is the distinctive voice of a solitary thinker, a versatile mind, at once mathematician and physicist, philosopher and theologian. Pascal's voice may sound all too familiar to us: "*Le coeur a ses raisons, que la raison ne connait point.*"[12] Of course, we all know and readily agree that the heart can have its own reasons that are unknown to reason itself. But do we really understand what Pascal meant by this ingeniously formulated distinction? Can we reconstruct his intellectual universe that reveals what he took as reason and what was for him the function of the heart? Much has been written on the meaning of the Pascalian heart, less, perhaps, on Pascal's understanding of reason. However, the most

---

10. For one such view see Lobb, *T. S. Eliot and the Romantic Critical Tradition*. Another example: "Eliot's famous doctrine of 'dissociation of sensibility' refers to a disjunction between the intellect and the senses, and adumbrates a rather simple-minded and nostalgic view of cultural history." "Sensibility," in Preminger and Brogan, *The New Princeton Encyclopedia of Poetry and Poetics*, 1144.

11. "After Eliot, the term sensibility tended to widen its meaning still further, until the poet's sensibility came to mean little other than 'the sort of person he is.' But in the 1980s, sensibility has almost disappeared as a critical term, as structuralism and post-structuralism have increasingly directed attention away from the creating subject toward factors inherent in the language and in codes and discursive practices. Sensibility can be said to have lost its centrality as a critical term not because changing theories of the creative process have proposed other terms, but because criticism has turned to look at different problems." Ibid., 1144.

12. Pascal, *Thoughts*, fr. 277.

difficult problem of all is disentangling an imbroglio: the relationship between Pascal's reason and the mysterious heart. It is all the more a thorny problem, since, obviously, Pascal did not construct a neatly outlined theory. What he preferred was a disorderly system that does not, however, lack a distinctive design and yet has no discursive structure. Consequently, Pascal's *Pensées* are a constant challenge for someone wishing to comprehend the "real" design of the fragmentary trains of thought, sometimes even at the cost of too hastily reducing ambiguities.

Apparently, Pascal believes in the majesty of reason that for him distinguishes human beings from the inanimate world and all other living beings. The use of reason is constitutive of our humanity, it belongs to our inner nature; one could not conceive humans without the faculty of thought for we would be like stones or brutes if we lacked the capability of reasoning.[13] In the famous metaphor of the thinking reed, Pascal compares humanity to the entire universe, admiring humanity's essential frailty but also its unalienable nobility. While the human being is set in the universe as nature's weakest creature like a delicate reed, he is nonetheless nobler than the entire universe for he is endowed with the faculty of thought; the human person is a thinking reed who is conscious of his state, whereas the universe knows absolutely nothing of its own existence.[14] Therefore, the use of reason displays our ultimate dignity: human reason is a wonderful and unparalleled source of humanity's delicate greatness. It also reveals our fundamental duty to use our intellect in the right manner. Pascal opens up a theological horizon beyond his philosophical observations by insisting that the right order of human thinking starts with ourselves and then reaches forward towards our creator and to the scrutiny of our ultimate goal. If we use our reason in this manner, we experience our essential greatness since *"pensée fait la grandeur de l'homme."*[15] Our grandeur lies in the fact that we are able to think.

What we have here is an open admission of the grandeur of reason, a eulogy of its power and strength, an appraisal of its glorious might. As Philippe Sellier has argued in his seminal study on Pascal and Augustine, Pascal is not the isolated, solitary thinker one would be inclined to imagine,

---

13. "I can well conceive a man without hands, feet, head (for it is only experience which teaches us that the head is more necessary than feet). But I cannot conceive man without thought; he would be a stone or a brute." Ibid., fr. 339.

14. "Man is but a reed, the most feeble thing in nature; but he is a thinking reed. The entire universe need not arm itself to crush him. A vapor, a drop of water suffices to kill him. But, if the universe were to crush him, man would still be more noble than that which killed him, because he knows that he dies and the advantage which the universe has over him; the universe knows nothing of this." Ibid., fr. 347.

15. Ibid., fr. 346.

but works within the tradition and consciously draws on Augustine (among others), whose insights he at times modifies and further develops to fit his own distinctive vision. In appraising the grandeur of reason, Pascal obviously joins Augustine and, through him, the entire theological tradition.[16] The comparison between the human person and the unthinking brute is also part of Augustine's repertoire.

What distinguishes Pascal's vision however, I would argue, is his own underlying anthropology that is, of course, largely shaped by the age he lived in. Pascal's human person is ridden with paradoxes, moving between the twin abysses of the infinite and the nothing. His existence is woven from disproportionate proportions: against the infinite, humanity appears as nothing, and yet we infinitely transcend the nothing. Pascal's human being is placed in a vast middle between two extremes where he hovers as an indeterminate entity, not finding any stable resting point to clutch.[17] Such a vision explains why reason is also frail and insufficient for Pascal, who maintains that the real grandeur of reason shines forth in the recognition of its ultimate failure to grasp all of reality. Reason is paradoxically at its greatest when it humbly admits of being weak.[18] Yet what is precisely the cause of reason's essential deficiency?

In my view, one can distinguish two basic arguments in Pascal's project, both of which are intended to demonstrate the causes of reason's weakness: we may describe the first as external and the other as internal. The external argument is heir to the philosophical-theological tradition in appealing to the idea of the two infinites: things that are infinitely greater than reason and those that are infinitely small escape the human intellect and cannot be known exhaustively. Pascal often resorts to this argument, illustrating it in his own manner with examples taken from

---

16. Sellier, *Pascal et Saint Augustin*, 110.

17. "This is our true state; this is what makes us incapable of certain knowledge and of absolute ignorance. We sail within a vast sphere, ever drifting in uncertainty, driven from end to end. When we think to attach ourselves to any point and to fasten to it, it wavers and leaves us; and if we follow it, it eludes our grasp, slips past us, and vanishes for ever. Nothing stays for us. This is our natural condition and yet most contrary to our inclination; we burn with desire to find solid ground and an ultimate sure foundation whereon to build a tower reaching to the Infinite. But our whole groundwork cracks, and the earth opens to abysses." Pascal, *Thoughts*, fr. 72 ("Man's Disproportion").

18. "The last proceeding of reason is to recognize that there is an infinity of things which are beyond it. It is but feeble if it does not see so far as to know this. But if natural things are beyond it, what will be said of supernatural?" Ibid., fr. 267. And also: "All the dignity of man consists in thought. Thought is, therefore, by its nature a wonderful and incomparable thing. It must have strange defects to be contemptible. But it has such, so that nothing is more ridiculous. How great it is in its nature! How vile it is in its defects!" Ibid., fr. 365.

the world of mathematics.[19] By contrast, the internal argument does not approach reason from the point of view of external objects, but rather investigates the mechanisms of reason's inner workings. We may see this argument as arising from Pascal's own experience as a scientist and relying on observations concerning the nature and dangers of a newly evolving, scientific rationality. Such rationality is necessarily discursive: it proceeds in a straightforward way, step by step, judging and evaluating every detail according to the logic of scientific argumentation, refuting counter-claims and keeping a diverse variety of assumptions constantly in view. However, to keep everything in mind simultaneously is an impossible venture; reason, therefore, is only able to work slowly, with frequent deviations and is clumsy in holding all details together in a deeper unity. Furthermore, reason is unable to account for its own first principles, the axioms on which reasoning is based. For who would claim to know what space, time, movement, or numbers are? Who could discursively demonstrate their ultimate meaning? Pascal is eager to show that discursive reason facing ultimate reality is insufficient on its own because it lacks an important dimension which precedes it and on which it is based: intuitive immediate knowledge that is open to the unknown, the infinite and eventually to the divine. In one word, it is the Pascalian heart that is set so enigmatically against reason. To understand better this strange dichotomy, we follow Sellier's advice and, with his help, trace Pascal's vision back to Augustine's account of the faculties of the soul.[20]

As we shall see, while retaining much of Augustine's terminology and basic insights, Pascal nonetheless modifies Augustine's scheme at an important point: he deconstructs the Augustinian hierarchical structure of knowledge and turns it into a two-dimensional phenomenon: the twin-poled unity of reason and the heart. For Augustine, reason (*ratio*) provides one with discursive knowledge by way of inference and deduction, association and comparison, whereas the intellect (*intelligentia*) is

---

19. Pascal writes: "Thus we all see that all the sciences are infinite in the extent of their researches. For who doubts that geometry, for instance, has an infinite infinity of problems to solve? They are also infinite in the multitude and fineness of their premises; for it is clear that those which are put forward as ultimate are not self-supporting, but are based on others which, again having others for their support, do not permit of finality. But we represent some as ultimate for reason, in the same way as in regard to material objects we call that an indivisible point beyond which our senses can no longer perceive anything, although by its nature it is infinitely divisible. Of these two Infinites of science, that of greatness is the most palpable . . . . But the infinitely little is the least obvious." Ibid., fr. 72.

20. I base my account on Sellier's own account and scattered remarks. See Sellier, *Pascal et Saint Augustin*, 107–39.

a kind of "higher reason" that completes reason's activity by offering a higher, intuitive knowledge of truths and God. Intuition then, in Augustine's scheme, is at the top part of the soul (the famous *apex mentis*), a site where the highest possible metaphysical and religious knowledge can be gained. In this manner, Augustine holds all the different types of knowledge together—discursive and intuitive, rational and affective—in one single and complex act. Conversely, Pascal—in endorsing the Thomistic-Aristotelian epistemology that works with the notion of a two-step knowledge where sense perception and primary intuition is followed by discursive reasoning—first reverses the Augustinian order and then flattens out the Augustinian hierarchy by envisioning two contrasting but interrelated intellectual faculties: reason and the heart. What for Thomas Aquinas is still a distinction without separation between two operations of the human soul—intuitive understanding (*intellectus*), on the one hand, and discursive reasoning (*ratio*), on the other—appears, for Pascal, as the forced union of contrasting and sometimes even competing faculties. While the Thomistic *ratio* is surrounded by the understanding processes of *intellectus*—intuitive understanding being the origin and final end of discursive reason's movement—Pascalian discursive-scientific reason eventually finds itself boldly unsheltered in being juxtaposed to the intuitive understanding of the heart.[21] Pascal must willy-nilly concede a certain autonomy to reason; reason and heart can certainly cooperate and although neither is self-sufficient, they nonetheless can act on their own.

Obviously, Pascal's heart is also very biblical in the sense of being the seat of intellectual activity as well as the source of emotions and the memory; it can think and feel, reflect and be passionate. It is much like the inner dynamism of a person's integral inner life. The biblical heart has, of course, a pivotal role in Augustine's thought as well, where it is, however, spiritualized, inspected in its depths, and turned into a site of encounter with God. Remarkably, Augustine does not contrast reason and heart; for him, both are aspects of the one undivided soul that turns towards God in a single act of comprehension. And it is here that Pascal departs from Augustine in one important respect since Pascal's heart does not include reason in the narrow modern sense of the word; it excludes both discursive thought and the imagination (site of the unreal for Pascal), and becomes a kind of half-intellectual flattened-out and inflated *apex mentis* that houses scientific, aesthetic, and religious intuitions and, as such, is also the site *par excellence* of religious faith.

---

21. On the *intellectus-ratio* distinction in Thomas Aquinas's philosophy see for example O'Reilly, *Aesthetic Perception*, esp. 43–47.

Heart, instinct, sentiment, soul—Pascal's varying terminology denotes the same faculty that is not slow in comprehension like reason, but is able to take fundamental decisions in a single instant, unfailingly sensing the right way and reliably comprehending ultimate truths: "We know truth, not only by the reason, but also by the heart, and it is in this last way that we know first principles; and reason, which has no part in it, tries in vain to impugn them."[22] The heart acts differently than reason; it knows something that reason does not, or rather, the heart also "feels" while reason only "knows." It seems that, for Pascal, the act of sensing or feeling has primacy over the act of discursive knowing and he places faith that feels before reason that understands: "It is the heart which experiences God, and not the reason. This, then, is faith: God felt by the heart, not by the reason."[23]

So what do we make of Pascal's mysterious heart? Hervé Pasqua suggests that heart and reason here are not two separate faculties, but that they both constitute interrelated levels of the same faculty of knowing.[24] Hélène Michon, however, argues that the heart designates the faculty that is open to a mystical encounter with God and is also the seat of the will.[25] Apparently, it is very difficult to give a clear-cut account of the complex reality of the heart. What comes to the fore in the variety of opinions is the ultimately double-faced nature of the Pascalian endeavor, which aims to maintain the traditional unity between intuitive and discursive understanding and, at the same time, is aware of the ever growing prestige of a new type of rationality at the expense of what is seen as irrelevant or useless intuition. What is at stake is the integrity of human knowledge concerning the created world and God. Hans Urs von Balthasar has words to the effect that Pascal's *coeur* is the sensory organ of the Whole: ultimate values, the realm of religion, and God.[26] According to him, Pascal's major concern was to expose human sensibility—simultaneously on every level of existence and in all possible ways—to the depths of reality. Von Balthasar sees Pascal as a thinker who, boldly facing the evolving fatal dualism between modern science and human interiority, relentlessly struggled to unite disintegrating parts of reality into one unique baroque form where opposing elements are reconciled in a wholesome tension. A typically Balthasarian vision—we might say.[27]

22. Pascal, *Thoughts*, fr. 282.
23. Ibid., fr. 278.
24. Pasqua, *Blaise Pascal*, 85–103.
25. Michon, *L'Ordre du Coeur*.
26. Balthasar, "Pascal," 172–238.
27. Balthasar thinks that Pascal's attempt is a remarkable one: "It is the

And we may add that—given the nature of the task—Pascal's achievement is both a success and a kind of failure. Pascal's heart has undoubtedly become an emblematic notion that now indispensably belongs to our intellectual vocabulary, reminding us of the insufficiency of reason and offering an alternative vision. In contrasting the activity of reason and the heart, Pascal has analyzed the act of human knowing in a lastingly challenging way. And he is certainly one of the first to diagnose and try to prevent the impoverishment of reason and the concomitant degeneration of sensibility. Paradoxically, however, in trying to bridge the growing fissure between scientific rationality and human sensibility, and in attempting to scrutinize the nature of the gap, he made it disturbingly and irrevocably visible. By revealing reason's missing dimension and making it the seat of intuition, faith, and sensibility, he also legitimated a certain narrative that speaks in terms of separation and which eventually relegated faith, in important respects, to the domain of human affectivity. In trying to complement reason by recuperating its missing self, Pascal strangely doubled what was once seen as an indivisible whole. Since the age of Pascal, and despite his reconciliatory efforts, reason has relentlessly disentangled itself from the dubious bonds connecting it to the heart and has tried to sever every tie with knowledge inspired by ultimate (religious) intuitions. And, sadly against Pascal's original intention, the rich notion of the biblical heart—the unifying centre of human knowing and feeling—has gradually waned into the thin concept of the seat of mystical emotionality, pietist religious feeling, or unearthly spiritual sentiment.[28] It is as if the biblical heart, which originally comprised reason together with volition and sensibility, forming an indivisible unity, broke up and gave way to independent self-supporting modern reason and the juxtaposed modern and emancipated, purely emotional heart.

---

attempt—which in its way the great German romantics continued—of human sensibility, employing all its resources of judgment and taste, to depict reality at every level of being without abridgement or concealment. This ideal of a heart attuned to every level of the universe—*le coeur a son ordre*—manifests itself to Pascal as the human imitation of that archetypal and inimitable consuming of the heart of God in the death of love and in Christ's eternal transfiguration of love." Ibid., 238.

28. Placide Deseille, author of the entry "soul—heart—body" in the *Dictionnaire Critique de Théologie* notes that the impoverishment of the biblical richness of the metaphor of the heart can be detected already in Thomas Aquinas's account, which makes it simply the metaphorical seat of the will; although he does not ignore the realities expressed by the biblical notion, he treats them under other concepts (such as *intellectus*). Deseille also argues that modernity changed the notion even further by seeing it as the exclusive site where doctrine is transposed in the affective mode, but it did not work out a proper Christian framework for the understanding of human emotionality. Deseille, "Ame—Coeur—Corps," 30–31.

Here the three voices (Ottlik, Eliot, and Pascal) join in one single word of warning: our present condition is indeed sickly and is not what it ought to be. The "pathological hyperthrophy" of reason seems to have shattered the essential unity of the human mind and such disintegration of the intellect has brought with it the concomitant "dissociation of sensibility." Is there still hope to recover from such an awful state? Could we remind hyperthrophic reason of its real dimensions, its grandeur that lies in the recognition of its essential insufficiency and ultimate frailty when faced with the ever greater mystery of reality? Can we recuperate the original strength of the currently too feeble heart by re-exploring its rich dimensions and corroborating the truth of its indispensable contribution to the human knowledge of ultimate reality? And above all, can reason and heart be seen again as essentially forming one indivisible theological unity?

Reason and Sensibility Re-examined

All this seems an impossible venture, given the enormous conceptual difficulty inherent in the task. However, in an interesting recent convergence between long isolated fields, there is a growing sense among philosophers and theologians that a theological account of reason and also of the human heart is indispensable for a proper understanding of the relationship between reason, faith, and sensibility. Such an account must be theological in the sense of transcending secular immanentist accounts of self-founding reason and autonomous emotion closed off from transcendence, and in the sense of directing attention towards reason's, faith's, and sensibility's ultimate ground and goal: the Triune God of Creation. As Paul J. Griffiths and Reinhard Hütter have argued in the introductory essay of a recent book, which aims to rethink the relationship between reason and faith in the Christian mode (and informed by currently often overlooked pivotal principles of the Christian tradition), reason from such a perspective must be seen as having "distinct theological contours" and a "theological constitution" in being a human property that, however, is possessed by humans as a gift from God.[29] The theological contours of reason include then autonomous reason's essential relatedness to its Creator, who has typically been considered in the Christian tradition as the ultimate source of rationality. Someone thinking from within this tradition must not be oblivious of the fact that the God of Christianity is believed to be rational and that human rationality is not primary but is traditionally thought to be participating in God's divine *ratio*.

---

29. Paul J. Griffiths and Reinhard Hütter, "Introduction," in Griffiths and Hütter, *Reason and the Reasons of Faith*, 1–23.

Reason, understood theologically, and therefore working theologically, is then anchored in the Triune God—the principle of all reason—and doubly so, for God is conceived as its ultimate ground as well as the final goal of inquiry. Reason must recognize itself as turned towards God, who is always greater than what reason is able to think. Moreover, reason, understood theologically, also involves the recognition of its fallenness, its postlapsarian corruption by sin. Reason is corrupted by human sinfulness; it does not function according to God's original intention, and cannot avoid the fallacy and self-delusion that constantly threaten reason's confidence in its own essential trustfulness. Clearly, the account of Griffiths and Hütter offers an antidote to modern secular reason's hyperthrophic hubris by re-situating it within the original theological framework from which it has too long broken away. Reason, situated theologically, rediscovers its real dimensions and becomes deflated by constantly keeping its createdness, as its outside source, in view. At the same time, it regains its long-lost dignity in acknowledging analogical likeness with God's *ratio*.

Such a theological account of reason allows Griffiths and Hütter to make an interesting move and argue for a new understanding of faith as being a specific instantiation of generic reason, rather than a more or less equal counterpart to reason. Understood in this manner, faith and reason have much in common, and, we could even say, are structurally similar. Faith too, like reason, is God's gift, a natural and universal disposition that is not self-sufficient or self-founding but receives completion from outside itself. Faith, as a special mode of reason, is distinguished by being more than a simple assent to truths; besides the intellectual element it also involves an affective component: as a disposition it requires trust, the activity of trusting in God's promises. It is by trusting God's word that faith arrives at assent to claims about the way things are and as such it also involves the pivotal affective-cognitive component of relation, that is, relation to the Creator. Griffiths and Hütter thus enlarge impoverished modern reason's horizon by placing faith—together with its intellectual-affective component—within the normal range of general reason's operation as one of its possible working modes.

As part of the same project directed to the reconfiguration of the modern secular self-understanding of reason and its relation to faith, Charles Taylor speaks of the allure and shortcomings of what he calls the secular Enlightenment citadel of reason.[30] According to the long-standing Enlightenment prejudice, reason must accept nothing from outside that has not

---

30. Charles Taylor, "A Philosopher's Postscript: Engaging the Citadel of Secular Reason," in Griffiths and Hütter, *Reason and the Reasons of Faith*, 339–53.

passed the test of its control. Taylor sees the idea of reason's ruthless and all-encompassing critical duty as conjoined with the specific Enlightenment use of the metaphor of light. In contrast with earlier uses of the image of light in Plato (as ambient illumination) or in Christianity (for example, in John's Gospel, where the redeeming light comes from God), for Enlightenment thinkers the source of light is exclusively internal to reason: it is reason that casts its harsh and inexorable beam on all that falls dimly outside its territory, checking and testing everything that resides in the darkness outside. Against such a self-sufficiently critical stance of reason, Taylor suggests that, in order to expand the restricted notion of Enlightenment reason, the idea of reason's duty to check everything entering its domain must be corrected and reason must be allowed to take openly and legitimately what it is not disposed to check. And, obviously, in Taylor's understanding, such an outside includes also what faith can deliver to reason by revelation. Moreover, what also lies outside the scope of secular materialistic reason is the volitional-affective and moral component; it cannot give an adequate account of the innate human inclination towards the good and it is also unable to provide a satisfactory answer to the question of what gives human beings their ultimate dignity. For how could materialist reason in its self-imposed conceptual limitation grasp the dignity of mentally handicapped people, for instance, who lack proper human use of reason? How could secularist human reason recognize its own dignity in those who ultimately do not fit a utilitarian philanthropic scheme? Taylor here makes an interesting point by insisting that reason insensitive to love (for example, the love that handicapped persons are capable of giving to their helpers), that is, reason that does not let itself be touched by a reality outside its critical scope, remains forever blind to a fuller and deeper dimension that is only visible for a nonobjectifying and compassionate look. It is only reason touched and moved by love that can open up to receive a sense of the ultimate ground for human dignity, something it cannot deliver on its own.

And this leads us to questions concerning the heart. While the theological tradition furnishes helpful conceptual resources to account for the theological nature of reason, the disposition of human sensibility is much harder to conceptualize in a theological manner in our time. Whereas the contours of secularist Enlightenment reason have recently been widely explored and so have become clearly recognizable for the contemporary eye, the underlying secularist-immanentist stance of the majority of current treatments of human affectivity is just now beginning to come to the fore. For too long, theology has abandoned the project of exploring the human heart and has left the problematic job of mapping the domain of human emotionality to secular philosophy. Even philosophy has been oblivious of the issue of the emotions for a long time and has only recently regained a lively interest in the subject. The recent boom of emotion theories, however, reveals the existence of curious impasses, unexpected aporias that these theories seem to be unable to resolve within the scope of their own competence and resources. What they do offer is an impressive achievement, an indispensable, newly refined, and constantly enriched conceptual framework that is suitable for grasping the phenomenology of emotions and the complex relationship between cognition and emotionality. They are informative about the connections between human morality and the emotions, the role of feeling and judgment in emotional experience and the essentially narrative structure of human affectivity. What they lack, however, is a treatment of what could be called the theological contours of human sensibility, the ultimate ground and final teleology of the human heart. Seen from a theological perspective, just as reason needs the recognition of its createdness and participation in God's divine *ratio* in order to regain its real grandeur, so too the human property of emotional life needs to be conceived as a gift received from God and as participating in God's grounding and anticipatory love. Without this, the emotions appear as ultimately arbitrary and inexplicable movements of the heart.

Recent explorations of the nature of love are paradigmatic of the impasse that emotion theory is admittedly unable to resolve. For example, Bennett Helm's overview of recent theories of love discloses at least two major difficulties that contemporary accounts of love must face.[31] As he notes, these accounts (and Helm's is in this respect one of them) typically focus on personal love (as contrasted to the analogous concept of love of objects, animals, or abstract entities) and so they omit Christian conceptions of God's love for persons and persons' love for God. Love here is understood as an attitude we take towards other persons, including romantic love. The first difficulty that comes to the fore in Helm's survey is the fact that the exact nature of love defies definition, and none of the existing partial explanations can do full justice to the complex reality of love. The view of love as a union of two persons is unable to account for the integrity of the freedom of the respective partners; the view of love as a robust concern for a person falls short in explaining the emotional depths of love, making it a mere attitude of volition. If we consider love as being an appraisal of the values that the beloved possesses or as a bestowal of values on the person by the one who loves her (making her valuable, so to speak), it is the unique and irreplaceable status of the person loved that escapes clarification. There is an additional difficulty in viewing love as emotion, namely, the fact that there is no established consensus concerning the nature of this term either, and

---

31. Helm, "Love," in *The Stanford Encyclopedia of Philosophy (online)*.

so various theories provide sometimes widely different understandings of emotion.

The second difficulty indicated by Helm is already foreshadowed by the first: there can be no satisfactory account of the motivation underlying the attitude of love, a difficulty Helm calls "the problem of the justification of love." For ultimately there is no adequate answer to the question of why we love at all. Is our love intended to promote self-knowledge or to increase our sense of well-being? Do we love without any rational reasons, moved simply by the will and our feelings? Is our love influenced by the qualities of the beloved or is it steadfast, enduring irrespective of changes in the person we love? Is love rational, irrational, affective, or purely volitional? All these questions then culminate in the problem of what emotion theories call fungibility. What justifies the claim that love is directed to one specific person as someone unique and irreplaceable? Why cannot the "object" of our love be replaced by someone having the same values? Helm ends by claiming that, ultimately, it is preconceptions concerning the nature of justification that ought to be adequately addressed. If we take justification as the appeal to general objective properties that can be shared by others, we are led back to the question of fungibility and the argument becomes circular. Helm therefore concludes that the solution to this problem "requires somehow overcoming this preconception concerning justification—a task which no one has attempted in the literature on love."[32]

So where does that leave us? Apparently, secular emotion theories run into the same difficulty that atheistic Enlightenment conceptions of reason must face: they become aporetic concerning the ultimate ground of human emotionality. As Thomas Dixon has argued, current emotion theories are atheological in the sense of taking a "scientifically" neutral stance towards theological assumptions and, consequently, they are also largely oblivious of the Christian theological tradition concerning human emotionality.[33] While they provide far better means for the articulation of human emotional experiences than was available a century ago, they are isolated from the resources of Christian theology and so cannot address questions that are only meaningful from a theological stance. And we may add that atheological discoveries of secular theories unwittingly mirror traditional Christian ideas such as the essential goodness and yet dangerousness of the passions

---

32. Ibid.

33. Dixon, "Theology, Anti-Theology and Atheology," 297–330. Dixon holds: "Our current concept of emotion relies on atheological myths and models drawn not just from brain science, behavioral psychology and physiology, but also from cognitive science, existentialist and Anglo-American philosophy, and from social constructionist thought." Ibid., 312.

that can at times seriously disturb reason's activity[34]—an idea that has a parallel in the Christian claim of the postlapsarian corruption of human emotionality that, after the fall, does not seamlessly cooperate with reason's commands. Recent cognitive theories of emotion also remind Christian theology of those largely forgotten resources that viewed the passions in conjunction with reason and saw emotional experience as a unity of thinking and feeling.[35] These developments invite Christian theology to take its own tradition seriously in the light of current secularist theories and yet independently of their atheological self-imposed limitations and immanentist biases.[36] In a theological framework, human emotionality, like human reason, is directed to God as the source and completion of human desire and the ultimate ground and goal of creation. Seen in this light, the passions, like reason, are acknowledged to be functioning deficiently, not according to God's original intention, but manifesting in various ways the condition of sinfulness: they can be the source of self-delusion and fallacy. Nonetheless, viewed theologically, human sensibility is an invaluable property, a precious means of making us capable of receiving God's self-gift of love.

---

34. For example, in a panoramic survey of the current state of emotion research, Ronald de Sousa notes an interesting development: after a euphoric appraisal of the helpful and cognitive nature of the emotions, philosophers have recently come to recognize their less trustful aspect: "we should not infer that emotions act consistently as aids to rational thought and action. Researchers in recent decades have identified a large number of cases where emotions are indeed guilty of the lapses in rationality imputed by traditional prejudices of philosophers." Sousa, "Emotion," in *The Stanford Encyclopedia of Philosophy*.

Petri Järveläinen observes that the idea of mixed feelings (love of God and fear of eternal punishment) in the presence of God has been handed down through history as an almost unbroken tradition. Järveläinen, "What are Religious Emotions?," in Lemmens and Van Herck, *Religious Emotions*, 16.

35. See, for example, Corrigan, "Cognitions, Universals, and Constructedness: Recent Emotions Research and the Study of Religion," in Lemmens and Van Herck, *Religious Emotions*, 42. Corrigan also sees a strange oscillation in the history of theories of emotion: "From the Enlightenment into the twenty-first century, the subsequent development of theory about religion and emotion veered back and forth between theologically informed analysis and interpretation which thought other grounds—and especially materialist grounds—for understanding emotion." Ibid., 36.

36. Eleonore Stump realizes such an approach by bringing Thomas Aquinas's theory of love in conversation with modern secular accounts and offering a theological corrective to their aporias. See Stump, "Chapter Five: The Nature of Love," in Stump, *Wandering in Darkness*, 85–107. Paul Gondreau too draws attention to the overlooked richness of the Thomistic theory of the emotions and its potential for the metaphysical completion of current models. Gondreau, *The Passions of Christ's Soul*, 101–34. Charles Bernard's study is likewise an attempt to see the theological tradition in the light of modern psychology; however, in my view, it draws too heavily on contemporary secularist emotion science. See Bernard, *Théologie Affective*.

"Our Most Serious Deficiency-Disease"

At this stage of my tortuous intellectual journey, I may conclude that the narrative of intellectual and emotional dissociation is indeed a meaningful way to describe the actual mental and, concomitantly, linguistic situation of our (post)modern state. Yet, what is more important for this inquiry is the lamentable fact that Christian theology too is guilty in having forgotten its own rich tradition, a tradition that has the potential to contribute to the development of a new vision where the dissociation could be overcome on the plane of a theological narrative of divinely grounded and imparted unity. Regrettably, modern theology, in the wake of modern philosophy, has internalized the growing fissure between intellect and sensibility by approaching God alternately as either *Logos* or *Agape*, or by regarding these as independent of one another, and only in rare moments as both, thereby overlooking the multidimensional depth of the Triune God who is traditionally, and also in a truly biblical sense, Reason and Love and the mutual inter-mediation of both in a dynamic, distinct, and unifying manner. In the Triune God, both human intellect and sensibility find their ultimate justification and source. Secular reflection on "passional thought" and "cognitive emotion" paves the way for the conceptualization of the essential interrelatedness of reason and emotionality. Christian thought about *Logos* and Love as being (for our perception) two distinct yet simultaneous aspects of God's internal mystery should advance the development of a new vision that does more justice to both aspects in one complex narrative. To do this, Christian theology ought to undertake the difficult job of elaborating a new theological account of human emotionality, in conversation with secular theories and yet in contradistinction to them, faithful to its own God-oriented stance and resourcefully conscious of its own rich tradition. Human sensibility should not be left entirely to mystical, spiritual, or moral theology either, but ought to form an integral part of the systematic articulation of Christian faith as such, and understood as a property that works in conjunction with reason in the attempt to see everything in reference to God.

In his *Love Alone*, Hans Urs von Balthasar attempts to realize such a unifying account when—in a panoramic survey of the history of Christian philosophy and theology—he registers the existence of two basic trends in the articulation of Christian revelation: one emphasizing God's *Logos*-character (as we might put it) and the consequent *Logos*-character of revelation on cosmological grounds, and the other stressing God's subjective Love-character (as we may term it) and seeing revelation as credible on anthropological grounds and as something that satisfies the innate desires of the human heart.[37] Against these two traditional trends, Balthasar inaugurates a "new" vision that, in fact, has always been part of Christian tradition. What needs to be done, according to Balthasar, is to read various scattered manifestations of this trend together as a meaningful third way, a way he terms "the way of love" but that I would prefer to call the way of *Logos*-Love within the context of this study. Balthasar then sets out to explore the complex manner in which love and *logos* intertwine in Christian revelation and in the mystery of the Triune God. However, it must be acknowledged that his account admittedly outlines only the formal methodological contours of the third way and does not aim to fill in details concerning its realization. Hence, it is perhaps best seen as a pivotal diagnosis and a bold attempt to overcome the dissociation between reason and sensibility within a theological framework.

Such attempts are indispensable if we want to recover from the serious deficiency-disease of our age. As the Hungarian poet Ágnes Nemes-Nagy (1922–91) makes us feel and understand, what we lack is not simply an intellectual grasp of the existence of God as our Creator, but also the emotional apprehension of this message; we need to be capable of interpreting the significance of how we feel as humans in the created world. And we also have to harmonize what we grasp about God by reason, and what we feel of God's reality in our senses and the heart. Nemes-Nagy speaks in a Pascalian tone: "Admit it, Lord, this cannot be right. This cannot be the/ way to create. To plant an eggshell-earth like ours into space,/ an eggshell-life like ours onto earth, and into this life, as an/ absurd disciplinary measure: consciousness. This is too little/ and too much. This is a loss of proportion, Lord."[38] While our secular age is capable of constructing the idea of God by means of conceptual thought, such a God remains a moral absurdity when one is faced with the allurements and the concomitant suffering present in this world. Our intellect and sensibility are in discord, and we are left with a purely intellectual vision that lacks the dimension of love; we are desperately perplexed and cannot reconcile disparate elements into a meaningful whole. Nemes Nagy, like a modern psalmist, complains: "Your existence is not a scientific but rather a moral/ incongruity. The assumption that You are the creator of such/ a world is blasphemy."[39] Her poem is a constant reminder that the neatly constructed rational idea of God, shorn of its emotional import, becomes a dreadful

---

37. Balthasar, *Love Alone: The Way of Revelation*.

38. Nemes-Nagy, "About God, Our most serious deficiency-disease," in Nemes-Nagy, *51 Poems*, 115.

39. Ibid., 115.

riddle for the modern dissociated mind, since such an idea of God, in the end, sows the nagging suspicion that the experiences of our affective nature have no interpretative value in approaching God's mystery. With such a God in view, our human predicament too becomes incomprehensible. God, as a rational construct, is suspected of being completely meaningless in the face of the suffering and sense experiences of human life: "Do you know about living with hypoglycaemia? . . . What do you know of fear? Or/ physical pain? Or living in disgrace? . . . Have you ever swum in a river? Eaten a crab apple? Held/ a pair of compasses? . . . Do you have an 'up' there where you are? And an 'above you'? Sorry."[40] And here the poem ends and the flow of poetic laments ceases abruptly, for at the end of the day, it is not even certain whom we are questioning, the living God or a figment of our minds. It is no surprise, then, that ultimately everything depends on the way we interpret the enchanting allurements of the created world: either as traps of illusion or as signs of a Love-*Logos* that in the theological tradition has been thought to be regulating the entire universe lovingly and reasonably.

---

40. Ibid., 117.

2

The Essential Polarity of the Human Condition

> As sorrowful yet always rejoicing.
>
> —2 Cor 6:10

How can reason and sensibility fit together? What would be an adequate anthropology for capturing the essential unity of our humanity? For a full-fledged philosophical account of the tensile and delicate unity of the primordial human condition, I propose that we turn to Paul Ricoeur's philosophical anthropology in his unjustly neglected early masterpiece, *Fallible Man* (1960).[1] The book was written as part of a vast project that Ricoeur named philosophy of the will and that was initiated with an impressive study of the phenomenological structures of the will, entitled *The Voluntary and the Involuntary* (1950), and followed by the two-part meditation on the possibility of human freedom and its actualization in cases of good or bad will in the two volumes *Fallible Man* and *The Symbolism of Evil* (both in 1960) bearing the overall title *Finitude and Guilt*.[2] Ricoeur's initial intention

---

1. Ricoeur, *L'homme faillible*; in English: Ricoeur, *Fallible Man*.

2. The realized volumes of the projected philosophy of the will are the following: *Philosophie de la volonté*. I: *Le volontaire et l'involontaire*, translated as *Freedom and Nature: The Voluntary and the Involuntary*; *Philosophie de la volonté. Finitude et*

was to write a third part to his philosophy of the will which would have treated the relation of human willing to Transcendence, or, in his phrasing, "the poetics of Transcendence." The planned grandiose trilogy, however, remained incomplete as only the first two parts were realized and the study on Transcendence and the will was never written in the originally projected form due to Ricoeur's growing and lasting conviction that philosophy must not mix *genres* with theology, but has to stay within its own confines, refraining respectfully from working with a concept of the god of philosophers which never corresponds to the reality of the living God of the Bible. Another reason for the abandonment of the original plan was Ricoeur's shifting interest, which made him turn away from purely phenomenological concerns and pursue a more hermeneutically informed method, one that allowed him to investigate human action as the site of a dialectic between explanation and understanding instead of the more traditionally restricted, individual-based concept of the will. This does not mean, however, that the early project of the philosophy of the will should be considered as a kind of failure. Ricoeur himself recognized that the lasting concerns of the early project accompanied him throughout his career and turned up in surprising new forms and contexts.[3] While his interest in an eidetic description of the will shifted towards the "graft of hermeneutics onto phenomenology," the broader concern animating both endeavors remained: how could one formulate an anthropological account of the essential fragility of the human condition that is capable of mediating between the, for him, equally unsatisfactory positions of substance monism or dualism?

Clearly, *Fallible Man* occupies a middle place in the vaster project of the philosophy of the will, and yet it must by no means be considered as a transitory step between the early philosophy and the later works since, in important respects, it lays down solid foundations for the late masterpieces such as, for instance, *Oneself as Another* (1990) and *The Course of Recognition* (2004),[4] both of which take up and explore the theme of human frailty in a renewed form. One can draw a clear trajectory starting with the initial interest in the operations of consciousness extended to the spheres of affection and volition (and in this manner complementing and correcting Husserl's more restricted project) in *Freedom and Nature: The Voluntary and*

Culpabilité. I: *L'homme faillible*, translated as *Fallible Man, Philosophy of the Will*; and *Philosophie de la volonté. Finitude et Culpabilité*. II: *La symbolique du mal*, which appeared in English translation as *The Symbolism of Evil*.

3. Ricoeur, "Intellectual Autobiography," in Hahn, *The Philosophy of Paul Ricoeur*, 3–53.

4. *Soi-même comme un autre* (in English: *Oneself as Another*); *Parcours de la Reconnaissance* (in English: *The Course of Recognition*).

the Involuntary (1950), through an anthropology of the finite historical will appearing in the human ontological situation of disproportion and manifested in the three median sites of human frailty: the imagination, respect, and feeling in *Fallible Man* (1960), and finally culminating in the theme of self-identity in *Oneself as Another* (1990), where the threefold site of human frailty reappears as zones of otherness: one's own body, other people, and conscience. Ricoeur considered the last chapter of this late masterpiece as a return to the central theme of *Fallible Man* where reflection on the human condition comes full circle. In retrospect, he saw his entire philosophical project as a consistent, even if inquisitively non-linear, endeavor. And indeed, a clearly unfolding trajectory can be traced: questions of the will led Ricoeur to consider ontology and the field of practice, that is, human action as suspended within the dialectic of explanation and understanding. Problems of the phenomenology of the will pointed in the direction of a hermeneutics of the symbol and even forward toward a hermeneutics of the text. The text, in turn, referred him back to the *hors-texte* of human action and questions of the will in the renewed context of intersubjectivity and the dialectic of sameness and otherness. While Ricoeur did not later return to the theme of human disproportion and fallibility in the form it was initiated in *Fallible Man,* the underlying concerns of this early work kept shaping his philosophy in many important respects. All the more so, because *Fallible Man* is a kind of pivot between *Freedom and Nature* and *The Symbolism of Evil*. As Walter J. Lowe has noted, all three books were written with an underlying concern to counter some "gnostic" tendencies in the thought of the period.[5] While *Freedom and Nature* fights contemporary trends that over-value human transcendence, the latter two volumes together challenge the gnostic drift of thought that conflates finitude and guilt. Against the tendency towards the over-valuation of human transcendence, Ricoeur demonstrates, through the meticulous analysis of case after case, that human transcendence is correlative with finitude and binding factors of human experience (such as, character, the unconscious, and birth). Transcendence is inconceivable without the finite in human experience. Accordingly, against the tendency of the conflation of finitude and guilt, he writes two separate yet connected studies (*Fallible Man* and *The Symbolism of Evil*) which demonstrate the essential difference between the condition of human finitude and actual sinfulness.

Up to the present, this early volume in which Ricoeur meditates on the ontological situation of human "fallibility," a situation of disproportion and frailty, has received relatively little attention since it has been

---

5. Lowe, "Introduction," in Ricoeur, *Fallible Man*, xxiv–xxv.

overshadowed by the later works. One reason might be the obvious difficulty in approaching the enormous corpus of the French philosopher's works, which is among the largest of contemporary leading philosophers. It is also the, at first glance, disparately rich variety of themes and approaches that perplexes one wanting to find an entrance into this vast philosophical universe: phenomenology, anthropology, philosophical and biblical hermeneutics, hermeneutics of the symbol and of the text, problems of narrativity and time, reflections on the self, ethics of human action, and many other issues are present in various combinations throughout the writings. While there are many piecemeal treatments of Ricoeur's wide range of topics, until very recently it has been more difficult to trace the underlying unity of concern.[6] Because Ricoeur's later period treats issues that are closer to current Anglo-American philosophical themes (e.g., the problem of the self), this later framework seems to offer contemporary readers an easier access to his thought. While his first period is acknowledged as already mature, it is still seen as more dependent on the tradition and less resonant with questions of the current intellectual climate.[7]

Nonetheless, the last few years since the completion of this extraordinarily rich oeuvre seem to have brought a deeper understanding of the lasting central concern which weaves the seemingly disparate threads of philosophical issues into a masterly composition. It has been suggested that the entire magnificent edifice of Ricoeur's thought can best be understood as philosophical anthropology, as a sustained meditation on the human condition in various contexts and from various perspectives: the interpretative key to the writings is nothing other than the omnipresent anthropological

---

6. For example, Dan R. Stiver confesses that he was struck by the fact that "despite his influence in various areas, there were few attempts to understand Ricoeur comprehensively. Indeed, it seemed to many that he was not offering a comprehensive philosophy." Stiver, *Theology After Ricoeur*, ix–x.

7. Don Ihde divides Ricoeur's career into three periods. The first, earliest (and in Ihde's view already mature) period spans 1950–60 when *Freedom and Nature*, *Fallible Man*, and *The Symbolism of Evil* were written. This is the time when the phenomenological approach prevails, which, however, in Ricoeur's case is always combined with non-phenomenological aspects that significantly enrich his phenomenology. The second phase runs between 1965–75 (with the works *Freud and Philosophy*, *The Conflict of Interpretations*, *The Rule of Metaphor*) and can be characterized as having a marked interest in a theory of the self and self-understanding and, consequently, in language. The third period starts around 1975 when *Time and Narrative* and *From Text to Action* (and, we may add, *Oneself as Another*, *Memory, History, Forgetting* in 1990 and *The Course of Recognition* in 2004) were written and which is marked by a renewed interest in narrativity and the self as constituted by otherness and in conversation with other disciplines. Don Ihde, "Paul Ricoeur's Place in the Hermeneutic Tradition," in Hahn, *The Philosophy of Paul Ricoeur*, 59–69.

framework which can be traced from the first to the very last writing and which connects all phases of development, making them a coherent whole. As Bernard Dauenhauer—author of an encyclopedia entry on Ricoeur—has recently argued, there is surely a considerable shift in the development of the anthropology, away from purely existential phenomenology towards hermeneutic interpretation. However, with the shift, earlier basic insights were not discarded. Rather, their implications were more comprehensively explored.[8] Taking the standpoint of anthropology as an essential clue to the overall shape of this complex philosophy, Dauenhauer has discerned seven central themes of Ricoeurian anthropology: 1. discourse and action, 2. selves as agents, 3. the temporality of action, 4. narrativity, identity, and time, 5. memory and history, 6. ethics, 7. politics. In all these fields of inquiry, as Dauenhauer suggests, one can observe the initial underlying concern to reject substance dualism, and the early conviction about the essential fragility of the human condition—both of which received a seminal early treatment in *Fallible Man*, we may add.

In response to the charge that his understanding of the human situation as fallible transgresses the limits of purely philosophical investigation, Ricoeur emphasized the clear borderline between a philosophical anthropology of human fragility and the actual theological claim of the condition of fallenness.[9] He made it clear that what was developed through the notion of fallibility in *Fallible Man*, received a different expression in the later anthropology, one less associated with theological discourse. In the later works, Ricoeur speaks in terms of human capability and the concomitant incapacity as the potential source of evil in man. The early anthropology of fallibility which was expressed through Pascalian terms such as "disproportion" had been turned, in this manner, into an anthropology of "fragility," one of essential human frailty, which results from a tension, a radical rift between the voluntary and the involuntary structures of human action. Thus, on the one hand, we see Ricoeur insisting on the essential continuity with the basic

---

8. Dauenhauer, "Paul Ricoeur," in *The Stanford Encyclopedia of Philosophy (online)*.

9. See Bourgeois, "The Limits of Ricoeur's Hermeneutics of Existence," in Hahn, *The Philosophy of Paul Ricoeur*, 550. In his reply Ricoeur argues: "I do not believe I have ever violated the rule of thought introduced in *Finitude and Guilt*, namely that philosophy can advance as far as the idea of fallibility, which still belongs to a philosophical anthropology, which I then described in a Pascalian style as an anthropology of disproportion.... More recently, I have developed an anthropology of the capable man, based on the analogy of acting, the latter circulating among being-able-to-speak, being-able-to-make, being-able-to-recount, being-able-to impute to oneself the origin of one's own action. I now see evil as an incapacity belonging to the capable man, an incapacity that does not abolish capability but presupposes it as the very thing that has ceased to be available to man as we know him historically." Ricoeur, "Reply to Patrick L. Bourgeois," ibid., 568–69.

insights of Pascalian disproportion, and, on the other, recognizing a shift away from the initial framework and the terms through in which it was expressed. Obviously, the early foundations of Ricoeurian anthropology have never been retracted or rebuilt substantially.[10]

The Pascalian Language of Disproportion

In *Fallible Man*, then, Ricoeur, borrowing Pascal's language of the essential disproportion of man, outlines a vision of the human condition. We already touched upon the theme of disproportion in the first chapter, in our discussion of Pascal's concept of reason and his understanding of the heart. There, our treatment concerned the wider context of the Pascalian opposition between scientific rationality and a holistic grasp of reality as an indivisible whole. What interests us here is the specific issue of existential disproportion which is disclosed through the account of human epistemological insufficiency as developed in one of the longest discursive fragments in the *Pensées* (fr. 72). This fragment, subtitled "The Disproportion of Man," is usually grouped by editors under the heading, "Section Two: The Misery of Man without God." Within the projected structure, fragment 72, on man's disproportion, belongs to the context of the first large unit which treats of the human condition (nature) in purely philosophical terms, that is, in methodological abstraction from the theological claim of human teleology in the happiness offered by a life-giving relationship with God (grace) and the salvific message of divine revelation in Scripture. In this manner, this celebrated fragment can rightly be seen as containing the gist of Pascal's distinctive philosophical anthropology.

In the fragments preceding fragment 72, we see Pascal rehearsing two of the central ideas: the necessity and the concomitant impossibility of full self-knowledge, and human disposition as set in the centre between the two infinites of too much and too little.[11] These five-finger exercises all playfully point in the direction of the grand theme: the idea of disproportion. The

---

10. Interesting evidence of Ricoeur's return to an early theme which was first outlined in *Fallible Man* is his late meditation on the concept of recognition in *The Course of Recognition* (2004). Here he further develops the analysis of esteem/recognition/worth put forward in *Fallible Man*, 183–91.

11. See, for example: "One must know oneself. If this does not serve to discover truth, it at least serves as a rule of life, and there is nothing better (fr. 66); *The infinites, the mean*. When we read too fast or too slowly, we understand nothing. (fr. 69); Nature has set us so well in the centre, that if we change one side of the balance, we change the other also. . . . (fr.70); Too much and too little wine. Give him none, he cannot find truth; give him too much, the same. (fr. 71)."

opening sentence of fragment 72 resumes the idea of human (self-)knowledge. The entire fragment is built on comparisons between the human person and the universe, the human person and the microcosmic organisms of nature; between intellect/mind/soul and body. Disproportion runs across all the domains of human knowing and existence since neither things as vast as the universe nor things in nature smaller than the human person prove to be proportionate to the knowing power or the basic constitution of humanity. Both in the direction of vastness and in the direction of smallness an ultimate horizon of the infinite is revealed. Pascal's discourse is cast in the language of the traditional philosophical-theological claim that had for long been used by theologians who argued for the ultimate unknowability of God on the basis of the ultimate unknowability even of ordinary earthly realities. According to this traditional argument, if one obviously fails to obtain exhaustive knowledge concerning the life-processes of small creatures (e.g., an ant) in nature, one can by no means aspire to comprehensive knowledge of God, the almighty Creator of the universe.[12]

Pascal, having had recourse to the traditional argument of the infinite vastness of the universe and the inscrutable smallness of a tiny mite, sets the problem in the perspective of the sciences and, from the epistemological arguments, draws conclusions concerning humanity's existential situation.[13] His existential vision is strikingly (post)modern; the traditional arguments are squeezed to communicate the specific flavor of early-modern experience of human frailty: "For, in fact, what is man in nature? A Nothing in comparison with the Infinite, an All in comparison with the Nothing, a mean between nothing and everything" (fr. 72). While, in the theological tradition, humanity is indeed regarded as a mean between supra-human

---

12. A brilliant example of the argument of the ultimate unknowability of created things is provided by Gregory of Nyssa in his *Against Eunomius* where he argues from the unkowability of such a small and simple-looking creature as an ant. See Schaff, *Gregory of Nyssa: Dogmatic Treatises*, 220–21.

13. Pascal's own example of the mite is structured according to the logic of division ad infinitum: "But to show him another prodigy equally astonishing, let him examine the most delicate things he knows. Let a mite be given him, with its minute body and parts incomparably more minute, limbs with their joints, veins in the limbs, blood in the veins, humors in the blood, drops in the humors, vapors in the drops. Dividing the last thing again, let him exhaust his powers of conception, and let the last object at which he can arrive be now that of discourse. Perhaps he will think that there is the smallest point in nature. I will let him see therein a new abyss. I will paint for him not only the visible universe, but all that he can conceive of nature's immensity in the womb of this abridged atom. Let him see therein an infinity of universes, each of which has its firmament, its planets, its earth, in the same proportion as in the visible world.... Let him lose himself in wonders as amazing in their littleness as the others in their vastness." Pascal, *Thoughts*, fr. 72.

intelligent beings (angels) and lower animate yet non-rational creatures (animals and plants), Pascal's mean runs across the very constitution of humanity; it affects his capacity of knowing but also the scope of his sense experiences, his entire mind and body, intellect and sensibility. The infinitely large and the infinitely tiny exhaust both the power of outward knowledge of the world and inward self-knowledge. The imagination, wanting to reach forward into the abyss, eventually runs out of resources due to a lack of sufficient concepts. All this results in a paradoxically unstable situation where humanity's frailty becomes truly palpable: "We sail within a vast sphere, ever drifting in uncertainty, driven from end to end. When we think to attach ourselves to any point and to fasten to it, it wavers and leaves us; and if we follow it, it eludes our grasp, slips past us, and vanishes for ever. Nothing stays for us" (fr. 72). Pascal registers a deep-seated inner conflict within the human predicament, one that originates in the irresolvable tension between desire and actuality: "This is our natural condition and yet most contrary to our inclination; we burn with desire to find solid ground and an ultimate sure foundation whereon to build a tower reaching to the Infinite. But our whole groundwork cracks, and the earth opens to abysses" (fr. 72). While many postmodern thinkers would readily welcome Pascal's diagnosis of the impossibility of finding solid foundations, the equal importance of the claim that our inclination runs contrary to the actual situation would likely be taken as a sign of illusory hubris. Nonetheless, it is an essential part of Pascal's rhetoric of misery, that is, a moving account of the miserable human situation, one in which the transcending inclination points towards an ideal which is not altogether illusory but serves as a valuable clue to faith in God's recreating might.

The ultimate cause of disproportion is traced by Pascal to the very texture of human existence, in the fact that the human person recognizes himself as a composite being consisting of two different natures: a rational and a spiritual part. Such a mysterious merging of two opposite natures issues in an insurmountable, ultimate incapability, a condition of weakness (*faiblesse*) that affects both the knowledge of outside reality and reflective knowledge of oneself. As a composite of mind and matter/body, the human person is neither wholly proportionate to spiritual realities nor fully attuned for grasping material things in material terms since matter cannot know itself. Consequently, humanity's self-knowledge is hindered by the same weakness; the human person is never transparent to himself: "Man is to himself the most wonderful object in nature; for he cannot conceive what the body is, still less what the mind is, and least of all how a body should be united to a mind. This is the consummation of his difficulties, and yet it is his very being" (fr. 72). These insights are also heir to the philosophical/

theological tradition.[14] What makes them specifically Pascalian, however, is the way they are summoned to support a distinctive vision of human weakness in terms of a foundational disproportion that appears not only with regard to the human-world relationship, but also deep within the human subject who is not entirely knowable for him- or herself. In sum, for Pascal the misery of humanity stems from a sheer inability to cope with the consequences of being captive to the finite and the Infinite dimensions that so curiously merge at the heart of human existence. This is Pascal's intuition, and the language of the misery of the human person, expressed in terms of disproportion and frailty, will serve as a major source of inspiration for Ricoeur's own distinctive philosophical anthropology.

Ricoeur's Reading of the Pascalian Discourse on Misery

Why does Ricoeur find the Pascalian account of human disproportion so appealing? I suggest that the answer lies in the specific exigencies of Ricoeurian anthropology, which necessitate an account of the possible site, the "locus," where "evil" can be conceived as entering human existence. As we have seen, *Fallible Man* occupies a middle position between a general meditation, a purely abstract description of the most fundamental possibilities of the human will as moving between the voluntary and the involuntary (in *The Voluntary and the Involuntary*), on the one hand, and, on the other, the actual mythic avowal of guilt and fallennes in *The Symbolism of Evil*. While the neutrally abstracted exploration of the will outlines "the undifferentiated keyboard upon which the guilty as well as the innocent might play,"[15] the hermeneutic interpretation of myths of fallenness, through symbolic expression, testifies to the innate self-understanding of the human person as being primordially captive to guilt. In between these two opposing poles there is a gap which the anthropological reflection of *Fallible Man* is intended to fill. Here, in contrast to the purely abstractive and more restricted analysis of the structures of the will, the whole of the human being—in Ricoeur's own phrasing, "the global dispositions of man's being"—are explored (in the fields of knowing, acting, and feeling) and the narrow dialectic of the voluntary and the involuntary is broadened in

---

14. Pascal quotes at this point Augustine to the effect that man is a mystery to himself: "*Modus quo corporibus adhaerent spiritus comprehendi ab hominibus non potest, et hoc tamen homo est.*" See Augustine, *City of God*, 21.10. ["The manner in which the spirit is united to the body can not be understood by man; and yet it is man."] Pascal, *Thoughts*, fr. 72.

15. Ricoeur, *Fallible Man*, xvi.

order to include the much vaster dialectic of the polarity of the finite and the infinite. It is such an all-encompassing polarity that is seen by Ricoeur as manifesting itself in the idea of humanity's disproportion and the idea that disproportion is ceaselessly sought to be overcome by a human activity of mediation. In order to explore the nature of the inner dynamics of the human person as a mediatory and mediated being, a comprehensive anthropological account is necessary, and this is what *Fallible Man* sets out to articulate.

What is of interest for us in this specific anthropology is Ricoeur's conception of the unity of the human person that is realized in spite of, or in the midst of, opposing inclinations. Therefore, it is not so much the framework—the question of fallibility and the problem of the insertion of evil into the human situation—but rather the outcome, the actual anthropology developed as an aid, a working hypothesis in answer to this question, that will form the focus of my investigations. What is the human person? And of what precisely does humanity's constitutional weakness consist? These are the questions that Ricoeur has in mind when he reads Pascal (and as we shall see, also Plato, Aristotle, Descartes, and Kant). His re-reading of these authors is animated by an aspiration to find supporting evidence in the philosophical tradition for the following two major claims: first, that in his own self-understanding the human person is fallible, that is, fragile and liable to err; and, second, that according to such a first-order self-awareness, the reason for fallibility is seen to be located in an essential non-coincidence of the human being with himself. In Ricoeur's view, a distinguished example of pre-philosophical precomprehension is offered by Pascal's meditations on the misery of the human predicament, which Ricoeur dubs the "*Pathétique* of Misery" and which he obviously reads through the spectacles of his own philosophical presuppositions.

An early forerunner to the idea of misery is detected by Ricoeur in Plato's notion of the soul as a transitory being set between the Ideas and perishable things.[16] The soul is a mixture of the sensible and the intelligible, and in this manner, the intermediate being *par excellence*. It is exposed to a system of tensions, a non-determined movement, and its misery stems from a hybrid existence: it is pulled apart by both what desire demands and the attraction of reason. In the much later discourse of Descartes, Ricoeur finds evidence for a graspable awareness of human intermediacy, even if, in his view, such awareness is an insufficiently articulated one. Descartes's intermediacy is unsatisfactory because it is cast in purely spatial terms; it

---

16. Ricoeur examines Plato's changing perspective with respect to the idea of the soul in the *Symposium*, the *Phaedrus*, and the *Republic*. Ibid., 12–20.

envisages the human person as being intermediate in space between the inifinite God and nothingness.[17] Such a schema does not do justice to the rift that the human person experiences in himself: a deep-seated sense of constitutional disproportion. In Ricoeur's view, it is against these embryonic formulations that Pascal's *pathétique* can be fully appreciated since it goes further than any of the former articulations in that it comprehends more profoundly what human intermediacy and, consequently, misery consist in. It is, nonetheless, only a *pathétique*, the tone of which is not that of conceptual philosophical argument, but one of rhetoric, that is, exhortation, opinion, persuasion. Therefore, it can only serve as raw material for the more articulately conceptual edifice of Ricoeur's anthropological thought.

In the Pascalian account, Ricoeur pinpoints a progression away from a purely spatial scheme towards the interiorization of the vexing experience of the two infinites.[18] First, spatial symbolism of the very great and the very small is introduced in the image of nature and the vastness of the universe. Next, the same spatial arrangement is seen as inhabiting human knowledge about external things. Then, the purely spatial schema of the two outside infinites is gradually turned into the interiorized existential scheme of disproportion: the infinitely great appears as the teleology of human existence, while the infinitely small signifies the origin, the nothingness from which humanity comes. In this manner, the idea of external spatial disproportion—which, in Ricoeur's view, reflects an empty notion of infinites ungraspable for the imagination—is filled with meaning when it is applied to the two existential infinites that frame human life between the origin and the end. Finally, in internalizing spatial symbolism, a new insight emerges that discloses the ultimate opacity of knowledge concerning the real significance of the human situation, originating in the nothing and tending towards the infinite. It is against such a background that Ricoeur understands Pascal's statement: "This is our natural condition, and yet most contrary to our inclination."[19] The rhetoric of misery remains ambiguous as a means used to account for the precise contours of human disproportion. However, with the key ideas of mediation, limited infinity, and transcending

---

17. Ricoeur refers here to Descartes's *Meditation IV*, where Descartes writes: "I note that in addition to the real and positive idea of God, that is, of a Being of sovereign perfection, there is also present to me a certain negative idea so to speak, of nothing, i.e., of what is infinitely far removed from every kind of perfection, and that I am intermediate between God and nothingness, that is to say, placed between sovereign Being and not-being . . . ." Ibid., 5–7.

18. See ibid., 12–25.

19. See ibid., 23.

finiteness, the stage is set for Ricoeur to construct his own distinctive philosophical account of the fragile unity of human disproportion.

The Imagination of Innocence

As we have seen, the occasion for the elaboration of a coherent philosophical anthropology is prompted by a quest for the ultimate roots of human fallibility and the search for the site where evil can be conceived as entering the human world. Such a site, however, is imaged as part of a pre-fallen state where the global dispositions of the human being are understood as existing primordially beyond the fall, that is, as being at the root of the fallen without actually being under the regime of guilt.[20] In Ricoeur's view, the task of philosophical anthropology is to explore the primordial state through an actual situation of fallenness and to reconstruct—by way of the imagination of innocence—the primordial grandeur that underlies the actual human experience of guilt as a contrastive background against which downfall, deviation, and the inordinate receive their real significance and can be interpreted. Such a primordial pre-fallen state can only be construed with the help of the imagination, without, however, being in any respect purely illusory. The work of the imagination here is not one of nostalgic escapism from the given and the unalterable; it is rather an indispensable means of understanding the possible which is inherent in the given and the actually realized. The imagination offers the freedom available in the midst of and despite a captive state of actual fallenness. Ricoeur envisages a process of complex intermediation between the fallen and the imagined primordial state. Since, on the one hand, the primordial can only be glimpsed through the fallen as being intentionally beyond the failure of guilt, yet, on the other hand, the very concept of guilt can only be constituted as failure, digression, deviation in the light of the primordial and in reference to an original state of innocence which serves as a starting point for one's understanding of the fallen. Obviously, the relationship between the fallen and the primordial is not understood in temporal terms, but the primordial is seen as offering the constant pattern and paradigm that makes the—in Ricoeurian terms—pseudo-genesis of fault possible: "I can think of evil as evil only 'starting from' that from which it falls."[21] What we have here is not two phases of

---

20. The idea of primordial innocence and the necessity of exploring philosophically the primordial constitution of the human being prior to and beyond the downfall can be found in various passages throughout *Fallible Man*. A summary of these ideas is given in the "Conclusion: The Concept of Fallibility" 203–24.

21. Ibid., 221. See also: "We have access to the primordial only through what is

the human condition, not a temporal sequence; it is rather the coincident grasp of the actual and the ideally possible through one indivisible act of the philosophical imagination.

It is against the background of such intermediation of the fallen and the innocent that one can understand Ricoeur's attempt to isolate, in a hypothetical manner, through the imagination, a philosophically construed representation of the primordial, which is for him the true object of a philosophical anthropology. A primordial imaginary condition of innocence is one without fault and yet, at the same time, it is a state of fallibility. Fallibility is taken here—in abstraction from the specific theological meaning—in a general philosophical sense as constitutional weakness, as essential fragility inherent in the human disposition. Ricoeur emphasizes on many occasions that such a primordial state of fragility is not yet fallen; it just makes humans capable of failing in the sense of representing a power to fail that, however, does not deterministically lead to guilt. Between a condition of fallibility and actual evil there is a mysterious leap that can only be captured by particular narratives, symbolic expressions, and is not open to general philosophical explanation. Consequently, Ricoeur sees essential human disproportion in terms of a caesura, a rupture, a rift, that is, fault (*faille*) in the neutral geological sense: it is break, breach, something akin to *faillibilité*.[22] French terms synonymous with *faille*, in Ricoeur's usage, are *écart* ("gap, digression") *fêlure* ("rift") and *déchirement* ("a tearing, torn"). All these terms are meant to highlight the nature of human disproportion prior (even if not in a purely temporal sense) to the religious notion of fallenness and sin. What is at stake here, is the working out of a concept of limitation, a specifically human limitation, which may be used to outline a fitting ontology of human reality, one that is capable of giving a faithful account of the disproportionate relation of finitude to infinitude in the human disposition. Human disproportion is thus simply fragility, weakness, or fault in the geological sense. Such a break or rift is a non-sinful characteristic of every level of the human set-up: it can be detected in the rational powers as well as in human sensibility and the affective realm. And this has important consequences for the entire shape of Ricoeurian anthropology which does not see a particular part of the human "soul" as having more inclination to sin than any others; knowing, vital sensibility and affectivity are all distinctively human in essence, according to this scheme, and they are all free from sinfulness, representing primordial modes of non-fallen possibility. Fallibility is

---

fallen. In return, if the fallen denotes nothing about that *from which* it has fallen, no philosophy of the primordial is possible, and we cannot even say that man is fallen." Ibid., 116–17.

22. See Charles Kelbley's explanation in "Translator's Introduction," Ibid., xiii.

essentially conflict which manifests itself at every level of human existence. Nonetheless, it is conflict that is not destructive, but beneficially constitutes the core of humanity's (self)-transcending inclination.

The Ricoeurian Version of the Idea of Dissociation

In making the idea of fault as rift or breach the guiding concept of his anthropological account, Ricoeur opts for a position that starts from the essential duality/polarity of human existence as a positive given that is the result of the ultimate non-congruence of the finite and the infinite. Thus, the Ricoeurian version of the idea of "dissociation"—while giving an accurate diagnosis of the nature of the dissociation—offers at the same time its antidote through exploring ways of mediation that are seen as overcoming the divide. Duality or polarity are not simply deplored in such an account, but are celebrated as a valuable source of synthesis and mediation in the human mediatory zone where the finite and the infinite merge. The analysis proceeds step by step through an examination of the three traditional "parts" of the "soul"—reason, will, and affectivity. All of this, however, is set in a new perspective, beyond the old framework of faculty psychology, which in Ricoeur's conviction is insufficient for capturing the all-encompassing complexity of the disproportion of the finite and the infinite. While Descartes famously connected the perspective of finitude to one specific faculty, namely, the understanding, and associated the perspective of infinitude with the will, the present analysis argues for the double-sided nature of both will and understanding and, as we shall see later, adds a completely novel approach to affectivity as also open not only to the finite, but likewise to the infinite. Consequently, Ricoeur's main contention is to step out of the traditional framework of a faculty psychology without, however, discarding altogether its pivotal insights. The central concern is thus expressed in the following question: "how can we retain the driving force of the Cartesian distinction between the finite and the infinite in man without going back to a philosophy of the faculties, without assigning the finite to one faculty and the infinite to another?"[23] Instead of endorsing the old view, which divided the soul into the faculties of reason, the will, and the sensitive part, Ricoeur distinguishes three types of synthesis, parallel to and yet not identical with the function of the former faculties: the transcendental synthesis, the practical synthesis, and a third one dubbed the mediating

---

23. Ibid., 39. Ricoeur writes: "In a sense it was Descartes in his celebrated (and obscure) analysis of judgment, who first brought this relation of the finite and the infinite to the centre of philosophical anthropology. . . . But the distinction between a finite understanding and an infinite will is not a good point of departure for us." Ibid., 38.

function *par excellence*, namely, affective synthesis or affective fragility. The structure of the book is obviously reflective of Ricoeur's specific concern, in view of the fact that the first two syntheses (the transcendental and the practical) receive shorter treatment together than affective fragility alone. As we shall see, the discussion proceeds from a consideration of the hidden potential in traditional views towards the elaboration of Ricoeur's own distinctive vision in the third part, which discusses the central role of feeling in the human constitution of disproportion.

The first kind of disproportion appears in the theoretical order, in the power of knowing, where Kant had registered a break between sensibility and the understanding. In this part of the discussion, Ricoeur acknowledges his indebtedness to Kant's philosophy in terms of thinking a divide that can, however, be overcome by mediation. So what shape does the duality of understanding and sensibility take in the Ricoeurian account? This initial duality can only be observed indirectly, in the dynamics of synthesis in the object that is effected by the mediatory third term that Kant identified as the transcendental imagination, transcendental here meaning transposed into the object from pure subjectivity.[24] It is Kant's notion, then, that Ricoeur invests with a new meaning in his own scheme of mediated synthesis.

For Ricoeur, at the core of the initial duality lies a process of scission and division whereby reflection takes place. One side of the divorce is constituted by reception in various ways in the body and in the cultural linguistic sphere of signs: reception of meaning, ideas, that is, the perspectival limitation of (corporeal) perception which accounts for the passion-like constitution of appearance within sensibility. By means of a set of examples, Ricoeur analyses the specific passive-receptive nature of the body, of looking/seeing, the primary significations of nouns and the workings of language, all of which outline for him the graspable limits of understanding/reflection within the framework of a theory of the sign (instead of a philosophy of the faculties as we saw). This side of the divide therefore represents the finiteness of knowing in the theoretical order: "Primal finitude consists in *perspective* or *point of view*. It affects our primary relation to the world which is to 'receive' objects and not to create them[,] . . . a principle of narrowness

---

24. Ricoeur quotes Kant's *Critique of Pure Reason* to the effect that the transcendental imagination is the mediator between intellect and sensibility. Kant writes: "there must be some third term, which is homogeneous on the one hand with the category, and on the other hand with the appearance and which thus makes the application of the former to the latter possible. This mediating representation must be pure, that is, void of all empirical content, and yet at the same time, while it must in one respect be *intellectual*, it must in another be *sensible*. Such a representation is the transcendental schema." Ibid., 63.

or, indeed, a closing within the openness."[25] This is what Ricoeur names the finitude of the infinite.

On the other side of the dissociation lies the infinitude of determining, meaning, and expression: examples range from naming, saying, to verbal expression as an act of super-addition to the noun of the open dimensions of tense and the additional verbal signification of attribution to a subject, and finally, the volitional linguistic freedom of affirmation and negation. All these instantiations of a theoretically limitless choice reflect the infinitude inherent in knowing, in the power of will and freedom. As we can see, Ricoeur is cautious to avoid the one-sided classification of a philosophy of the faculties; duality is not conceived here as something prior to the actual synthesis in the objective sign or within the linguistic process of signification where both the understanding and sensibility or understanding and the will form an indivisible unity of passive appearance and active expression. In this manner, the dangerous dichotomy of will and understanding, freedom and truth, the finite and the infinite is overcome in verbal expression and the objectivity of the sign. Transcendental imagination, the mediatory third term, brings about a transcendental synthesis in the objective realm of linguistic signs between understanding and sensibility. This common root of understanding and sensibility (meaning and appearance, speaking and looking), invisible in itself, assimilates to both sides of the divide and is generated by the initial polarity, where it brings about multiple mediations. It represents consciousness and a mean between the finite and the infinite. The essential features of the transcendental synthesis, then, are seen by Ricoeur as illuminating for both the practical and the affective synthesis in determining the basic pattern and paradigmatic issues for the rest of the discussion, or, in his own terms, in providing the melodic germ of all the subsequent developments.

In sum, the first stage of an analysis of human disproportion in the theoretical realm yields the following central insights. First, the Pascalian *pathétique* of misery can be meaningfully transposed into philosophical discourse as the conceptual analysis of a dissociation in the power of knowing which comprises in itself characteristics of both finitude and infinitude. Second, the twin functions of understanding and sensibility reveal the twofold nature of knowing, which has both an active meaning-creating and a passion-like (in the traditional sense of the word) receptive-affective aspect. In this manner, the duality of reason and passion is somehow mimicked within the power of the intellect. Third, such a duality is not seen as a deficiency, but is viewed as occasioning mediation within the human being and is evidence of humanity's intermediate position at the intersection of

---

25. Ibid., 37.

the finite and the infinite. In framing the problem in this manner, Ricoeur furnishes the conceptual framework for the subsequent analysis of the practical synthesis of human action traditionally assigned to the realm of the will. The conceptual triad of finite perspective, infinite meaning, and mediatory synthesis—elaborated with regard to the theoretical order—continues to play a pivotal role in the practical sphere of human action as well.

The second step of Ricoeur's anthropology of disproportion involves a move away from the theoretical field to the practical sphere, resulting in a shift from a theory of knowledge to a theory of the will. While the theoretical synthesis was viewed as a dialectic taking place in the thing, in the object of the understanding, the practical synthesis comes about in the flesh and blood human person who not only thinks, but also wills and feels with regard to the world of things and, more importantly, other humans. We register here the constant enrichment of Ricoeur's anthropological vision, which starts from an abstract conceptual framework and becomes more refined along the way, when analysis addresses an always wider spectrum of phenomena in actual worldly existence. The key triad of perspective, meaning, and synthesis is associated here with the notions of character, happiness, and respect, which form the two respective sides and the third, mediatory term within the divide.

The finitude of character in the practical realm corresponds to the limited openness of perspective in the theoretical order. Perspective in character manifests itself as practical receptivity and represents the (hitherto) absent dimension of feeling in the abstract rational perspective. The movement of the will within character—that is, desire—discloses the very same ambiguity we detected in the passive (passional) and active (determining) function of the understanding. The dynamics of desire reveals both an active intentionality and a kind of "passion" of the will that is best captured by the term "inclination." Just as theoretical receptivity is characterized by a passive acceptance of ideas and meanings that are delivered to it from a source outside of its own, so too practical receptivity consists in the will's being inclined to action, moved by a project as a goal different from its own scope. And, in this sense, the finite aspect of the human will finds itself aroused and motivated in a passion-like state where outside effects are "suffered" and add up to a mood, a feeling of primordial difference or self-attachment that the will cannot intentionally target or intend and that constitutes the affective finitude of the person. Ricoeur proceeds here in small tortuous steps in order to explore every aspect of the finitude and the concomitant infinitude inherent in the notion of character. Leaving aside details that are not directly relevant for our present scheme, I therefore limit the discussion to an examination of the key insights of Ricoeur's analysis.[26]

While character represents the limited perspective and the finite openness of human existence as a whole, the notion of happiness stands for the infinitude of the field of human desire and action in stepping out of the horizon of the world, which is still a horizon of *the thing*, and by opening it up from every point of view as a totality directed towards completion. In other words, happiness is not simply a sum total or an ultimate accumulation of fulfilled human desires, but consists in the ancient quest for the supreme good itself, which represents the idea of totality, an all-encompassing and indivisible whole. Ricoeur finds Aristotle's concept of happiness illuminating for his own idea. According to Aristotle, "what we are aiming at with the term happiness is not a particular form of transgression or human transcendence but the total aim of all the facets of transgression . . . ."[27] While character gives the zero origin of our total field of motivation, happiness embodies its infinite goal and direction. Ricoeur contrasts the theoretical field with the practical realm throughout the analysis of the notion of happiness, registering an important expansion of the horizon. First, the theoretical disproportion between speaking and perspective is broadened here to encompass the global character of disproportion. Next, the idea of totality—traditionally seen as an inherent dynamism within theoretical thought—is viewed by Ricoeur as being an essential component of the will as well. And, third, a certain division of labor is envisioned whereby reason has the job of aiming for totality and of opening up infinite dimensions that, however, it cannot inwardly sense or interiorize, leaving the performance of these tasks for the instinct for happiness. Clearly, this insight already points to Ricoeur's major concern in the book: an elaborate account of the mediating role of human affectivity.

How do the finitude of character and the infinitude of happiness come together in a practical synthesis in the human person? Ricoeur finds the mediatory third term in Kant's notion of respect, which he fashions to suit his own anthropological scheme by bringing out its hidden implications.[28]

---

26. Ricoeur approaches the theme of character in concentric circles by examining affective perspective first, then the practical perspective, and last, character itself. The section on the finitude of practical perspective too is subdivided into three consecutive steps: the finitude of perspective, the finitude of self-dilection, and the "closing" of habit or perseverance. These subdivisions make the argumentation rich in insightful detail, yet difficult to condense into a linear argument. See ibid., 72–121.

27. Ibid., 98–99.

28. Ricoeur explains: "I am fully aware here of changing the gist of the Kantian analysis of respect. For Kant respect is respect for law, and the person is one example of it. Consequently, I am using Kantianism freely by putting respect and person in a direct

Since the human person, in Ricoeur's understanding, is given primarily as an intention, a project, that is, an ideal of what the person should be, the synthesis that constitutes the person can best be understood as a projected synthesis. Such a practical synthesis comprises actual human existence as well as the forward-looking dynamism of the realization of essential humanity—characterized by Ricoeur as the human quality of the human person. In this sense, the person or the Self embodies the synthesis of reason (as the regulative and end-projecting principle) and existence (actual realized presence), the experience of which is epitomized in the moral feeling of respect. Respect or self-esteem is at once a feeling of obligation that subdues the self to its own ideal and a sense of endless desire in the horizon of possibility. Respect is thus both attuned to practical reason through the acknowledgment of obligation and also to sensibility as the faculty of desiring, and in this manner it fulfills a specific mediatory function. The mediation of respect is akin to the mediation of the transcendental imagination in the theoretical order. Just as the transcendental imagination is homogeneous with both reason and sensibility, so too respect comes about as the result of the mutual influence of practical reason and sensibility, as the all-encompassing human faculty of desiring.

So where does that leave us? Our survey of the first two steps in the analysis of disproportion yields an important conclusion. We register a growing tendency in Ricoeur's thought to think in terms of fissures, not only on the macro level of an essential duality between reason and sensibility but also on the level of micro-structures within the two opposing poles: reason is seen as having both an active and a receptive aspect and therefore incorporating the rift between finitude and the infinite. Sensibility too appears as consisting of two opposing dynamics; it is the sphere of infinite desire, on the one hand, but also shows a tendency to side with the finite obligation of reason, on the other. Bifurcation and disproportion, that is, a non-coincidence with its own self characterizes the entire human disposition in this anthropological framework. Human existence has a texture ridden with multiple cracks in all respects and even mediation between the rifted sides rearticulates and interiorizes the primal fault lines. However, despite the strong emphasis on dissociation, Ricoeur's account is by no means a pessimistic one. Quite the contrary, it aims to correct pessimistic accounts, which see in the disproportion a sign of fallenness and consider sensibility in particular as the pre-eminent site of possible evil, ultimately

---

relation of intentionality. However, in betraying Kantian orthodoxy, I think I bring out the Kantian philosophy of the person which is outlined in the *Foundation* and stifled in the *Critique of Practical Reason*, the latter being wholly devoted to the elucidation of the synthesis of will and law in autonomy." Ibid., 111, note 24.

presupposing an already fallen sensibility.[29] For Ricoeur, both reason and sensibility bear the same ambiguity of limitedness and infinity and, as such, are prior to sinfulness or guilt. The two diametrically opposed syntheses of the theoretical and the practical set the Ricoeurian stage for the final analysis of the most crucial phase of disproportion: affective fragility.

A Philosophy of the "Heart" and the Novelty of Ricoeur's Approach

As we have seen, the trajectory of Ricoeur's thought led from an examination of the disproportion displayed in the objectivity of the thing towards the disproportion experienced within the practical human project of personhood. The missing link between these two, for Ricoeur, is to be found in feeling, which he sees as having a unitive function where, in his view, disproportion becomes fully observable. While the two former types of disproportion (the theoretical/transcendental between understanding and sensibility, and the practical between character and happiness) were only graspable through the specific syntheses that overcame them (the synthesis in the object and the synthesis of respect in the person), this last form of disproportion does not radiate from a specific type of synthesis between two opposing poles, but is the synthesizing or mediating function itself, or, as Ricoeur puts it, "the median function *par excellence.*" This is why he abandons talk about synthesis with regard to the realm of feeling and speaks about primordial affective fragility instead.[30] What comes to the fore in this part of the analysis is the inner polarity within mediation itself, wherein lies the ultimate fragility of what is essentially human in us. From now onwards, Ricoeur also consciously distinguishes between the notions of disproportion and fragility, assigning the latter term in an exclusive manner to the affective sphere, where it becomes analogous with what had formerly been described as theoretical and practical disproportion. Characteristic features of the realm of feeling come to the fore in the Ricoeurian "heart," which, I

---

29. Ricoeur, returning to the underlying concern of the entire project of his book, translates it into the terms of the practical synthesis in this manner: "The problem could be stated in these terms: to rediscover, through the consideration of an ethical dualism and prior to its condemnation of sensibility, the structure of fallibility which has made this dualism possible. Such a regression could be called a reconquest of the primordial 'practical' dimension over its derivative dualist and 'ethical' aspect. Is this movement from the 'ethical' duality to the 'practical' disproportion possible?" Ibid., 117.

30. The chapter in which Ricoeur develops his theory of feeling has the title "Affective Fragility" in contradistinction to the two previous chapters bearing the respective titles "The Transcendental Synthesis" and "The Practical Synthesis."

suggest, is akin to both the Augustinian *cor inquietum* (the restless heart) and the Pascalian sensitive *coeur*, and yet differs from them significantly at the same time. The challenge for Ricoeur here is to elaborate a "philosophy of feeling" or, in other words, a "philosophy of the heart" which transposes into the conceptual realm of philosophical discussion the former symbolic or rhetorical formulations. Such a "theory of feeling" will represent the third step of an anthropology of fallibility and must be seen as the culminating point of the entire Ricoeurian anthropological quest.

Ricoeur's theory of feeling starts from the consideration of the universal function of feeling in relation to knowing. First, feeling is seen as connecting what the understanding separates: in the process of knowing, subject and object emerge as two sides of a divide where intention from the subject posits and reaches for the object of knowledge. By exteriorizing its object and setting it against the background of being, knowing brings about a cleavage between subject and object and in this manner creates an initial epistemological duality. Feeling, in turn, as the counterpart of the objectification of knowing, manifests a relation to the world beyond duality. Such a relation, as Ricoeur notes, is very difficult to grasp since "[t]his relation to the world, which is irreducible to any *objectival* polarity, can certainly be named but not recaptured in itself. We can name it ante-predicative, pre-reflective, pre-objective, or hyper-predicative, hyper-reflective, hyper-objective as well."[31] Our language, which is structured according to the logic of subject-object duality, can only express the relation embodied by feeling in an indirect way. Feeling not only establishes connectedness to the object in knowing, it also binds us to other persons in the interpersonal realm of human action and, as a whole, it binds us to being itself.

Next, as the counterpart of objectification, feeling has a complex relation to knowing. In a "reciprocal genesis," feeling and knowing explain each other: knowledge—hierarchized by the power of the understanding—imprints the same hierarchical structure on affectivity by patterning the degrees of feeling and ridding feeling of its initial chaotic state. Thus, knowing can be seen as generating feeling in presenting objects where feeling can be anchored. Feeling, in turn, elicits the intention of knowing on all levels, portraying the object of knowledge as desirable for the intellect. Both knowing and feeling proceed in such a mutual genesis where one pole is elicited through the other in a process of cross-fertilization.

And here Ricoeur pinpoints a curious paradox. The binding function of feeling is at once the correlative and the inverse of the sundering objectification of knowing. Obviously, it is the inverse due to the fact that, as we

---

31. Ibid., 129.

have seen, it connects what knowing divides; the connecting pre-objective and hyper-objective feature of feeling transcends and counters the objectification that is characteristic of knowing. Moreover, it is inverse also in the sense that while knowing sets over against the subject an objectivity of things and beings, feeling, conversely, interiorizes and personalizes the "outward" movement of objectification: "While we oppose ourselves to objects by means of the representation, feeling attests our coaptation, our elective harmonies and disharmonies with realities whose affective image we carry in ourselves in the form of 'good' and 'bad.'"[32] Ricoeur refers to the scholastic term "connaturality," to the effect that scholastic philosophy already saw a bond of mutual coaptation of the human person to goods that are suitable for him and things that are bad and do not suit him. Inherent in the idea of connaturality is thus the essential mutual attunement of knowing and feeling.

And yet, the binding function of feeling would not be possible without a movement that is correlative with the polarity of knowing. In overcoming the objectivizing gap, feeling interiorizes this gap; in adhering to the duality of knowing, feeling mimics the same epistemological duality. This is the case because feeling, too, like knowing, is intentional; it is associated with an object such as the loveable or the hateful. Such feeling-objects, however, lack the epistemologically posited existence of the objects of knowing; they are no more than the intentional correlates of the objects objectified by knowing. Nonetheless, such a dynamics parallels the intentional trajectory of knowing and represents the outward movement and transcending aim of feeling, establishing thereby one side of a divorce. On the other side lies the inward movement of feeling inasmuch as it registers the way in which the person is inwardly affected by the qualities that are "felt" to attach themselves to, or are attached to objects (or other persons, the world, that is, being as such). Ricoeur identifies this two-way dynamic as a paradox or an aporia: "an intention and an affection coincide in the same experience, a transcending aim and the revelation of an inwardness."[33] This mysterious bifurcation of feeling as, on the one hand, a mimetic repetition of the intentionality of

---

32. Ibid., 133.

33. Ibid., 127. See also: "We can see why feeling, thus intermingled with the adventure of knowledge and objectivity, must present to reflection the paradoxical intentional texture we described. For it is *on* the things elaborated by the work of objectification that feeling projects its affective correlates, its felt qualities: the lovable and the hateful, the desirable and the loathsome, the sad and the joyous; thus it seems to play the game of the object. But since these qualities are not objects facing a subject but the intentional expression of an undivided bond with the world, feeling appears at the same time as a coloring of the soul, as an affection: it is the landscape which, in turn, is the sign and cipher of my inwardness." Ibid., 134.

theoretical reflection through the creation of the feeling-correlate of objects of knowing and, on the other, an inward-turning affection that registers and gives expression to the inner disposition of the self in relation to the world, is at once analogous to the bifurcation displayed by reflection, but also runs counter to it. In other words, the paradox of feeling boils down to the following question: "How can the same experience *designate* a thing-quality and, through this thing-quality, manifest, express and reveal the inwardness of an I?"[34] Ultimately, feeling that binds is at the same time feeling split in two; the unity of feeling is not a simple homogeneous unity, it contains an inner tension in spite of, or rather, on account of, its binding function. This is the recognition that forms the central tenet of Ricoeur's reflection on the human person's affective fragility. The division inherent in feeling, or in other words, the initial polarity of feeling, culminates in a site of affective disproportion, a locus of affective mediation, a part of the self that Ricoeur names the heart.

Ricoeur sees an archetypal expression of his own notion of the heart in what Plato calls *thumos* when he speaks about the parts of the soul.[35] On Ricoeur's exegesis, the half-mythical, half-philosophical understanding of the Platonic *thumos* envisions an enigmatic, ambiguous power of the soul set between reason and desire and undergoing double attraction from both the reflective and the desiring powers. Plato's description of the soul in Book IV of the *Republic*, as Ricoeur points out, is dominated by the idea of unstable movement and a system of tensions that culminate in the median power of the *thumos*, which is not so much a mean, but rather a mixture or "*mélange*" of reason and desire: it sides both with reason (in the form of indignation and endurance) and it also sides with desire (in the form of irritation and fury). Ricoeur sees in this description of the soul a significant alternative to the more static Platonian account in a previous section of Book 4 of the *Republic* where the soul is likened to the three orders of the city: rulers, auxiliaries, and craftsmen. What is missing from the static political symbol of the soul is the dynamism of the soul, that is, its unity in the movement towards the Ideas and the Good. By contrast, in the dynamic *thumos*, Ricoeur welcomes a versatile force that occupies a middle position between sensible desire (*epithumia*) and reason's specific desire (*erōs*) and, in this manner, forms a kind of "affective node," constituting the field of human feeling *par excellence*. Therefore, Ricoeur's key contention is to transpose

---

34. Ibid., 129.

35. Ricoeur refers to Plato throughout *Fallible Man*. More discursive passages concerning Plato's *thumos* are in the sections 12–19, 138–41, and 161–71.

Plato's intuition into the mode of philosophical reflection by working out a modern theory of feeling where *thumos* as the "heart" assumes a pivotal role.

Why is the notion of *thumos* so illuminating for Ricoeur? I think that it is important on two counts. First, *thumos* epitomizes the duality we have pinpointed above with regard to feeling, where feeling was seen as interiorizing the duality of reason and sensibility. Just as the Platonian *thumos* is capable of binding reason and desire by way of assimilating itself with one or the other, so the Ricoeurian heart is pulled by the two contrary attractions of reflective intentionality and affective inwardness. Second, and more importantly, from this first duality, which is the continuation of the theoretical duality of knowing and receiving in the field of feeling, Ricoeur shifts to a more fundamental duality, which he detects as lying at the core of the human heart. In fact, he seems to trace both the reflective and the affective dualities back to a primordial duality within our humanity prior to its manifestation in the theoretical, practical, or affective orders. Plato's *thumos* offers him in this respect a valuable intuition to the effect that the unity of the human soul is constituted through an essential polarity in a dynamic process. Ricoeur's heart, in turn, both symbolizes and realizes the specific nature of human affectivity, which is for him not simple but dual right from the outset.

Wherein, then, lies the specific duality of human affectivity, epitomized by the human heart? Ricoeur's working hypothesis is that affectivity itself veers between two extremities: vital affectivity or desire (what in Plato's term was *epithumia*) and spiritual affectivity (*erōs* for Plato), or, in other words, between vital desire and intellectual love. This initial polarity determines the entire outlook of specifically human affectivity and has important consequences for the function of the Ricoeurian heart. As we saw in the case of the theoretical and the practical syntheses, Ricoeur proceeds first by an analysis of the two opposing poles (pleasure and happiness, corresponding to character and happiness in the practical order) and from this he derives the characteristics of the mediation, in this case the "restless" heart, that is, "the fragile moment par excellence."[36]

Human affectivity consists in the tensile unity of two opposing movements. At one extreme we find sensible desire (Plato's *epithumia*), which is directed so as to terminate in pleasure. Pleasure is the finite pole of affectivity

---

36. Ibid., 124. Ricoeur describes his itinerary in the following way: "Our path is therefore clear: First we will proceed to the extremes—ἐπιθυμία [*epithumia*] and ἔρως [*erōs*]—in order to understand the range of feeling through the image of that of reason. Then we will come back to the middle term—θυμός [*thumos*]—in order to reach an understanding of the whole of man's fragility through that of feeling." Ibid., 139.

in the same way as character was the finite closing off, or a perspectival narrowness, of happiness in the practical order. The same procedure that disclosed the finitude of point of view in both the theoretical and the practical orders, reveals the finitude of pleasure in the affective order. While the narrowness of perspective becomes visible against a background of infinite horizon, the finitude of pleasure is understood as pleasure against the totality of the transgressing movement of ultimate happiness. Ricoeur sees in this phenomenon a sign of the hidden potential of feeling to relate itself to pleasure in a pre-reflective manner in the form of "second-degree feelings": "I can suffer from enjoying and rejoice in suffering. . . . This affective doubling ushers in and begins a kind of immanent critique of the principle of pleasure, quietly worked upon by the principle of happiness."[37] The finitude of pleasure can best be understood in terms of its partial perfection (in the instant) against the horizon of the whole; seen in the light of the totalizing aim of happiness, pleasure is happiness and perfection in the transitory moment. The finitude of pleasure also accentuates our bodily nature, our organic rootedness in the world. Pleasure binds us to life; "[i]t magnifies the dilection with which I cherish the life which passes through me and this center of perspective that I am."[38]

Pleasure as "the instantaneous perfection of life," for Ricoeur, is "primordial enjoyment" and, as such, belongs to our essential humanity. We find him carefully distinguishing the "innocent" primordial form of pleasure, which always keeps the wider horizon of happiness in view, and pleasure as deviation from the initial spontaneous enjoyment of living where the horizon gets closed off and pleasure becomes a substantive, an end in itself, and one loses sight of the activity that is its source and transgressing goal. Here Ricoeur takes Aristotle as his guide. In *The Nichomachean Ethics*, the latter highlights the close connection between pleasure, activity, and the good life: "Pleasure perfects activities and consequently the life to which one aspires."[39] When pleasure gets separated from the dimension of the overall life-project, then it becomes static and is imprisoned in the instant; it hinders further activity and petrifies into a false totality. It is only in its distorted form that pleasure occasions evil as pleasure sealed off from the dynamics of life and ultimate happiness.

At the other extreme of the opposing movements that constitute human affectivity, there is spiritual desire or intellectual love (*erōs* for Plato), which aims at happiness. While pleasure stood for the finite moment of

---

37. Ibid., 141.
38. Ibid., 143.
39. Aristotle, *The Nichomachean Ethics*, 10, 1175a, quoted ibid., 145., note 6.

human affectivity, happiness comprises aspects of infinitude. The principle of happiness is in seamless continuity with the principle of pleasure: happiness retains the enjoyment aspect of pleasure, but instead of finding it in the fleeting moment, it restores the dynamism of activity that is directed at the supreme good, the supremely pleasant. In this sense, happiness includes a "suspension of pleasure" in the instant in order to reach "the most excellent form of pleasure itself," that is, happiness. Ricoeur finds evidence in Plato's and Aristotle's thought for the intuition that, in happiness, pleasure is hierarchized toward the supremely pleasant and that the drive to retain the pleasure encapsulated in the instant is countered by the opening up of momentary pleasure to a final lasting totality. What Ricoeur wants to stress is that happiness is pleasure in its most genuine form. It is the highest degree of pleasure in the context of the ontological destination of human desire; it is the fulfillment of both vital feelings and spiritual love. The infinitude of happiness is revealed by the existence of "spiritual" feelings, which transcend the scope of finite satisfaction. Our fundamental attachment to existence as Eros is expressed through the schematization of ontological feeling which houses feelings in the noetic realm, far-removed from what finds satisfaction in the instant. Ricoeur distinguishes two forms of fundamental Eros: *philia*, that is, "inter-human participation in the various forms of a 'We,'" on the one hand, and "participation in tasks of supra-personal works that are 'Ideas,'" on the other.[40] The finite and the infinite, the vital and the spiritual, are ultimately intermingled in the human quest for pleasure and happiness. The symbolic organ that regulates both aspirations and becomes therefore the source of the human person's affective fragility is the human heart.

As we have seen, *thumos*, the heart is the "median region" of affectivity. Contrary to the implicit mediation of the transcendental imagination—which was not in itself detectable, but was grasped only in the synthesis of the object—the mediation of the *thumos* is clearly experienced in itself as conflict in the affective realm. The conflict dramatized in the heart is the reflection of the duality that is overcome in the synthesis of the object in the theoretical order. The conflict of the heart is due to the fact that human affectivity is caught up in the initial dialectic of two affectivities: the vital and the intellectual, the sensible desire of pleasure and the intellectual desire of happiness, in other words, the affectivity belonging to living (*bios*) and the affectivity attached to thinking (*logos*). This median region is crucial for Ricoeur as the site where the self is constituted (and we know how important a role the self plays in his later meditations). It is the heart where the multiple transitions between the vital and the spiritual take place; therefore,

---

40. Ibid., 156.

it is a site of restless quest and endless pursuit. The mediation of the heart is never complete; it displays a constant oscillation between the finitude of pleasure and the infinitude of happiness, and the merging of these two aspirations results in an unstable balance that always has a "note of indefiniteness." From this analysis of the *thumos*, Ricoeur concludes that conflict is a primordial dimension of humanity's constitution; the human person is a fragile synthesis mediated through an essential polarity. The ultimate disproportion of the vital and the spiritual is thus epitomized in the curious symbolic organ of the heart.

Throughout his account, mostly in scattered statements, Ricoeur himself indicates the points where his position goes against the grain of traditional interpretations. I see them as crystallizing around two major issues, both of which are closely interrelated. The first one, which I shall call the problem of fallenness, has already been adumbrated in the foregoing discussion. As we have seen, in an attempt to trace the outlines of the cause of human fallibility, Ricoeur imaginatively reaches beyond actual fallenness and construes the primordial characteristics of the "innocent," essential human disposition, which is not fallen and yet bears the mark of fallibility as fragility. The fallen and the fallible explain each other in a complex process of cross-reference where the primordial furnishes the pattern and paradigm against which the deviation of the fallen can be comprehended. What comes to the fore in such an analysis is the specific nature of our humanity. Applied to the issue of human affectivity, such a quest culminates in the problem of the nature of vital desire, namely, the question of whether the drives of sensible and corporeally determined desire must be viewed as fallen and sinful right from the outset or whether its primordial and specifically human grandeur can be reconnoitered through an actual situation of fallenness.

Ricoeur's position challenges two traditional solutions to this problem. One, the Thomistic scheme, avoids the pitfall of considering sensible desire as sinful at the cost of relegating vital affectivity to the animal nature in man, which is seen in this framework as showing an essential continuity with bodily materiality. The other extreme, Kant's anthropology, starts from the fallen forms of specifically human passions (possession, domination, and honor) and describes them in terms of their inherent distortion as they appear in history. For Kant, *Habsucht*, *Herrschsucht*, and *Ersucht* are all rooted in the vital human desire of greed and egotism; they cannot be extricated from the texture of evil woven into history and culture. Although Kant avoids in this manner the natural fallacy of Thomas Aquinas (that is, the attribution of human vital affectivity to the animal nature of man), he at the same time commits what we could term the cultural fallacy in seeing fallen tendencies in neutral natural drives. That is why Ricoeur, wishing to counter these two opposing fallacies, argues, on the one hand, against Aquinas, for the distinctively human character of both vital and intellectual affectivities and the essential non-continuity of human pleasure with animal satisfaction, and, on the other, contests Kant's pessimistic anthropology, which is unable to see the primordial grandeur in specifically human affectivity. As we have seen, Ricoeur re-reads Plato and Aristotle in order to find support for his own claim that sensible pleasure is part and parcel of the dynamism towards the totality of spiritual happiness; vital pleasure is not closed-up satisfaction reduced to the instant, but an anticipation and partial realization of the highest form of pleasure: happiness. The distorted forms of pleasure-seeking and the mistaken human effort to idolize vital pleasure as if it could yield ultimate happiness, do not disqualify the fundamental claim that vital desire is a valuable and constructive component of our essential humanity. Ricoeur's own elaboration of Kant's triad of human passions (possession, domination, and honor) is meant to correct a vision of fallenness and is destined to demonstrate the beneficial intermingling of the vital and the intellectual in the realm of feeling, termed by him *thumos*. These "*thumic* quests," for Ricoeur, are revelatory of the essential goodness of human affectivity beyond and "prior" to fallenness.

The second issue is already implied by the first. I shall call it the issue of the uniqueness of human affectivity. Throughout *Fallible Man*, Ricoeur makes a powerful case for the essential discontinuity between human and animal affectivities. It is all the more interesting because such a stance seems to challenge not only traditional views, but also some modern theories of the emotions. Ricoeur makes clear, however, that the hypothesis he is working with differs from both old and new assumptions: "Man's humanity is not reached by adding one more stratum to the basic substratum of tendencies (and affective states) which are assumed to be common to animal and man. Man's humanity is that discrepancy in levels, that initial polarity, that divergence of affective tension between the extremities of which is placed the 'heart.'"[41] Obviously, this statement does not question an essential biological continuity between human feelings and animal sensitivity. What it stresses, though, is the ontological specificity of human affectivity, which cannot be understood from the perspective of simple biological continuity or a naturalistic understanding of our bodiliness; in his view, the human situation radically differs from the animal environment.

Wherein, then, lies the specificity of human affectivity? If, in a traditional manner, we simply add to the basic substratum of vital desire—seen as in common with the animal world—the extra human stratum of spiritual/

---

41. Ibid., 140.

intellectual/ontological feelings, then we must ascribe all that is specifically human to this added extra layer and we run into difficulties in interpreting the humanity of pleasure, or of sexual love, for example. If, on the other hand, by means of a modern scheme, we opt for the construal of the human predicament entirely within the framework of finitude and materialistic physicality, the same problem occurs with regard to the spiritual aspect of human affectivity. What is missing on both counts, as Ricoeur contends, is a dialectic of finitude and infinitude and the consequent dialectic of the vital and the spiritual in all layers of human feeling. Human existence is polar right from the outset and specifically human affectivity is a mediated and mediating tension between two fundamental tendencies where the sensible and the spiritual internally divide desire. The sensible reverberates in the spiritual and the spiritual resounds in the sensible; human pleasure is open for the infinite and spiritual happiness is weighed down by the finite. And, here again, the importance of the Ricoeurian *thumos*-heart becomes obvious in providing the key to an anthropology that offers a distinctive framework where the traditional problem of the double-edged character of our humanity can be adequately treated. It is within the heart that the geological rift between the animally vital and the spiritually human is overcome in a polar and specifically human dynamic unity. The ancient dictum that Ricoeur chooses as the subtitle of the chapter discussing affective fragility, "*Homo simplex in vitalitate, duplex in humanitate*" ("man simple in vitality, dual in humanity")—an idea that has its origins in Platonic and Stoic thought and occurs as an explicit formula in hermetic Gnosticism[42]—is implicitly turned around to indicate duality right through vitality and to point towards the twofold character of the human disposition. Thus, fashioned to suit Ricoeur's implicit intention, we may rightly modify the ancient saying as: *homo duplex in vitalitate et humanitate* (man dual both in vitality and humanity)—which, in my view, would aptly point out the ultimate intent of the Ricoeurian anthropological quest.

It is on these grounds that Ricoeur challenges the traditional framework of various treatises on the passions (whether Stoic, Thomistic, or Cartesian) that work with the common assumption that a number of simple, elementary passions add up to complex feelings/"affections," as if human

---

42. See François Azouvi's article on the long and tortuous history of the idea in which various trends of thought intersect from Plato to Saint Paul and from Hermes Trismegistos, through Renaissance thinkers like Pico della Mirandola to medical doctors like Paracelsus in the sixteenth century and Boerhaave in the eighteenth century. Azouvi traces the development of the idea from antiquity up to Maine de Biran's reappropriation in the nineteenth century. Maine de Biran had an admitted influence on Ricoeur's thought. Azouvi, "Homo Duplex," 229–44.

affectivity was just a complication of basic vital-animal affectivity. For the same reason, Ricoeur also criticizes what he describes as the Thomist or Cartesian "love–desire–pleasure cycle," where desire is understood in the limited terms of finite satisfaction as observed in the alimentary union. This schema works with an implicit notion of finitude associated with vital desire and presupposes a closed-up cycle where "satiety" is the ultimate (and finite) goal as if desire were not itself open to an infinite quest even in its most basic form. And here we touch upon the next crucial element of the uniqueness of human affectivity. The ultimate reason for Ricoeur's discontent with traditional views is that they do not build into their system (although they sporadically recognize) the implications of the inter-human character of human feeling. As Ricoeur observes in a long footnote on Thomas Aquinas, in speaking about the two kinds of love—concupiscence and friendship—while Aquinas introduces the notion of the other person as the beneficiary of one's love, he misses the full implications of the distinction between love of a thing and interpersonal love.[43] His notion of satisfaction and union revolves around the idea of the good as *thing* and not as the good implied by a relation to another person. When he defines love of friendship as directed toward *the one to whom* one wishes good, in contrast to concupiscent love, which is directed toward the *good* one wishes to another, he seems to be half-aware of the revolutionary difference made by the appearance of another person in the love–desire–pleasure cycle, but he ignores the consequences it would have for a basic understanding of desire. In other words, he keeps thinking in terms of the finite satisfaction model and does not see the full import of "satisfaction," which is brought by love for another person. Aquinas works with a finite pattern of the sensible appetite and so does not have suitable theoretical means to interpret the fact that "the encountering of another person is what breaks the finite, cyclic pattern of the sensible appetite."[44]

The Ricoeurian interpretation of sexual love is illuminating at this point. Human sexuality for Ricoeur is not animal sexuality tamed by the human intellect, but epitomizes the interconnectedness of the vital and the human at the level of desire. It is instinct "traversed, reconstituted and penetrated by the truly human quest."[45] It is transformed through and through by the triple Ricoeurian passional projects of having, power, and worth, which illustrate the complex interplay of the vital and the human. In sexuality one finds an element of all the three *thumic* quests: "a note

---

43. Ibid., 167–68., note 17.
44. Ibid., 168.
45. Ibid., 195.

of possession, some nuance of domination, as well as a seeking of mutual recognition."[46] The last element, the need for mutual recognition, clearly indicates the site where human reciprocity enters sexuality. While the desire of possession and domination are the first two components halfway through the process of humanization, the desire of mutual recognition introduces the truly human aspect by bringing in the experience of equality and reciprocity. Sexuality which is permeated by the truly human does not represent satisfaction simply on the physical level; it cannot be adequately grasped within the "love–desire–pleasure" cycle. The cycle opens up towards the infinite: "The human being, through pleasure, beyond pleasure, and sometimes by sacrificing pleasure, pursues the satisfaction of the quests with which 'instinct' becomes overlaid; a certain indefiniteness thus enters into it while it is being humanized. Instinct becomes open and without end instead of cyclic."[47] Human sexuality is thus situated in the *thumos* or heart, which reconciles the disparate pulls of the vital and the human in a restless and never-ending process.

Because human sexuality is rooted in the heart, it displays the same duality that is characteristic of the *thumos*. Freud's notion of libido—read in the light of Plato's idea of *thumos*—is a clear indication, for Ricoeur, that sexuality sides both with desire (*epithumia*) and the heart (*thumos*). In human sexuality, libido stands for genital desire, which is sublimated into affection beyond sex, while the desire for recognition, embodied as tenderness, assumes a sexual coloring. As "desire of the other's desire," sexuality is both vital and human and therefore has a unique place in anthropology.

Besides being distinctively inter-human, human affectivity is also unique because of its cultural character. Ricoeur illustrates the nature of specifically human feelings through the analyses of the three basic human quests: having, power, and worth.[48] Each of these three fundamental quests revolves around cultural objects and engenders clusters of feelings that are thus culturally shaped. The cultural objects have a "thing" character, an interpersonal level, and an institutional aspect. Feeling, as the "correlative and the inverse of the process of objectification," comes about as the counterpart of culturally determined objectivity which becomes interiorized in the self. Ricoeur here makes a strong case for the contention that the objective counterparts of human feelings are not to be thought of in terms of objects in the natural environment or in continuity with animal tendencies. Human affectivity is directed towards objects within a cultural setting and therefore also

---

46. Ibid., 195.
47. Ibid., 195.
48. See ibid., 168–91.

has economic and political dimensions. The feelings associated with possession have as their object the "available good" that comes about as the result of human work through the transformation of the animal environment into a human world. Such a relation to the economic object engenders a cycle of feelings that interiorize the experience of having within the self as feelings of possession. The feelings connected to power are more intersubjective and have an institutional-political dimension as well. They orbit around the socially and culturally institutionalized patterns of commanding and obeying and they also involve the political sphere where power is an essential component. The feelings attached to the quest for worth (also identified as honor or esteem) are seen by Ricoeur as the most obviously inter-human and cultural of all human feelings. What may cause difficulty at first sight is the identification of the specific object of these feelings, because they appear to be too intersubjective to crystallize in a clearly objectified form. Objectivity, however, is given by the regulating formal idea of esteem, on the one hand, while, on the other, cultural works (works of art and literature and all human works included) appear as material "objects" for the nebula of feelings aroused by the quest for esteem. Objectivity in this case is "cultural objectivity": it is "the very relation of man to man represented in the idea of humanity."[49] Ricoeur's account of the three basic "*thumic*" quests in which vital needs and human ambitions merge into an indivisible whole convincingly proves the importance of a cultural framework for the understanding of a distinctively human affectivity.

Last but not least, it is noteworthy that all the previous distinctive features (discontinuity with the animal environment, intersubjectivity, and cultural determination) converge in Ricoeur's specific conception of the human passions. His own concept is elaborated in contradistinction to the traditional idea that the passions, as modes of passivity, are involuntary movements "suffered" in the soul. This old notion of the passions comprises a wide variety of phenomena from instinctive drives to moods, feelings, and emotions. Ricoeur does not take the word passion in this traditional sense. His re-interpretation of the notion of passion follows directly from his theory of *thumic* feelings, which we saw as gravitating around the three basic human quests of having, power, and worth. Ricoeur does not think in terms of simple passions (such as love, hate, desire, hope, fear, etc.) that combine to form more complex feelings. Rather, he thinks along the lines of human projects (such as having, power, and worth) that are interiorized in a complex web of corresponding feelings or structured patterns of affectivity that do not have finite pleasure as their goal, but are open to the infinity of

---

49. Ibid., 188.

the human desire for happiness. The Ricoeurian passions are all connected to the desire for happiness and, in their ideal form, in "their grandeur," are not negatively obsessive or irrational, but represent the positive transcending movement of the human pursuit that is attracted by nothing less than the totality of ultimate happiness. It is in this sense—as revelatory of the attraction of the ultimate goal of human existence—that Ricoeur understands passions: "we are thinking of those great ventures which constitute the dramaturgy of human existence, of Othello's jealousy, of Rastignac's ambition"—in the sense that they are signs of an underlying commitment to life and happiness.[50] Primordial passion, beyond fallen passionality, is life devoted to the quest for happiness: "A passional life is a devoted life, dedicated to its theme; this 'passivity' is more primordial than passional captivity and sufferance; all the other passive modalities of passion are grafted onto this first 'passion.'"[51] Such an interpersonal, cultural, and, we could say, dramaturgical understanding of the passions fits in well with contemporary trends of emotion theory, which have recently put a growing emphasis (besides intersubjectivity and culturality) on the essentially narrative character of the emotions.[52]

Interestingly, Ricoeur's distinctive contribution to the theory of the passions has not always been fully recognized and was certainly overlooked by even one of the leading emotion theorists. In an ambitious programmatic article (in a volume of collected essays devoted to the appreciation of Ricoeur's philosophical achievement!), Robert C. Solomon has claimed that Ricoeur's understanding of the passions is completely inappropriate for a modern emotion theory since it is permeated by old-fashioned views that reflect an entirely hostile attitude towards passion and emotion. Solomon announces the following ruthless verdict:

> Like so many other philosophers, Ricoeur treats passion and emotion as an addendum or a parenthetical aside, at best, to his more sweeping philosophical theories. But what emerges from that brief sketch is a portrait of the passions so unappealing that it is no wonder that they play a minimal part in the rest of his philosophy. At one point he says, "all passions make us unhappy." In general, and like his predecessor Descartes, he finds emotions and passions to be less than wholly human . . . . In a

---

50. Ibid., 197.
51. Ibid., 199.
52. See for example, Frijda, *The Emotions*; Oatley, "From the Emotions of Conversation to the Passions of Fiction," in Manstead et al., *Feelings and Emotions*, 98–115; Pugmire, *Rediscovering Emotion*; Goldie, *The Emotions*.

philosophy devoted to intellect and will, the apparent "pathology" of the passions plays little positive part.[53]

The "brief sketch" of emotion theory that Solomon is alluding to can be found in Ricoeur's *Freedom and Nature: The Voluntary and the Involuntary*, the second part of which is dedicated to a philosophy of human action.[54] In this second major part, Ricoeur has a section on "emotion," classed under the subtitle "bodily spontaneity." Apart from scattered allusions to the *Symbolism of Evil*, Solomon's essay concentrates exclusively on this particular section, which he considers as the key text for an understanding of Ricoeur's somewhat deficient theory of the emotions. Consequently, the problem of the *thumos* and affective mediation in *Fallible Man* seems to have entirely escaped Solomon's attention as he complains about the difficulty one must face in delineating the contours of Ricoeur's theory, which is "tucked away" "in the middle of that mammoth volume" (that is, in *Freedom and Nature*). Solomon is indignant about the fact that "Ricoeur, unlike Descartes, has never bothered to write anything like a 'treatise on the passions,' [or developed] a theory of emotion, despite the fact that his entire philosophical enterprise is, in an important sense, supported by them."[55] Solomon in fact finds several clues in Ricoeur that, if consistently followed, in his view, could make up what he sees as a proper theory of the emotions, but which remain undeveloped.

Besides the fact that Solomon completely overlooks what can be seen as a unifying thread in Ricoeur's endeavor (which is made so clear, for example, in *Fallible Man*), he also obviously misreads the passage he refers to in *Freedom and Nature* where Ricoeur distinguishes between the term passion and emotion, anticipating a similar distinction made between the two senses of passion, as we saw, in *Fallible Man*. In the "General Introduction" to *Freedom and Nature*, Ricoeur clearly states that, for him, passions do not differ from emotions in terms of being more complex emotional formations or more systematic and durable forms of emotion. Instead, what Ricoeur takes as passion is the distortion of emotion, an obsession, the disfiguration of both the voluntary and the involuntary in man.[56] That is why one finds

53. Robert C. Solomon, "Paul Ricoeur on Passion and Emotion," in Reagan, *Studies in the Philosophy of Paul Ricoeur*, 2–3.

54. See Ricoeur, *Le volontaire et l'involontaire*, 235–64.

55. Solomon, "Paul Ricoeur on Passion and Emotion," 2.

56. *Le volontaire et l'involontaire*, 7–36. See also a footnote in the section on the emotions where Ricoeur explains that he does not take the word passion in the wide sense of, for example, Descartes, who understood everything as passion which is the counterpart of action and included both emotions and passions in the same category. Ricoeur takes passion in the specific narrow sense of obsessed desire. Ibid., 237–38.,

derogatory terms with regard to the passions in the book; they are criticized for being detrimental for a wholesome emotionality and an ultimately free will. The passions "make us unhappy" (as Solomon cites Ricoeur who literally says: "*Toute passion est malheureuse*"[57]) because they promote the servitude of the free will and generate a never-ending pursuit that leads towards a "bad" infinite of meaningless quest and respects no limits.

Obviously, Solomon finds Ricoeur's negative assessment of the passions useful for his own overall claim that the passions have hitherto been regarded in the philosophical tradition as irrational, dangerous, and harmful. In the fervor to clear the ground for his own cognitive theory of the emotions, Solomon has simply overlooked the fact that, besides the negative account of the passions, one also finds in Ricoeur a positive appreciation of the emotions. The latter represent, in his scheme, a natural human disposition and display basic human affectivity as "the neutral fundamental keyboard upon which both innocence and fault may play."[58] In fact, what Solomon registers as a deep-seated ambiguity in Ricoeur's evaluation of human passions is nothing but the overall presence of this presupposed basic distinction between passion and emotion (in *Freedom and Nature*) and the same distinction between two forms of passion, one as primordial desire for happiness and another as pathological deviation from the primordial innocent quest (in *Fallible Man*).

With regard to Solomon's charge that Ricoeur does not develop a coherent theory of the passions, we may reply that the apparent absence of a "proper" treatise on the passions in Ricoeur's oeuvre is not due to a failure in treating the issue in an adequate manner, but is totally consistent with the holistic anthropological account in question, which, aiming to step out of the restricted framework of a "treatise," situates the issue of the emotions in the wider context of the entire disposition of the human person and the interaction of *bios* and *logos* (cognition and sensibility, emotion and cognition) in the human quest. Ricoeur's theory of the passions is woven into the fabric of his general account of the nature of the distinctively human, and his specific understanding of what makes human existence essentially fragile. The passions, as residents of the intermediary *thumic* heart, are not to be interpreted on their own as independent entities or phenomena in the soul. They are intricately tied to the mediation between the vital and the spiritual, the finite and the infinite, reason and the heart.[59] Taken in isolation and

---

note 2.
    57. Ibid., 27.
    58. Ibid.
    59. It is remarkable how much Ricoeur in his later hermeneutical writings still

separated from the theoretical synthesis that (as has been seen) they interiorize or the practical synthesis that they enact, they become lifeless (in the sense of losing their rootedness in *bios*) and meaningless (because of losing reference to *logos*) like pressed flowers randomly arranged in an album. Instead of a theory of the emotions/passions, Ricoeur elaborates a theory of the heart that is by no means an anti-theory of reason, but is a complex account of the problem of mediation between disparate movements and tendencies in the human self. Therefore, the best way to appreciate Ricoeur's distinctive contribution to emotion theory is to turn to his "exegesis of disproportion," which culminates—as we saw—in a philosophy of the heart.

Ultimately, in what ways can Ricoeur's philosophy be appropriated by theological reflection? This is a question Dan R. Stiver poses in his study, *Theology After Ricoeur*.[60] While he thinks that Ricoeur's philosophy would offer an excellent and largely untapped resource for postmodern theology in many respects, he at the same time registers theologians' reluctance to deal with this complex philosophy in a comprehensive manner. What one finds are mostly piecemeal appropriations of a handful of key insights in the Ricoeurian account that, however, renounce more extensive engagement with his thought as a unified whole. Such reluctance is understandable, as Stiver explains, since Ricoeur is a philosopher who followed many ways and dialogued with a great variety of authors, touching upon a wide

---

thinks essentially in terms of the early anthropological account elaborated in *Fallible Man*. For example, in the essay "The Metaphorical Process as Cognition, Imagination, and Feeling," Ricoeur transposes into a linguistic-hermeneutic framework the basic early insight: "To *feel*, in the emotional sense of the word, is to make *ours* what has been put at a distance by thought in its objectifying phase. Feelings, therefore, have a very complex kind of intentionality. They are not merely inner states but interiorized thoughts. It is as such that they accompany and complete the work of imagination as schematizing a synthetic operation: they make the schematized thought ours. Feeling, then is a case of *Selbst-Affektion*, in the sense Kant used it in the second edition of the *Critique*. This *Selbst-Affektion*, in turn, is a part of what we call poetic feeling. Its function is to abolish the distance between knower and known without cancelling the cognitive structure of thought and the intentional distance which it implies. Feeling is not contrary to thought. It is thought made ours. This felt participation is a part of its complete meaning as poem." Ricoeur, "The Metaphorical Process as Cognition, Imagination, and Feeling," 156. In *Oneself as Another*, addressing the problem of the body and the consequent passivity inherent to the self, he writes: "In a sharp-edged dialectic between praxis and pathos, one's own body becomes the emblematic title of a vast inquiry which, beyond the simple mineness of one's own body, denotes the entire sphere of *intimate* passivity, and hence of otherness, for which it forms the centre of gravity. In this perspective, one would have to review the conceptual labor that has been done from the classic treatises on the passions . . . on embodiment, the flesh, affectivity, and self-affection." Ricoeur, *Oneself as Another*, 220.

60. Stiver, *Theology After Ricoeur*, 30.

THE ESSENTIAL POLARITY OF THE HUMAN CONDITION 57

range of themes. He is also an author whose texts do not lend themselves to easy synthesis or paraphrasing. The richness of his writings lies in the details rather than the overarching structure; his thought is more analytic than synthetic and he also draws on many great figures in the philosophical tradition. In order to understand his overall project, one would have to be trained in various fields in philosophy and the social sciences; therefore, "it is no wonder that scholars found Ricoeur enormously helpful in sporadic ways but frustratingly difficult to grasp in general."[61]

Stiver joins the opinion of those who see Ricoeur's anthropological interest as the unifying thread of his somewhat disparate writings and he contends that Ricoeur's philosophical quest must be regarded as an anthropology that is mainly directed to the investigation of questions connected with the embodied self as an interpersonal and social reality. In contradistinction to the already existing works on Ricoeur, Stiver stresses the importance of seeing his entire inquiry in essential unity, as one following a single overarching trajectory from beginning to the end. Consequently, he claims that the earlier works form an indispensable part of Ricoeur's edifice of thought and must be consulted if one wishes to understand later developments since they contain pivotal themes that occur in later works in the form of presuppositions and inherently shape the rest of his work.

What Stiver sees as a major "untapped resource" for theology in Ricoeur has to do with the notion of the embodied, intersubjective, and socially-constructed self, which could be constructively rethought in a threefold theological direction: first, the unity of the self in biblical terms, as contrasted to the Hellenistic dualistic and intellectualistic framework; next, the self as the image of God understood in its social dimensions and not as an individual entity; third, the Ricoeurian self as analogous to the sociality, mutuality, and communality of the trinitarian communion. Stiver only highlights these themes as important topics for theological inquiry; he does not give any further detail concerning the implementation of this task. His aim in the book is simply to draw the overall hermeneutic framework within which a postmodern theology may progress, and he mainly develops his own view with regard to the relationship between philosophy and faith as it is formulated in Ricoeur and as it may be complemented from our present perspective.

Regrettably, we can take Stiver to task for not being fully consistent with his own principles since he seems to give only a cursory glance at the early work, *Fallible Man*, and concentrates almost exclusively on *Freedom*

---

61. Stiver, *Theology After Ricoeur*, 28.

and Nature.⁶² Owing to this omission, he cannot see the full import of the Ricoeurian theory of the heart because he misses the link that connects the part on the emotions in *Freedom and Nature* with the later more hermeneutical works. It is on these grounds that he maintains that while Ricoeur "elaborated in that work [*Freedom and Nature*] the integral role of the body in willing, and particularly the mediation of the emotions," he "has not developed these ideas in terms of epistemology as much as he could have, given that the importance of the body and the emotions to knowing has been strengthened more and more since the time of that book."⁶³ I suggest that, with the missing link of Ricoeur's theory of the mediating *thumos*, the picture of Ricoeur's epistemological vision of human affectivity can be adequately drawn.

Stiver's approach is most remarkable for the account it gives of the relationship between philosophy and theology. He explores the clear contours of Ricoeur's philosophy, which deliberately brackets theological concerns and respects the autonomy of the two independent disciplines. Stiver calls for taking Ricoeur's philosophical account for what it is, as genuine philosophy, which is open to theological appropriation but resists attempts at reading into it crypto-theological claims. Although Ricoeur openly confesses his personal Christian faith commitment, he consciously pursues a philosophy that does not venture into the territory where faith has the most important word to say. Stiver rightly sees philosophy and theology as dialogue partners that are neither subordinate to one another, nor absolutely separate from one another. For just as Ricoeur was always careful to distinguish his philosophical conclusions from his theological views, we must likewise regard his theology as different from his philosophy. Ricoeurian philosophy can at best serve as a constructive dialogue partner for theology, which, in turn, needs to construct in a creative manner its own distinctive account built on Scripture, the tradition of the church, and the experience of faith. And we may add that the danger with *Fallible Man* is that it might be appreciated by theologians and dismissed by philosophers respectively for the wrong reasons. For a philosopher's ear, the idea of "fallibility" may smack suspiciously of a theological agenda, while theologians might err in too hastily welcoming helpful philosophical "proof" for the doctrine of human fallenness, thereby misreading the underlying Ricoeurian intent.⁶⁴ In

---

62. While *Freedom and Nature* receives a relatively longer treatment in Stiver's book (160–66), *Fallible Man* is referred to in a short paragraph and in very general terms (166–67).

63. Stiver, *Theology After Ricoeur*, 203.

64. Patrick L. Bourgeois's essay shows signs of such a philosophical suspicion when he claims that in his philosophy "Ricoeur has chosen to look at religious symbols within

order to steer clear of these twin dangers, one must find a middle course of respectful appropriation, a difficult venture, of course.

Apart from Stiver's suggestion that certain themes in Ricoeur are open to creative theological appropriation, we must also recognize a more general open-endedness present in his thought, which I would call a basic methodological openness to all that transcends the limits of philosophical reflection. As Walter J. Lowe has pointed out, Ricoeur's philosophy is uncompromisingly holistic in that it resists every kind of reductionism that restricts the human phenomenon to a partial aspect instead of addressing the paradox of the whole, while likewise resisting overarching interpretations where the concrete particulars of the distinctively human are lost for the sake of an abstract metaphysical scheme.[65] It is this "humanist dilemma," says Lowe, that forms the background to Ricoeur's entire project and is augmented by an acute feeling for mystery in the Marcelian sense. For Ricoeur's eminent mentor, Gabriel Marcel, "problem" and "mystery" differ in the sense that the former is a matter of technical proficiency that can be resolved in time, while the latter proves ultimately intractable for pure philosophical inquiry, partly because of the deficiency of our conceptual means to explore it fully, and partly because we are part and parcel of it and cannot detach ourselves from it completely. That is why the "mystery of being," for instance, will never lend itself to exhaustive theoretical reflection, and yet it is such mystery that must be the primary theme of a truly challenging philosophy. Ricoeur is fully aware of such a sense of mystery throughout *Fallible Man* and in his other works as well, turning it into a lasting methodological concern. And we might add that only a philosophy that is respectful of mystery in such a manner can be a truly adequate dialogue partner for theology in the common quest for a never fully exhaustive understanding of the place of the human being in the totality of existence. And this is why, as Lowe rightly comments, Ricoeur's philosophy addresses totality right from the outset and does not proceed from an assumed simplicity towards complexity. The totality of the human being and the totality of the "mystery of being" can be seen here as concurring in one inextricable knot that may be experienced and observed, but that cannot be neatly untied.

---

a theistic option and within a specific tradition. Admitting this, he then allows certain assumed philosophical tenets full play, as for instance, radical evil and the captive will, and hope of regeneration. A more neutral account is necessary, thus posing the corrective element to Ricoeur's thought. . . . Ricoeur should perhaps be more open to a basic level of unity and a neutral place for the possibility of evil and of good in the existential possibilities of Dasein." Bourgeois, "The Limits of Ricoeur's Hermeneutic of Existence," in Hahn, *The Philosophy of Paul Ricoeur*, 562; 564.

65. Lowe, "Introduction," in Ricoeur, *Fallible Man*, vii–xxxvii.

Taking all into consideration, in my view, a (post)modern theological anthropology may creatively engage with the following central insights of Ricoeur's philosophical anthropology. First, there is his insistence that the ancient rift between what is vital/corporeal and what is intellectual/spiritual in the human being must not be regarded as a deficiency, but must be seen as a primordial given that occasions multiple mediations, forming in this manner the texture of our humanity. In other words, Ricoeur's acknowledgment of the essential polarity of human existence—while avoiding a dualistic anthropology—is a valuable clue for a non-dualistic and yet equally non-monistic theological vision. Within such a framework, the key idea of mediation must receive an eminent status and, in this respect, Ricoeur's idea of the *thumos* provides a wealth of precious insight.

Second, the consequent appreciation by Ricoeur of affectivity as a specifically human property both in its orientation towards the vital and also as the source of spiritual feelings—where these two realms are seen as mutually interpenetrating one another—can be usefully appropriated by a theological account.

Third, the idea of the human being as mediating mediation between *bios* and *logos* can serve as an inspiration for a renewed theological account of the traditional doctrine of human createdness in the image of God. It is especially illuminating with regard to the question of whether human affectivity may be included in the image-like aspect or whether it is only our intellect that bears likeness to God.

Fourth, Ricoeur's philosophy of the heart in itself is a remarkably unique attempt at the conceptualization of genuine human experience, which has so long been relegated to the domain of intractable sentimentality. Such a framework may also offer new grounds for a more holistic emotion theory that has in view the entire human person as made in the image of God.

And, last but not least, the Ricoeurian philosophy of the human person provides a useful background for a renewed understanding of the notion of human and divine love in presenting a systematic framework for the analogy between trinitarian and human love and gathering various aspects of the issue of love in a revealing unity.

3

Human Likeness to God

You have made us for yourself and our hearts are restless until they rest in you.

—Augustine, *Confessions* 1.1.1.

Dialogue between Philosophy and Theological Anthropology

That there is no seamless continuity between philosophies of man and a theological vision of the human being is a case often made by theologians. What are, then, the distinguishing marks that delineate a truly theological anthropology? Is not the object of the two disciplines the same human being as situated in the world and as being in relation with the material, the natural, and the human sphere to which theological anthropology adds the dimension of relatedness to God in turn? What difference does a religious perspective make in our judgment of the true nature of the human person? Can theological anthropology build on the insights of philosophy for its own distinctive vision of what makes us human? Or should it rather start construction from the foundations on its own, distrustful of the ultimate immanence of philosophical inquiry? These are questions that have elicited a plurality of answers among theologians and which therefore do not lend themselves to an easy consensus. One thing is admittedly clear, namely, that theological anthropology as a separate branch of study owes its existence to the anthropological turn of philosophy, that is, the philosopher's growing interest in the human autonomous subject with the appearance of modernity, a discussion where theological anthropology is an obvious latecomer in the twentieth century. On the other hand, theology from the very beginning has been permeated by a wealth of reflection on human nature (both philosophically and theologically) and as such has long been a source of inspiration and a true dialogue partner for philosophy. As both a latecomer and an age-old partner, theology must come to terms with the fact that it willy-nilly shares much of its subject matter with philosophy: the problem of human freedom, the issue of evil, the questions of suffering and the ultimate goal of human existence, or the nature of personhood, for example, are all crucial points of debate for philosophers and theologians alike. And yet, theological anthropology need not fear the eventual loss of its competence over these shared issues because, although the subject of philosophical anthropology and theology may be the same, both have their unmistakable voice on these matters and the manner of their respective treatments is markedly different.[1] They are twin discourses that look like one another and yet bear non-interchangeable individuality that lends both of them their distinctively unique character.

So what are the distinguishing features of theological anthropology? As a young branch of study that cuts across various fields of systematic theology, theological anthropology does not easily situate itself within the theological discipline.[2] On Karl Rahner's view, it belongs to fundamental theological reflection where the human being as hearer of God's word and the addressee of God's salvific action is treated, and which, accordingly, is intended to prepare the ground for the treatment of more specifically theological issues within systematic theology. Wolfhart Pannenberg, on the other hand, avoids talk of an expressly and distinctively theological anthropology, using the term "contemporary anthropology in theological perspective" instead.[3] He too associates theological discourse on the human

---

1. As Dan R. Stiver has noted: "The 'flavor' of the treatments of virtually the same issue by a theologian and by a philosopher can vary tremendously," due to "their differing tradition and ethos." Stiver, *Theology After Ricoeur*, 245.

2. For a definition of theological anthropology and its various forms see, for example, the dictionary entry on theological anthropology [*Theologische Antropologie*] by Georg Langemeyer in Beinert, *Lexikon der katholischen Dogmatik*, 502–4.

3. As is indicated by the title of his book *What is Man? Contemporary Anthropology in Theological Perspective*.

being with fundamental theology. On another view—one that is perhaps the most consistent with the theological tradition—theological anthropology must be included in the discourse on creation (this is an option followed by the second volume of the handbook *Mysterium Salutis*,[4] for instance). Otto Hermann Pesch, by contrast, claims that issues concerning the human being are to be treated within the framework of a theology of grace, which regards the human person as addressed by God's word and in the light of the recognition of her/his sinfulness and the gift of God's saving grace. There are also those who insert anthropological discussion into the context of eschatology, emphasizing in this manner the eschatologically-oriented nature of human existence and the not yet fulfilled character of our essential humanity.

Despite the differences, however, there is considerable consensus on one important point: theological anthropology cannot claim to be capable of elaborating a once-and-for-all exhaustive vision of what constitutes our humanity. We, as human beings, are always on the way towards eschatological fulfillment, moving within the time of salvation history, never fully realizing ourselves in this life, and displaying essential openness to the *eschaton*. This is the theological reason, we may say, for the required modesty of anthropological inquiry within theology. The next reason is methodological, for the diversity of approaches in philosophy, the natural and the human sciences warrant healthy skepticism concerning the ultimate possibility to work out a comprehensive view of the nature of humanity. What may be theology's distinctive task is to set the whole issue of the human person in the light of the promise of the Gospels: human mystery receives final illumination through God and in God who is both our Creator and ultimate fulfillment. What theological anthropology puts forward as knowledge about humanity is gleaned from the overall context of faith in God's loving and redeeming goodness as it is understood in Scripture, the teaching of the church, and the lived experience of the faithful throughout salvation history. Human theological self-knowledge issues from a lived faith relationship with the Creator of the universe. And here lies the third limitation of a theological anthropological approach, one we may call tradition-determined constraint. By this I mean that, until recently, discourses on human self-understanding within theology itself have not been sufficiently organized to make up a comprehensive whole, but were indeed kept apart, compartmentalized in diverse theological contexts that were not integrated along the lines of a guiding idea. Theology has traditionally been orientated towards God and God's revelation and therefore has given the human being second-order or indirect attention, not feeling the need to work out a separate treatise "On

---

4. Feiner and Löhrer, *Die Heilsgeschichte vor Christus*.

Man" as a counterpart to the treatise "On God." If we look at traditional themes concerning the human being in theology, we find seemingly disparate issues, such as, our createdness in the image of God, the state of original glory, original sin, nature and grace and the various forms of grace, the issue of the immortality of the soul and the resurrection of the body, and the nature of the beatific vision. It comes as no surprise, then, that a major concern of contemporary theologians working in the field of anthropology is to pull together various strands of thought in a unified vision, notwithstanding the awareness that such a vision will never be exhaustive and that the projection back into the tradition of a modern idea of theological anthropology might turn out to be sheer anachronism.

Obviously, despite its own distinctive agenda, theology cannot work in isolation from philosophy, but must always be mindful of our humanity as it is expressed from the perspective of immanent human self-understanding. In a recent encyclopedic volume dedicated to theological anthropology, Franco Giulio Brambilla has distinguished three trends in philosophy, all of which set the issue of the nature of our humanity in a distinctive overall framework.[5] The first trend, characteristic of Anglo-Saxon philosophy and heir to psychological behaviorism, poses the question in terms of the mind-body problem, which it sees as a suitable conceptual means for the replacement of the traditional scheme of the duality of body and soul. Proponents of this trend regard the human person as an indivisible whole, whose mind is a function (even if spiritual) of the body. By means of this approach, they hope to overcome both anthropological dualism and material monism. The next trend originates in twentieth-century German philosophy (Max Scheler, Helmuth Plessner, and Arnold Gehlen), which finds the specifically human in our unique capacity to be open to the world (*Weltoffenheit*) in contradistinction to animals, which live a life closed upon their immediate needs and the exigencies of the species. The idea of a foundational openness that distinguishes the human from the animal world is also a reaction to behaviorism and all sorts of psychological naturalism, which consider the human being in seamless continuity with the animal and the biological. The emphasis on *Weltoffenheit* restructures anthropological discourse around the pivotal idea of human uniqueness without, however, having to place the distinctively human into an old notion of the soul as distinguished from the body. The third trend is the fruit of phenomenological reflection on the lived body in the wake of Edmund Husserl, Maurice Merleau-Ponty, Gabriel Marcel, Michel Henry, and others, and it is here that we may include Paul Ricoeur and Jean-Luc Marion as well. These philosophers reject both

---

5. Brambilla, *Antropologia teologica*, 361–82.

an objectifying scientific and naturalistic interpretation of our bodiliness and also a spiritualistic understanding of the soul as superadded to the body or the idea of consciousness immediate to itself, without the mediation of the body. In a polemical fashion, they aim to retrieve, for philosophical discussion, the ultimate significance of the lived human body (as opposed to an object of detached scrutiny) and work out a phenomenological framework where one's own (human and lived) body is regarded as the unifying center and the zero origin of consciousness and the self. In this perspective, embodied human existence embraces the experienced duality of consciousness and the body; it gives such duality continuity and a new unifying design.

While the latter two approaches (the one of *Weltoffenheit* and the philosophy of the body) seem the most suitable for theological appropriation, the question arises whether theology may truly profit from the full endorsement of one of these philosophical stances. After all, theological anthropology obviously grapples with the same problems—the need to overcome dualistic schemes of soul-body relation and the necessity to step out of an old hierarchical framework of faculty psychology. Could it not, then, rely on philosophical anthropology for a convincing new integral vision that promises to avoid the twin dangers of spiritual dualism and material monism? Besides the fact that none of the philosophical approaches lack certain significant shortcomings and therefore cannot claim to have resolved the age-old problem of soul-body dualism completely or without remainder, theology must also be conscious of the fact that it cannot travel entirely free of the at once beneficial and yet thwarting weight of its own tradition and of certain inherited patterns that house pivotal truth claims and that cannot be jettisoned altogether but have to be re-thought and cautiously adapted to new insights. Therefore, theologians in our day are looking for a broader organizing idea around which a theological vision of the distinctively human can be constructed. The notion of relationality (itself, of course, largely indebted to modern philosophical elaborations but also essentially and truly biblical) proves to be fruitfully open for adaptation to a theological agenda. As F. LeRon Shults—a theologian undertaking the challenging job of reforming theological anthropology—has insisted, after "the philosophical turn to relationality" theological anthropology too must embrace the concept of relationality as a hermeneutical tool for creating the adequate conceptual space within which discourse about the human being must be conducted."[6] It must be relationality taken in a comprehen-

6. Shults, *Reforming Theological Anthropology*. Shults examines traditional topics of theological anthropology in the light of the modern idea of relationality as it is indicated by the titles of almost all the chapters of his book. Just to mention a few: "The Philosophical Turn to Relationality"; "Relationality and Developmental Psychology";

sive sense and covering all aspects of the human experience: "Late modern theological anthropology must take into account not only our psychological and social relations to other persons, but also the physical and cultural relations that compose the matrices within which our lives are dynamically embedded."[7] And, clearly, human relationality must be seen as originating in divine trinitarian relations, which are the archetype and pattern of our actual disposition as relational beings. To carry out reform along the pathway of these ideas is pivotal for Shults' argument, because the theological tradition has obviously neglected basic dimensions of relationality, placing the focus often "on the abstract nature of the individual and the intellectual and volitional powers of one's soul."[8]

While clearly accepting the centrality of the idea of relationality for theological anthropology, the Italian F. Giulio Brambilla follows a different path by choosing the concept of freedom as the pivot of his own account of our human condition in the light of God's revelation.[9] What he stresses is the importance of the fact that God's self-communication is inscribed into the texture of human freedom and is made comprehensible by the divine gift of the Holy Spirit. Christian existence is essentially trustful freedom, consciously at the disposal of God's salvific action. It is freedom both given and realized through acceptance; both a gift and a task. It is a given, inherent in the state of our essential creatureliness, which, however, becomes one's own only in responsible action with regard to oneself, others, and God. Naturally, freedom in this sense is internally related to the idea of relationality, both in terms of its origin and its goal. Brambilla's "anthropology of freedom" (his own phrase) posits human beings as essentially relational and Brambilla even risks equating the idea of freedom with relationality: "So freedom appears as structurally being 'in relation,' or even as 'relation' (first donated, then willed)."[10] In his scheme, the human self is constituted by relational freedom through the body, the experience of the other, and the mediation of culture and society, and, at a more fundamental level, through the all-embracing faith-relationship with Christ as the second person of the Trinity. Such a self is not viewed as immediate presence to itself, but is recognized to be mediated through other selves, time, and human culture.[11]

"Constitutive [Trinitarian] Relationality in Barth and Pannenberg"; "Relationality and the Doctrine of Sin"; "Relationality and the Doctrine of *Imago* Dei."

7. Ibid., 2.

8. Ibid.

9. Brambilla, *Antropologia teologica*.

10. Ibid., 383. My translation.

11. Brambilla acknowledges his indebtedness to Ricoeur's idea of the self and his analyses of human freedom (among other influences) in *Oneself as Another*

What emerges from even this cursory overview of the present state of theological research in anthropology is the fact that certain basic philosophical stances and key concepts prove to be open for theological appropriation and so foster human self-understanding in the theological perspective of human createdness in the image of the Triune God. And here lies the ultimate difference between anthropologies constructed as part of a philosophical framework, and ones emerging as the result of theological inquiry: the latter, unlike the former, work with a traditionally inherited idea that structures and determines theological discourse on the human being. With the idea of *imago Dei* (human createdness in the image of God), theology is equipped with a pivotal interpretative tool that creates the conceptual space within which theological reflection on the human being is made possible. As an overarching hermeneutic principle, the idea of our (not easily definable) likeness to God governs all the partial accounts arranged around the traditional themes of original sin, grace, resurrection, beatitude, and so forth, while being, at the same time, the particular distinguishing mark that gives theological discussion its specific "flavor" as distinct from philosophical discourse.[12] The theologically-conceived human being sees him/herself in reference to the Creator as an ultimate source of meaning and an ultimate ground of interpretation; she or he is not only in relation with the world and other humans, but is in a mysterious kinship with the source of all relationality: the divine community of the Trinity. Does this mean, then, that whatever we assert with regard to the nature of the human person must apply in some way also to God? Where exactly does our likeness become apparent; is there an aspect of our humanity that is the eminent locus of our image-character? How does the principle of analogy enter the picture if one is to specify the nature of the likeness? These are questions theology has long been grappling with, and if we wish to bring Ricoeur's anthropological vision of human polarity into dialogue with theological anthropology, they may serve as a good starting point.

---

and *Freedom and Nature*. Interestingly, in his theological anthropology, he makes no reference to Ricoeur's *Fallible Man*.

12. Ostensibly, the arrangement of traditional topics of theological anthropology into a consistent structure causes considerable difficulty for authors writing on the subject. I disagree, however, with Shults's proposal that "the three traditional loci of theological anthropology [are] human nature, sin and the image of God." Shults, *Reforming Theological Anthropology*, 163. I would rather suggest that the traditional locus of the idea of the image of God is the comprehensive hermeneutical device that has internally governed theological reflection throughout the ages and has given the specific backdrop to the sub-issues of human nature and sin. Nonetheless, it is clear that the treatment of the issue of the *imago Dei* in a separate chapter is, for Shults, a methodological rather than a hermeneutical necessity.

The Biblical Idea of Image of God

The phrase in the book of *Genesis* (1:26) has traditionally been seen as vital for the perspective theology adopts when it poses the question concerning the human being. If we are made in God's image and likeness, we can only understand ourselves with reference to the Creator in a reciprocal relationship where knowledge about God and knowledge concerning humans mutually presuppose and illuminate one another. The human being, understood theologically, is not a lonely enigma set within and yet over against nature and the universe as the sole rational and bodily being who must boldly face the unbearable burden of not knowing his/her ultimate origin or final destination and of not having a dialogue partner other than him/herself. The human subject of theological reflection is not seen as engaged in a monologue on her baffling state, but is someone who speaks in God's presence and with the confidence (faith) of receiving answers to her vexing questions from the ultimate source of meaning and reason. This is the gist of the traditional teaching. However, the nature of the likeness has not always been easy to determine, as it is obvious from the long and tortuous history of interpretation that goes back to the early church fathers in the second half of the second century. To start the story with the testimony of the Scriptures, in a sense anticipates the current position, since the reading one gives of the Bible narratives is conditioned by the account contemporary exegesis provides concerning the meaning of "in God's image" in the Genesis narrative. Nonetheless, our cursory overview, which concentrates on just one aspect of this complicated issue (the status of human reason and emotionality with regard to our image character), cannot ignore as a first foundational step the testimony of the first-order biblical reflection on the enigma of woman and man. The biblical narrative is vital for two interconnected reasons: on the one hand, because contemporary theology is fully aware of the key importance of Scripture as an indispensable foundation for the work of theoretical construction; and, on the other, because our present awareness results from a re-discovery of the theological method of the church fathers, whose theology issued from a practice of reading and interpreting biblical texts and who therefore essentially thought in biblical terms and along the lines of questions posed by biblical authors. And this is particularly true in the case of the issue of the *imago Dei*, which owes its origin to the creative New Testament appropriation of the Old Testament Genesis narratives and the subsequent patristic reflection on these biblical texts. As Adalbert G. Hamman—an astute commentator on the anthropology of the church fathers—has noted, it was always Scripture that the first Christian believers turned to for an answer to the question, "What is man?"[13] Taking all this into consideration, the purpose of my overview is to glean ideas from various contexts and, by pulling together various strands of thought, to draw a clearly recognizable trajectory of the development of views concerning the nature of human likeness to God. Consequently, I will leave out all unnecessary detail that would further complicate this already difficult problem.

Both of the Old Testament creation narratives (the later Priestly one of Gen 1:1—2:4a and the earlier Yahwist one of Gen 2:4b–25), which reflect on God's creating activity in a theological manner—in contrast with other non-doctrinal Old Testament texts, where the idea of creation appears in the context of praise and prayer—reach their climax in the account of the creation of the human being, that is, man and woman.[14] These two otherwise stylistically and conceptually widely differing texts have one important feature in common: both picture the world as orientated towards the human being who is seen as Yhwh's principal masterpiece. This underlying idea is expressed in different ways by each narrative, either by placing man/woman in the centre around which God constructs all the things of the world (in the case of the Yahwist's narrative), or by situating the first two human beings at the top of a cosmological hierarchy after the creation of lower beings (according to the Priestly narrative). Despite the considerable differences in detail and perspective, the two stories converge in their anthropocentric stance, that is, in the fact that both view the act of God's creation as having the human being as its ultimate goal. Hence, both accord the creation of man/woman the most prominent place in the narrative.

That being said, the idea that the human being was created in the image of God appears only in the Priestly narrative (in Gen 1:26), which surveys various creatures in their relation to God according to an ascending scale of bonds, where the chaos from which the world is formed has the loosest connection in being formless and dark, and night and day, plants and animals represent gradually stronger connectedness to ʿelōhîm (God). While these former are only in an indirect relation with God, the human being, who is situated at the top of the ascending scale, has a uniquely intimate relationship with the Creator, and even the rest of the world, which was created for him/her, and is connected to ʿelōhîm in and through him/her. The creation of man/woman forms the climax of the story when, having created the world and furnished it with various living creatures, God solemnly

---

13. Hamman, *L'Homme, Image de Dieu*, 7.

14. From the extensive literature on the issue of the "image of God" in the Old Testament, I base my account on the following synthesizing key works: Rad, *The Theology of Israel's Historical Traditions*, 135–54; Wolff, *Anthropology of the Old Testament*, 159–65; Schreiner, *Theologie des Alten Testaments*, 132–83.

announces: "Let us make man in our image, in our likeness, and let them rule over the fish of the sea and the birds of the air, over the livestock, over all the earth, and over all the creatures that move along the ground" (Gen 1:26). While God creates all things—over which the human being receives the power of dominion—with his word ("Let there be . . ."), God creates man/woman using a different expression, which expresses God's intimate decision, a cherished divine wish: "Let us make man" (Gen 1:26). In the next verse, the narrative repeats the idea and solemnly emphasizes the fact of its realization: "So God created man in his own image, in the image of God he created him; male and female he created them" (Gen 1:27). As Gerhard von Rad has observed, apart from the fact that the creation of the human being is introduced by a distinctive divine wish (as contrasted to the creation of other creatures), the unique position of man/woman within the created world is also highlighted by the suggestion that he and she have their model outside of creation, in God's transcendent world, to which they bear special likeness.[15]

And here we arrive at the crucial question: what exactly does the phrase "in our image, in our likeness" mean? In what way does man/woman bear resemblance to God? Can it be satisfactorily interpreted in the light of the creation narrative? It seems that the answer is partly positive and partly negative, depending mostly on what we are looking for. Rad stresses the fact that the text does not furnish further information concerning the exact nature of the likeness; it is simply assumed that the meaning of the statement is evident and there is no further clue given as how to understand it. On the other hand, and this is a consensual recognition of modern exegetes, in the story we are given ample information concerning the purpose of the likeness, that is, the reason why God presents the human being with such a distinguished state and the idea of what role he assigns man/woman within the created world. The purpose is clearly expressed by the injunction inherent in the consequent blessing: "Be fruitful and increase in number; fill the earth and subdue it. Rule over the fish of the sea and the birds of the air and over every living creature that moves on the ground" (Gen 1:28). Human likeness to God is given so that man/woman may act as God's stewards in the world; they are called to rule over living and non-living creatures

15. Rad, *Old Testament Theology*, 144. Rad writes: "On the topmost step of this pyramid stands man, and there is nothing between him and God: indeed, the world, which was in fact made for him, has in him alone its most absolute immediacy to God. Also, unlike the rest of Creation, he was not created by the word; but in creating him God was actuated by a unique, solemn resolve in the depths of his heart. And in particular, God took the pattern for this, his last work of Creation, from the heavenly world above. In no other work of Creation is everything referred so very immediately to God himself as in this." Ibid., 144.

in God's name as caretakers of the created world. They represent God and it is in this sense that they are God's image on earth. Just as ancient Near Eastern kings had their "images," their statues, set up in their kingdom, as representatives of their sovereignty over the given territory, so God places the human being on earth as God's own image, as a sign and agent of his sovereignty.[16]

Nevertheless, the idea of image/statue suggests more than simple functional likeness. There must be a more inherent relation between the human being and God, some kind of correspondence, a certain kind of likeness that accounts for the special place God allocates man/woman with regard to the entire creation. Even Gerhard von Rad and Hans Walter Wolff acknowledge the presence of indirect indication concerning the nature of the likeness in Old Testament texts. Obviously, in pointing in the direction of where characteristics of the likeness may be found, their aim is partly polemical. What they have in mind is a long history of interpretations where likeness was associated with one particular aspect of the human being, namely, the human intellect (and will) and where the human corporeal state was excluded from the image-character. It is in this vein that Rad insists that likeness refers to the entire human person, body and intellect alike, and that he even goes so far as to add that evidence in various parallel texts (e.g., Ps 8:6 or Ezek 28:12) points to the existence of interpretation that relate the idea of image "equally, if not first and foremost, to the splendor of his bodily form."[17] Ostensibly, Wolff too has both ideas in mind when he sums up the different aspects of the notion of image with regard to the anthropological vision inherent in the Old Testament. We might describe Wolff's view as involving a "constitutive" and a "functional" likeness. For him, the human being is God's image because he/she in some sense bears likeness to God. In other words, there is a certain correspondence between man/woman and God. However, Wolff also tries to avoid essentialistic interpretations and, instead of identifying likeness with one specific aspect of the human being, regards it rather as a divinely allotted capacity to enter into relationship with God. God creates the human being as someone who comes to life through God's divinely uttered words and who is in turn summoned to hear God's word addressed to him/her in obedient responsive action. In a similar manner,

---

16. It is also worth considering the now-common proposal that Genesis 1 depicts creation as a cosmic temple, just as Genesis 2 depicts Eden as a temple sanctuary. In this scheme, the claim that humans are in the "image" (*tselem*) of the deity would suggest that humans function in a role somewhat analogous to that of a cult statue in an ancient Near Eastern sanctuary. Humans would thus be the cultic icons of God, filled with the spirit of the deity, mediating divine presence and rule into the temple-cosmos.

17. Rad, *Old Testament Theology*, 145.

human correspondence to God, in Wolff's view, comprises the capability of communicating with God, made possible by the unique gift of speech, but it also extends to the human relation to the rest of creation. Just as God is engaged in creating activity with regard to all things in the world, so the human being too must enter into a creative relationship with all the things of the world.[18] In this manner, constitutive and functional likeness converge in the key idea of relationality, which aptly expresses their interconnectedness: human likeness to God as a given of human nature can only be realized through free purposive action, through the fulfillment of the mission inherent in the creational gift.

Is there a difference between the idea of image and the connected expression of likeness? This is a question that has ceaselessly vexed commentators on the Priestly creation narrative. What meaning does the text seek to convey with the juxtaposition of the two phrases "in our image, in our likeness"? There have been innumerable suggestions made on how to distinguish image from likeness. However, one thing is clear: the two connected expressions are in Hebrew a stylistic device named parallelism, a widespread stylistic characteristic of biblical language in which synonyms are employed to render various aspects of the same meaning. The Hebrew *selem*, meaning "image" in the sense of a "statue" or "a work of plastic art," and the word *demut* meaning "likeness," "something like," do not differ in any significant manner. The latter is simply a specification of the former in pointing to the nature of image-character as inner kinship and similarity.[19] As Josef Schreiner explains, according to modern exegetes, *selem* has the concrete and well-definable meaning of "statue," while *demut* attenuates the clear-cut primary sense—which originates in the plastic arts and therefore is evocative of the forbidden Israelite practice of image-making—and focuses on the idea of comparison instead. On this view, *demut* is added in order to preclude a literalistic interpretation of *selem* and is employed to pinpoint the associative field in which image can be understood properly.[20] As we can see, the meaning of the two phrases can be defined with considerable clarity and yet a certain indefiniteness remains. The questions of

---

18. Wolff explains: "When man enters into relationship to the things of the world, whether in his day's work, or in his meals, or in his discoveries, he also enters objectively into relationship with God, as their Creator, who has appointed these things to him. Accordingly, the relation of correspondence, to which his destiny as 'God's image' points, is also to be seen in the fact that man has to cope in the world with the very things that God has created." See Wolff, *Anthropology of the Old Testament*, 160.

19. Rad, *Old Testament Theology*, 144.

20. Schreiner, *Theologie des Alten Testaments*, 158, note 145.

constitutive and functional likeness in various interpretations oscillate and issue in irresolvable ambiguity.

In sum, the Old Testament idea of the image of God remains open for interpretation with regard to the specific content of the likeness. However, it provides more indications concerning the implementation of the likeness as a divinely entrusted task. It focuses on the relationship with God and man/woman which is one of unique communication and human action in the created world in the name of God: humans are called to connect the entire created world to God by virtue of their special status and their distinctive ruling and governing action. Nevertheless, the few parallel texts within the Old Testament that reflect on creation in the light of the Genesis narrative at a later phase, give witness to an interesting development that culminates in the sapiential literature of the first century BC, which was itself influenced by Hellenistic Greek thought.[21] In these few texts, one can trace a tendency of moving towards a more ontological interpretation of the idea of likeness to God. The original relational and functional interpretation is reinterpreted as being suggestive of a certain constitutive likeness inherent in the nature of man: "Because God created man for incorruption/ And made him an image of his own proper being" (Wis 2:23)—it is in this manner that the author of this passage reinterprets creation in the light of the *eschaton*, setting the idea of likeness in the perspective of the divine nature that is mirrored in the human image. As we shall see, the ontological interpretation gradually takes precedence over the functional one during the period of the church fathers and reaches full citizenship in medieval thought.

While there are only a few passages in the Old Testament that reflect on the idea of the human being as God's image, and so this theme can by no means be regarded as central to Old Testament thought, it occupies a uniquely central place in New Testament thinking, where it occurs in a christological perspective in the form of an explicit image-theology in the Pauline letters and in a more indirect, allusive form in John's Gospel.[22] The two loci where Christ is expressly called God's image in the entire New Testament can be found in two Pauline texts. One phrase is in the second letter to the Corinthians: "The god of this age has blinded the minds of unbelievers, so that they cannot see the light of the gospel of the glory of Christ, who is the image of God" (2 Cor 4:4). The other statement can be found in the letter to the Colossians: "He is the image of the invisible God, the firstborn over all creation" (Col 1:15). The idea of Christ being the image

21. See, for example, Hamman's account in *L'Homme, Image de Dieu*, 9–18.

22. See ibid., 19–33. On the Johannine rendering of the idea of image see Brambilla, *Antropologia Teologica*, 337–38. Brambilla draws on Udo Schnelle's "Johannische Anthropologie," in Schnelle, *Neutestamentliche Anthropologie*, 134–70.

of God, according to exegetes, may have been part of the teaching of the apostolic community and so both Pauline *loci* are most probably quotations from already existing faith formulations. Besides these two key passages, Paul elaborates a real image-theology prompted by the creation narrative in the book of Genesis. He applies to Christ the notion of image in two distinctive and yet interrelated manners. On the one hand, there are Pauline passages that confess Christ to be God's image; on the other, a variety of texts speak about the community of believers as one founded by the resurrected Christ and renewed in its likeness to God. In both cases, Paul has the figure of the first man, Adam, in mind, who was created in God's image and in whom the image-character was marred because of the fall. On the Pauline comparison, Christ is the true Adam who is *the* Image of God (as contrasted to Adam who was created *in* God's image) and in whom creation is fulfilled and the image becomes clearly visible again. In Christ, God's glory shines forth with a renewed splendor and receives its most perfect expression. Christ, as the true man, restores and re-creates through his death and resurrection the image that was blurred as a consequence of sin in humanity. Those who follow Christ and participate in his mystery through baptism are transformed in him to become images of God like him: "Do not lie to each other, since you have taken off your old self with its practices and have put on the new self, which is being renewed in knowledge in the image of its Creator" (Col 3:9–10). By means of this exhortation, the letter to the Colossians connects the analogy of the baptismal vestment with reflection on the idea of image, in the light of the Genesis story. It is not only in this life that the Christian, in an eminent sense, is transformed through Christ into God's image. He will also share in Christ's resurrection eschatologically: Christ's resurrected body is the model (image) for all believers in the double sense of being both the cause and also the exemplar of the transformation of the earthly body into the glorious body. It is likewise the question of the resurrection that is elaborated upon in the most important text of Paul's image-theology. In the first letter to the Corinthians (1 Cor 15:45–49), an antithesis is once again set up between the first man, Adam, who was of "the dust of the earth" and who "became a living being" (here Paul quotes Gen 2:7) and the second Adam, the second man who is from heaven and who gives life:

> So it is written: "The first man Adam became a living being," the last Adam a life-giving spirit. The spiritual did not come first, but the natural, and after that the spiritual. The first man was of the dust of the earth, the second man from heaven. As was the earthly man, so are those who are of the earth; and as is the man from heaven, so also are those who are of heaven. *And just as we*

have borne the likeness of the earthly man, so shall we bear the likeness of the man from heaven.[23] (1 Cor 15:45-49)

In this text, too, it is Christ who is the pivot of the comparison between the earthly and the heavenly, the natural and the spiritual. He is both the reason and the goal of transformation in the resurrection, and the prototype of the new creation. In contrast to Platonic conceptions, the opposition here is not between body and soul (or mind, that is, *noûs*), but between two conditions of the entire person—the present earthly condition and the future heavenly condition—that are thought of as being continuous with one another, not in spite of, but on account of, the body.[24] As we can see, the Pauline theology of the image is a complex re-reading of the Genesis idea from a soteriological, christological, and ecclesiological perspective, which intertwine throughout the texts, thereby forming a multidimensional vision.

The Johannine anthropology of the image reflects the profound appropriation of the Genesis theme, expressed now, however, in a more indirect, allusive manner within a christological context. Christ is characterized as the perfect human being, the true Adam, who is the Son in a perfect relation of harmony with the Father's being and acting. Here, too, Christ is the perfect image of God, but this truth is conveyed indirectly through subtle allusions to the Genesis creation narrative throughout the Gospel. When Pilate presents Jesus to the crowd with the words, "Here is the man!" (John 19:5), he indirectly and unwittingly highlights the key claim of the Gospel: Christ, the obedient Son of the Father, represents the fullness of our humanity. When blood and water are reported to be flowing from Jesus's pierced side (John 19:34)—as signs of the new life which Christians experience by living a life in Christ—the reader recognizes the hint at the Genesis story where Eve is created from the rib taken from Adam's side (Gen 2:21-22). And when Christ breathes the Holy Spirit on the disciples (John 20:22), he imitates God's creative act of blowing the breath of life into Adam's nostrils (Gen 2:7) thereby making him alive. The underlying governing idea of John's Gospel is that Christ, the perfect human being, through his life, death, and resurrection, embodies our eschatological fulfillment, recapitulating the beginning, that is, creation, and realizing the fullness of our image-character with regard to God. With the complex New Testament interpretation of Christ as the true meaning and the real dimension of the human image, the stage is set for further reflection on the full import of the Genesis text in the light of Christ's revealing mission: in Christ the functional and the ontological

23. My emphasis.
24. See Hamman, *L'Homme, Image de Dieu*, 32.

interpretation of the image unite in a revelatory manner. As we shall see, the church fathers read the Genesis narratives through such a thoroughly christological lens.

The Place of the Image in Patristic Thought

Because the perspective of the church fathers is essentially christological and revelation-oriented, they do not develop a systematic anthropological account on its own. Neither do they engage in a philosophical debate on the nature of the human being.[25] Their anthropological ideas issue from theological debates concerning the person of Christ, his redeeming work, and the nature of eschatological fulfillment in the resurrection, and are set in the perspective of salvation history. In an effort to defend the orthodoxy of faith from what they see as distortions in the teachings of their adversaries, their anthropological vision is largely determined by the Genesis text, which describes the human being as created in God's image and in his likeness. And here we touch upon a pivotal point. As we saw on analyzing the meaning of the Old Testament phrase (Gen 1:26), image and likeness are synonyms in the text and are employed to illustrate the same basic idea—that humans are God's caretakers in the created world and that they are unique in having their model outside of the world, namely, in God's transcendence. Famously, in the Septuagint Greek translation of the Hebrew text (used by the authors of the New Testament and most of the church fathers) the two expressions (image, likeness) are conjoined by an inserted *kai* and so the phrase becomes: "Let us make man in our image *and* in our likeness."[26] This slight change in the text then triggers a long history of interpretations where two ways of human resemblance to God are distinguished: one according to image and another according to likeness. This distinction is then combined with an interest in discerning the place of the divine image in the human constitution, an interest that will determine the shape of a long tradition.

The first writer who develops a wealth of precious insight concerning our image character and so can be regarded as the first "systematic" theologian of the image is Irenaeus of Lyon (130–202), who is also the first to elaborate the theological difference between image and likeness. His entire reflection on human nature can be seen as the refutation of gnostic-philosophical dualism on the basis of a deeply biblical understanding of the

---

25. On the image theology of the fathers see Hamman, *L'Homme, Image de Dieu*; Shults, "Relationality and the Doctrine of *Imago Dei*," 217–42; Puskás, *A teremtés teológiája* [Theology of the Creation], 114–26.

26. See, for example, Hamman, *L'Homme, Image de Dieu*, 18–19.

fundamental unity of the human person. Against gnostics, who devalue the body as a material and therefore perishable, irredeemable, and accidental part of the human person, and who claim to find biblical justification for this view in Paul's words, "Flesh and blood cannot inherit the kingdom of God" (1 Cor 15:50), Irenaeus argues for the essential goodness of the body, which is created by God in God's image and which is made alive by the Spirit of God.

Interestingly, in his view, human beings, their bodies included, are modeled in the image of God through Christ, who is the archetype and model of each human person; as a consequence, human beings, who bear the imprints of God's hands on their body and soul, glorify their creator also in their bodily nature, which is an indispensable part of their humanity.[27] Irenaeus conceives of the unity of the human person—body and soul intimately linked—in a manner that is genuinely faithful to the anthropology of the biblical vision where neither the body nor the soul is regarded as constitutive of the human person on its own: both body and soul are called to life by God's life-giving breath or spirit. Just as in the Genesis story, where God breathes his breath into Adam's nostrils, making him a living human being whose "body" and "soul" come alive through one indivisible creative act, so too, in a deeply Christian vision, Irenaeus assigns the life-giving act to the Spirit of God, who keeps the unity of body and soul alive and makes the resurrection of the entire human person possible on the last day. In this boldly theological vision, it is God's Spirit who guarantees the unity of the human person and holds body and soul together in an indivisible and dynamic unity.

The distinction that Irenaeus famously makes (as the first among Christian writers) between "image" and "likeness" is likewise revelatory of his hard-line stance concerning human likeness to God. Against gnostic conceptions, which assign image and likeness to two distinct types of people (image to those governed by matter, and likeness to the ones ruled by the soul), Irenaeus insists on the possibility of the simultaneous presence of both of these features in every person. He interprets the Genesis expression, "in our image and in our likeness," to the effect that it discloses two distinct manners of human likeness to God: the visible unity of body and soul is

---

27. Irenaeus writes: "Now God shall be glorified in His handiwork, fitting it so as to be conformable to, and modeled after, His own Son. For by the hands of the Father, that is, by the Son and the Holy Spirit, man, and not [merely] a part of man, was made in the likeness of God. Now the soul and the spirit are certainly a part of the man, but certainly not the man; for the perfect man consists in the commingling and the union of the soul receiving the spirit of the Father, and the admixture of that fleshly nature which was molded after the image of God." Irenaeus, *Against the Heresies*, 5.6.1.

created in God's *image* and is a divine gift for every human being, while *likeness* is attained through the imitation of the model of our true humanity, namely, Christ, in a dynamic inner process whereby God's Spirit forms the human person to reach an ever-greater likeness to God. The divine gift of the Spirit—which animates Christians on the way towards assuming an ever-fuller unity with Christ, and through him with the Triune God—is imparted by baptism, which is the start of the dynamic process leading towards full likeness. On this view, visible bodily existence, created in the image of God, is indispensable as a foundation upon which the ultimate and still-to-be-accomplished perfect likeness is built. Here again, the importance of the entire person is confirmed as a site where human likeness to God is eminently displayed.

Tertullian (c.155–c.240), in the wake of Irenaeus and fighting against Marcionite Gnosticism, likewise argues for the essential goodness and image-character of the body that for him too constitutes an indivisible unity with the soul. The entire human person is seen by Tertullian as an integral unity where, much in the way Irenaeus argued, body and soul cannot exist apart, but form some kind of inseparable fusion. God's Spirit, the Spirit of life is "entwined" and "commingled" with the "flesh" "and so intimate is the union, that it may be deemed to be uncertain whether the flesh bears about the soul, or the soul the flesh; or whether the flesh acts as *apparitor* to the soul, or the soul to the flesh."[28] In this manner, because the entire human being is the carefully made and beloved artefact of God, to whom God gives his own breath (*flatus*) to make him alive, it is the entire human person who is created in God's image and who bears essential likeness to God. Tertullian, just like Irenaeus, thus situates the image character in the whole of the human person, body and soul alike, and defines it, first of all, as ultimate freedom endowed by God.[29]

However, things are not so simple for Tertullian, since he also makes an important qualification of his claim that image is a global characteristic of the entire person, by asserting that, were one forced to assess the degree of likeness in the case of the body and of the soul, it might be the soul that would carry the day. As someone who is first among Christian writers to reflect on the nature of the soul in a separate treatise (*De Anima*), while not parting ways with Irenaeus, does, however, modify the picture slightly when he gives pride of place to the soul (and in some passages to reason) in

---

28. Tertullian, *On the Resurrection of the Flesh*, 7.

29. "I find, then, that man was by God constituted free, master of his own will and power; indicating the presence of God's image and likeness in him by nothing so well as by this constitution of his nature." Tertullian, *Against Marcion*, 2.5.

terms of attributing to it a greater degree of likeness than to the body.[30] On this idea, just as God can be characterized as spirit/intellect, so the human being too bears a likeness to God in having a soul and being endowed with reason. With this, human likeness—while fully accorded to the body—is attributed in an eminent sense to the soul (and reason) in Tertullian's thought. That being said, Tertullian's position remains squarely within the confines of a genuinely biblical anthropology and is free of an imposed, dualistic, philosophical stance.

With their holistic view of the place of the divine image in the human person, Irenaeus and Tertullian remain exceptions, rather than the general rule among patristic authors, whose vast majority subscribes to a more restrictive notion of our image character. One can register an early and influential development of such a restrictive notion in the work of the Jewish philosopher Philo of Alexandria (15 BC–50 AD), whose biblical exegesis combines various elements from Platonic thought. While Plato famously held that image—as a way of relation—is characteristic of the sensible world only in being a reflection of the intelligible world of Ideas, Philo turns the idea around and situates the image of God in the intellectual part of the soul (*noũs*) of the human person.[31] For him, it is the spiritual *noũs* alone that bears a recognizable likeness to God, who is likewise invisible immaterial intelligence. *Noũs*, the mind—as the seat of the human faculty of knowing—is God's gift and enables humans to obtain an ever fuller, though never exhaustive, knowledge of God. Consequently, the body—which belongs to the sensible and visible world, and is material and mortal—is entirely excluded in Philo's scheme from being part of the image. Interestingly, while Philo opposes Plato's vision concerning the sensible nature of the image, he nonetheless fully endorses Plato's anthropological dichotomy of body and soul. In Plato, the soul (taken in itself as originating in the divine *noũs*) is superior to the body in being simple, immobile, immortal, and without passions (*apathēs*)—attributes akin to the divine nature—and it is only through contact with the body that the soul is forced to enter into a world of mortality and misery and undergoes the influence of the passions. The soul is therefore not seen by Plato as united to the body, but as existing in tension with it, wanting to escape from the body and desiring to return to its model, the divine eternal intellect. The ultimate aim in this scheme is the liberation of the soul from the miserable body and the influence of the

---

30. See, for example, ibid., 2.5.

31. For an account of the elements of Platonic Greek thought appropriated by Philo, see Hamman, *L'Homme, Image de Dieu*, 103–13.

passions aroused by the body and the final return of the soul to the divine model through a gradual purification from all material hindering impurity.

It is this line of thought that underlies, as a detectable presumption, Philo's interpretation of the Genesis narratives in his treatise on the creation (*De opificio mundi*). Like Plato, Philo too opposes the intelligible to the sensible world and therefore situates likeness with God exclusively in the intellectual soul. On his interpretation, the two Genesis creation narratives refer to two kinds of human beings: one heavenly and another earthly. Heavenly, ideal man (a generic personification of ideal human nature)—as depicted in the first (Priestly) creation narrative—is said to be created in the image of God and indeed bears likeness to God in having an immaterial intelligent *noũs* and wearing the imprint of the divine spirit. Earthly man (as the concrete historical instantiation of the human being characterized by the Yahwist's narrative), however, is not said to be created in God's image, but is said to be fashioned from the soil of the earth and therefore is mortal, sensible, consisting of a body and a soul and gendered as man and woman. In Philo's interpretation, the body is just a temporary and provisional addendum that will disappear when the state of full likeness is attained with God through the intellectual soul. Philo's account is a curious amalgam of Platonic thought and Jewish biblical exegesis and had a great impact on Christian writers who either wanted, like him, to reconcile philosophical ideas and biblical revelation, or were unwittingly working with ideas received from Philonian thought.

An interesting example of the impact of Philonian exegesis and its modification within a Christian scheme, resulting in a controversial approach to the body, can be detected in the works of Clement of Alexandria (c.150–c.215). Clement, who—often uncritically eclectic in his philosophical assumptions—like Philo, situates the divine image in the *noũs*, that is, reason within the immortal soul, excluding in this manner the mortal body from a likeness to God and he too distinguishes between earthly and heavenly man in the Genesis narratives. His Christian account, in contrast to Philonian exegesis, however, differs on an important point. In his anthropological remarks, Clement does not oppose, but rather combines, the two creation narratives, arguing (still in a thoroughly Philonian fashion) that they portray two simultaneous dimensions of man: his earthly character as being modeled from the dust of the earth and his heavenly nature as being animated by God's life-giving breath. Through such life-giving breath, God communicates to man an intelligent soul (*noũs*), which governs the human person (*hēgemonikon*), and it is in this respect that he is said to be created according to God's image and likeness.

One could say that Clement's exclusion of the body from the likeness to God is more of a formal, logical necessity—resulting from the inner dynamics of the philosophical ideas he uncritically borrows—than a genuine expression of his own conviction concerning the actual status of the human body.[32] On several occasions he also counters a too intellectualistic interpretation of the image by highlighting the importance of the practical sphere where likeness to God can be realized as the fruit of lived and active charity.

While Clement's exclusion of the body from the likeness to God may not reflect a consistent theoretical decision, but is rather the unfavorable consequence of his borrowed and eclectic philosophy, Origen's (184–254) similar insistence on the non-participation of the body in the divine likeness solidifies into a consciously embraced philosophical stance. Origen consciously breaks with the tradition of the two previous centuries (and Irenaeus and Tertullian within it) when he plainly rejects the image-character of the body and, in the wake of Philo and Clement, situates the image in the *noūs* of the soul. The philosophical necessity that makes him so fervently oppose the idea of finding the image in the body, comes from the rejection of an anthropomorphic notion of God, which, however, for Origen, is unavoidable if one assumes that the body bears likeness to God: if the body is created in God's image, then God must have a body, which is an idolatrous thought.

Origen, like Philo, interprets the two creation narratives as describing respectively corporeal earthly man and (heavenly) inner man, both of which remain, however, a characteristic of the human being after the fall. Corporeal man (as the second creation narrative suggests), in being modeled from the earth, is subject to *pathē* (passion) and undergoes the pernicious influence of the material body. The part of the soul that is forced into interaction with the earthly body is therefore inferior and is slave to irrational bodily motions. Inner man, according to the first Genesis narrative, is said to be created in the image of God and is governed by the *noūs*—the exclusive seat of image and likeness for Origen.

The consequences of this option also affect the shape of his Christology, which does not recognize the connection between the incarnation and the creation of man, but considers Christ's saving work as necessitated exclusively by the fall. In apparent discontinuity with the creation, Christ came to restore the image and likeness lost due to the sin of the first humans. For Origen, it is the trinitarian Word and not the incarnate Christ who is God's image (the Logos is "the image of the invisible God" Col 1:15)

---

32. See ibid., 122. Hamman also observes how—in surprising discontinuity with his endorsed stance concerning the inferior status of the body—on various occasions, Clement praises the beauty of the physical body as the "image of the Logos." Ibid., 122.

and so Jesus's visible humanity is just secondary or mediated image in this sense.[33] While his trinitarian interpretation of the image initiates a tradition that culminates in Augustine's trinitarian reflection on the traces of Trinity in the human mind, his Christology, which does not take into account the link between the creation and the incarnation, awaits correction by later thought.

One such correction can be detected in the evolution of the thought of Athanasius of Alexandria (c.297-373), whose theology displays an interesting shift of emphasis. Athanasius, although initially following in Origen's wake, eventually moves away, towards a more biblically faithful and less philosophically determined interpretation, identifying the image of the invisible God with the incarnate Christ, who, fully human and truly divine, exemplifies our true humanity and is also the agent of our divinization. In this manner, through a complete reversal of perspectives, the creation no longer serves as an ultimate point of reference: within the new perspective of the Word made flesh, the incarnation is seen as the renewal and accomplishment of the creation, which receives the status of just a first sketch in comparison to the full richness realized by Christ. The idea of image and likeness at the initial creation gives way to the idea of divinization whereby humans are transformed to become participants in the divine life and are transfigured—by virtue of the salvific gift of the incarnation—to become similar to God. In order to demonstrate what human likeness to God means for the Christian, one need not turn to the Genesis stories in the first place, but must rather contemplate the mystery of the divine Word made truly human and the consequences this has for our humanity.

This new scheme allows Athanasius to work out a renewed conception of the human body with respect to its likeness to God. Athanasius's entire Christology is a plea for the reintegration of the body in the image and a unifying vision of body and soul. If Christ did not have a real human body, then we have not been redeemed and there is also no bodily resurrection. It is a Christology—consistent with Scripture and the tradition—that compels Athanasius to argue for the true and full humanity of Christ, his body, senses, and passions included: "the Savior had not a body without a soul, nor without sense or intelligence; for it was not possible, when the Lord had become man for us, that His body should be without intelligence: nor was the salvation effected in the Word Himself a salvation of body only, but of

---

33. As Hamman notes, Origen is the first to develop a Word-Image theology by transposing the idea of the image from the plane of anthropology to the plane of trinitarian reflection. His biblical sources can be found in the sapiential literature, in the letter to the Hebrews and the letter to the Colossians (1:15), which he quotes 129 times throughout his works. Ibid., 137.

soul also."³⁴ Only if one assumes the true humanity of Christ, can one hope for real salvation and the ultimate divinization of the entire human person. Athanasius's anthropology, which is entirely governed by his Christology, joins Irenaeus's holistic vision in providing the conceptual means with which to avoid the dead-end of a body-soul dichotomy. There is no need to situate the christologically understood image in the *noūs* at the expense of the body within such a theology, since the emphasis here is put on the body that is united to the soul, despised by Greek philosophy, but rehabilitated and transfigured by the incarnate Christ, the eternal Logos.

At the same period, we find an eminent example of image-theology in Gregory of Nyssa (335–94), who reflects on the issue of human likeness to God extensively, both in his theological treatises and his pastoral sermons. As a result of such a sustained meditation on the relationship between God and the human person, a veritable anthropology unfolds which takes into account the role of man in the universe and inquires about the ultimate basis of the resemblance with God. Gregory seeks to be faithful to the biblical teaching, while his philosophical training allows him to set the scriptural message in the light of theoretical reflection, out of which issues a theology of outstanding richness. Gregory's theoretical speculation extends as far as a reflection on the place of man in the universe and the claim that the human being is set in between two extremes: between the sensible and the intelligible, the inanimate and animal world and the divine life of God, corporeal irrational beings and incorporeal divine Logos. Man, as a borderline creature, is set in the middle and is called to harmonize in himself these two opposing orders. Entrusted with free will, the human person can either choose to tend towards God and so assimilate to the divine nature by sharing in the divine light, or join the tendencies of irrational animal life and darken in himself the likeness to God. Gregory freely employs here a term borrowed from Philo (*methorios*—"forming a frontier") to elaborate his own distinctive vision.

Within his scheme it is not a similarity with the elements of the universe or the indisputable continuity with the material world that forms the basis of human likeness to God. Gregory rejects the "pagan" attempts that argue for the unique position of man on the basis of the Middle Stoic idea that man is a microcosm in being composed of the same elements as the universe.³⁵ Such logic, besides concealing a non-Christian pantheism, does not account appropriately for the unique position of the human being in

34. Athanasius, *Synodal Letter to the People of Antioch*, 7.

35. Hamman explains that the idea of man being a microcosm comes from Posidonius, a Middle Stoic thinker. Hamman relies on Rudolf Allers's study *Microcosmus: From Anaximandrus to Paracelsus*. Ibid., 207., note 43.

God's creation: if man is on a par with the rest of the inanimate and irrational creation, what is one to make of the Genesis claim that he (alone) was made in the image of God?[36] Gregory's logic proceeds through a strict adherence to the teaching of Scripture, which for him is also the indispensable hermeneutic tool for answering the questions asked by philosophy. Perfectly conscious of the difficulty inherent in the claim that finite and mortal man could be the image of the eternal infinite God, he concludes that our image character is by no means due to a continuity with the universe, but is God's gift by which God communicates the attributes of his nature to the human being in such a manner as to make man similar to God.

In his view, the rational and intelligent element in man is created in the image of God, while the sexed body, which is also irrational, does not bear likeness to God because God transcends the distinction of male and female and does not have a body.[37] He interprets the Genesis account of the creation of man (Gen 1:26-28) to the effect that creation took place in two consecutive steps, where the generic human being—or more precisely, collective mankind—was created first, that is to say, man/mankind in its totality is created in God's image and is characterized by the use of reason and has a rational soul.[38] The concrete human person, who is sexed according to the added division of male and female, is made only as a second step of the creation. Therefore, Gregory concludes that sexuality, taken in the narrow sense of "reproductive function," does not belong to the human attributes that bear likeness to God.

Nonetheless, apart from Gregory's strangely negative view of reproductive sexuality, his overall stance concerning the significance of the body for our image-character is far from a negative one. While he aligns himself with the Alexandrian tradition by attributing to the *noūs* the image in an eminent sense, he also attenuates the hard-line Alexandrian position by making room in his account for the body, which at the resurrection will even

---

36. Gregory does not dispense completely with the idea of man as microcosm, but he employs it in most cases implicitly. What is important for him is that the ultimate reference in the analogy between the cosmos and man must be the doctrine of the image of God in man, which alone explains the unique status of the human being with regard to the rest of the cosmos. See Thunberg, *Microcosm and Mediator*, 135-36.

37. See Gregory, *On the Making of Man*, 16.

38. Lars Thunberg thinks that the first creation exists only in God's foreknowledge as an ideal type: "There is, thus, to Gregory one ideal man, who is after the image of God, and who is in fact a type of a future blessed humanity. This man is not sexually differentiated.... The 'second' creation, on the other hand, divides humanity into man and woman, though this does not change the pre-sexual character of the divine image in this 'second' man, for the sexual distinction in the creation of Adam is made by God in view of the coming fall." Thunberg, *Microcosm and Mediator*, 148-49.

share in the soul's likeness to God. The soul is viewed as being directly God's image, while the body shares in the soul's image nature in a secondary way, through mediation; the body is just "the mirror of the mirror" (in Gregory's favorite mirror-analogy). In his holistic and unifying vision, Gregory rejects both the possibility of the pre-existence of the soul and the pre-existence of the body, claiming their essential and simultaneous interdependence.

In the wake of Gregory of Nyssa, Augustine of Hippo (354–430) develops his own distinctive and innovative theology of the image, which exerts a lasting impact on later Western tradition. His account is neither systematic nor homogeneous, however, since his discourse on the image is embedded in various contexts and therefore displays a diversity of perspectives.[39] Like Origen and the Alexandrian school of theology, Augustine, too, claims that it is the intellectual soul, the soul's spiritual faculties, residing in the highest point of the soul named *mens* (a Latin term corresponding to the Greek *noūs*), where the site of the image is to be found in the human being. The *mens* is immortal and it has a capability to reflect on its own situation and to recognize and know God, the Creator. To the objection of the Manicheans—who insisted that the orthodox reading of the Genesis story, where emphasis is put on man's being made in the image of God, reflects an anthropomorphic idea of God—Augustine replies that it is not the outer shape, the body, that is created in God's image, but the inner spiritual and rational soul. This is what makes humans superior to the brutes and capable of knowing God. Nonetheless, the body may bear some likeness to God in view of its upright position, which distinguishes man from the animal world.

In his investigations concerning the image, Augustine is guided by the renowned Johannine verse: "We know that when he appears, we shall be like him, for we shall see him as he is" (1 John 3:2), and also by Paul's idea in the letter to the Romans: "For those God foreknew he also predestined to be conformed to the likeness of his Son" (Rom 8:29). To this is added his famous aspiration to get to know both himself and God in the light of the mystery of the Trinity. What makes his inquiry unique is its trinitarian orientation: for Augustine, unlike his predecessors, it is the Triune God in whose image the human person is created and, therefore, the perfect model-image is not solely the Son, the second person of the Trinity. When Augustine famously asks in what way the *mens*, the intellectual part of the soul, may be the image of God, his underlying central assumption is that our

---

39. Augustine's image theology is scattered in various works. See, for example, his commentary *On Genesis Against the Manichees*; *Unfinished Literal Commentary On Genesis*; *Literal Commentary On Genesis*; and his *On the Trinity*.

mind is capable of recognizing God's traces within itself because God gave it the capacity to know its Creator.

Despite the importance Augustine gives to the mind with regard to the image, thereby excluding the body from the site where our likeness to God becomes manifest, he nevertheless does not undervalue the crucial significance of the body, which he sees as intimately linked to the soul by forming with it an indissoluble unity. As a biblical underpinning, he often refers to the Pauline dictum that "No one ever hated his own body" (Eph 5:29), to the effect that the body is good (*bonum*), even if the soul is a greater good (*bonum magnum*).[40] The body is the instrument of the soul and its most intimate ally; the two cannot be thought apart in the living human person.

Augustine's theology of the image, with its emphasis on the intellectual *mens* and the exclusion from the image of the body, displays an Origenean influence, but it also distances itself from the Origenean negative judgment concerning the body and elaborates a more positive vision, arguing for its ultimate goodness and indispensability.[41] Intellectualism and an acute sense of the reality of the human constitution make his anthropology deeply fascinating and challenging.

As a last significant example of the Eastern tradition in this respect, one must make mention of Maximus the Confessor (580–662), whose entire vision can be seen as being determined by the doctrine of the *imago Dei*, although he makes only rare references to the explicit doctrine itself.[42] While his entire anthropology points in the direction of the re-integration of the body into the image of God, on the formal level of discourse concerning the actual site of human likeness to God, Maximus does not break with the inherited Alexandrian tradition that clearly places the image in the *noūs*, the higher part of the soul, which is rational and is alone capable of contemplating God by enjoying a certain familiarity with God. What he does, however, is to emphasize the close interconnection between the mind (*noūs*) and the rest of man. That is to say, the mind is not set in a sharp contrast with the passible part of the soul or the body, but is seen as integrated into the overall unity of the human constitution. The mind is not

---

40. In his view concerning the relationship between body and soul, Augustine is influenced by Plotinus's ontology when he holds that body and soul both belong to different levels of God's good creation. The perfection of the bodily-sensual level, however, is realized to a fuller degree in the spiritual-intellectual level. See Puskás, *A teremtés teológiája*, 118.

41. Hamman traces one single occurrence of the idea that the body too is made in the image of God in Augustine's writings in his *Eighty-Three Different Questions*, a work from Augustine's early period. See Hamman, *L'Homme, Image de Dieu*, 259, note 129.

42. See Thunberg, *Microcosm and Mediator*, especially "Chapter Three: Maximus's Anthropology in General," 95–168.

just a part of man's soul, but is his "thinking subject" or "spiritual subject."[43] For Maximus, the *noūs* represents the whole of man who is in relation with God. This important emphasis on the unity of the human person and the interrelation of the mind with the whole of man is what makes his account, we may say, distinctively unique among the Christian writers.

It is such a unitary approach that governs his own distinction between image and likeness, a significant contribution to the theology of the image. While the "image" in Maximus is the natural gift with which man is endowed at creation, "likeness" completes what is of nature and in this process the whole of man is at play. Likeness unfolds as the result of man's good use of freedom, as the outcome of his positive self-determination where not only mind but the activities of the body and the senses are also crucially important. Likeness realizes a total loving relation to God, mind, and body alike, through the appropriation of virtues and the individual accomplishment of the presence of the incarnate Logos in the world. The Maximian concept of likeness thus extends (even if only implicitly) the image character of the mind to the whole of man: his body and his soul as an indissoluble unity. The mind radiates its likeness to God onto the body, while the body is an ally in the realization of the likeness. At the end of the day, Maximus's theology implicitly, even if not professedly, continues the Irenaean tradition, where the body too participates in the image.

So where does all of this leave us? Our survey of patristic authors, both from the West and the East, discloses an interesting common tendency. While there is a clear shift away from earlier attempts to integrate the body into the image (e.g., in Irenaeus and Tertullian), we also register a more or less united effort (with the one exception of Origen) to counter a too hard-line philosophical exclusion of the body from the image. Obviously, in early Christian reflection on the issue, where the body is explicitly seen as the place of the image (together with the soul in an indissoluble biblical unity)—even though the content of the message is truly in accordance with the scriptural vision—the vision is vulnerable to the charge of anthropomorphism, since God, as a divine model for man, might be mistakenly conceived as having a body. Probably due to the anthropomorphist weakness of the holistic position, this line of thinking was not carried further in this form. Instead, almost unanimously in the West and the East, and among members of various theological schools, the same common stance was adopted that localized the image within the immortal and incorporeal soul, the part of man that distinguishes him from the animal kingdom and

---

43. As Thurnberg explains, "thinking subject" is Hans Urs von Balthasar's term, which Balthasar coins to describe the nature of *noūs* in Maximus. See ibid., 112.

directly connects man to God. Within this common trend, the Alexandrian tradition introduced a restriction by placing the image in the higher part of the soul in a narrow sense, i.e., the intellectual mind (*noūs*), which alone is capable of receiving and knowing God. The endorsement of the view that it is only the soul that bears God's image was also more amenable to the Hellenistic anthropological vision, which likewise saw the immortal and intellectual soul as the part of man that has a relation to the divine.

What strikes one, however, in the varying views of Christian writers, is their almost universal effort to soften a too narrowly philosophical exclusion of the body from the image. Except for Origen—whose theoretical option for the pre-existence of the soul does not allow for a more lenient stance concerning the body, which he sees as the consequence of punishment necessitated by the fall—the rest of the authors in our survey look for ways whereby the image, in one way or another, can be extended to the body and the sensual aspect of human existence. While they all formally profess the tenet of the spiritual nature of the image intimately linked to the soul, they also attenuate the theoretical import of this claim by implicitly making room for the body within the image on theological grounds. We saw how Clement of Alexandria recognizes the importance of the body in the practical sphere where likeness to God is attained as the fruit of lived and active charity in imitating God's own loving action. Athanasius likewise includes the body as the consequence of his wholesome Christology: only if Christ becomes truly incarnate, assuming our true humanity in the unity of body and soul, can he truly obtain the salvation of the whole person, body and soul alike. Gregory of Nyssa likewise allows for the body's participation in the image character of the soul. The soul as the image of God *par excellence* radiates its likeness also onto the body, which is even seen as sharing eschatologically in the image character of the soul after the resurrection, where the ultimate eternal unity of body and soul will exist in an accomplished likeness to God. Augustine too emphasizes the indissoluble unity of body and soul and the essential goodness of the body as the soul's intimate ally and indispensable instrument that will participate in the resurrection, receiving an incorruptible form. Maximus the Confessor, in the wake of Gregory of Nyssa, elaborates an impressive theological vision where man's bodily existence has a crucial role in the mediation between the intelligible and the sensible, between heaven and earth. Man, as a borderline creature consisting of both body and soul, is called to reconcile in himself the fundamental divisions of the world. To actualize his vocation as a likeness to God, he must make good use of his freedom wherein mind and body are equally involved and wherein both play a pivotal part in the realization of a loving relationship with God.

What we have here is a sustained effort to make room for the body in the theology of the image. Christian writers, on the one hand, counter Platonic dualism and try to avoid a too spiritualistic concept of man, and on the other, aim to supersede Manichaeism, which despises the body and maintains the pre-existence of the soul. While both the Platonic and the Manichean vision conceive of an accidental unity of body and soul, Christian writers argue for the substantial unity of the bodily and the spiritual parts of man, who is created as one indivisible unity.[44] According to this Christian vision, the body is essentially good as God's gift given at the creation and as redeemed by Christ. It is certainly not regarded as a punishment due to the fall. The theological fact of Christ's incarnation and resurrection entails a positive view of the body and results in the inclusion of the body in the image character of man, even if only in an implicit manner. We may discern two major trends in the attempts directed at the inclusion of the bodily and the sensible into the theology of the image.[45] Both attempts share the same ambition to establish the lasting and indissoluble unity of body and soul. However, they differ in their views concerning the way such a unity is theoretically conceived. One trend aims to reconcile the division of body and soul by establishing their stable unity through God's Spirit who is thought to keep both body and soul alive in a divinely imparted unity. Irenaeus is a prominent exponent of this view.[46] In Irenaeus's vision, the Holy Spirit enlivens both the human body and the soul and also makes them conform to the image of God. Proponents of the other option (and most church fathers fall within this camp) make room for the body by subordinating it to the spiritual soul. Through such subordination they can account for the participation of the body in the soul's image character: the soul is seen to radiate its primary image character onto the body, which becomes in this manner a second-order image on account of the soul. Thus, the bodily and the sensible alike—in complete unity with the soul—are drawn within the dynamics of the soul's image-bearing activity.

This second trend (the one that subordinates the body to the soul) takes two distinct forms in the East and in the West, depending on the respective discourses and contexts where the idea of subordination is inserted. In

---

44. See Brambilla, *Antropologia Teologica*, 339.

45. See Puskás, *A teremtés teológiája*, 117–18.

46. While one finds aborted attempts and passing remarks to the effect that the body too is included in the image, the overwhelming majority of patristic authors, both in the Greek and the Latin tradition, locate the image in the soul. Those authors who admit of the body being in the image, however, remain largely inarticulate on the exact manner in which such a claim is to be understood. See Burghardt, *The Image of God in Man according to Cyril of Alexandria*, 14–19.

the East (in Alexandrian theology), it is the ultimate goal of contemplating God that governs the discourse on the unity of body and soul. The Eastern contemplative vision speaks in terms of the necessary restraint exerted by the soul on the sensible and the bodily, and the indispensable discernment of the spiritual within the sensible, in order that the person may remain unhindered in the contemplation of the divine. The soul thus disciplines the sensible and the bodily so that they may become a suitable means for the ascent to the divine archetype. In the West the same idea of the subjection of the body to the soul is embedded in an ethical discourse in which the body is viewed as a necessary means for the accomplishment of good deeds. The emphasis here does not so much lie on the dominion of the soul over the body, but it is put rather on the process of attaining likeness to God through ethical action, which requires an effort of the whole person, body and soul.

Thomas Aquinas and John Paul II's "Theology of the Body"

With Thomas Aquinas and other great medieval thinkers, the theology of the image takes a distinctively different shape, not only due to the systematizing effort with regard to its elaboration, but also because—in Augustine's wake—it becomes almost exclusively part of trinitarian reflection and so loses its former connectedness to Christology.[47] The framework for the issue of the image is now the famous Augustinian claim that man created by the Triune God—who eternally knows and loves himself—bears the image of the Creator within his created intellect inasmuch as it is capable of remembering, knowing, and loving God. The human mind imitates God's acts of self-knowledge and self-love through the workings of its intellectual powers: remembering, knowing, and willing. The human person is conceived in terms of this intellectual triad as a "created trinity" (*trinitas creata*) whose image character is given with his created nature and is never lost in spite of sin. Such a presupposed interrelation between the human intellectual nature and the inner life of the Trinity largely determines the perspective of medieval theology of the image: Christ's central role in the process of imitation and transformation to an ever-fuller likeness to God is lost from view, together with the soteriological and existential considerations it would

---

47. For an overview of Aquinas's anthropological concerns see Mondin, "Immagine (di Dio nell'uomo)," in Mondin, *Dizionario enciclopedico del pensiero di San Tommaso D'Aquino*, 347–51; "Uomo," in ibid., 696–708; "Corpo umano," in ibid., 156–59; and Puskás, *A teremtés teológiája*, 132–38.

also imply, while a one-sided emphasis is put on a fixed ascending scale of likenesses that the Christian must follow in order to reach perfect likeness to God.

Thomas Aquinas's anthropology is centered around two major claims: the intellectual nature of man and the essential unity of body and soul. His primary concern is to work out a philosophical/theological transposition of the biblical vision, where the human person is portrayed as God's unique and cherished creature who is endowed with a specific status within the created world and who appears as one indivisible unity of bodily-sensible and spiritual-intellectual nature. Among various Christian anthropologies, it is Thomas's account that exerted the greatest influence on official church doctrine and was regarded as the clearest theoretical expression of traditional biblical faith. The theme of the image figures prominently in Aquinas's theology and he returns to the question on several occasions throughout his works.[48] The most well-known discursive treatment of the issue can be found in the First Part of his *Summa Theologica* where it is embedded in a discourse that (after the doctrine of God and the Trinity, the teaching concerning the angels, and consequent comments on the biblical creation narratives) inquires about the nature of man and that reflects Aquinas's own distinctive anthropology. The famous *Question 93*, which provides a discursive treatment of man's image character, is entitled, "The End or Term of the Production of Man," and comprises nine articles where Aquinas refutes various objections that may be raised against his tenets and also puts forward his own distinctive account concerning the nature of human likeness to God.[49] What becomes clear from the text (in accordance with Aquinas's other treatments of the issue) is the fact that Aquinas joins Augustine and, as we saw, almost the entire theological tradition, in situating the image in the intellectual soul, that is, the human intellect. Interestingly, responding to the objection that man does not consist of mind alone

---

48. For example, Aquinas treats of the issue of the image in a work as early as the *Commentary on the Sentences of Peter Lombard* (written around 1257 when the young Dominican commenced lecturing in the university of Paris). See Mondin, "Immagine," ibid., 350.

49. *Summa Theologica*, Ia.93.1–9. (Hereafter abbreviated as *ST*). The articles are entitled as follows: 1. Whether the image of God is man?; 2. Whether the image of God is to be found in irrational creatures?; 3. Whether the angels are more to the image of God than man is?; 4. Whether the image of God is found in every man?; 5. Whether the image of God is in man according to the Trinity of persons?; 6. Whether the image of God is in man as regards the mind only?; 7. Whether the image of man is to be found in the acts of the soul?; 8. Whether the image of the Divine Trinity is in the soul only by comparison with God as its object?; 9. Whether "likeness" is properly distinguished from "image"?

and that, therefore, when Paul says that "the man is the image . . . of God" (Aquinas quotes 1 Cor 11:7) he obviously means the whole of man and not only his mind, Aquinas replies that "there is no need to consider the image of God as existing in every part of man" because "the image of God is impressed on his mind; as a coin is an image of the king, as having the image of the king."[50] The whole of man is not God's image in an essential sense; it is only his/her intellect or mind (Aquinas stresses the inclusion of both sexes in the image) that bears the image of God and he quotes Augustine to the effect that it is the intellect—the site of human knowing and understanding—that distinguishes man from other terrestrial creatures and makes the human being "near to God in likeness."[51] Like Augustine, Thomas too extends the comparison both ways: to lower creatures, but also to God. The human intellect bears God's image also on account of the fact that it "can best imitate God in his intellectual nature," which is to say that, like God, it is capable of understanding and loving itself.[52]

He allows for a scale of likenesses within creation where the highest degree of likeness, "likeness of image," is reserved, from among bodily creatures, exclusively for man, and not even all dimensions of man, but only man's intellect. According to a lower level of likeness—one due to cause and effect—the rest of the human being (the lower parts of the soul and the body) also refer to God by way of a "trace" (*vestigium*). While Aquinas concedes that the upright position of the human body shows man's unique position (referring again to a remark by Augustine), he nonetheless concludes that "this is not to be understood as though the image of God were in man's body; but in the sense that the very shape of the human body represents the image of God in the soul by way of a trace."[53] Likeness according to trace is characteristic of all created things, which by way of existing, having a definite form, and being directed towards a destination all point to the

50. Ibid., Ia.93.6.

51. To the objection that "the distinction of male and female is in the body, therefore the image of God is also in the body and not in his mind"—Aquinas replies that the Scripture text does not imply that "the image of God came through the distinction of sex, but that the image of God belongs to both sexes, since it is in the mind, wherein there is no sexual distinction of sex, but that the image of God belongs to both sexes, since it is in the mind, wherein there is no sexual distinction." Ibid., Ia.93.6. Ostensibly, Aquinas (echoing the logic of the traditional idea of two phases of creation, but without endorsing its actual claim, namely, that intellectual man was created first and bodily sexed man was made as a next step) presupposes a common intellectual nature beyond sexual division (and bodily constitution) and it is here that he localizes the image, which therefore both man and woman are claimed to possess.

52. Ibid., Ia.93.4.

53. Ibid., Ia.93.6.

Creator and bear the trace of their ultimate cause. All things considered, in Aquinas's refined scheme, the body is accorded merely a second-order likeness, i.e., that which is common to all things in the created world, animate and inanimate alike, and which is the result of God's creative activity manifesting itself in equal measure in all existing things.

Aquinas's position determines later reflection on the issue up to the twentieth century, when John Paul II's catechetical lectures, given at papal audiences between September 1979 and November 1984, foment a budding revolution in church doctrine concerning the theme of the image.[54] More than twenty years after the lectures were delivered, their teaching today appears as a strikingly bold re-interpretation of human bodiliness in the light of human likeness to God, the implications of which are just starting to enter the focus of wider theological reflection. In fact, the term "theology of the body" was coined by John Paul II himself, who makes extensive use of the expression in his teachings, describing his own meditations on marriage and love in the audience speeches as "reflections on the theology of the body." The cycle of catechesis given during a time span of a little more than five years displays a level of academic sophistication that largely exceeds the scope of the occasion, where the audience consisted of members of the entire universal church and included just a small number of experts in the field. Notwithstanding the general nature of his public, John Paul II elaborates here his own distinctive and daring vision of human sexuality and love in conscious dialogue with the Christian tradition and personalist philosophy.[55] As Michael Waldstein has pointed out, what is at stake in the papal teaching is a reaction against Enlightenment Cartesian-Kantian conceptions of personal subjectivity associated with a mechanistic view of the natural world. In such a scientific-rationalistic framework, there is a growing split posited between body and soul, matter and spirit, nature and subjective human consciousness. Body in this scheme sides with the

---

54. John Paul II, *Man and Woman He Created Them*. John Paul II commented on the theological significance of the human body and human sexuality in various other official writings as well, for example, in his *Mulieris Dignitatem* (1988); *Letter to Families* (1994); *Veritatis Splendor* (1993); *Letter to Women* (1995). While commentators of John Paul's theology of the body usually concentrate on his vision of sexuality and marriage, I focus here on the new emphases in his underlying anthropology of likeness to God. For a general introduction into the background and structure of this pope's theology of the body, see Michael Waldstein, "Introduction," in John Paul II, *Man and Woman He Created Them*, 1–128. See also West, *Theology of the Body Explained*.

55. John Paul II is influenced by the personalism of the mystical poetry of St. John of the Cross and he also dialogues with the personalist philosophy of Max Scheler and the concept of subjectivity in Immanuel Kant. See Waldstein, "Introduction," in ibid., 1–128.

natural, material, and therefore scientifically observable and manageable natural objects and loses its intrinsic meaning as an inherent part of an intellectual person who is the indissoluble unity of both body and spirit. The human body is regarded on a par with all other bodies as part of the material neutral and value-free world; it is disconnected from the value-charged intellectual-spiritual and subjective dimension of man. Against such a dualistic understanding, the pope appeals to the theological tradition, which has always held that the body is a good and essential part of the human person on account of the incarnation of Christ and as an indispensable concomitant of the resurrection and final beatitude. While appealing to the Christian tradition, John Paul II, however, also surpasses the tradition, not so much by breaking with its general tendency, but by drawing out potential implications and in this manner complementing earlier anthropological visions. While the line of interpretations that placed the image in the human intellect is not negated, a new perspective—which views the human body as also part of the image—is thoughtfully added.

We recall that, except for early Christian writers on the issue and especially Irenaeus (and perhaps Tertullian) in this regard, the entire Western and Eastern theological tradition connects God's image with the human soul and, more specifically, its highest part, the human mind or intellect. We have also seen how Thomas Aquinas endorses, in the wake of Augustine, this same traditional stance and elaborates a complex account in which the body and the lower parts of the soul (on a par with all created things in the world) bear likeness only according to trace, while the human intellect alone owns the image. In Aquinas, our maleness or femininity does not enter into consideration with regard to our likeness to God because our bodiliness is excluded from the image as such. It is at this point that John Paul II resumes the conversation, so to speak, and makes his pivotal contribution to the discussion. Like his patristic predecessors, he too elaborates his own teaching on the body (which is obviously a fully fledged theological anthropology of the entire person and not just the human body) through a sustained commentary on Scripture: the Genesis creation narratives seen through the spectacles of Jesus's own Scripture interpretation, Jesus's own teaching in the Sermon on the Mount and concerning the resurrection, and the Pauline teaching on the body and marriage in the letter to the Ephesians (5:21–33).[56] The telling title, "Man and Woman He Created Them," already anticipates the central perspective from which the issue of bodiliness, the image, and the spousal meaning of the body (in John Paul II's own phrase)

---

56. The second chapter of the volume contains a commentary on the Song of Songs, and reflections on the book of Tobit.

is approached. On his reading, there is no caesura between the biblical assertion that the human being is created in the image of God and that this same human being is created male and female. Far from joining Gregory of Nyssa's insistence that it is our intellectual unsexed nature that was created first and that the division of sexes as apparent in our bodily form was added afterwards, and maintaining a certain distance even from Thomas Aquinas, for whom our bodily constitution does not enter the image character, John Paul II sets out to explain how, at the root of likeness to God, one finds the sexually marked body, which *is* precisely one created in the image of God. He proceeds in small, carefully pondered steps that keep close to the meaning that emerges from a close reading of the biblical text. While the insights of biblical critical scholarship are incorporated, what emerges here is rather a theological reading of the text that keeps in view the implied truth claims. In a back and forth movement between the text and a hermeneutics of philosophical/theological assumptions, and in the style of patristic models, John Paul II's exegesis takes a distinctive shape.

In an original move, distinctively the pope's own, he turns to the "beginning" indirectly, through Jesus's reply to the question of the Pharisees in the Gospel of Matthew (19:3–8), who—wanting to test Jesus—ask him whether it is "lawful for a man to divorce his wife for any reason." To which question Jesus replies by referring to both creation narratives in the words: "Have you not heard that from the beginning the Creator created them male and female and said, 'For this reason a man will leave his father and his mother and unite with his wife, and the two will be one flesh'? So it is that they are no longer two, but one flesh. Therefore, what God has joined let man not separate." Obviously, Jesus's answer contains a combination of Gen 1:27 and Gen 2:24 and, as the pope notes, Jesus gives here a normative teaching concerning the spousal relationship between man and woman. Jesus's words then give the framework to the discussion of the creation narratives in John Paul II's exegesis. Interestingly, his reading focuses on the body and the image from the very outset and it is already at this initial phase of his interpretation that he introduces the idea that the image is in the body marked by sexual difference. He is aware that the text itself does not speak about body but about man, yet, as he explains, "the account taken as a whole offers us sufficient bases to perceive this man, created in the visible world, precisely as body among bodies."[57]

Throughout his voluminous teachings on the scriptural meaning of spousal love, John Paul II makes ample reference to the issue of God's image and, in deepening concentric circles, he elaborates the idea of the

---

57. John Paul II, *Man and Woman He Created Them*, 152.

essential mediation of our bodily nature in our being the image of God. Going against the grain of long centuries of neglect, the pope is determined to demonstrate the crucial theological significance that the body has in the creation narratives, which is for him indicative of the fact that the body has an indispensable role, not only in our relation to one another, but also in our relation to God, namely, a relation of likeness to God. Both the body and God's image are gifts to the human being donated at creation. Far from obscuring the likeness to God, the human body, given as a gift, is an enduring and forceful token of the image and testifies to the never failing presence of the image: "in the mystery of creation, the human body carried within itself an unquestionable sign of the 'image of God' and also constituted the specific source of certainty about this image, present in the human being."[58] This is at least the ideal meaning of the body beyond sinfulness in its intended integrity at the creation. But even the body of our actual historical humanity has the image inscribed in it, that is, inscribed in the whole human being. The human vocation is linked up precisely with the fact of our being created in the image of God: it is "*the theological basis of man's truth . . . that springs forth from the eternal mystery of the person as the image of God, incarnated in the visible and bodily fact of the masculinity and femininity* of the human person."[59] The theme of the image, and the idea of the body having an indispensable role in our image-character, are universal leitmotifs in the catechesis.

However, the question arises as to the way in which the human body bears God's image? Is there no danger of anthropomorphism if we extend the image even to the sexually marked bodily aspect of the human being which is apparently in the most seamless continuity with the rest of the created world? Does such a move have support in the theological tradition—given the fact that it seems to contradict long centuries of reflection from a markedly different perspective? The theological reason for the image character of the body is seen by the pope in the fact that the body functions as a kind of archaic sacrament that renders visible the invisible intellectual/spiritual nature of the human being, on the one hand, and the transcendent reality of God, on the other. The human body, which is in seeming continuity with the rest of the created world, is also significantly different from it in that it has a specific and unique relation to God:

> The sacrament or sacramentality—in the most general sense of this term—intersects with the body and presupposes the "theology of the body." According to the generally recognized

---

58. Ibid., 241.
59. Ibid., 356. Original emphases.

meaning, the *sacrament* is, in fact, a *"visible sign."* "Body" also refers to what is visible; it signifies the "visibility" of the world and of man. In some way, therefore, even if in the most general way—the body enters into the definition of sacrament, which is "a visible sign of an invisible reality," namely, of the spiritual, transcendent, and divine reality. In this sign—and through this sign—God gives himself to man in his transcendent truth and love.[60]

The human body then, like the sacraments, is an effective sign of a transcendent reality: it symbolizes and realizes at the same time the spiritual reality of the human being and the transcendent creative love of God, which has eternally been hidden in the mystery of the trinitarian community. While the human body obviously differs from the sacraments in the narrow sense in that it does not function *ex opere operato* with universal efficacy, and its sign character may fail or become blurred or obscured, nonetheless it *is* a forceful primordial sign of divine grace and love lying at the heart of elemental human experience.

John Paul II's theological vision of the body as image of God is also fundamentally relational. For him, the deepest meaning of the body is "spousal" (a key term in his theology of the body); the true meaning of the body is only revealed through its spousal directedness to the other person in love. Therefore, the image that is inscribed in the human person is primarily found in the communion of bodily-expressed love between persons, which reflects (as a visible sign of an invisible reality) the communion of trinitarian divine love.[61] The long-neglected dimension of the significance of our bodiliness for our image character is thus masterfully retrieved once again for theological discussion.

The foregoing survey of the anthropological status of the divine image in the theological tradition, which stays admittedly cursory on account of the fact that our intention was not to give an exhaustive history of the

---

60. Ibid., 468. Elsewhere he writes: "Man appears in the visible world as the highest expression of the divine gift, because he bears within himself the inner dimension of the gift. And with it he carries into the world his particular likeness to God, with which he transcends and also rules his 'visibility' in the world, his bodiliness, his masculinity or femininity, his nakedness.... The sacrament, as a visible sign, is constituted with man, inasmuch as he is a 'body,' through his 'visible' masculinity and femininity. The body, in fact, and only the body, is capable of making visible what is invisible: the spiritual and the divine." Ibid., 3–5, 202–4.

61. As Puskás notes, both teachings, the one concerning the image character of the body and the analogy of family as the image of the Trinity, have entered official church teaching (see *Catechism of the Catholic Church* no. 364, no. 2205). See Puskás, "A házasság antropológiai alapjai" [The Anthropological Foundations of Marriage], 48.

theology of the image, but simply to indicate some pivotal stages in its evolution, has nonetheless yielded an impressive wealth of detail, which allows us to draw some important conclusions. First, it has become clear that the idea of our createdness in God's image belongs to the heart of anthropological reflection in the patristic period and continues to play a less central yet important role in later reflection. It is often assumed without explicit reflection or taken for granted without further explanation: the idea of God's image is omnipresent and universally shapes theological reflection concerning the nature and destiny of man. Next, because the distinguishing feature of human image-character has long been localized in the intellectual mind, despite all serious and sustained efforts to view man as an essential unity of body and soul or to attenuate a too rigidly philosophical exclusion of the body from the image—together with the essential theological claim of the radically bodily nature of Christ's incarnation and the indispensability of the body at the resurrection—the body has long remained in the twilight of reflection, while the shaft of interpretative light was primarily cast on the eminent site of likeness with God, the highest part of the soul, which alone is capable of knowing and contemplating the divine. The body in this scheme is accorded just a derivative role in the realization of the likeness to God and therefore is regarded as a second-order beneficiary of the intellect's privileged status with regard to the image. As an indispensable yet intellectually subjected instrument of the good or the contemplation of God, the body has not been considered as being specifically revelatory of the mystery of the divine reality in its own right and as an indissoluble unity of matter and spirit. Even in the fascinating account of Maximus the Confessor—where man is claimed to a have pivotal role of mediation between the differing orders of the sensible and the intelligible, the earthly and the divine—the body is associated with the material and the sensible and is regarded as in continuity with the rest of the created material world. The idea that the body is the "animal" and earthly part of the human person, while the immaterial soul and the intellect in particular have community with God's spiritual nature seems to be an unquestioned premise running through various periods of theological-anthropological reflection. The concept of the double nature of man (partly terrestrial and partly spiritual) seems to originate in a perennial human experience that, however, gives rise to differing interpretations and this is where John Paul II's theology of the body has an important word to say.

Obviously, John Paul II's theology of the body could not have been conceived without the background of philosophical and especially phenomenological reflection on the importance of the lived body as the site and also the most intimate originary experience of our humanity. Such a non-objectifying view of the body reveals the ultimate transcendence of the spirited body and the non-reducibility of the human body to its biological-animal-material dimension. The renewed philosophical interest in the specific humanity, and even transcendence, of the body provides John Paul II with the conceptual framework within which a retrieval of the body with regard to the image can be adequately thought. The shaft of light cast on the intellect is now directed to the spirited body and in this new light appear surprising dimensions of human likeness to God. Far from simply displaying continuity with the rest of creation, the body becomes the site *par excellence* where our likeness to God becomes truly and clearly visible. While in the theological tradition, the intellect is God's invisible image only—a way of thinking that is, in fact, unfaithful to the biblical function of the image as visible representation—John Paul II's bold move of making the real visibility of the body the pivot of his understanding of its image function also retrieves the original meaning that the biblical idea has in view: the idea of effective sign (that is, a statue representing and actualizing the dominion of a ruler in a particular land). In such a sacramental way of thinking (in the original sense of the word, where sacrament is an effective sign), the traditional hierarchy between body and soul becomes subverted and the body—as the sign and agent of human spirituality and intellectual activity—is accorded pride of place. While true visibility becomes the interpretative key for our likeness to God, the invisible soul and the human intellect within it lose their privileged position of having a more direct relation to God and are now seen as being dependent on the body in the process of attaining visibility and fulfilling the role of image.

Is it not the old danger of anthropomorphism that lurks behind such a vision? Hardly so. In my opinion, the key concept of sacramental sign can safeguard a necessary distance between God and the world, and between God and the human being within John Paul II's framework. The body is viewed here as being completely different from God: the visible sign of an invisible reality, the material sign of immaterial divine life. The safe distance implied between the visible body and the invisible divine reality maintains a wholesome difference between immanence and transcendence. In fact, it even avoids the opposite danger where the intellect would be regarded in a too seamless continuity with God's intellectual nature. And this is a potential danger, I think, in traditional image theology. One gets the impression at times that—although a greater difference despite the apparent likeness according to the principle of analogy is claimed—nonetheless, implicitly, a smaller difference is posited between God's spiritual nature and the human intellect than between the rest of the person and God. It is at this point that a "theology of the body" may offer an important corrective because it obviously does not view the body as being at a farther remove from God than the mind, but places both instead at an equally safe distance from God's transcendent reality, constantly reminding one of the unbridgeable and greater difference on the side of God in the analogy. This is also what Georg Langemeyer seems to be suggesting when he toys with the idea that the age-old Western hierarchy of body and soul—which builds upon a presupposed qualitative difference between them—may have to be revised completely.[62] Insofar as the body-soul antinomy constitutes a fundamental feature of human creaturehood, God cannot be adequately conceived as pure spirit, but must be viewed as somehow transcending the human antinomy of which God, the Creator, is the absolute origin. As Langemeyer notes, the ultimate inscrutability of our bodily-cosmic roots (and not only of our intellect) points equally to God's incomprehensible mystery, who both transcends and encompasses human duality. And all this leads us to another question: once we have outlined a framework within which the human being as God's image may be meaningfully thought, what place may we accord to human emotionality within such a scheme?

---

62. Georg Langemeyer, "Leibhaftigkeit des Menschen," in Beinert, *Lexikon der katolischen Dogmatik*, 345–46.

4

Human Emotionality and the *Imago Dei*

Thus without knowledge of the heart of God man's real situation is incomprehensible.

—Hans Walter Wolff, *Anthropology of the Old Testament*

Fallen Man and the State of Original Innocence

If, as our survey has clearly shown, a long theological tradition had located God's image squarely within the human intellect, what place was left for the emotions and human emotionality in conceptions regarding the human constitution? The answer largely depends on the way the role of the emotions is defined within human life, namely, whether they are seen as belonging essentially to the body or whether they are viewed as being rooted in the soul.[1] Whether they are feared as irrational and harmful or whether they are

---

1. As Paul Gavrilyuk has noted, one can register the presence of a centuries-old debate in Greek psychology which revolved around the following questions and which never arrived at real consensus: "How is the soul united to the body? Do passions arise from the body or from the soul? Do they form a separate part (Plato) or a faculty (Aristotle) of the soul? Can the passionate faculty operate in the soul without the body, or is it activated only through the body? There was no agreement among different philosophical schools on these issues, which fact is also registered by the Fathers." Gavrilyuk,

thought to be an indispensable dimension of our rational humanity. The answer is also shaped by the two fundamental options—as we saw, one of the East and another of the West—with respect to the subordination the body to the soul: the Alexandrian way is to stress the importance of temperance and the right command over one's own body with a view to the ultimate goal of the undisturbed, purely intellectual contemplation of God; the Western way is to make of one's body a reliable ally in the process leading to the attainment of virtuous life. For a theological answer concerning the characteristics of the ideal human constitution, we shall turn to some accounts of what in the theological tradition is described as the state of original innocence, that is, the imagined and imaginary situation of the first humans before the fall. Was emotionality an integral part of the human person in Paradise before the tragic sin of Adam and Eve? And what exactly is implied by the idea of original sin, the cause of the fall, with regard to the passions? These will be our guiding questions in the following inquiry.

The question of the image of God is intricately bound up with the question of the nature of the fall and an ideal vision of an originally uncorrupted state previous to the fall in patristic and scholastic theology. In my survey of the place of the image in the human person, for the sake of clarity, I have deliberately left the issue of sinfulness and the concomitant idea of original innocence aside, although certain allusions to these tenets could not entirely be avoided, given the fact that the theology of the image is intimately connected with considerations regarding the primeval "events" in the Genesis creation narratives. It is time for us now to examine key formulations in patristic and scholastic thought in order to understand the role they assign to human emotionality in the pre- and postlapsarian state.

Among patristic authors, Gregory of Nyssa's account is a truly remarkable attempt at the reconciliation of an inherited strictly intellectualistic concept of the soul and the biblical vision where love, compassion, and, we may say, human emotionality in general have pride of place.[2] While eventually remaining faithful to the traditional view, which excludes the emotions from the essence of the intellectual soul and therefore also from the divine image, he nonetheless makes some important concessions to a distinctively Christian stance. To the question of whether emotions (such as anger and desire) belong inherently to the essence of the soul or whether they just enter the soul from outside as accidental properties, Gregory gives a cautiously formulated answer, aware that either way, there is much at stake. If emo-

---

The Suffering of the Impassible God, 32–33.

2. See Gregory's *On the Soul and the Resurrection* and also his *On the Making of Man*.

tions are seen as belonging entirely to the body, then the scriptural vision, where desire and love for God is a paramount feature of human personhood (the centre of which for Gregory resides in the intellectual soul), becomes distorted. If, on the other hand, were one to argue for the intellectual and inherent nature of the emotions within the soul, one would also have to state their likeness to God—and this is something Gregory is not willing to concede because it directly contradicts his inherited philosophical-theological stance.[3] Human emotionality for him is excluded from the image, even if it is linked up in some mysterious manner with the intelligent soul. What then is the status of the emotions with regard to the human constitution?

One can see Gregory's answer as being a cautious compromise between biblical-ethical necessity and philosophical consistency. While admitting of the indispensable character of the emotions in the concrete human person, he nonetheless argues for their secondary role with regard to the ideal form of man characterized by the human constitution before the fall. In this manner, the emotions are (in his words) borderland phenomena in the soul: they are not of one essence with the soul, however they belong to our actual human existence just like the wheat and the tares necessarily belong to a field and must not be eradicated before the harvest.[4] Remarkably, and it is here that the impact of a truly biblical vision can be traced, Gregory does not seem to endorse the influential philosophical view of the time according to which the passions, as negative disturbances in the soul, should be avoided at all costs. Instead, he argues for the essential twofold nature of the emotions, which can either incline towards the good and so, in serving the intellect, side with the intelligent soul, or tend towards the irrational animal world (bad instinct) and so, in subjugating the intellectual soul, side with the "brute creation."[5] They can be good or bad depending on their

---

3. Gregory is well aware of the difficulty: "In fact, while all equally allow that these principles [the principle of desire and the principle of anger] are to be detected in the soul, investigation has not yet discovered exactly what we are to think of them so as to gain some fixed belief with regard to them. The generality of men still fluctuate in their opinions about this, which are as erroneous as numerous." *On the Soul and the Resurrection*.

4. See ibid.

5. Gregory characterizes the double nature of man in the following manner: "I may be allowed to describe the human image by comparison with some wonderful piece of modeling. For, as one may see in models those carved shapes which the artificers of such things contrive for the wonder of the beholders, tracing out upon a single head two forms of faces; so man seems to me to bear a double likeness to opposite things— being molded in the Divine element of his mind to the Divine beauty, but bearing, in the passionate impulses that arise in him, a likeness to the brute nature; while often even his reason is rendered brutish, and obscures the better element by the worse through its inclination and disposition towards what is irrational. . . . So, likewise, on the contrary,

objects: they either incline towards what is brute-like in the human person, or strive for what is of divine origin in the human soul.

What then is, for Gregory, the original state of innocence like? He distinguishes between two types of man at the creation: the ideal type, who is created in the image of God, is intellectual and incorruptible, has a spiritual body, and does not bear the bodily marks of sexual difference; and the empirical type, who is man in his concrete historical appearance, is mortal, embodied, the bearer of sexuality and liable to passions. It is not easy to dissolve the equivocity inherent in Gregory's account. Are we dealing here with an example of the argument for double creation in an Origenean manner whereby spiritual man is made in God's image first and then material mortal man is shaped from matter? One certainly cannot find here the idea of a prehistoric fall in between the two creations of the first and the second man as is the case with Origen. Do we have then two aspects of the same creation: ideal man as existing only in God's foreknowledge and destined to be realized through the gradual historical process of deification and accomplished in the ultimate community with God, and the concrete man of salvation history? Evidence gleaned from the context of Gregory's arguments seems to support this second interpretation and it is also supported by the fact that, according to Gregory, the fall takes place within history and after the creation of the concrete man.[6] In his vision of the two aspects of created man, Gregory seems to combine a description of the original state with one of the world to come in the *eschaton*. While the state of innocence is linked to the creation of the first historical man, ideal man displays the characteristics of the blessed state that is still to come at the end of world history. On the basis of what has been said so far, it may not be wide of the mark to conclude that emotionality, while it is regarded by Gregory as an inherent part of the actual and empirical human constitution, does not, however, belong to the original state of innocence and the final state of blessedness. Gregory's own words seem to confirm our assumption when he states that "it is not allowable to ascribe the first beginnings of our constitutional liability to passion to that human nature which was fashioned in the Divine likeness"—this we can safely interpret to the effect that liability to passion does not belong to the original state, but is a consequence of the fall.[7]

What happened, then, at the fall? Gregory sees the consequences of original sin in the impediments that the human intellect and will must face: both are weakened and tend towards earthly things instead of striving

---

if reason instead assumes sway over such emotions, each of them is transmuted to a form of virtue." *On the Making of Man*, 18.3–5.

6. See Thunberg's interpretation in *Microcosm and Mediator*, 148–51.

7. Gregory of Nyssa, *On the Making of Man*, 18.1.

for the contemplation of God. Sin causes the deviation of the will, which from now onwards gives the lead to earthly sensuality and pleasure-seeking emotionality instead of reason, and gives in to the temptation of a curious mixture of good and bad represented by the tree of the knowledge of good and evil in Paradise. In Gregory's view, it is such a mixed disposition of the human person that characterizes our fallen constitution. Namely, the order of the parts, that is, the interaction between the intellect and emotionality is deeply disturbed because sin causes disharmony between thoughts and feelings and, consequently, between the intellect and the will.

His inexorable logic leads Gregory to work out meticulously all the implications of his initial question concerning the status of the emotions with regard to our likeness to God. If one maintains that the emotions are indispensable for the realization of the good and the attainment of virtue, can one also hold the view that they will disappear when the soul enters God's life after the resurrection? If virtue is necessary for a living relationship with God and if desire is crucial for spurring the soul towards God, how is one to conceive of the state of the final assimilation to the Divine without the beneficial role of the emotions? If the human person's final destiny is to find eternal bliss in the love of God, who is himself said to be Love, can one imagine heavenly love without the passion of desire? In answering these questions, Gregory employs the same logic underpinned by the idea that it is the "speculative and critical faculty" that forms man's godlike part. Since God is pure spirit and full intellect, God's love is likewise intellectual and lacks the element of desire, which would seek an object outside of itself. God's self-love originates in the recognition of his Beauty, which is lovable. In eternal blessedness, the human being becomes the full image of the archetype and so his human love is assimilated to God's emotionless/desireless intellectual love.[8] Gregory's vision of the integrity of the resurrected body seems to fit in well with the idea that the final state of likeness to God lacks emotionality and yet is characterized by the fullness of love.[9]

---

8. "Whenever the soul, then, having divested itself of the multifarious emotions incident to its nature, gets its divine form and, mounting above Desire, enters within that towards which it was once incited by that Desire, it offers no harbor within itself either for hope or for memory . . . and thus the soul copies the life that is above, and is conformed to the peculiar features of the Divine nature; none of its habits are left to it except that of love, which clings by natural affinity to the Beautiful. For this is what love is; the inherent affection towards a chosen object." Gregory, *On the Soul and the Resurrection*.

9. It is difficult to decide whether Gregory's concept of divine love has an erotic dimension. In his impressive study, J. Warren Smith has recently suggested that Gregory thinks in terms of the erotic dimension of our agapeic love of God even in the *eschaton*, where desire is much like a paradoxical impossible stasis. Smith, *Passion and Paradise*,

Maximus the Confessor, who in many respects follows the tradition of the Cappadocian fathers, puts forward a vision of human fallenness along very similar lines.[10] In the primitive state of original innocence man was incorruptible, without sin, and had spiritual freedom. He was not subject to needs caused by outward circumstances and therefore had detachment (*apatheia*); that is, he was free from passions in the general sense of changes caused by external mechanisms, but also in the narrower sense of emotional disturbances. He had no pain. Neither did he experience sensual lust. However, he had an ability for spiritual pleasure. Before the fall there was no physical birth or sexual intercourse, which came only as the consequence of Adam's sin.

In Maximus's view, the passions were not created together with the rest of primeval man, but were placed into the irrational part of his soul as a consequence of the fall. Since, through original sin, man turned away from the contemplation of God and the intellectual world and the concomitant spiritual pleasure towards the sensible world and sensible pleasure, God introduced pain into man as a counterpart of sensible lust.[11] Man's preference for sensual pleasure above spiritual pleasure results in a new state in which he experiences passions and becomes corruptible and mortal. The consequences of the fall entail a dialectic of pleasure and pain that becomes a lasting characteristic of the decisive mechanisms of human life. In seeking pleasure man must experience its ephemeral nature and the ultimate impossibility of satisfying desire; despite all human efforts, pleasure cannot be made lasting and proves to be corruptible: the turn towards sensible lust brings the inextricable fusion of pleasure with pain. Maximus interprets Adam's curse in Gen 3:17–19 ("To Adam he said, 'Because you listened to your wife and ate from the tree about which I commanded you, "You must not eat of it," Cursed is the ground because of you; through painful toil you will eat of it all the days of your life'") in the same spirit and in an allegorical fashion. The cursed ground represents Adam's body, which is damned to infertility due to Adam's improper works, influenced by the passions and vices of his earth-bound mind. Virtues, the works of God, cannot flourish on the cursed ground, which abounds in vices and so man eats the products

---

see esp. 183–227.

10. See Thunberg, *Microcosm and Mediator*, 144–68.

11. The background to Maximus's thought is the Stoic conception of four cardinal passions: desire (*epithūmia*), pleasure (*hēdonē*), fear (*phobos*), and grief (*lupē*), which were grouped to form antithetical pairs, such as, lust–grief, desire–fear. Maximus modifies the Stoic scheme by arguing for the existence of "good" spiritual pleasure. Thunberg, *Microcosm and Mediator*, 152; 157.

of this soil in great pain and grief, which is alleviated by just a small amount of pleasure accompanying pain.[12]

Maximus pinpoints three fundamental evils that characterize the human predicament after the fall and that give rise to a wide range of vices and passions. The first one is ignorance (*agnoia*), a lack of knowledge of God as the good cause of things. Due to ignorance, the healthy movement of the soul towards divine perception is curbed and man is unable to discern what is truly good; he is impeded in carrying out works according to the divine purpose. That is why he keeps searching for satisfaction in the corruptible world of the senses. The next fundamental evil that determines postlapsarian human life is self-love (*philautia*), the root of all vices. The host of vices connected to self-love involve passions of bodily lust and manifestations of human pride. Man receives contradictory sensations through the senses that give rise to competing imaginations and cognitions dividing in this manner the one human nature and deviating him from the only true love: the love of God. The third evil is named tyranny (*turannis*) by Maximus. It extends in two directions. On the one hand, it implies the tyranny of the passions in the soul of the individual, on the other, it also designates the tyranny against other human beings as a consequence of the transformation of the love for God into egotistic self-love where the neighbor is excluded from such a love. Tyranny occurs due to the twofold division of mankind: the inner rupture of man and the consequent discord among people.

Despite the negative role the passions play in Maximus's account of the fall and in the description of the actual human situation, in his overall judgment the passions are not regarded as completely harmful or superfluous. Like Gregory of Nyssa, Maximus likewise thinks that they can be good if they serve a good purpose and are used in obedience to Christ for the attainment of virtuous Christian life. His generally positive view of the unity of body and soul as an indispensable means of mediation between the sensible and the intelligible prevents Maximus from an overly pessimistic outlook concerning human emotionality, and leads him to a rather realistic evaluation of the perennial ambiguity of, and the ultimate inseparability of, the passions from human pleasure and pain. The importance of pleasure is also clearly indicated by Maximus's distinctive idea of spiritual pleasure as an experience of unfallen man and as a reward of the blessed who reach the deificatory state after the resurrection. The dialectic of earthly pleasure and pain must be viewed as the fallen actualization of a primordially divinely instituted gift for the first human person.

---

12. Maximus the Confessor, *Quaestiones ad Thalassium*, 5. See Thunberg, *Microcosm and Mediator*, 160–61.

From the Western tradition we choose Augustine of Hippo, whose influence on later developments has been decisive and whose ideas, as we shall see, Thomas Aquinas also used in his own description of the original state of innocence. Augustine represents a position considerably different from the ones we have examined so far, arguing for the indispensability of emotions even in the pre-fallen state of the first human couple. One can glean some pivotal elements of his general view concerning human emotionality from Book 14 of his *City of God* (chapter 8–12) where he takes issue with the Stoic ideal of a passionless state (*apatheia*), which, in Stoic philosophy, is regarded as the only state fitting a sage who wishes to lead a good life. Augustine makes a head-on attack against the Stoic classification of the emotions, which distinguishes between "good feelings" (*eupatheiai*)—in the soul of the wise man, who through self-discipline is required to get rid of all emotional disturbances, experiencing emotions only in the form of cognitive states, such as will instead of desire, contentment in place of joy, and caution as an alternative to fear—and the four main types of bad passions (*pathē*), pleasure, grief, desire, and fear, which are thought to be harmful and disturbing movements to be eradicated from the mind of the sage.[13] Against such a Stoic proposal for the total avoidance of real emotions, Augustine marshals ample biblical evidence to the effect that the citizens of the holy city of God experience fear and desire, grief and joy. For, obviously, one finds numerous passages in the New Testament that register the emotional states of the first Christians who experience all four kinds of passions rejected by the Stoics. Moreover, these passions are not presented by Scripture as harmful provided that they do not contradict the overall motive of love for God: "And because their love is rightly placed, all these affections of theirs are right," Augustine asserts.[14] Furthermore, it is clear from the Gospels (and Augustine collects a handful of examples here too) that even Jesus Christ, who was completely sinless, "exercised" emotions according to his human nature. By using the term "exercise" Augustine obviously intends to stress the (for him) important fact that, in the case of Jesus, the emotions were under the control of reason, unlike the emotions of sinners, which break loose of reason's control. In contradistinction to us, whose emotions arise as the result of "human infirmity," Christ's infirmity was a consequence of his power and not a sign of weakness. This fact conceded, a recognition of

---

13. It is not easy to specify the exact nature of what the Stoics term a "good feeling" (*eupatheia*) in contradistinction to what they see as a bad passion (*pathē*). Ostensibly, there are various interpretations among modern scholars directed to the reconciliation of the Stoic claim concerning the complete avoidance of the passions and the idea of the existence of cognitive states analogous to the passions. See Knuuttila, *Emotions*, 68–71.

14. Augustine, *City of God*, 14.9.

Christ's true humanity must necessarily entail the idea that he had human emotions.

Based on firm evidence in Scripture, Augustine argues that the Stoic ideal of life without emotions, apart from being unattainable, is also fundamentally inhuman since were one able to get rid of all emotionality, then, instead of becoming a perfected human being, one would lose all humanity. His main argument against the idea of a passion-free life appeals to the centrality of love generally, in human and particularly in Christian existence. For Augustine, love implies various emotions, such as joy, concern, and compassion for others. Contrary to what the Stoics say, an impassible person, who has extirpated all such emotions from himself, is lacking any virtue or humanity. Therefore, Augustine opines that the emotional experiences of love and joy will be an indispensable part of the heavenly state of the blessed where sadness and fear will be completely absent, but, he asks, "who that is not quite lost to truth would say that neither love nor joy shall be experienced there?"[15] Perfect blessedness as our "eternal condition" has nothing to do with insensible apathy except for the fact that in this final state no terrifying fear or annoying pain will disturb the blessed. One has the impression that Augustine's covert aim is to give a new meaning to the Stoic distinction between "good feelings" and bad "passions," which for him no longer signifies a distinction between emotionless cognitive states and the entire gamut of passions, which are viewed indiscriminately as harmful, but a division between positive emotions rooted in love and negative emotions arising out of a lack of love or the suffering caused by evil.

Having outlined the foundations for a biblically based Christian account of human emotionality, Augustine proceeds to a discussion of the state of original innocence. His main question is whether the pre-fallen state is reconcilable with the idea of experiencing emotions. Unlike Origen, who—as we remember—attributed a spiritual body to the first man before the fall, Augustine assigns a real "animal" (meaning somatic and therefore sensitive) body to Adam and Eve on the basis of the Genesis text, which explicitly tell us that they required drink and food, for they felt bodily thirst and hunger. Having such an animal body, Adam and Eve did experience emotions that are rooted in love. As a loving couple, "[t]heir love to God was unclouded, and their mutual affection was that of faithful sincere marriage; and from this love flowed a wonderful delight, because they always enjoyed what was loved," Augustine explains.[16] What was absent from their complete happiness were emotions connected to suffering and evil since these

---

15. Ibid., 14.10.
16. Ibid.

negative emotions are the consequence of sin, which did not yet disturb the ideal state of paradise. Thomas Aquinas will refer to this passage concerning the delightful emotions connected to love, which he sees as supporting his own view of the human condition in the state of original innocence, as we shall see soon.[17] Augustine also stresses the fact that man's happiness in paradise was equally physical and spiritual. The importance of real bodily bliss in the state before the fall and the presence of "good" emotions associated with love is made very clear in Augustine's account.

What role do the emotions play in the postlapsarian state? The fall of Adam and Eve changed the initial undisturbed happiness and even human nature itself was changed. The animal body of humans, which was destined to become immortal, assumed mortality and suffered decay and pain. The perfect harmony between the body and soul was disturbed too and man began to experience a curious inner conflict, a kind of "disobedience to himself"; his mind and his flesh did not obey his will any longer and the soul's original effective control over the body was lost, so much so that "man, who by keeping the commandments should have been spiritual even in his flesh, became fleshly even in his spirit."[18] Moreover, it was not only a question of the soul losing control over the body, but also of the soul becoming divided against itself and losing control over itself. The human person experienced an inner discord that ran across all parts of his constitution: intellect, will, and emotionality alike. Disobedience to God resulted in a strange "disobedience to himself" where one acts against one's will, reason and feelings. In a nutshell, this is the Augustinian diagnosis of the state of concupiscence, which characterizes the human condition after the fall.[19]

17. Aquinas, *ST* Ia.95.2.
18. Augustine, *City of God*, 15.15.
19. Augustine gives a concise description of the state subsequent to the fall in the *City of God*, 13.13: "For, as soon as our first parents had transgressed the commandment, divine grace forsook them, and they were confounded at their own wickedness; and therefore they took fig-leaves (which were possibly the first that came to hand in their troubled state of mind), and covered their shame; for though their members remained the same, they had shame now where they had none before. They experienced a new motion of their flesh, which had become disobedient to them, in strict retribution of their own disobedience to God. For the soul, reveling in its own liberty, and scorning to serve God, was itself deprived of the command it had formerly maintained over the body. And because it had willfully deserted its superior Lord, it no longer held its own inferior servant; neither could it hold the flesh subject, as it would always have been able to do had it remained itself subject to God. Then began the flesh to lust against the Spirit, in which strife we are born, deriving from the first transgression a seed of death, and bearing in our members, and in our vitiated nature, the contest or even victory of the flesh." On Augustine's idea of the fall see Katherin A. Rogers, "Fall," in Fitzgerald, *Augustine through the Ages*, 351–52.

Concupiscence as a harmful disharmony affecting the core of the human person is central to Augustine's theology. In some way, it is obviously bound up with human emotionality, yet the crucial question is whether it is due exclusively to an emotional disorder. As Peter Burnell has argued, there are three fundamental problems concerning concupiscence, none of which, however, make one conclude that the emotions are solely at fault in the fragility caused by such an inward conflict.[20] The first problem concerns the nature of concupiscence, namely, the question whether concupiscence is a moral weakness or simply an emotional disorder in the first place. Burnell's suggestion, that it is best regarded as the disorder of the entire mind that cuts across both human morality and emotionality, fits well in the overall context of Augustine's theology of sin. Within such a scheme, while concupiscence is emotional, it is also closely connected with the soul's moral behavior and, through morality, with the intellect. Therefore, it would be a misguided attempt to take the unruly emotions alone to task for a deep-seated disjunction within the human person. The second problem is one of locating concupiscence: is its seat in the soul or in the body? As Burnell points out, in interpreting the Genesis text, Augustine takes it as obvious that the body has an essential role in concupiscent desire. What he aims to show in his exegesis, is that the soul is likewise involved in concupiscent acts. His overall stance is that the seat of concupiscence is both in the soul and the body, in the spirit and the flesh. The third question concerns the effect of concupiscence on human nature: is it primarily bound up with sexuality or is sexual concupiscence just one form of a general malfunction in the human disposition? Augustine treats of this question in his later works where he seems to suggest that, while in an obvious and immediate manner, it is manifested by sexuality and is linked to the operation of the sexual parts of the body, nonetheless it cannot be reduced entirely to the sexual mode since it is a more general disorder which is transmitted even to children and affects the whole of what we are.

Thomas Aquinas, in the anthropological part of his *Summa Theologica*, making ample reference to Augustine, takes up the question of man's situation in what he terms the original state of innocence.[21] This primitive state of rectitude and perfection was characterized by the special supernatural gifts with which the first human persons were endowed. They possessed extraordinary wisdom and—in addition to natural knowledge—the supernatural knowledge of truths that were necessary for the attainment of their

---

20. See Peter Burnell, "Concupiscence," in ibid., 224–27.

21. See esp. *ST* Ia.94–97. On Aquinas's anthropology see Mondin, "Antropologia Filosofica e Teologica," and "Uomo," in Mondin, *Dizionario enciclopedico del pensiero di San Tommaso D'Aquino*, 55–58; 696–708.

supernatural end. They were also fully virtuous in having all of the virtues and displayed a high degree of sanctity. The rectitude of this pre-fallen state consisted in the right ordering of the parts of the human constitution as a result of the obedient submission to God of the entire human person. Reason subjected itself to God and, as a consequence, the powers within man's soul were ordered in a hierarchical fashion: reason held control over the lower powers and the soul over the body. Aquinas gives a logically neat description where each part has its place and the parts are ordered according to a descending scale: "For this rectitude consisted in his reason being subject to God, the lower powers to reason, and the body to the soul: and the first subjection was the cause of both the second and the third; since while reason was subject to God, the lower powers remained subject to reason."[22] He then proceeds to ask the question concerning the existence of passions in the perfect state of rectitude, devoting one article entitled "Whether passions existed in the soul of the first man?" to this disputed issue.[23] According to an objection made against the presence of passions in the state of innocence—which Aquinas quotes—the passions induce the rebellion of the flesh against the spirit; therefore they could not belong to man's soul before the fall. For a contrary opinion, Aquinas quotes Augustine to the effect that undisturbed love and other passions of the soul did exist in the first humans. The passage Aquinas refers to in Augustine is the one we saw in connection with Augustine's idea that the complete happiness of the first couple involved true mutual marital love and emotions of delight and joy.[24] Having referred to a variety of views, Aquinas himself takes the side of Augustine in arguing for the presence of passions that have a good object (such as, joy, love, hope, and desire) in the primitive human soul. As we can see, the distinction between passions with a good object and ones having evil objects also follows Augustine's classification, where it is only love and the related emotions that are considered as part of paradise and from which evil, fear, and pain are absent. Like Augustine, Aquinas holds that the passions linked with the existence of evil did not disturb the ideal state of pre-fallen humans. Aquinas refines the Augustinian scheme and transposes it into his own intricate taxonomy of the human soul. The passions—belonging to the sensual appetite—in the state of perfect rectitude were seamlessly integrated into the whole of man since then "the inferior appetite was wholly subject to reason: so that in that state the passions of the

---

22. Aquinas, *ST* Ia.95.1.
23. Ibid., Ia.95.2.
24. Aquinas refers here to Augustine's *City of God*, 14.10.

soul existed only as consequent upon the judgment of reason."[25] Therefore, the presence of passions with a good object is completely reconcilable with the paradisiac state and does not involve the rebellion of the body against reason, as is certainly the case in the state of concupiscence.

At the fall the neat hierarchic order of obedience (reason obeys God, the lower powers of the soul obey reason, and the body obeys the soul) was disturbed and the passions became capricious, so to speak, in their attitude of relating to reason. Instead of a full submission to reason—a reason in turn obedient to God—the lower sensual part of the soul inclines to objects at hand and is not always in harmony with man's supernatural ultimate goal. As commentators note, in his understanding of the consequences of the fall Aquinas moves away from the Augustinian framework of concupiscence, which starts from the existence of bodily lust and from that argues for the existence of concupiscence in the soul and the mind.[26] He places the root of the disorder caused by original sin directly in the human mind, which—due to rebellion against God's will—becomes disorderly and alienated from God and so also loses control over the lower faculties. Aquinas's version of concupiscence is an "infirmity of the mind" in the first place, and only as a consequence does it affect the emotions and the body. A disorder in the highest part of the soul (reason) escalates downwards to the lowest part (the body). Within such an intellectually-oriented scheme, the passions have only second-order responsibility in the precarious situation in which man finds himself after the fall. Aquinas thinks in terms of a tension, a discord, a fracture between sensibility and reason as well as body and soul.[27] In his view, the original harmony of the teleologically ordered parts of the human person is lost and, with the loss of reason's unified control over the lower powers, human affectivity too becomes "corrupted," that is, it displays the signs of division or destruction. Such a regrettable division (as a consequence of original sin) occurred against the original intention of the Creator, who initially willed the complete harmony of reason and sensibility which was given as a supernatural gift of grace for the first humans in the state of rectified innocence. Life without the disturbing sundering effect of concupiscence meant the complete penetration of reason into the movements of sensibility whereby nothing could arise in the soul that was not subject to reason. This perfect dominion of reason over the sensible parts belonged to a state of supernatural grace where human nature was aided in

---

25. Aquinas, *ST* Ia.95.2.

26. See, for example Mondin, "Uomo," in Mondin, *Dizionario enciclopedico del pensiero di San Tommaso D'Aquino*, 704–5.

27. See Gondreau, *The Passions of Christ's Soul*, 291–300.

the preservation of the perfect harmony between the lower and the higher powers thanks to God's immediate operative grace. Therefore, the division between reason and sensibility does not characterize pre-lapsarian, ideal human nature in Aquinas's thought.

All things considered, at first sight it seems clear that Aquinas, in Augustine's wake, acknowledges the constitutive role of the emotions in the state of original rectitude: they belong to the nature of Adam and Eve from the moment they receive life. However, we have also seen that both Augustine and Aquinas claim the complete absence of negative emotions connected to evil and suffering from the soul of primeval man. Does this mean that human emotionality after the fall, as it appears to us in its actual form, is regarded by Aquinas as being somehow contaminated by sin, or at least, by the consequences of sin? While—against the aftermath of the Stoic rejection of the passions—Aquinas on the whole rehabilitates affectivity as an indispensable part of our natural human constitution, he nonetheless retains the traditional caveat concerning the harmful effects of the negative passions for the integrity of the God-searching soul. On a closer look at Aquinas's theological assumptions, a strange ambiguity comes to the fore: alongside a positive overall outlook concerning the passions, one finds in him also traits of a more negative approach, especially in his Christology, with regard to the issue of the passions of Christ's soul. Since Aquinas's general theory of the emotions can only be properly understood within the theological context of Christ's humanity, for which it serves as an introduction, we turn first to his general theory of the human passions, and then to his christological considerations. Within the context of the general theory, we find the full array of the finest traditional theological thought concerning human affectivity. Aquinas's reflection on human emotionality is exemplary also in the sense that it recapitulates the best of patristic speculation concerning the place of the passions in the life of a Christian and, at the same time, far surpasses in scope, depth, and method earlier existing accounts. It also offers a truly systematic framework concerning the nature and place of the passions within the human stature.[28]

The Christological Contours of Human Affectivity in Thomas Aquinas

While Thomas Aquinas's treatise on the passions has received considerable attention in recent (mostly philosophical) scholarship, his christological

---

28. For a recent comprehensive account of Aquinas's emotion theory see Lombardo: *The Logic of Desire: Aquinas on Emotion*.

considerations concerning Jesus's human affectivity have been largely overlooked. This is the conclusion of Paul Gondreau who, in a monumental study on the passions of Christ's soul in Aquinas's theology, claims the essential interrelatedness of Thomas's general anthropology of the passions and his specific christological doctrine concerning the nature of the passions that Christ experienced as a human being.[29] In his view, there is a two-way relationship between Aquinas's conception of general human affectivity and his doctrine of Christ's emotional experiences. These mutually condition one another: the christological tenets are influenced by a conception of human passion in general, whereas the general theory of the passions is elaborated in order to serve as a backdrop to his Christology. To consider just one side of the discussion is to sever a strong logical tie and, as a result, obtain an incomplete and even distorted picture. Philosophy and theology are closely linked up here and are mutually illuminating for a proper understanding of Aquinas's real position concerning the role of the passions in our humanity. Therefore, one must be familiar with both aspects in order to see the full theological import of this complicated issue. That is why we shall turn to Aquinas's general theory of the passions first, and then complement the picture with his distinctive contribution to Christology concerning the real humanity of Christ, something that also sheds light on the nature of what is conceived by Aquinas as our ideal humanity.

Thomas Aquinas treats of the passions at great length in his *Summa Theologica*, in a section within his general anthropology which is intended as a preparation for the discussion of the virtues and the nature of sin subsequent to the treatise on the passions.[30] Before discussing the passions, Aquinas examines questions concerning the will (the voluntary and the involuntary) and the good or bad nature of human acts. The immediate context for the long systematic treatise on the passions is provided therefore by Aquinas's general interest in the moral quality of human acts and the attainment of human happiness. The reason why Aquinas's extensive treatise has been recently recognized as an important source of original insight is because, on the one hand, in contradistinction to several previous spiritual authors influenced by inherited Stoic ideas, Aquinas argues for the essential goodness of human emotionality, and on the other, because of the unparalleled depth and detail of his inquiry. As a matter of fact, the treatise on the passions is the largest one in the entire *Summa*, revealing its author's intense interest in the workings of human affectivity. While it is obviously indebted

---

29. Gondreau, *The Passions of Christ's Soul*, see esp., 35–135; 191–259; 288–300.

30. *ST* IaIIae.22–48. The entire section on the passions consists of twenty-seven questions (*quaestiones*) and 132 articles in total, making up the largest treatise of the *Summa*.

to a handful of already existing works on the issue, in many respects it contains Aquinas's own insight due to a lack of previous reflection on the matter.[31] The overall stance is Aristotelian, where body and soul are seen as forming an indissoluble unity, the soul being the form of the body which is in turn the material constituent. Within such an intricate unity and interaction between body and soul, the passions are not regarded as additional and harmful intruders into the life of the soul, but are viewed as part and parcel of the natural human constitution. Like Augustine, Aquinas takes a firm stand against Stoic conceptions, where the passions are nothing else but inimical obstacles to virtuous activity or even "sicknesses of the soul." Aquinas refuses to assign human passion simply a marginal role; instead, he sets out to show to what extent the passions play a vital role in the attainment of virtuous life. Moreover, his Aristotelian stance allows him to keep the sensible dimension of the human soul in a complete continuity with the rational and spiritual dimension and explore the points of convergence between the two. There is no isolation in his thought of the rational-spiritual from the sensible-corporeal. And, most importantly, Aquinas sets the issue in a theological light: the passions are teleologically ordained to happiness in God as indispensable means in the realization of virtues.

What are the passions according to Aquinas? His definition is faithful to the tradition, and Nemesius of Emesa via John of Damascus in the first place. On this view, the passions are actions or operations of the sensitive appetite directed to a good or an evil object: "Passion is a movement of the sensitive appetite."[32] In order to understand the full import of the definition and dis-

31. Among the influences are Aristotle (*The Nichomachean Ethics*, *Rhetoric*, and the *De anima*) and Christian anthropologies that in some ways continue Aristotelian thought, such as, Nemesius of Emesa's *De Natura Hominis* (written between 390–400 AD) via John of Damascene's *De fide orthodoxa* (a work from the eighth century) which appropriates in an extensive manner Nemesius's account. Augustine's influence is decisive (especially the *De civitate Dei*, books 9–14.) and Aquinas's mentor, Albert the Great (in the *De bono* and the *De homine*) with a predominantly Aristotelian approach to the passions had also a deep impact on Thomas's work. See Gondreau, *The Passions of Christ's Soul*, 101–35.

32. ST IaIIae.22.3 *sed contra*. Gondreau points out that the definition is a quotation from John of Damascus's *De fide orthodoxa*, 2.22. See Gondreau, *The Passions of Christ's Soul*, 203. According to Knuuttila, Aquinas's position (that the passions are movements) was criticized by Albert the Great for being imprecise on the analogy between natural movement and the nature of the passions: "One obvious problem of the movement terminology is that of the stages of natural processes (inclination, movement, rest) the first precedes a temporal process and the third follows it. Only the middle part seems to be a movement.... Aquinas's comments on the nature of emotional passions as movements remained somewhat sketchy—he apparently thought that the problems associated with the details of his conception were less important than its systematic weight." Knuuttila, *Emotions*, 248–49.

sipate a suspicion of contradiction concerning the idea of the passions being actions at the same time, one must explore the intricate taxonomy Aquinas assigns to the human soul. On Aquinas's complex account—inspired by Aristotelian philosophy—the one indivisible intellectual human soul acts as the form of the human body on three levels of operation, starting from a level common to all living beings (plants, animals, and humans alike), leading to the second level characteristic of animals and humans, and culminating in the third and highest level, which is exclusively human. These three levels of operation give the following three dimensions: the vegetative, the sensitive (animal), and the intellectual operations of the soul. The passions thus belong to the middle, sensitive part of the human soul, which houses actions of sense knowledge and sensible desire. Within two operations (the sensitive and the intellectual) a crucial distinction is made between knowledge and appetite or inclination, that is, between knowing and desiring. The difference between the two lies in the fact that while knowledge takes an outside object into the inner dynamics of the intellectual soul, appetite or desire goes out to the object presented by knowledge first. In this manner, affectivity is essentially a movement towards things, whereas knowledge is an inward movement of appropriation. Applied to the two kinds of operation of the human soul (for the lowest, vegetative part is pre-cognitive and lacks any degree of reflection), the distinction then gives a knowing and a desiring aspect on both (distinct) levels: the sensitive level displays knowledge gained through the senses (sense knowledge being particular in nature and connected to the actual sense experience), and sensitive desire (sensitive appetite), which draws this part of the soul towards the object presented by the senses.[33] The intellectual level is characterized by intellectual knowledge (of an abstract or universal nature, possessed only by humans who have a spiritual intellect or mind), and the corresponding intellectual appetite or the will, which inclines towards things known by the intellect. The passions then, according to the definition Aquinas employs, belong to the desiring aspect of the sensitive soul (that is, the sensitive appetite), and so are intimately linked both to the body and the operation of the senses and to the specific kind of knowledge obtained by the senses. Therefore, they are—in a modern term—psychosomatic, since only creatures with bodies can experience passions. Aquinas goes as far as to say that, techni-

33. As Peter King explains, the vegetative part of the soul is a category apart in this scheme: "The sensitive and intellective parts of the soul sit astride another fundamental cluster of principles accounting for nourishment, growth, and reproduction, known as the vegetative part of the soul. There are psychological experiences founded solely on the vegetative part: for instance, hunger, thirst, and sexuality (as mere physical reactivity). But medieval philosophers, along with modern psychologists, do not classify these together with the passions of the soul or emotions." Peter King, "Aquinas on the Passions," in MacDonald and Stump, *Aquinas's Moral Theory*, 101, note 1.

cally speaking, the bodily change that accompanies a passion is the "material" element of passion, whereas the movement of the sensitive appetite gives the "formal" aspect of passion. He also introduces another important distinction between what Gondreau describes as "body-first" passion and "soul-first" passion. While both types are movements of the soul, their origin is different: body-first passion (*passio corporalis*) originates in bodily pain (important here is Aquinas's one-sided emphasis on the negative aspect of passion, which we shall examine later) and such physical pain necessarily affects the soul; soul-first passion (*passio animalis*) arises directly in the soul and has repercussions in the body. The latter is passion in the proper sense, signifying a movement of the sense appetite that involves a bodily modification.[34]

And here we arrive at our next question: if the passions are movements or operations of the sensitive appetite, in what sense can they be thought as passive (as their name would clearly suggest)? The answer lies in the distinction between the knowing and the desiring aspects of the soul. While the sensitive appetite moves towards the object presented to it by sense knowledge, and in this sense it acts in an active manner, it is passive in the more important sense that it does not act upon its own initiative, but is moved by something outside itself, namely, information construed by sense knowledge. The passions are thus passive responses to received information and, as such, also subjective experiences; they color our perception of realities: "When a man is affected by a passion, things seem to him greater or lesser than they really are; thus, to a lover, what he loves seems better, and to him that fears, what he fears seems more dreadful."[35] Therefore, the primary characteristic of passions is their actual passivity, the fact of their being reactions to data presented by sense knowledge. Apparently, the Latin term for passion "*passio*" causes considerable difficulty for translators because it does not have the connotation of strong passionate emotion that its English counterpart necessarily implies. *Passio* is just any kind of movement of the sensitive appetite, no matter how slight, and in a broad sense it can also mean change in one's state occurring when something is received and something else is taken away. Its meaning could best be captured by the technical phrase "affective response," which however has no real equivalent in English since the term "emotion" cannot render the exact meaning of *passio* properly either, because it does not indicate passive change (especially for the worse, as we shall see), which is, however, essential to the Latin meaning.

In sum, Aquinas's general theory of the passions reveals his positive regard for human affectivity. This is also clear from the fact that no other

---

34. Gondreau, *The Passions of Christ's Soul*, 208.
35. *ST* IaIIae.44.2. See ibid., 211.

author treats this issue at a comparable length or depth. The treatise on the passions demonstrates the central role of affectivity in human life and the fundamental goodness of the human constitution where—as a consequence of the unity of body and soul—changes occurring in the body involve movements of the soul and conversely, affects of the soul cause bodily change. Aquinas holds that, analogous to the passions of the sensitive soul, there are "passions" in the intellectual soul too, spiritual passions, among which the greatest is charity. With this he posits a constant synergy between the sentient and the intellectual, sensibility and rationality. However, his narrow conception of passion within the context of his Christology shows a markedly different concern.

As Gondreau observes, Aquinas's analysis of Christ's human affectivity contains a negative conception of passion rooted in the original and proper meaning of the term, which associates passion with the suffering of change for the worse, regarding it therefore as "defect," "weakness," "disability," "limitation." On the one hand, the treatment of the issue of the passions of Christ's soul undergoes a remarkable progress in Aquinas's thought. On the other hand, he does not seem to go far enough in coming to terms with the positive nature of Christ's human affectivity. While in his early *Commentary on the Sentences of Peter Lombard* (written between 1252–56), he does not admit of the fully human and passible nature of Christ's sensitive soul (since the joyful state of the blessed vision in which Christ constantly finds himself would exclude the influence of the passions), in the mature synthesis of the *Summa Theologica* he concedes the fully human and therefore passible nature of Christ's soul. Such a concession is all the more significant because in the theological tradition, and even among Aquinas's contemporary opponents, one finds a strong tendency to deny suffering and pain to Christ. Due to the long-lasting influence of Stoicism, which held *apathy*, a state unswayed by passions, as an ideal for the virtuous life, throughout the patristic period and up to the seventh century, Christ's possession of a fully human soul was not unanimously accepted and his victory over suffering and death was understood in Stoic terms as complete freedom from the harmful effects of passion. While we find sporadic patristic comments on Christ's emotional experiences in Scripture texts, the reality of his emotions was almost completely ignored. The fight against affective suffering and even passibility in general was set as an ideal before the Christian believer by many patristic authors who adopted the notion of impassibility as an optimal state for one wishing to follow Christ. Therefore, Aquinas's move, whereby he affirms the full human reality of suffering and pain in the soul of the incarnate Christ, goes boldly against the grain of a long tradition to the contrary effect.

However, and this is Gondreau's central insight, quite unlike his general theory of the passions, Aquinas's account of Christ's affectivity is conceived exclusively in negative terms in accordance with the inherited theological tradition.[36] While, in his general theory, the passions are a neutral phenomenon naturally belonging to the unity of body and soul, when speaking about the passions of Christ's soul, Aquinas takes the traditional negative meaning of passion as weakness and defect: "Christ came in the weakness of the flesh, which is manifested in the passions," Aquinas openly states, and he discusses Jesus's passions under the heading "Of the Defects of Soul assumed by Christ."[37] The passions according to the primary, proper meaning of the word are "sufferings" caused by external influences that disturb the equilibrium of the soul and involve the loss of harmonious disposition and therefore entail deterioration in the state of the soul. The primary passions in this sense are manifested in pain and affective suffering, and the possibility of the soul appears as a defect and a disagreeable experience of human nature. Aquinas's emphasis is on the fact that the incarnate Christ took up such a passible human nature "in the weakness of the flesh," although—as someone who was entirely sinless and stayed in the state of original rectitude and perfection (just like Adam before the fall) he need not have assumed the disagreeable consequences of original sin. Passion in the narrow sense of affective suffering must ultimately go back to the original sin of Adam because it is with sin that suffering has entered the world. Suffering is a sign of corruptibility, that is, deterioration with regard to an ideal situation. We remember that, in Aquinas's view, in the state of original innocence no negative passions linked with the existence of evil disturbed the bliss of the first humans who lived in mutual love and joy. On this view, the disagreeable passions are not part of God's initial intention with regard to our humanity.

Such a narrow conception of passion and human passibility gives rise to the following question: does passibility belong to the essence of human nature (as it was created before the fall) or must we ascribe it to an unfavorable consequence of the fall? As Gondreau astutely observes, at this point there is a certain ambiguity in Aquinas. He seems to be aware of the danger in taking original sin to task for the appearance of the human passions (at least in the narrow sense of pain and suffering) since such a move would necessarily imply the indispensability of sin for the experience of

---

36. Gondreau registers the surprising fact that Aquinas scholars have overlooked almost completely the notion of passion as defect in Aquinas's Christology. Ibid., 220. The passions Aquinas treats with regard to Christ's soul are: pain, sorrow, fear, wonder, and anger.

37. *ST* III.43.1 ad 2.; *ST* III.15.

true and proper passion. Therefore, through complex arguments, he tries to demonstrate that, while passion as affective suffering is a natural feature of the human condition, it did not belong to man in the prelapsarian state, which is characterized by immunity to affective suffering (that is, impassibility in the proper sense) thanks to the operation of divine grace given to pre-fallen man. Nevertheless Aquinas remains somewhat ambiguous on the issue, maintaining elsewhere that passibility is a natural human state directly reflective of the creative will of God.[38] His entire account of the passions is constructed upon the ambiguous premise that, on the one hand, the passions are an essential and morally neutral feature of our humanity and, on the other, that they represent weakness and vulnerability and are therefore defective. As a consequence of such a hesitant stance, Aquinas treats of Christ's passions under the rubric of defect that is, in his view, a natural outcome of Christ's assumption of a fully human soul (with its entire intellectual, sensitive, and vegetative dimensions) together with a corruptible and so passible body.

At the end of the day, Aquinas attributes to Jesus an affectivity markedly different from ours: on his account, Jesus experienced only "consequent" passions, ones that issue as a result of the command of reason and, therefore, he was free from "antecedent" passions where the sensitive appetite acts before the consideration of reason. Jesus's soul was ordered in the ideal way that must have characterized the state of original rectitude and perfection: his reason held perfect dominion over the lower parts of the soul, he experienced no unforeseen passions and the ones he did experience were never unruly, but always respected the bounds of reason. Moreover, he only had passions whose objects were aligned with higher rational goods. In him the complete penetration of reason into the movements of sensibility was realized at the highest degree since nothing could arise in his soul that was not subject to reason. His sensibility and his reason were in a perfect harmony. At times Aquinas terms Jesus's passions "propassions," stressing their difference from ordinary passions due to their complete rootedness in reason, which, in the case of general human passions, is never completely accomplished.[39] Interestingly, while Aquinas daringly argues for the full

---

38. See Gondreau, *The Passions of Christ's Soul*, 231. Gondreau quotes from Aquinas the following passage to this effect: "All natural things were produced by the Divine art, and so may be considered God's works of art. Now every artist intends to grant his work the best disposition—not absolutely the best, but the best in relation to the end, even if this entails some defect." *ST* Ia.91.3.

39. Aquinas apparently borrows the term "propassion" from Jerome and he also relies on the widespread use of the term in thirteenth-century Christology. Nevertheless he only employs it in a christological context and never in relation to general human affectivity. See Gondreau, *The Passions of Christ's Soul*, 366–72. Gondreau's account must

integrity of Christ's sensitive soul, which is capable of experiencing passion in the proper sense of pain and affective suffering (besides, of course, good emotions, which are attributed to Christ without any difficulty), he nonetheless does not go far enough (at least to our modern judgment) when he only half-concedes the presence in Christ of passions in the form that they occur in actual human life. On his account, Christ is immune to the moral effects of original sin on human affectivity. Aquinas ostensibly keeps the fragile fissure between sensibility and reason, a characteristic feature of our natural condition, at a safe distance from the perfect humanity of Christ. While—contrary to opposing views—he resolutely argues for the passible nature of Christ's soul in being subject to the negative effects of passions, such as, pain, fear, wonder (a subtype of fear on Aquinas's classification), and even anger, he nonetheless ascribes to Jesus a more perfect sensibility than ours on account of his complete sinlessness.[40] With this option Aquinas also intimates that human emotionality is deficient in a significant manner, since it does not seem to be functioning the way it was originally intended to function. Therefore, it is to be suspected and subjected by reason. The question of whether the vulnerability of human affectivity belongs to the primordial constitution of man or is it rather a consequence of the fall eventually remains open in Aquinas's thought. Despite the outright rejection of the Stoic contempt for natural human emotionality, one has the impression that some residue of the Stoic ideal of *apatheia* still haunts the background inherent in the idea that Jesus's passions were not exactly like ours, but were under the complete and seamless control of reason, never occurring unforeseen, but always following the lead of reason. Or can we rather say that there is a Christianized version of the ideal of *apatheia*, one that Aquinas inherits from the previous tradition and that therefore guides his discussion of Jesus's emotionality?

The Ideal of Human Impassibility

Throughout our inquiry concerning the seat of our likeness to God and the role of human emotionality with regard to the image, we have made ample reference to the notion of *apatheia* as an ideal for perfect human life and

---

be complemented with the fact that the idea of "propassion" probably originates in the Stoic notion of "pre-passion," which is introduced by the Stoics to denote emotional reaction that, however, is not an emotion proper since it is not assented to by reason. The concept of Christ's "propassion" is most likely a modified version of this Stoic conception. See Knuuttila, *Emotions*, 6–7.

40. See Gondreau, *The Passions of Christ's Soul*, 438–41.

an essential feature of God's divinity. In order to get a clearer picture of this disputed and difficult issue, we first attempt to outline the essential features of the human ideal of a passionless state as it appears within the works of some prominent representatives of the ancient philosophical and theological tradition and then, as a next step, we examine the Christian theological claim concerning God's freedom from change and passion: divine immutability and impassibility. Does the ideal of freedom from the passions involve the complete eradication of the emotional part of the soul? If this is so, is there any place for love and the concomitant emotions in human and divine life? Is there a divide between sensible and spiritual affectivity according to the Christian vision? Is an impassible God insensitive towards humans according to this view? If God is impassible, can he still feel and have emotions such as love? If God's emotions differ from human emotions, what makes them different? And, last but not least, is the ideal of *apatheia* reconcilable with the ideal of love in the final resort? Part of the answer to these questions has already been implied in the foregoing discussion. What we need here is a more synthetic vision that highlights some important underlying assumptions and pinpoints important points of ambiguity without, however, attempting to give an exhaustive account of all details of this complex issue.

For a careful analysis of the status of emotions in ancient (and medieval) philosophy and Christian theology, we turn to Simo Knuuttila's comprehensive study, which draws a vast panorama of views from Plato up to late medieval compendia, tracing a genealogy of influences and pointing out intriguing implications.[41] Knuuttila writes as a philosopher who is interested both in properly philosophical accounts and Christian theological views containing philosophical elements. What makes his book particularly interesting is the fact that, contrary to most philosophical investigations, which aim to stay within the confines of a strictly philosophical approach, he gives equally careful attention to early Christian views of the emotions and he aims to respect and understand the theological contexts in which these views are embedded. This method makes his account capable of tracing a revealing traffic of ideas between philosophy and theology. His main contention is that ancient and medieval views have had an all-pervasive influence on subsequent modern developments, which fact, however, is often overlooked by scholars of the modern period. There seems to be a considerable discontinuity between what researchers of ancient-medieval theories say and the findings of modern theorists. Moreover, there is a significant lacuna in research concerning medieval theories (one that Knuuttila sets

---

41. Knuuttila, *Emotions*.

out to fill), where, apart from piecemeal approaches, there are no comprehensive studies of emotion theories.[42] A lack of adequate acquaintance with ancient and medieval thought on this issue (much of it embedded in a theological context) on many occasions results in misconceptions concerning modern theories. We shall read Knuuttila's account in the light of the series of questions listed above, looking also for hidden implications in between the lines of Knuuttila's analysis from our own theological perspective, in order to discern the driving force behind Christian theological views concerning the state of human and divine freedom from the emotions. We shall restrict our inquiry to the sole issue of *apatheia* and closely related problems that we glean from the wider panorama of emotion theories presented in Knuuttila's study.

While Plato and Aristotle—although differing on several crucial points—equally consider the emotions as acts of natural potencies and so part and parcel of human nature that cannot be eradicated, the Stoics argue for the integrity of the rational soul without the emotional part and therefore believe that one can learn to live completely without emotions.[43] The thought of Plato displays an interesting evolution concerning the role of affectivity in the human person. He famously divides the soul into three parts: the reasoning part (*logistikon*), which strives for knowledge and is able to love knowledge and wisdom; the spirited part (*thumoeides*), that is, the intermediate part and the seat of emotions connected with self-assurance and self-affirmation; and the appetitive part (*epithumetikon*), which pursues immediate sensual pleasure and aims to avoid suffering. Plato sees these parts as almost separate agents at times and he imagines a constant struggle between them. In his earlier dialogues (e.g., *Phaedo*) the emotions are placed outside the reasoning part and are regarded as belonging to the body. Here, one finds a strong dichotomy between body and soul, which entails the fundamental distinction between the immortal rational soul and the mortal irrational parts. In this first phase, Plato's asceticism is strongly manifest. In his view, there is nothing positive in the desires and emotions of the body. The best attitude a philosopher can adopt is to be detached from them. The later *Republic* displays a modified view in the acknowledgment of desires and passions as movements of the soul. On this later more lenient view, the appetitive part is not completely instinctive or biological, but also houses more cognitive attitudes, such as the desire for wealth. However, this lowest part of the soul remains a potentially disturbing factor for Plato, who claims

42. In recent years, however, there has been a growing interest in Aquinas's emotion theory and Lombardo's study (*The Logic of Desire*) has filled an important gap in this respect.

43. For a discussion of ancient philosophy see Knuuttila, *Emotions*, 5–110.

that it must be continuously held under the control of reason. The spirited part in the *Republic* receives an interesting mediatory role, since—although it is the seat of aggressive self-assertion—it can be habituated to become an ally of reason. In this respect it differs from the appetitive part, which can never act in harmony with reason on its own accord and therefore must be constantly held hostage to reason. It seems that Plato treats the emotional responses of the spirited part as cognitive, although, as we saw, he grants a certain degree of cognitivity even to the appetitive part (e.g., in its having not only biological desires but also the more intellectual desire for wealth). Neither the appetitive nor the spirited parts are irrational in Plato's scheme. Nonetheless, the fact remains that the appetitive part can be a hindrance to the attainment of good life, which requires the improvement of the intellectual, immortal part of the soul through philosophizing. Moreover, as Knuuttila suggests, it seems that Plato admits of the existence of specific intellectual desires and pleasures also in the rational part, one crucial example being the love for truth and wisdom. Another emotion located in the reasoning part is shame. In the *Symposium* and the *Phaedrus*, we find a more detailed description of rational *erōs* that is analogous to the sexual desire of the appetitive part. Rational *erōs* has the same element of the feeling of possession and fascination typical of erotic love and it serves as a basis for love of the objects of the rational soul. The search for knowledge is described in passionate and erotically colored terms. On this account, emotional responses likewise belong to the rational and immortal soul. In sum, Plato has a reserved attitude towards the emotions, regarding them as hindrance in the contemplation of higher realities, which is the only goal worthy of the immortal soul. The emotions, although belonging indispensably to human nature, tend to fill the soul with inappropriate attachment to contingent temporal matters and distract it from what it should ideally cling to in the realm of the Ideas.

Aristotle has a diametrically opposed view concerning the role that emotions play in human life. According to him, the detachment from the emotions cannot be a meaningful goal of philosophy since the emotions are part and parcel of rational and social human action directed to the good life. Although he too recognizes the essential contingence and fragility that affectivity represents for our humanity, he nonetheless gives a positive evaluation of our necessary attachment to temporal and contingent things as a natural outcome of our basic human condition. Since his stance is not one of seeking ultimate fulfillment outside the visible world in transcendent realities, he can be more welcoming towards those realities that do not seem to be completely under our rational control. In accordance with the intimate relationship he posits between body and soul (the soul being the form of the body), he does not so much divide the soul into separate parts or separate agents (as is the tendency in Plato's case). He rather speaks of various capacities that operate within the same undivided soul. In this manner, the reasoning and emotional parts are supposed to be making use of the same faculty of reason in different ways. What emotions do is to guide human behavior and help in the habituation of the virtues, which are based on dispositions to feel emotions aright. Consequently, a state of *apatheia* where no pleasure, pain, fear, pity, and like emotions are felt is a doubly deficient state. First, it is unnatural because insensibility is basically inhuman; it resembles more of the state of a fool who displays mental retardation and whose emotions are either completely lacking or do not correspond to their object. Second, a state of *apatheia* is also deficient for being immoral, since feeling no pity over someone's suffering is a moral failing; no one who is morally sane can claim to rise above the consequences of suffering. The acceptance of our natural condition of vulnerability is a prerequisite for the realization of our true humanity. Therefore, the virtues cannot be defined on the basis of complete freedom from the emotions, for even anger is a necessary element in virtuous life.

The emotionless state of *apatheia* or detachment from the emotions is therefore far from being an ideal state of perfect humanity in Aristotle's philosophy. No matter how much Aristotle's and Plato's positions differ on the issue of the usefulness of emotion, Plato nonetheless sides with Aristotle in viewing the emotional part as an ineradicable component of human nature.

The Stoic ideal is similar to the theories of Plato and Aristotle in the sense that all three posit, even if in different ways, the cognitivity of emotions. More specifically, the Stoic theory shows much similarity with Plato's early view of the ascetic ideal of detachment from disturbing affectivity. However, what makes the Stoic view differ, in a significant manner, from Platonic and Aristotelian accounts is its more radical conception of cognitivity: while in Plato and Aristotle the emotions are associated with beliefs, the Stoics view emotions as judgments. According to the Stoics, emotions are false judgments; they are irrational, contrary to nature, and excessive; they represent deviation from the norms of nature and reason by being unruly motions disobedient to reason. Underlying such a negative evaluation of the emotions is the Stoic conception of the soul viewed as radically unitary, that is, entirely rational and corporeal. The soul operates as a centralized system where the governing faculty (*hēgemonikon*) is the centre of all sensations and psychic activities, extending to and mixing with every part of the body. On this model, the ideal wise man relies on his completely rational, cognitive mental contents and objective value judgments, undisturbed by any false judgments, namely, emotions. Freedom from the emotions (*apatheia*) is therefore seen as the ideal situation of those wishing to lead a good life on philosophical principles. Philosophy is regarded as a medicine for the emotional diseases, and the Stoic cognitive therapy includes the unremitting supervision of one's thoughts and actions. Emotions, as false judgments, are to be extirpated by changing the beliefs at the root of false judgments. Emotional responses are thought to be neither necessary nor natural and they are by no means constituents of virtuous acts.

To charges against the actual impossibility and inhumanity of such an emotionless state, the Stoics forwarded two specific qualifications to the idea of *apatheia*. On the first, to the widespread charge that it is simply impossible to live completely without emotional reactions to events occurring in life (the most typical example being anger), the Stoics elaborated the idea of pre-emotions, that is, involuntary motions preceding an emotion. These motions are not yet emotions as such, they are just preliminary to emotions. Only when such a preliminary feeling is rationally assented to by the mind, can it be considered as voluntary and so is regarded as an emotion proper. The third step in this process (the first being the involuntary motion, the second the assent of the mind) takes place when the rational assent is followed by blind insistence and the conscious upholding of the embraced emotional state. In this manner, the Stoics could argue that anger can indeed occur as an involuntary motion even in the soul of the wise man. However, it does not become an emotion if it is not assented to in his mind. Therefore, *apatheia*, a state free from emotions, is not an unattainable ideal, but can be realized by someone wishing to lead a good life. Knuuttila stresses the often overlooked fact that the idea of feelings preceding an emotion was the basis of the late Stoic doctrine of the so called "first movements" or "pre-emotions" (*propatheia*, in Latin *antepassio*, or more commonly *propassio*), which was appropriated in a modified form by many Christian writers (for example, Origen and Jerome) and had a long-lasting influence on Christian moral teaching in the form of investigations of the voluntariness and involuntariness of emotional reactions.[44] We remember that Thomas Aquinas on occasions likewise employs the notion of propassion to describe the moral quality of the emotions that the incarnate Christ experienced according to his human nature.[45] According to Aquinas, in Christ the passions were not complete or perfect in the sense that—unlike real perfect passions—they did not dominate his mind and did not prevail over his entire soul. Christ's passions were incomplete (and therefore nobler than ordinary full-blown passions that must be understood in negative terms here in accordance with

---

44. See Knuuttila, *Emotions*, 2.
45. *ST* III.15.4.

the original meaning of the term), in being rooted entirely in reason and in fully respecting reason's judgment. Jesus's propassions strictly harmonized with reason and were entirely directed towards higher rational goods. This is a clear modification of the Stoic idea, which held that the first movements are but a preliminary to emotions, not being emotions themselves. Christ's propassions, while not reaching the (negative) status of complete passions, are nonetheless real emotions in Aquinas's view.

The other qualification the Stoics made to the charge of the impossibility and inhumanity of having no emotions at all is the idea of the existence of "good passions" (*eupatheiai*). There is much debate in current emotion scholarship on how to understand the Stoic claim that, while the soul of the sage is undisturbed by emotions (*pathē*), it can nonetheless have good passions that are in some way analogous to real passions, but—contrary to ordinary passion—are entirely cognitive, reason-ruled states. We recall Augustine's indignant attack on the Stoic legerdemain whereby terms denoting proper emotions are substituted by terms suggesting positive cognitive states (will instead of desire, contentment in place of joy, and caution as an alternative to fear).[46] As Knuuttila observes, one can put forward arguments either for the legitimacy of the Stoic claim or its nonsensical character depending on one's interpretation of the Stoic intent and the idea of cognitivity in Stoic emotion theory.[47]

So, does the state of *apatheia* require the complete eradication of human emotionality? The answer largely depends on one's understanding of emotionality. For it seems that even the Stoics, the most radical champions of the ideal of impassibility, admit of the necessary presence in the soul of positive cognitive states in the manner of emotions: such as good will,

---

46. Augustine, *City of God*, 14.8. Augustine here writes: "Those emotions which the Greeks call *eupatheiai* and which Cicero calls *constantiae*, the Stoics would restrict to three; and, instead of three 'perturbations' in the soul of the wise man, they substituted severally, in place of desire, will; in place of joy, contentment; and for fear, caution; and as to sickness or pain, which we, to avoid ambiguity, preferred to call sorrow, they denied that it could exist in the mind of a wise man. Will, they say, seeks the good, for this the wise man does. . . . But sorrow arises from evil that has already happened; and as they suppose that no evil can happen to the wise man, there can be no representative of sorrow in his mind. According to them, therefore, none but the wise man wills, is contented, uses caution; and that the fool can do no more than desire, rejoice, fear, be sad."

47. "It was said that the sage may react to things with well-reasoned elation which is joy, with well-reasoned shrinking which is caution, and well-reasoned reaching out which is wishing. There was no good feeling corresponding to distress. In more detailed accounts of the *eupatheiai* it was said that wish includes good will, generosity, kindness, and love; caution includes respect and cleanliness; and joy includes delight, merriment, and cheerfulness." Knuuttila, *Emotions*, 68–69.

generosity, kindness, love, respect, cleanliness, delight, merriment, and cheerfulness. Most of the Stoic *eupatheiai* in this list would readily qualify as real emotions to our modern mindset. What makes them differ, however, on the Stoic conception, from emotions (passions) in the negative sense is their fully cognitive status: they do not contain involuntary or uncontrolled impulses; there is nothing irrational or visceral about them; they are fully compatible with the activities of the higher intellectual part of the soul.

Due to an interesting development, the Stoic idea of *apatheia*, combined with key elements from Platonism, results in a curiously ambiguous notion in Middle Platonic theories. There we can detect a telling bifurcation. While Stoic *apatheia* is criticized for its impracticability as a practical attitude to things in everyday life, it is nonetheless endorsed in another sense, where it is linked to the idea that the highest good for humans is the state of likeness to God (*homoiōsis theōi*). In the process of *homoiōsis*, a state of final *apatheia* is reached for those who are perfect in likeness to the emotionless God and who thus turn away from mundane matters and contemplate eternal truths through the purified eyes of the soul in a Platonic manner. Interestingly, such a state does not include the complete loss of emotional dispositions in Middle Platonic conceptions. Plotinus, for example, believes that the impassibility of the soul is perfectly compatible with the idea that some part of the soul is involved in emotions as their cause or as their perceiver. Even purified souls can have pleasures and appetites that arise spontaneously, without a cognitive judgment, and so do not disturb the apathy of the highest part of the soul. Plotinus thinks that the perfect soul ideally resides in the intelligible spheres where human emotions are not elicited. Nevertheless, it does not lose the capacity for emotional dispositions, which is a natural outcome of human bodiliness.[48] In addition to such an odd combination of impassibility and emotionality—a theory that became a central doctrine of later Neoplatonic philosophy—one also finds in Plotinus the idea of noetic senses, that is, special faculties corresponding to sense faculties through which supersensitive experiences of the transcendental origin of being can be enjoyed by those who have ascended to the higher spheres and have left the visible world behind. As Knuuttila notes, a long mystical tradition, with Origen at the start, will make use of this influential Plotinian idea.

While Christian authors obviously work with borrowed Platonic and Stoic ideas when they treat human emotions and set up rules for the way of moral perfection, the notion of *apatheia* seems to have undergone a

48. Plotinus believed that the highest part of the soul, of which one is seldom conscious, never left the intelligible world and is completely *apathēs* by nature. It permanently contemplates eternal truths and the divine. See Knuuttila, *Emotions*, 102.

thorough change within the Christian context. Elements from Platonic and Stoic thought are set in an entirely new perspective when the Plotinian idea of likeness to God (*homoiōsis theōi*) is transformed into the Christian idea of deification (*theiōsis*). The Christian God of Scripture is radically different from the Plotinian transcendent and impassible deity. The application of the philosophical idea of *apatheia* to God who is primarily understood as Love changes the entire Neoplatonic picture, entailing a specifically Christian version of impassibility, which is universally regarded as perfectly reconcilable with love. It is the unique combination of love and the idea of *apatheia* that governs Christian discourse concerning ways of attaining perfect likeness to God. What is at stake here is no longer the reconciliation of the possibility of a state completely free from emotions and the existence of reason-governed emotion-like experiences (the Stoic good feelings or *eupatheiai*). The major question of Christian discourse concerning the attainment of likeness to God hinges on the idea of love, which takes the place of the Stoic *eupatheiai* and reconfigures Plotinian *apatheia*.

Our foregoing survey of various conceptions concerning the place of emotionality clearly points in this direction. We have seen that the basic Christian distinction was made between emotions with a good object and emotions with an evil object, the first type being intimately connected to love and the concomitant emotions, such as, joy, delight, hope, and desire, whereas the latter were seen as unnecessary emotional disturbance, such as, pain, sorrow, and suffering, which does not constitute our ideal humanity as expressed by the concept of original innocence. Even authors like Maximus the Confessor, who describe the state of original innocence as a perfect state of *apatheia*, admit of the presence of love and spiritual pleasure. What is absent from such a blissful state is passion in the negative sense: emotional disturbance, sensual lust, and the suffering caused by pain. Augustine likewise argues for the presence of love and associated emotions rooted in love, both in the primeval state and in ultimate beatitude. He also expressly employs the distinction between positive and negative passion where passion in the negative sense includes both mental perturbations and bodily discomforts. We recall his claim that complete insensibility to the emotions cannot be set as a high ideal for the Christian. Aquinas also stresses the presence of passions with a good object in the original state of innocence. Undisturbed love, joy, hope, and desire could by no means be absent from such a blissful state. Within such an overall framework, there is nothing surprising in the insistence of Evagrius (345–399), for example, that the victory over the passions leads to the desirable state of *apatheia* where the soul's sole nourishment is divine knowledge and where love, the fruit of ascetic practice, is born as *apatheia*'s daughter.[49] Is it not the case that the discourse on love eventually absorbs talk about impassibility concerning Christian moral practice? Can we say that Christian agapaic love ultimately assumes the characteristics of *apatheia*, changing at the same time the entire original meaning?

Knuuttila's meticulous account of the twists and turns of various Christian emotion theories seems to be telling proof of such an intriguing development. What comes to the fore is a two-way movement. On the one hand, the discourse on love starts to govern the reflection concerning the human relation to God and neighbor; on the other, the Christian theological conception of love is marred by a curious division between what is seen as earthly, passible love, and divine impassible love. But can there be love for neighbor and God without compassion or grief or the feeling of pity? While the Christian reply definitely acknowledges the indispensability of these emotions for truly philanthropic love, it also speaks in terms of detachment, moderation, or even extirpation of the emotions as an ultimate goal of perfect Christianity. There seems to be a sharp divide between two kinds of emotionality: one mundane, biological, and therefore common with animals, attached to sensible contingent and finite things of the visible world, and another, understood analogously and associated with the fully intellectual love of the eternal and unchanging God. Whereas the first type of affectivity, the seat of sensitive psychosomatic passions, is entirely excluded from the image that bears human likeness to God (the highest, intellectual part of the soul) and is therefore seen as an aid for life in the sensible world at best, the second type of completely intellectual "affectivity" (claimed to be understood metaphorically) resides within the image, in the highest part of the soul, and involves spiritual and mystical feelings regarded as fundamentally different from their sensible counterparts. Such a basic dichotomy results in a curious doubling of perspectives. While early authors of the Alexandrian tradition, such as Clement and Origen, under the heavy influence of Stoic and Platonic philosophy, when speaking about the Christian road towards moral perfection, argue for the cutting away of the emotional part of the soul—which attaches to contingent, earthly things—and stress the complete mortification of natural emotions as unnecessary impediments on the way towards moral and spiritual perfection and the final goal of deification, at the same time they describe human love for God in highly emotional terms. The mystical union of the soul with God

---

49. See Aimé Solignac, "Passions et Vie Spirituelle," in Viller and Cavallera, *Dictionnaire de Spiritualité*, 344.

is expressed throughout Christian literature in the terms of the passionate spousal love of the biblical Song of Songs.

Moreover, the philosophical ideal of human *apatheia* (in the sense of the extirpation of the emotional part or detachment from the emotions) does not seem to play an important role in the theology of the West and practically disappears from medieval emotion theories.[50] This must be due to the fact that the significance of the body is viewed differently in the Eastern and the Western theological traditions. As we have seen, in the East, emphasis is placed on the disciplining of, and strict control over, the body in order that the soul may be capable of contemplating God in a purely intellectual manner without hindrance. In the West, the body is regarded as more of an ally or an instrument for the accomplishment of the good and the attainment of virtue. These two differing stances obviously influence the respective visions concerning the role of the emotions in human life with a view to the ultimate goal of Christian perfection.

One intriguing and often overlooked example of the Western approach is Lactantius (c.250–317), who in many respects anticipates Augustine's critique of the Stoic idea of *apatheia*. Lactantius, a great master of the Latin language, whose philosophy is rather eclectic and whose expertise in theology stays far behind that of his later fellow countryman, Augustine, nonetheless gives a uniquely positive account of human emotionality, arguing for the indispensability of the emotions in the human soul.[51] He tellingly avoids the negative term "passion," and uses the word "affections," the Latin *affectus*, instead. His main contention is that the affections cannot be cut out in a Stoic manner, but need to be regulated since they are implanted in man by nature, that is, by God at the creation. Lactantius illustrates his point with the forceful metaphor of a lush meadow:

> An affection therefore is a kind of natural fruitfulness of the powers of the mind. For as a field which is naturally fruitful produces an abundant crop of briars, so the mind which is uncultivated is overgrown with vices flourishing of their own accord,

---

50. In a panoramic survey of the role of the emotions in spirituality, Solignac registers a considerable decline in interest in the problem of the fight against the emotions in Western theology in contradistinction to Easter treatments of the issue. As he notes, Eastern theology is more markedly influenced by philosophical conceptions, while Western discussions are more inspired by Scripture texts, which have a different perspective on the unity of the human person and, consequently, on the role of affectivity. Solignac, "Passions et Vie Spirituelle," in Viller and Cavallera, *Dictionnaire de Spiritualité*, 340–57.

51. While Knuuttila makes only passing remarks on Lactantius, Solignac gives him pride of place in his own account of the role of the emotions in spirituality. Ibid., 345–46.

as with thorns. But when the true cultivator has applied himself, immediately vices give way, and the fruits of virtues spring up. Therefore God, when He first made man, with wonderful foresight first implanted in him these emotions of the mind, that he might be capable of receiving virtue, as the earth is of cultivation; and He placed the subject-matter of vices in the affections, and that of virtue in vices.[52]

Here we have a clear expression of the idea that the emotions are indispensable for virtuous life and that all they need is cultivation and proper guidance. It is only misguided sensual desire that is at fault, that is, desire of an unlawful object. Lactantius vehemently opposes the idea of impassibility, which he characterizes as the state of an "immovable insensibility of the mind," and maintains that whoever wants to deprive man of the affections is mad because it is in the affections that humanity exists. His main argument against the idea of *apatheia* is the claim that the soul cannot exist without movement because life itself is not immobile, but is "full of activity": "For as water which is always still and motionless is unwholesome and more muddy, so the soul which is unmoved and torpid is useless even to itself: nor will it be able to maintain life itself; for it will neither do nor think anything, since thought itself is nothing less than agitation of the mind."[53] Importantly, impassibility and immovability are here viewed as synonymous with an emotionless mental state. Lactantius's anthropology at other points reflects traditional views and is entirely couched in a traditional anthropological framework. For example, his idea of the composition of the human being from two opposing substances displays nothing original with regard to the thought common to the period: one substance is sensual and earthly (the body), the other heavenly (the soul), the heavenly part being the seat of the image of God.

Although the insistence on *apatheia* is, with time, absorbed by the discourse on love, what does remain is a strong sense of the assumed dichotomy between psychosomatic emotions and intellectual/spiritual passions; the higher feelings are sharply separated from lower ordinary emotions and are considered as being free from the negative effects of ordinary emotions. Such a theoretical dichotomy, then, as we shall see in the following chapter, largely determines Christian theological approaches to love. Despite the neat classifications and categorizations of types of love, one pivotal question concerning the nature of divine impassible love remains. Is God's divine love truly reconcilable with the idea of God's impassibility?

52. Lactantius, *Divine Institutes*, 6.15.
53. Ibid., 6.17.

God's Impassibility

If, as we saw in the case of Evagrius, human love is seen as issuing forth from human *apatheia*, then both ideas must be seen as mutually conditioning one another to the extent that they eventually merge in the more powerful concept of love. This is what happens in discussions concerning the idea of God's impassibility.[54] What comes to the fore from the history of the term is the curious fact that one is unable to find a meaningful way through the seemingly disparate aspects of the issue if one does not constantly keep in view the basic multiplicity of (to our mind contradictory) meanings associated with the notions of passion, impassibility, and immutability. On consideration of the various shades of meaning that converge in these terms, one thing becomes clear: just as the notion of human Christian *apatheia* by no means implies the complete absence of positive affectivity rooted in love, in a similar manner, the concept of divine impassibility does not primarily have to do with the negation of positive affectivity in God. I think that the distinction between the negative and the positive aspects of passion is crucial here. What is seen as lacking from God is connected to the negative effects of passion, which we saw in connection with the ideal state of original innocence. First, what is considered to be incompatible with God's eternal divinity is the occurrence of passion understood as involuntary movement originating in an external source, which engenders the loss of a suitable natural disposition (in the manner of Aquinas's definition of passion in the broad sense). Next, God is thought to be subject to no passion in the narrow sense of emotional disturbance or mental perturbation; in other words, God is believed to be completely free from the vexing limitation, weakness, or disability caused by the negative effect of passion. Thirdly, the suffering (as change for the worse or the deterioration of an ideal situation) caused by the two previous processes (the loss of a positive disposition and the pain resulting from emotional disturbance) is claimed to be absent from God's immutable nature since any kind of inert passivity is incompatible with the Creator's omnipotence. Behind such a negative understanding of passion lies a fundamental assumption common since the beginning of the Christian era: reason, a stable and relatively autonomous force, is opposed to the realm of affectivity, which is regarded as implying submission to an alien

---

54. This is the impression one gets from John Milbank's survey of the complex development of this concept throughout Christian theology. See John Milbank, "Immutabilité Divine/Impassibilité Divine," in Lacoste, *Dictionnaire Critique de Théologie*, 561-63.

force.⁵⁵ That is why affectivity in this sense is viewed as entirely incompatible with God's divine sovereignty.

As has become clear from our foregoing discussion of the state of original innocence, parallel to the traditional sense of passion and impassibility, a new and specifically Christian distinction between bad passion and good sentiment emerges, together with a new understanding of passivity and receptivity and a new conception of suffering. Obviously, at the root of the changing vision one finds the central idea of Christian love, which transforms the traditional philosophical concept of divine impassibility and calls for the inclusion of an idea of positive affectivity within the divine life. Interestingly, such a reworked notion of impassibility does not weaken the original idea that God is free from involuntary suffering, weakness, or limitation, and therefore is unmovable. Quite the contrary, the interplay of impassibility and love creates what we could term a strong concept of impassibility, which is now seen on biblical grounds as the constancy of love and the freely (and therefore actively) accepted suffering that, however, does not change in any manner the constant divine disposition of positive love. On such a curious paradox, the more God is thought as love, the more God is conceived as unmovable and impassible in a dynamic and active manner. Such a change in emphasis entails the redefinition of action, which from now onwards also includes the meanings of "freely letting oneself be influenced," or "receive," and it likewise gives rise to a renewed conception of suffering without passivity or resentment. Such suffering (Christ's redemptive suffering in an eminent sense) is not imposed from outside, but is a free gift from within, revealing the constancy of love. Such constancy is *apatheia* in an eminent sense: it is apathetic to the disturbing effects of evil forces that aim to deviate it from the ultimate accomplishment of the redemptory work of love through a free and active acceptance of suffering. It is only if one embraces such a notion of impassibility conditioned by love that claims about the effect of divine immutability truly make sense. Otherwise the biblical vision—where God obviously appears to be moved by the emotions of love, compassion, anger, and pity—is hopelessly irreconcilable with the idea of passionless apathy. The internal logic of orthodox Christianity does not allow for the abandonment of the claim that God is impassible and immutable in the sense of being firmly faithful to the constancy of his love. Were one to discard the idea of impassibility in this renewed Christian sense of the term, or were one to claim (as many theologians of the nineteenth and the twentieth century did) that, in Jesus Christ, the Triune God underwent

---

55. See ibid., 561. Milbank relies here on Herbert Frohnhofen's account *Apatheia tou Theou*, 13–123.

suffering in the same way as humans do, one would also necessarily imply that, with Jesus's suffering and death, the Logos lost its divinity and that the weakness, limitation, defects, and disability inflicted by passion (both in the sense of emotional disturbance and that of general physical and spiritual suffering) allow for no redemptive difference between God and the human being. In the last resort, it means the victory of evil passion over the primary and foundational, good passion of divine love.[56]

Just as human impassibility is a difficult concept, there is no easy answer to the question of divine impassibility either. One can only identify directions or trajectories that the discussion may optimally take. It is also a question of walking a tightrope between anthropomorphic conceptions and rigid philosophical concepts, in the hope of finding the living and loving God of Scripture. What one must do is listen to some distinctive voices from the theological tradition concerning the issue of affectivity in God. Can it be meaningfully held in an orthodox fashion that God has emotions analogous to ours? This is a question rarely put in current theological inquiry since, on the one hand, it is somehow taken for granted that God's love implies passionate involvement and concern for humans, and, on the other, the question of divine impassibility is usually asked from the perspective of divine co-suffering with the human being. Even if we take it for granted that God is passionate towards us, we must find adequate theological foundations in support of such a claim. While the attribution of pure intellect to God has not seemingly caused any problem for authors in the theological tradition, the idea that God also feels has proved to be more challenging. For a supreme example of the view that God is not impassible in the manner that Stoic and Epicurean philosophers imagine, we turn to Lactantius who famously argued even for the presence of the affection of anger in God.[57]

Lactantius's main interest does not lie in the metaphysical reality of God's divine nature, because he writes from a more practical perspective. The Epicurean and Stoic ideas of divine *apatheia* contain the underlying assumption that the impassible God is not influenced by men's deeds, that he neither rejoices nor is angry at what humans do. Lactantius sees a great danger in such a claim since it undermines the doctrine of providence and the notion of future punishment and reward, deconstructing the ultimate grounds of human worship of God. What is at stake, for Lactantius, is a proper idea of divine love, which, in his view, cannot be meaningfully conceived without the parallel affection of divine anger. Consequently, he

---

56. See Milbank, "Immutabilité Divine/Impassibilité Divine," in Lacoste, *Dictionnaire Critique de Théologie*, 563.

57. Lactantius, *A Treatise on the Anger of God*.

maintains that those who deny the deity both love and anger follow a more consistent logic than those who simply argue for the presence of love, kindness, and benevolence without admitting the possibility of divine anger, although both camps are manifestly wrong.[58] While, clearly, a God without any affections would be a logical absurdity for a Christian since it would imply the absence of care or providence with regard to the creation, the idea of a God who can only love without hatred for the wicked leads to an even more nonsensical conception. Therefore, love goes hand in hand with anger. Anger (or hatred) is an aspect of divine love and the integrity of the concept of God's love demands the equal acknowledgement of the existence of the twin concept of divine wrath. As Aimé Solignac notes, it is always from the perspective of God's relation to us that Lactantius speaks about love and anger in God.[59] There is no question here of the dynamism of inner divine life or the metaphysical attributes of God. Remarkably, Lactantius too makes the crucial distinction between good and "vicious" affections, asserting that desire, fear, avarice, grief, and envy cannot be found in God, who is entirely free from these negative emotions. He likewise distinguishes between human and divine anger. While human anger can be unjust and unruly, divine anger is always just, is entirely under the control of the divine will and is wholly contained by the divine love. In sum, Lactantius allows for the existence of two major emotions in God: love (and the related kindness, benevolence, joy, pity, etc.) and anger (that is, justified hatred and concern for the wicked). Notably, his positive view of human emotionality is coupled with a positive regard of divine affectivity. We get, nevertheless, no further clarification concerning the way the affections can be ascribed to God.

Surprisingly, in Augustine's treatise *The Trinity* (Book 14), in a passage that treats of the connection between traces of the Trinity within the visible creation and the divine characteristics of the Triune God, we find the intriguing claim that God both thinks and feels in a primary sense.[60] Having described the ascending hierarchy of the order of the universe where living things are more perfect than non-living ones and beings equipped with sense perception are on a higher scale compared to the ones without such a capacity, where creatures with intellect are superior those lacking reason, mortal beings are inferior to immortal ones, and where those having a body

---

58. "The arguments are found to be empty and false, either of those who, when they will not admit that God is angry, will have it that he shows kindness, because this, indeed, cannot take place without anger; or those who think that there is no emotion of the mind in God." Lactantius, *A Treatise on the Anger of God*, 16.

59. Solignac, "Passions et Vie Spirituelle," in Viller and Cavallera, *Dictionnaire de Spiritualité*, 346.

60. Augustine, *The Trinity*, 15.4–5.

are lower in rank compared to incorporeal beings, Augustine asserts that God the Creator of the universe possesses all the characteristics at the top of the hierarchy in the highest sense. God "lives in the highest sense.... He perceives all things, and understands all things."[61] By rendering the Latin *sentire* ("feel," "sense") with the word "perceive," the English translation cautiously attenuates the concrete directness of the original meaning, which, however proves to be a consistent choice throughout the passage on the part of Augustine (the text has the words *sensus*, "sense" and *sentit*, "sense, feel" and nowhere is the otherwise possible synonym *percepit* "perceive" employed)."[62] The governing image of the passage is the metaphor of life. God is life in the truest sense because his life is not received from an outside source but He lives "by the life which He Himself is to Himself." And since life is characterized by both the ability to feel and understand, God likewise feels and understands all things. Augustine also explains the difference between various degrees of life and the corresponding ways of sensation and thinking. While the life of a tree lacks both understanding and sense, and the beast [*pecus*]—although it possesses the fivefold sense—has no understanding, God "perceives and understands all things [*sentit atque intelligit omnia*], and it [that life that God is] perceives in a mind [*sentit mente*], not in a body [*non corpore*], because 'God is spirit' [see John 4:24]."[63] Interestingly, Augustine's comparison seems to omit man who, according to the logic of the text, ought to be treated between the "beast" and God. However, one can also argue that Augustine does include both humans and beasts in the category of "*animalia*," which primarily denotes a spirited being.[64] This could also be regarded as a telling option whereby human sense perception and sensitivity are viewed in seamless continuity with the animal world, having nothing specifically unique with respect to the rest of spirited beings. All things considered, the fundamental difference between the way God feels and understands and the operation of human feeling and understanding clearly lies in the presence or the absence of the body, ac-

61. Ibid., 15.4.6.

62. Augustine goes on to insist: "For who would venture to say either that the one God, which is the Trinity itself, or that the Father, or the Son, or the Holy Spirit is not living, or is lacking in perception [*sentientem*] or understanding?" Ibid., 15.4.7.

63. Augustine explains: "But not as animals [*animalia*] which have bodies does God perceive through a body, for He does not consist of soul and body, and, therefore, that simple nature, as it understands, so it perceives, as it perceives, so it understands [*sicut intellegit sentit, sicut sentit intellegit*], and in it perception is the same as understanding [*idemque sensus qui intellectus est illi*]." Ibid., 15.4.7.

64. This suggestion is supported by the interpretation of the Hungarian translator who renders *animalia* by "bodily creatures," that is, a category that may equally include humans and animals. See Augustinus, *A Szentháromságról* [On the Trinity], 441.

cording to Augustine. God feels in an intellectual/spiritual manner (and in this regard, the English rendering of *sentit* by the term "perceive" is to some extent justified); God's simplicity allows for the absolute convertibility of the (otherwise) two distinct acts of sense perception and understanding.

There is obviously no direct mention here of God's emotions. However, the attribution of a kind of spiritual emotionality that follows from the fact of spiritual sensing may not be wide of the mark on the basis of this text. Augustine, however, does not pursue this line of thought any further; what he importantly does, nevertheless, is to list the characteristics of the divine life. Here we are provided clear proof again that immutability or unchangeability are perfectly compatible with the idea of the dynamism of divine life in Augustine's thought, since God is equally "eternal, immortal, incorruptible, unchangeable, living, wise, powerful, beautiful, just, good, blessed, and spirit."[65]

If God is the fullness of life that, to our human understanding, can be represented by the inner dynamism of self-knowledge and self-love in an Augustinian fashion, can we still maintain the old premise that God is altogether immutable? This is a question Aquinas asks in his *Summa Theologica*.[66] In the reply he considers objections to the contrary. First, that, according to Augustine, God moves itself ("The Creator Spirit moves Himself neither by time, nor by place." *Gen. ad lit.*, 8.20). Second, that in Scripture Wisdom (who personifies God) is portrayed as being "more mobile than all things active." Third, that the letter of James speaks in terms of God's drawing near humans ("Draw nigh to God and He will draw nigh to you," Jas 4:8). Aquinas weighs these arguments against the Scripture claim that God does not change: "I am the Lord, and I change not" (Mal 3:6). The gist of his own intricate argument is, on the one hand, that movement in Scripture is ascribed to God not directly, but "by way of similitude" or "metaphorically," and, on the other, that the movement involved by God's moving Himself or in the acts of understanding and loving Himself does not mean movement that would make God mutable because such acts do not cause any change in God: God's eternal infinity is in no way altered by the dynamism of immanent divine life.[67] Consequently, Aquinas contends, there is no reason to question the traditional doctrine that God is altogether immutable.

65. Augustine, *The Trinity*, 15.4.7.
66. Aquinas, *ST* Ia.9.1.
67. It must be noted that, for Aquinas, the metaphorical sense of Scripture (*secundum metaphoram*) does not belong the category of spiritual sense (*sensus spiritualis* or *mysticus*) as one would expect, but to the one of literal sense (*sensus litteralis*). In the commentary on the letter to the Galatians, Aquinas explains that, while the spiritual sense (including allegorical sense, moral sense, and anagogical sense) comes about as

Elsewhere, Aquinas poses the related question whether love, which is obviously a passion and therefore involves movement and change, can exist in God.[68] His solution hinges on the crucial distinction we pinpointed throughout our discussion of the place of emotionality with regard to the image. Apparently, there are two types of love, bodily and intellectual: the first love is a passion insofar it is connected to the body and is seated in the sensitive appetite; the second love, however, is not a passion inasmuch as it is an act of the highest, intellectual part of the soul (which Aquinas terms the "intellective appetite"). Aquinas then concludes that it is such an intellectual love that we can ascribe to God, whose love is an act of his will and who therefore "loves without passion [*sine passione amat*]," similar to human intellective acts of love.[69] Here again one must recall the negative connotations of the concept of passion in the theological tradition that provides the proper context for Aquinas's otherwise startlingly odd claim. God loves without passion because passion involves the change of an ideal state for the worse, the loss of a good disposition, involuntary motion, emotional and mental disturbance, and therefore suffering, and ultimately weakness and limitation. These are incompatible with God's love, who nonetheless loves warmly and tenderly.[70]

To the objection that, because sorrow and anger are evidently attributed to God metaphorically, therefore, one cannot attribute to God love (in the proper sense) either, Aquinas replies that there is a basic difference between passions that imply imperfection and those that do not. Desire, for example,

---

a result of signification through things, that is, events and connections that God makes bearers of meaning expressed, of course, in the words of Scripture (for example, divinely given signs in the Old Testament are interpreted as pointing to Jesus Christ and to the church), the literal sense is given exclusively through words, that is, signification through words in language. The literal sense is then subdivided into two types according to the way a word can signify: 1. proper sense (*secundum proprietatem*), e.g., "That person laughs"; 2. in a metaphorical sense (*secundum metaphoram*), e.g., "a laughing meadow." See, for example, F. J. A. de Grijs, "Thomas Aquinas on *Ira* as a Divine Metaphor," in Schoot, *Tibi Soli Peccavi*, 28–29.

68. Aquinas, *ST* Ia.20.1.

69. Ibid., Ia.20.1.

70. As Michael J. Dodds argues, God's impassibility does not imply insensibility. God has compassion towards us without having passion, that is, without the imperfection of suffering within the divinity. God loves us with compassionate love by identifying with our situation and by beneficent action on our behalf. Dodds quotes Aquinas to the effect that in divine compassion there is no sorrow or suffering: "It is commonly said that in [God] there is not compassion according to passion, but according to effect. Nevertheless, the effect (*effectus*) proceeds from the affection (*affectu*) of the will, which is not a passion but a simple act of will." See *Sent* 4.46.2.1.1c. The simple act of will is love in Aquinas's scheme. See Dodds, "Thomas Aquinas, Human Suffering, and the Unchanging God of Love," 330–44.

implies imperfection inasmuch as it consists in longing for the good one does not have. Sorrow has to do with some evil one has, while anger presupposes sorrow over an evil situation or harm done to someone.[71] Since these passions are closely linked up with a state of imperfection linked to the body, they can only be attributed to God metaphorically (*metaphorice*), also because in God they do not have their body-dependent element, while passions without imperfection, such as love and joy, can be properly predicated of God. While Aquinas's meticulous logic seems completely clear at first sight, on second thought one may wonder what the exact difference between God's metaphorically understood anger, sorrow, and desire, and God's love in the proper sense, actually is. Is it really the body which makes all the difference?[72]

Among twentieth-century theologians, it is Hans Urs von Balthasar who famously takes up the question of God's anger and the relationship between anger and love.[73] He returns to the perspective of Lactantius, whom he expressly evokes to the effect that the Enlightenment claim of God having no "emotions" needs to be revised by modern theology along

---

71. Aquinas wrote extensively on these passions as human passions, and especially on anger, to which he devoted the lengthiest discussion in the *Summa Theologica* (IaIIae.158.1.). As Paul Gondreau has pointed out, Aquinas's positive regard concerning the passion of anger is outstanding in the theological tradition, which—going back to Gregory the Great—regarded anger as one of the capital sins or vices. Aquinas gives a complex account of the passion of anger, distinguishing its positive and negative elements and arguing for its essential neutrality and its vital importance for the formation of the moral virtue of meekness and its close relation to the sense of justice. Contrary to a strong tendency in the theological tradition, Aquinas does not hesitate to attribute the passion of anger to Christ, which he sees as compatible with Jesus's salvific mission directed to the reestablishment of the order of divine justice that has been perverted by human sin. However, unlike ordinary human anger, Christ's anger, in Aquinas's view, is always under the control of reason, never obstructing or impeding its operation. See Gondreau, *The Passions of Christ's Soul*, 429–41.

72. The difference obviously lies in the fact that anger is a passion and passions cannot be ascribed to God, that is why God's anger is understood metaphorically (within the literal sense); that is, God is not affected by the passion of anger, which involves bodily change and imperfection. Love belongs to the will in Aquinas's classification, and since it can be said in a proper sense that God wills, therefore one can also say in a proper sense that God loves, also because love does not involve any imperfection. See Grijs, "Thomas Aquinas on *Ira* as a Divine Metaphor," Schoot, *Tibi Soli Peccavi*, 19–46. However, one may wonder whether God's loving and willing displays such seamless continuity with human loving and willing as Aquinas assumes.

73. Balthasar, *The Action*, esp. 317–51. John Milbank judges that in Balthasar's account of the impassible immanent trinitarian life, which is at the same time deeply concerned with the world, one finds a forceful modern re-appropriation of the finest patristic thought. See Milbank, "Immutabilité Divine/Impassibilité Divine," in Lacoste, *Dictionnaire Critique de Théologie*, 563.

the lines of Lactantius's insistence that God's love is inseparable from his anger. Balthasar's own perspective likewise moves within the question of divine justice and punishment and it is from this perspective that he asks the question of divine involvement in the misery of the world. Ultimately, what is at stake here is the issue of the redemptive suffering of the Son and the Son's full acceptance of the crushing burden of divine wrath, which he bears as a consequence of the constancy of his love both for the Father and for us. Like Lactantius, von Balthasar argues that divine love does not make sense without the twin dimension of divine anger and he marshals ample scriptural evidence in demonstration of the fact that the theme of God's anger with the sinner on account of his sin is a central message throughout the entire Scripture. Contrary to any philosophically posited *apatheia*, the biblical God reveals "*pathos*," that is, he is involved and is deeply affected by the conduct of man; God never appears as detached from what goes on in his creation. Nevertheless, God's pathos is not anthropomorphic, since it is always an entirely free involvement and is never mere feeling or passive affection, but couples with the objective norm and active constancy of love, which also gives the ethos of the divine law. It is essentially a dynamic and active relation between God and the human being. In this context, Jesus Christ is the epitome of God's pathos expressed for us. It is not only through his teaching and his attitude towards sin that he reveals both God's love and anger; he also discloses the depths of God's affectivity through his loving acceptance of the increasing anger directed towards him, which eventually leads to his crucifixion. Balthasar thinks in terms of an inconceivable paradox: with Christ's passion the darkness of the world enters the inner light of the Trinity, without, however obstructing the eternal and unchanging flow of never-failing divine love. In Christ, "God's anger at the rejection of divine love encounters a divine love (the Son's) that exposes itself to this anger, disarms it and literally deprives it of its object."[74] What we are invited to reconnoiter in this theological universe, is the "vanishing point where the lines of God's anger and his love meet." Within such a soteriological and trinitarian perspective, God's affectivity proves to be impassible and immutable in a renewed sense, without being in the least apathetic to human suffering or unconcerned at the slightest with the misery of the world. Indeed, it discloses the fullness of everlasting, archetypal, divine love.[75]

74. Balthasar, *The Action*, 349–50.

75. Balthasar returns to the theme of divine wrath in his late work written as a recapitulation and an overview of his entire theological project of the trilogy of *The Glory of the Lord*. In this thin volume, entitled *Epilogue* (1987), commenting on the mystery of the cross, he again contests theological ideas that aim to separate love and anger in God's attitude towards us and maintain that "God is nothing else but love,

The themes of divine impassibility and the existence of divine emotions have been recently taken up by patristic scholar Paul L. Gavrilyuk. In his insightful and challenging study of these concepts in the writings of the Christian authors of the first five centuries, Gavrilyuk makes a convincing case for two claims. First, one cannot register a clear-cut and unified doctrine of divine impassibility in the fashion that some recent accounts have sought to do, with a view to dismissing this doctrine as an outdated theological tenet. Second, the idea of impassibility never meant the alleged absence of emotions or indifference to the world as is often mistakenly assumed by modern theologians.[76] The term impassibility is misinterpreted if it is taken to mean the complete absence of any "emotionally colored characteristics" or total unemotionality or impassive detachment, according to the etymology of the term. One reads more into this simply apophatic attribute than was intended if one thinks in terms of the claim that God has no emotions and is not moved by human suffering. As Gavrilyuk demonstrates, for the fathers, the thought that God is impassible was entirely compatible with the conviction that God has "select" (because analogically different from human) emotions, such as love, mercy, and compassion. While uncontrolled passion and the negative effects of the passions were believed to be absent from God, judicial anger and tender love, together with merciful compassion, were by no means regarded as alien to God. Moreover, divine impassibility must be interpreted within the context of apophatic theology, where it is just one of a series of interconnected negative qualifiers (e.g., infinite, invisible, immutable, incorporeal, incorruptible, incomprehensible, etc.) intended to highlight the greater difference (beyond similarity) between creatures and God. In this respect, divine immutability is not an isolated concept—despite the fact that it is often treated as such in the recent theological debate—but belongs to the overall framework of a theological effort to attribute truly and specifically divine emotions to God.

The Missing Heart

So where does that leave us? We have come a long way since our consideration of various forms of image-theology and the survey of the place of emotionality in the human person and in God. What has come to the fore

---

and all this talk about God's 'wrath' (think of René Girard and his epigones) is but a false transposition of human emotions onto God." Balthasar here once again emphasizes the inseparable mystery of divine love and anger, which mutually condition one another. Balthasar, *Epilogue*, 118–19.

76. Gavrilyuk, *The Suffering of the Impassible God*, esp. 1–63.

rather forcibly is the existence of a deep-seated dichotomy in the Christian understanding of affectivity, both with regard to its relationship to the intellect and with regard to its own inner coherence. Human affectivity, in being attached to the body and psychosomatic processes, has traditionally been regarded as lying outside the seat of human likeness to God, which has almost unanimously been located in the human intellect. Although the cognitive nature of the emotions, or at least the close connection between thinking and feeling, is generally not disputed, a hierarchical relation is posited whereby the passions are relegated to the lower part of the soul over which the intellect is ideally assumed to have full control. While reason is viewed as a relatively stable force, emotivity is feared as the site of unknown alien forces that threaten the constancy of reason by causing involuntary perturbation. Nevertheless, in the history of various Christian positions concerning the passions, one can register an interesting development from a negative to an increasingly positive attitude: after the neutral stance of the earliest Christian apostolic and subapostolic writings, comes an age of negative judgment with a strong emphasis on ascetic self-control and the eradication of the passions.[77] With the gradual evolution of Christology, however, the strict ascetic ideal of a general contempt for the body is largely relativized. A positive regard for the incarnation and Christ's bodily resurrection necessitates a more positive view of human bodily existence and bodily suffering. This also has important consequences for the assessment of the passions. These are no longer regarded as wholly dangerous intruders into the peace of the contemplating mind, but are accepted as part and parcel of our passible humanity, both in the sense that the body is capable of suffering and in the sense of our liability to having emotions. In addition to these developments, a new idea of passivity appears that is grounded in the recognition that passivity not only characterizes human affectivity but is an inherent feature of reason itself. This new idea of reason as passible in a fashion similar to the passions eventually attenuates the sharp divide between the two realms. On the whole, the theological (moral) status of human emotionality is gradually ameliorated, so much so that, as we saw, the passions are thought to be indispensable for virtuous Christian life.

We also detected signs of such amelioration in our survey of accounts concerning the state of original innocence and the cause of the fall. While Gregory of Nyssa and Maximus the Confessor, for example, both exclude human constitutional liability to bodily passion from the ideal state of original innocence (except for a capacity for spiritual pleasure, which they regard

---

77. See Thomas E. Breidenthal's survey in the entry "Passions," in Lacoste, *Dictionnaire Critique de Théologie*, 868–70.

as different from bodily passions, understood as negative emotional disturbances), representatives of a prevailing trend in Western theology, such as, Augustine and Thomas Aquinas in his wake, allow for the existence of real bodily passions with a good object (love, joy, delight, hope) in the pre-fallen primeval state. Nonetheless, the exclusion of the passions from the ideal state prior to the fall does not imply an overall negative outlook concerning human affectivity in the case of Gregory or Maximus either. Despite certain reservations concerning the role of the passions in primeval emotionality, they allow for the necessary presence of emotion in ordinary life and as inherent and indispensable movements of the soul. Their respective visions of the final beatitude is symmetrical to their accounts of the state of original innocence: supernatural love and spiritual joy are excluded by neither from a vision of God, however their opinions vary concerning the cause of joy, from predominantly intellectual to more emotional theories of ultimate love.

Interestingly, there is almost a unanimous consensus among the authors considered regarding the diagnosis of the state of fallen man. After the fall man is characterized by a certain weakness of intellect and will. Both are somehow deviated from their primary goal—the movement towards contemplative happiness in God—and become partly disoriented: without losing their supernatural aim completely from view, they nonetheless stray, reaching for earthly objects at hand and easily falling prey to bodily sensuality. While sensual pleasure, bodily passions, and self-love are taken to task for being the immediate cause of man's spiritual and intellectual deviation from his divinely projected ultimate end, nowhere does one find the claim that human affectivity or the body is to be blamed in the first place for the outbreak of the disorder. Various explanations of the postlapsarian deficient state of our humanity converge on the salient point that the primary cause of fragility, weakness, limitation, and defect must be detected in a malfunction of the highest part of the soul, in the intellect and the will, which are responsible for reasonable action and the right orientation of the entire human person. Therefore, it is the sinful confusion of these highest powers that is viewed as affecting the lower parts, leaving them partly uncontrolled and often without guidance. As a consequence of original sin, the intellect becomes to a great extent uncertain about what is truly good for man and seeks immediate satisfaction in the corruptible world of sense pleasure. Obviously, the body has an essential role in sinful desire; however, it is reason and the will that, by becoming disorderly and alienated from God, cease to exert wise dominion on bad inclinations, thereby abandoning the lower faculties to the final anarchy of the senses. Reason, which is also divided against itself, is unable to reconcile conflicting forces experienced within, or to resist the strong pull weighing it down from without. Within such a dynamics, the passions, sensuality and bodily lust have only second-order responsibility, since they are thought to be under the tutelage of the intellect and lack full maturity with regard to the discernment of basic human orientations.

One can detect traces of a negative judgment concerning human sensibility in Thomas Aquinas's Christology where Christ is claimed to have a more perfect sensibility than ours in that, in his case, reason is thought to penetrate the emotional part without remainder, leaving no quarter uncontrolled and allowing for no irrational outburst of passion, but taking the lead in all cases when emotions occur. Reason and emotionality are set in a sharp opposition in this manner, and a tension or discord, a kind of fracture, is posited between them that reason is expected to overcome. As F. LeRon Shults has rightly argued, the traditional claim that the intellect must rule over the other parts of the soul is suspect of concealing conceptual muddle at the point where continuity and discontinuity among the parts/faculties of the soul needs to be explained.[78] Put in our terms, inasmuch as continuity is stressed, arguments for the absolute superiority of the intellect are undermined; insofar as discontinuity is highlighted, it is the basis for dominion, which becomes ultimately unclear. What is eventually lacking in a hierarchical scheme of the faculties is mediation; the divide between the intellect and the lower faculties calls for an intermediary that these traditional theologies are unable to provide.

And here we have the next dichotomy, apart from the one between reason and emotionality. As has become clear from the foregoing discussion of the theological significance of emotionality, the concept of passion itself bifurcates between passion proper—understood as change for the worse, weakness, defect, emotional disturbance, and suffering (including emotions such as fear, anger, sadness, pain, etc.)—and the positive idea of passion or sentiment, which comprises emotions with a good object that are all rooted in love (joy, delight, merriment, hope, compassion, etc.). Such bifurcation becomes the basis for the idea of Christian *apatheia*, a state undisturbed by negative passion, but dominated by "passions" connected to love. We have also seen that the ideal of Christian love-governed *apatheia* eventually dissolves in discourses on love as a natural outcome of the fact that, in Western theology, the body is viewed as an ally in the exercise of virtue and the attainment of virtuous life and so the passions are seen as being part of this process. The tacit distinction between passion and sentiment inherently determines discussions of the passions and governs theological discourse

---

78. Shults, *Reforming Theological Anthropology*, 170–71.

on love. However, since this distinction is assumed rather than explicitly stated, it remains in the background and remains largely unarticulated.

The dichotomy of good and bad passions, or (bad) passion and (good) sentiment, is then cut across by another, more fundamental dichotomy between earthly, sensual, bodily passion, on the one hand, and, spiritual-intellectual sentiment, on the other, corresponding to the theoretical divide between intellect and sensibility. Both sensual and intellectual passion can be good or bad according to the respective objects they are directed to. It seems as if the rupture between reason and sensibility were internalized within sensibility itself, giving rise to an inner dissociation between two kinds of affectivity: one attached to the body and the senses, another connected to the immaterial intellect. Or shall we rather view it as a curious doubling of the notion of affectivity at the expense of any unitary vision: the first one being affectivity in the proper sense, the second denoting something like affectivity in the intellectual mode, affectivity in an analogous sense? If this is so, where lies the difference between the two? The reflections of the foregoing chapters have revealed ample evidence to the effect that it is the body that makes all the difference. More specifically, in the theological/philosophical tradition, emotions, in the proper sense, are held to be bodily and cannot be conceived without the body, whereas intellectual emotions are viewed as acts of the will, belonging to the intellectual part of the soul, and are therefore thought to be independent of materiality and bodiliness. Intellectual affectivity is assumed to be similar to God's divine spiritual love, differing only in the fact of its being created, in contradistinction to God's love, which is uncreated. Love as a bodily passion and love as the intellectual passion of the will, namely, charity, are treated in separate discourses by Aquinas, for instance, and the two are never brought to a real synthesis.[79] So much so that Peter King, a modern commentator on Aquinas's account of the passions, has remarkably noted that there is in Aquinas's theological thought a largely unexplored domain of what he terms "pseudopassion" (that is, "passions pertaining to the purely intellective part of the soul" and analogous to real passions), which would merit systematic investigation in its own right.[80] We

79. For example, in the most didactically ordered discussion of the *Summa Theologica*, we find a separate treatment of love as a passion (IaIIae.26-28) and of supernaturally infused intellectual love named charity, considered as a theological virtue (IIaIIae.23-27). God's love is treated also in a separate part that contrasts the passion of love and intellectual love, stating that love in God is not a passion, but is according to the will (Ia.20).

80. Peter King, who restricts his own account to real passions in Aquinas's moral philosophy, writes: "Aquinas holds that there are analogues to the passions pertaining to the purely intellective part of the soul—call them pseudopassions. These pseudopassions, unlike the passions, do not involve any somatic reactions or indeed any material

also found Simo Knuuttila registering a sharp divide in the emotion theories of Augustine and Aquinas, for example, between psychosomatic emotions and intellectual volitions (that is, intellectual emotions).[81] And, clearly, it is not only these two theologians who can be taken to task for such a theoretical separation. As Knuuttila points out, the separation of psychosomatic emotions from the naturally elicited or supernaturally influenced acts of the intellectual soul is practically present in the entire Western philosophical tradition and evolves in the direction of a growing acknowledgment of the structural similarities between emotions proper and intellectual volitions in medieval accounts. One can detect a growing sense of the similarity of these domains, namely, that the notion of love, fear, and similar emotions can be applied to both spheres. Late medieval theories even tend to regard affective experiences as one unified class of mental phenomena (consisting of bodily, intellectual, and mystical passions), which are then allotted to the various psychic powers. Notwithstanding the recognition of a pivotal link between various kinds of affectivities, the rupture is never overcome completely, the gap between animal sensuality and spiritual feeling remains as a constant reminder of the necessity of mediation. How could such mediation between intellect and sensuality be conceived? There is a symbolic (and, as we shall see, centrally biblical) organ the importance of which seems to have been almost entirely lost from view in the course of centuries of principally intellect-centered speculation. What we would need, then, may be the retrieval of the long-forgotten ministry of the heart.

At first sight the urgent necessity of retrieving an integral vision of the heart for modern theological discussion might not be obvious. One may immediately think of the vast amount of religious literature dedicated to the spiritual analysis of the devoted heart of the Christian or the mysteries of the sacred heart of Jesus. Starting with Pascal's famous aphorisms to the effect that the real seat of human knowledge resides not in reason but in the heart, has the heart not figured indeed very centrally during the past couple of centuries, viewed as an indispensable complement and corrective to cold scientific reason? Has the role of emotionality for authentic Christian faith—symbolized by the heart—not been emphasized enough

---

basis at all. They are located in the intellective appetite as rational acts of will. Angels and disembodied human souls experience only these pseudopassions; animals experience only passions; living human beings alone are capable of both. The *amor intellectualis Dei* is a pseudopassion, one that may be deeply held. Likewise, the dispassionate drive to destroy something evil, the reflective judgment that something—for example, smallpox—should be eradicated, is a pseudopassion." Peter King, "Aquinas on the Passions," in MacDonald and Stump, *Aquinas's Moral Theory*, 105, note 7.

81. Knuuttila, *Emotions*, 257–86.

since the birth of the Romantic movement and the rediscovery of human sensibility? Has not the job of correcting a one-sided focus on reason been adequately tackled in recent years by putting an equally strong stress on the hitherto neglected emotional aspect? And one can also think of the findings of recent emotion-research, which has convincingly demonstrated the ultimate interconnectedness of reason and the emotions and has likewise clarified the vital role emotions play in human intellectual processes. Is there still any need to make a persuasive case for the importance of the heart?

Notwithstanding the considerable attention the symbol of the heart may have received so far, it has still not been given the status it rightly deserves. This is at least the conviction of theologians who seek to retrieve an integral vision of the biblical heart for theology. From such a perspective it is not enough to appeal to the heart in an effort to complement a one-sided intellectual vision; what comes to the fore is the necessity to reconfigure lock, stock, and barrel the traditional conception of the seat of the distinctively human as located in the intellect by re-considering the biblical notion of the heart as the centre of every human life activity: including reason, emotion, and the will. Understood in holistic terms as the innermost core of the entire human person, the heart is regrettably marginalized in traditional theological discourse. As Georg Langemeyer has remarked, the notion of the heart does not figure with much weight in official church teaching and this fact may be partly due to the scholastic neglect of the—for the scholastic compartmentalizing and analytic mindset—conceptually too vague and unarticulated notion of the biblical heart.[82] Langemeyer goes so far as to reckon that the notion of the biblical heart defies any attempts at clear-cut definition, being outright "indefinable," since every definition involves the conceptual work of separation and distinction, whereas the notion of the heart—being essentially holistic—escapes all such efforts. In my view, Langemeyer regrettably slips into the very error he deplores when he eventually concludes that discourse on the heart can only serve at the margins of theological anthropology as a critical reminder of the ultimate impossibility of accounting for the fullness of reality through neatly organized conceptual systems. One gets the impression that Langemeyer's "heart" eventually remains captive to the old opposition between Enlightenment reason and Romantic sentimentality, not being able to fulfill the holistic function otherwise rightly assigned to it.

Commenting on the status of the heart in the theological tradition, Placide Deseille likewise argues that, after the essentially biblically-inspired thought of the patristic period and the subsequent scholastic

---

82. Georg Langemeyer, "Herz," in Beinert, *Lexikon der katholische Dogmatik*, 255–56.

impoverishment and neglect of the notion, the modern revival did not bring the retrieval of the early holistic vision. Instead, the heart was transformed into the centre of religious affections, hopelessly and tenaciously opposed to the rationality of faith.[83] And we may add that theologies of the heart simply complement rational theologies, without, however, overcoming the rupture between the two. Deseille pinpoints the absence of the biblical notion of the heart from Thomas Aquinas's theology, or at least from the conceptual theoretical level of discourse. What comes to the fore from Deseille's account is a two-way tendency in Thomas: on the one hand, the rich biblical notion is reduced to a metaphorical equivalent of the will, while, on the other, realities associated with the biblical notion are not overlooked, but are treated in various contexts and under different names in passages concerning the workings of the intellect or the will. The heart in this manner partly shrinks and partly disappears from view, giving way to a different taxonomy whereby its functions are distributed among the various faculties of the soul. Thomas's intellectualist climate, where the final beatitude is conceived as ultimate contemplation in intellectual terms, seems to leave little space for an all-encompassing heart in the earthly life of the Christian or in the eternal bliss of the resurrection.

In a similar vein, Andrew Louth argues that a renewed concept of the heart is indispensable for a wholesome understanding of spirituality, which can no longer identify itself in opposition to dogmatic theology or at best as its affective complement, but which must, in a truly patristic manner, appear as one of the integral dimensions inextricably bound up with the import of speculative thought.[84] Interestingly, Louth's account of the history and the current state of spiritual theology is, for the most part, nothing more than investigation into the reality of the heart, which he holds to be a key concept, capable of reconfiguring a narrow and one-sided modern understanding of the task and the scope of spiritual theology. In fact, starting from the twofold sense of the term "spiritual"—one being a reference to the Holy Spirit, the fount of our relation to God, the other being the human spirit in the sense of soul, interiority, the site of our openness to the divine, in one word, the heart—Louth looks for a corrective to an impoverished notion of the heart. On his account, such an impoverished understanding can be detected already as early as the twelfth century when the biblical notion was increasingly interpreted in emotional terms as the exclusive seat of human affectivity, which was then sharply opposed to reason. At the same

---

83. Placide Deseille et al., "Ame-Coeur-Corps," in Lacoste, *Dictionnaire Critique de Théologie*, 28–31.

84. Andrew Louth, "Spirituelle (Théologie)," ibid., 1116–18.

time, love was set against intellectual knowledge, and true knowledge was argued to consist in the knowledge love alone can give. Facing the lamentable consequences of these developments, Louth thinks that the two fundamental senses of spiritual theology indicate two interconnected, yet markedly different, paths leading towards the renewal of this field. The first sense, which is related to the activity of the Holy Spirit, is essentially biblical and trinitarian, while the second, based on the experience of interiority and the encounter with the divine, is more philosophical in character, showing affinities with Platonic thought. A renewed understanding of the biblical concept of the heart could offer a common ground where these traditionally different paths may eventually meet and a new synthesis may be formed. In what way can the concept of the heart bring together biblical and philosophical thought? Louth's solution to this problem seems to be to draw on the insight that the biblical reality of human interiority and the traditional philosophical concept of the soul epitomized by the *noūs* ultimately converge in the notion of the heart and so discourse on the heart might take over the function philosophically attributed to the *noūs*, evading at the same time the intellectualist drift of the tradition.

Finally, Jean-Yves Lacoste, who reflects on the status of the biblical vision of man (rendered by the biblical terms "soul," "heart," and "body") in current philosophical/theological investigation, highlights the body as a key concept that seems to regulate contemporary anthropological discourse.[85] Lacoste's survey of modern anthropologies gives the impression that the issue of the heart is currently subordinated to the more general question of the body regarded as the originating matrix of affection, knowledge, and desire. Do anthropologies of the body replace without remainder a biblically-based anthropology of the heart? What might be the exact function of the symbolic heart in a modern anthropology of the body? These are questions we need to keep in view as we proceed to the next part of our inquiry.

The "heart" of Scripture is far from being the simple seat of emotionality. Simple as it sounds, this is one of the major recognitions of modern biblical anthropology, which not so long ago had to face the stark fact that our understanding of the heart has been obscured for far too long by an Enlightenment- and Romanticism-conditioned preference for seeing in it an exclusive symbol of feeling and sentiment, over against the ruthless rationality of reason. Or, as Louth has suggested, this development might even be earlier, going back to the spiritual movements of the twelfth century when feeling started to be opposed to the intellectualism of dogmatic theology and a one-sided interpretation of the biblical heart was used as an antidote to

---

85. Deseille, "AmeCoeurCorps," 31–33.

the dire heartlessness of intellectualist doctrine. Read through such modern spectacles, biblical discourse on the heart gives the impression that the biblical person is primarily emotional in temper, even at the expense of rational consideration. As the classical account of Hans Walter Wolff knowledgeably demonstrates, the Hebrew terms for the heart (*lēb, lēbāb*) occur 858 times in the Old Testament and, apart from the statistically unparalleled rate of occurrences in comparison with other terms describing the human being, the notion also figures centrally as a key metaphor of biblical thought, so much so that it must even be regarded as "the most important word in the vocabulary of Old Testament anthropology."[86] Wolff's thoughtful study is a forceful plea for the reconsideration of narrowed-down modern conceptions of the biblical heart, which, he argues, originally encompasses a whole range of mental activities essentially linked to our humanity as reasonable beings. That is why he gives the chapter focusing on the term "heart" the telling title "Reasonable Man," which counters the one-sided emphasis on emotionality resulting from the modern rendering of the term by the only partially corresponding "heart." What is needed is a thorough semantic re-examination of the biblical notion and the conscious adjustment of our analytic mindset to the synthetic way of thinking characteristic of Scripture texts.

From a careful analysis that encompasses the entire gamut of Old Testament occurrences of this central notion, Wolff concludes that the wide range of shades of meaning crystallizes in an extremely rich symbol that "includes everything that we ascribe to the heart and the brain—power of perception, reason, understanding, insight, consciousness, memory, knowledge, reflection, judgment, sense of direction, discernment."[87] While affectivity is certainly part and parcel of the reality that the heart signifies, it is by no means its dominant aspect, because *lēb* first of all denotes "the centre of the consciously living man," who is called to reason in the presence of God. The basic shades of meaning that Wolff insightfully distinguishes are: 1. heart as a physical organ, 2. the seat of the emotions and irrational moods, 3. the symbolic organ of desire and longing, 4. the equivalent of the modern mind in the comprehensive sense of cultural, scientific, aesthetic rationality, and all kinds of intellectual functions, such as reasoning, reflecting, considering, understanding, and remembering, 5. the seat of the will and decision-making and the site of human planning. All these meanings converge without real separation in the one complex metaphor of the biblical heart.

---

86. Wolff, *Anthropology of the Old Testament*, 40.
87. Ibid., 51.

Since biblical anthropology is obviously theological in orientation, it is the theological significance of the heart that provides the key for a proper understanding of its utmost importance. As several commentators in Wolff's wake have noted, the heart is primarily the unified centre of the human being, the place of encounter with one's own interiority, the site where one faces one's feelings, conscience, reason, and decisions, and as such, the symbolic site of encounter with God.[88] The heart is the point where one can open up or close off from a relationship with God; the heart houses the fundamental decision of the religious person. It denotes the entire person viewed from the perspective of her basic stance towards the Creator. The heart is the *par excellence* dimension of relationality with regard to fellow-humans and God. And, most importantly, it is the heart that prays to God, representing therefore the deepest core of the human person.[89] The idea of profundity seems to be vital for a proper understanding of the mystery of the heart: the heart epitomizes the essence of our humanity in the perspective of the deep mystery of God. It is a focal point oriented towards the transcendent and situated at the crossroads of the horizontal and the vertical. However, according to biblical authors, the human heart is unable to understand its own secret. As Wolff astutely contends: "without knowledge of the heart of God, man's real situation is incomprehensible."[90]

It is noteworthy that the Old Testament not only speaks about the heart of man, but also tells us about the reality of God's heart.[91] Just as the human heart is first and foremost the seat of conscious life, in the same manner God's heart is the site of his consideration, memory, will, decisions, pleasure, and desire, and most importantly, the site of God's relation to man. It is in God's heart that his distinct will and plans for humanity are conceived. Such decisions are always conjoined with love, kindness, and mercy towards man; however, they also judge human evil deeds with just anger. The secret of God's heart is best revealed in his everlasting love and mercy that overcomes the anger over man's infidelity. God's heart is portrayed, first of all, as noticing, thinking, and planning, and less frequently as feeling; it is his determined merciful inclination towards man and the constancy of his determination that are most strongly emphasized by biblical authors. All in all, man's heart seems to be mysteriously attuned to understand—even if never in an exhaustive manner—God's tender heart.

88. See André Wénin et al., "Ame-Coeur-Corps," in Lacoste, *Dictionnaire Critique de Théologie*, 24–25.
89. See Andrew Louth, "Spirituelle (Théologie)," in ibid., 116.
90. Wolff, *Anthropology of the Old Testament*, 58.
91. Wolff notes that the term "heart" is used twenty-six times in connection with God in the Old Testament. Ibid., 40.

What, then, in a nutshell, is the theological significance of the biblical heart? In my view, its real significance can best be captured by the idea of mediation. The biblical heart is at once the concrete vital physical organ and the place of the spiritual. These two aspects are held in a tensile interplay, they are inextricably interconnected in the abstract concreteness of the metaphor. The heart, as the innermost centre of the human self, is the sensory organ of harmony and disharmony within the human person and the person's relation to God. As a symbolic sensory organ, it both senses and reconciles conflicting inclinations within the self and makes it capable of turning towards God. The heart senses both horizontally and vertically: it mediates between immanence and transcendence. As the fragile intermediary of the earthly and the heavenly, it marks out a site of human encounter with God.

Mediation, as we saw, is a key concept in Ricoeur's philosophical anthropology, which addresses the issue of the fragility of human existence stemming from an irreconcilable tension between finitude and infinity as lying at the core of the human disposition. The ultimate non-congruence of the finite and the infinite within man upholds an ineradicable polarity, an essential duality at every level of the human set-up: rationality and affectivity alike. What rescues such a lasting duality from tragic inertia is the presence of mediation in each level where a rift can be detected. Duality in this manner does not paralyze the self, but incites active mediation and a relentless effort to bring about synthesis, even if a lasting and final synthesis is recognized to be impossible. The mediating and synthesizing function *par excellence* is epitomized by the Ricoeurian heart, which, as an archetypal expression of a mixture of reason and desire and a restless site of endless pursuit, becomes the eminent locus where the sensual vitality of *bios* and the spiritual intellectuality of *logos* merge in endless transition.

The ontological significance of the heart is seen in the embodiment and the overcoming of the fundamental difference between vital affectivity and spiritual affectivity, that is, between the principle of finite pleasure and the principle of infinite happiness. The key Ricoeurian concept of the heart discloses the ultimate continuity between the vital and the spiritual. In the unstable balance established within the heart, vital pleasure reveals a dimension of infinity, while spiritual pleasure is conditioned by finitude. The sensible reverberates in the spiritual and the spiritual resounds in the sensible. This is what may be called the ontological destination of desire: there is nothing in man that would seamlessly correspond to purely vital animality; human bodily pleasure and emotionality is orientated towards the infinitude of happiness and is already an anticipation and a foretaste of the infinity it craves for. On the other hand, spiritual happiness is pleasure in the most fundamental sense; it is the lasting enjoyment of what vital pleasure already clearly foreshadows. The passions in this context are no mere modes of passivity in the vital realm. They are complex human projects interiorized in the transition zone of the heart and connected to a pursuit of infinite happiness. Their passivity lies in the fact that they require firm commitment, a complete dedication to their essential attractive force: the totality of ultimate happiness. The Ricoeurian exegesis of the heart pinpoints the site of the traditionally missing zone of the intermediary where vitality is transformed into spirituality. Although it is defined as the primary place of feeling, Ricoeur's heart is not purely emotional, as he explains: "I accord no primacy to affectivity over knowledge and the function of objectification. For philosophical anthropology, knowledge and feeling (objectification and interiorization) are contemporary; they are born together and grow together. Man conquers the 'depth' of feeling as the counterpart of the rigor of knowledge."[92] The Ricoeurian heart is the transition zone that connects our bodiliness and intellectuality both as emotion and as thought; it is the missing link "midway between the life of the body and the life of the spirit," not in opposition to, but in conjunction with, reason. Ricoeur's philosophical recuperation of the heart gives ample food for a renewed theological understanding of the twofold nature of human affectivity (vital and spiritual) that traditionally has been keen-sightedly detected and yet insufficiently explored or inadequately conceptualized. This fact, as we shall see, has had serious consequences for theological concepts of love.

---

92. Paul Ricoeur, "The Antinomy of Human Reality and the Problem of Philosophical Anthropology," in Reagan and Stewart, *The Philosophy of Paul Ricoeur*, 32.

5

The Unity of Love

However, the act of charity is especially enjoyable and especially inclines one to remain in charity, and through it everything we do or suffer is rendered pleasing.

—Aquinas, *On Charity*, Art. 1.

In our analysis of the place of human emotionality in the theological anthropology of the image, the discourse on love has emerged as a special point of reference around which thought on both the bodily passions and the spiritual feelings crystallize. The issue of love governs Christian reflection on *apatheia* and gathers various aspects of image theology in one coherent whole, providing an organizing principle for seemingly disparate discourses, such as, creation, the state of original innocence, the fall, human morality, Christian discipleship, redemption, and divine immutability. While love appears as a kind of universal that is present in and yet transcends all the fields of theological reflection, as a strange category of its own that cannot be subsumed under any larger name, love is at the same time strangely ripped by several antinomies, to the point that its essential unity becomes doubtful or is at least obscured. For, ultimately, it is very hard to tell where precisely we are to locate the unity of the disparate forms of love that have been traditionally distinguished: human and divine, self-love and love of neighbor, friendship and filial affection, bodily *erōs* and spiritual *agapē*, the love of food and the love of persons, the love of ideals and the love of one's enemy, romantic love and disinterested philanthropy, the passionate love of life and self-sacrificing generosity, the completely selfless willing of one's good and desperate egotic self-attachment. Why give the same name to such disparate acts and experiences? Would it not be more appropriate to dispense with a general idea of love altogether, keeping to the one, Christian idea of divinely inspired selfless *agapē*, and thereby eluding the difficulties such a generalized idea ineluctably creates? But is there a truly and specifically Christian idea of love that can be meaningfully contrasted with the rest of worldly loves? What needs to be emphasized most in a Christian context: continuity or discontinuity with what is "naturally" human? In what way does the Christian message bring the transformation of a general understanding of love?

These are questions that seem to be vexing contemporary philosophers and theologians alike. After a long period of meticulous distinction and theoretical separation, the burning issue of the ultimate unity of love has come to the fore again. There is a growing conviction among theorists of love that what is needed is a new unified vision that is capable of pinpointing the one distinguishing common feature of what appears, at first sight, to be strikingly different forms of love. One no longer takes for granted an essential division between two basic forms of love—one as a passion and another as an act of will—as in the case of a dictionary entry on love in 1906 (obviously revealing a Neothomist stance). The author of this entry finds no problem in maintaining that one can consider love under two separate aspects: either as a passion, that is, a movement of the sensitive appetite, or as an act of the will that seeks or attaches to the good.[1] From this distinction, then, follows another basic dichotomy for the author between "superior love" and "inferior love," that is, love governed by the rational will, and love that is purely sensible and is therefore a blind passion, the dominance of which over one's intellect must be avoided at all costs. Superior love must always obey the rational will and should never fall prey to purely sensible passion. Interestingly, this latter distinction (between superior and inferior love) does not seem to overlap completely with the former distinction between love as a movement of the sensitive appetite and love as an act of the will since the author of the article makes a laconic remark (which, however, he does not elaborate in more detail) to the effect that several laws applicable in the case

---

1. "Amour," in Blanc, *Dictionnaire de Philosophie Ancienne*, 56–57.

of sensible love are also the same laws operating in superior love, establishing in this manner a certain legitimate continuity between sensible and rational love.² As a philosopher, he ends on the note that—although one can list several philosophers who in the course of history had attempted to give a persuasive account of the nature of love—it is ultimately "Christian theology" alone that is capable of defining and explaining love "without error."

A Philosophical Plea for the Unity of Love

But is Christian theology really able to do the difficult job of "explaining" and "defining" what love truly is? Jean-Luc Marion has recently challenged an over-confident theological understanding of love that, by skipping the human phenomenon, starts immediately from above, from a direct understanding of God's divine kenotic sacrificial love: "Theology knows what love is all about; but it knows it too well ever to avoid imposing upon me an interpretation that comes so directly through the Passion that it annuls my passions—without taking the time to render justice to their phenomenality, or to give a meaning to their immanence."³ Marion, however, does not only take theology to task for a one-sided interpretation of the richness of love. He finds, first and foremost, philosophy itself guilty of the current reticence about love and in the relegation of the discourse on love to the margins of philosophical inquiry. The corrective he claims to offer to such a regrettable neglect is threefold. First, he proposes a univocal understanding of love that dispenses with any traditional dichotomies where "love and charity (ἔρως and ἀγάπη), supposedly possessive desire and supposedly gratuitous benevolence, rational love (of the moral law) and irrational passion" are distinguished, set in opposition or are thought to be irreconcilable.⁴ What Marion considers to be a "serious concept of love" is one powerful enough to keep all the disparate aspects of the one undivided phenomenon of love in a convincing unity since—as he argues—the "single garment of love" is seamless and essentially indivisible. The second philosophical corrective would be the acknowledgment of the alternative or "greater" rationality (compared to ordinary rationality) of phenomena occurring under the regime of love, that is, a narrative that does not see these phenomena as irrational, but seeks to understand their different and yet fully comprehensible

---

2. "Plusieurs lois de l'amour sensible, dont nous parlons d'abord, sont aussi les lois de l'amour supérieur." See ibid., 56.

3. Marion, *The Erotic Phenomenon*, 1. The French original appeared as *Le Phénomène érotique* (2003).

4. Ibid., 5.

"*erotic* rationality." The third corrective is closely related to the second and is characteristic of Marion's overall philosophical quest. What he looks for is a concept of "love without being" which is free from traditional metaphysical assumptions and the foreign horizon of beings and essentiality. Love has its own horizon (one without being) and the phenomena arising from love can only be made sense of by keeping to their own distinctive significance, independent of the metaphysical insistence on the primacy of being over loving. Marion goes so far as to suggest that love (understood univocally as erotic) is a determining feature of our humanity, so much so that one cannot imagine a human state without the "tonality of an erotic disposition": "we can never, without lying to ourselves, claim to arrive at a fundamental erotic neutrality."[5] Moreover, the fact that man loves—and not the traditionally accepted argument that he alone is capable of thinking—is the distinguishing feature that sets him apart from the animal world and the rest of creation.

Interestingly, Marion can only maintain the unity of the concept of love by amputating significations that in his view do not concern a truly univocal idea of love. His insistence that, within the one-way logic of erotic love, there is no place for multiple distinctions or analytic differentiation—since one who thinks in terms of divisions misses the point entirely and dissolves the one unitary concept into irredeemable equivocity—leads him into a significant narrowing down of the scope of what he recognizes as worthy of the name love. Challenging traditionally alleged dichotomies, his aim is to show their invalidity or unfounded character, safeguarding in this manner the integrity of the single indivisible concept of love. Love of objects—such as money, drugs, sex, or power—does not qualify in his scheme as real love; such a covetous craving is nothing but "desire for possessable worldly objects" and so it does not deserve the name love. The love of friendship, in the sense of a relation of equality on the basis of a reciprocal exchange of a worldly third party, that is, a common interest (for example, pleasure, utility, or virtue), must also be excluded from a seriously unitary concept of love as something irrelevant and not worthy of the name. It is only friendship characterized by the unequal relationship of self-giving without demand for reciprocity—where one cherishes a friend by the firm commitment of an oath—that belongs to a wholesome concept of love. As to the difference between *erōs* and *agapē*, Marion holds that they are ultimately one: *erōs* in the last resort is selfless, and *agapē* is in the end possessive and consuming; they are not two distinct realities, just two names to express the same phenomenon of (erotic) love. Instead of trying to stretch the concept in order to make room for exceptions and disparate senses, one must simply

---

5. Ibid., 7.

ignore them as phenomena foreign to the nature of love in the proper sense. This is so because, "[t]he difficulty does not consist in introducing exceptions to the erotic reduction and equivocations into univocal love, but in measuring just how far love's one way extends," Marion concludes.[6] One is left to wonder, however, whether such a swings-and-roundabouts approach, where the gain of a univocal concept is obtained at the price of giving up the comprehensive scope of traditional approaches, does not generate a new, even more hopeless dichotomy, one between a new, more or less seamlessly univocal concept and the rest of unclassifiable "loves" discarded as useless waste. What shall we make of a slimmed-down notion of friendship that excludes the reciprocal enjoyment of a common pursuit? Shall we see the notion of loving impersonal things—such as Isaac's loving of tasty wild game (Gen 27:4–7)—as hopelessly equivocal with regard to "real" erotic love? By restricting the circle where love proper is thought to legitimately operate, we also create a vast no man's land of phenomena of uncertain identity or status. Is it not the case that a neatly unified concept of love can only be attained by abandoning what traditionally has been regarded as integral to it?

On the one hand, Marion's ambitious project is admirably promising for a renewed self-understanding of our erotically conditioned humanity and the consequences it has for a renewed interpretation of the human being as the image of the Triune God who loves archetypally and eternally. On the other hand, one may wonder whether his pretensions to break the alleged philosophical silence concerning love are not misplaced, given the impressive amount of already existing philosophical attempts to conceptualize love if one considers only writers of the twentieth century and up to the present.[7] One cannot take previous authors to task for the compartmentalization of love into separate domains either, since most of them aim at showing the essential interconnectedness of various forms of love and the strong link between reason and the heart. What does distinguish Marion's attempt from many other explorations of the nature of love is his strong insistence on the primacy and paradigmatic character of bodily erotic love, which he sees as informing every aspect of the one undivided and, in this sense, univocal love: the love between man and woman, the love between

---

6. Ibid., 221.

7. Just to mention a few of the classic accounts: Rousselot, *The Problem of Love in the Middle Ages* (1908, trans. 2001); Nygren, *Agape and Eros* (1930–36, trans. 1953); Rougemont, *Love in the Western World* (1939, trans. 1983); D'Arcy, *The Mind and Heart of Love* (1954); Lewis, *The Four Loves* (1960); Pieper, *Faith, Hope, Love* (1972, trans. 1997); O'Donovan, *The Problem of Self-Love in St. Augustine* (1980); Brümmer, *The Model of Love* (1993). Some current accounts of love include: Brady, *Christian Love* (2003); Lindberg, *Love: A Brief History through Western Christianity* (2008); Jeanrond, *A Theology of Love* (2010).

friends and family members, the love between the human being and God. We shall subject the details of this novel approach to a closer scrutiny at a later stage of our investigation. What interests us here is the remarkable fact of a recent forceful plea for a unifying vision of love.

A Theological Re-Unification of Eros and Agape

In his first encyclical letter *Deus Caritas Est* (2006), Pope Benedict XVI likewise keeps the essential unity of love in view. The very fact that he chooses love as the first issue to be discussed at the beginning of his pontificate is not without importance for the present climate, where love is, on the one hand, dismissed as a sentimental attitude of the weak and, on the other, is exalted as a quasi-divine force capable of conferring auto-salvation in the midst of disillusioning rational apathy. In an effort to redirect Christian believers' attention to fundamental truths of the specific evangelical ideal of love and, in this manner, to lay the doctrinal foundations for a contemporary Christian practice of charitable action (which is the primary aim of the encyclical), the pope focuses specifically on "The Unity of Love in Creation and in Salvation History" in the first, theoretical part of the discussion. The unity of love envisaged in the encyclical partly resembles Marion's conception of erotic love as the common factor in all human types of love and is partly a markedly different attempt at the reintegration of erotic love into a world of purely Christian *agapē*. At the beginning of his reflection, Benedict XVI poses the question of whether one should see apparently different forms of love (such as love of country, love of one's profession, filial love between family members, love between man and woman, friendship, love of neighbor, and love of God) as manifestations of the same single reality or whether one should regard the word love as equivocally signifying ultimately disparate realities. His answer seems to come very close to Marion's suggestion that the one real epitome of love is the erotically-based loving bond between man and woman, "where body and soul are inseparably joined and human beings glimpse an apparently irresistible promise of happiness."[8] However, the pope's conception of the unity of love takes a distinctly different path than Marion's monism, in arguing for unity that encompasses essential and wholesome duality between body and soul, worldly *erōs* and faith-shaped *agapē*, possessive love and oblative love, ascending love and descending love, God's love for us and our love for God. Unity here is seen as underlying ineffaceable duality, and although love is set before us as "fundamentally a single reality," the old distinctions are kept as useful reminders of the differ-

---

8. Benedict XVI, *Deus Caritas Est*, note 2.

ent dimensions of the one single and indivisible love. *Erōs* is characterized as a common human experience, a natural worldly craving tinted by a desire for possession and yet tending ecstatically to a union with the other and the divine. Such a love has an original grandeur that only shines through if it is disciplined and purified; *erōs* "calls for a path of ascent, renunciation, purification and healing." *Agapē* is love informed and shaped by faith and as such contrasts at certain points with the basic instinct of natural human love; it is participation in the descending divine love and is the disinterested service of the good of all fellow humans without discrimination and reward. This traditional distinction is then overcome in the pope's claim that *erōs* and *agapē* are essentially interdependent since neither can exist purely on its own: true *erōs*, far from being merely egotistic, has a natural element of selflessness, a tendency to seek the happiness of the other through the attainment of its own happiness, while true *agapē* is always conscious of its gift-character and would surely turn into its own caricature if it pretended to self-sufficiently lack nothing and have no need to receive love in return. *Erōs* and *agapē* are so interrelated that the one indivisible love can only be realized in both at once, becoming lopsided if one pole suffers damage: "[t]he more the two, in their different aspects, find a proper unity in the one reality of love, the more the true nature of love in general is realized."[9] They are therefore inseparable and must be seen as mutually complementing one another, in no way being sufficient on their own.

Clearly, the reintegration of *erōs* into a Christian vision of love is not a self-evident gesture in a long tradition of reservation and suspicion towards the unruly power of erotic, worldly, and bodily love. Benedict XVI reminds us of the reasons why sober, selfless, and reliable *agapē* had to be set against the intoxicating force of divinized *erōs* and an ancient pagan understanding of the false ecstasy of ultimately dehumanizing love. And, although *erōs*, as such, was never expelled from a Christian understanding of charity, references to it were made sparingly and with caution, the emphasis being put on specifically faith-inspired *agapaic* benevolence. Such caution received much criticism from the side of philosophers influenced by the spirit of the Enlightenment, and Christianity was accused of poisoning and destroying *erōs* through a wholesale neglect and false charges against what is truly human and is a precious gift of nature. While rebutting the unjust exaggeration of the Enlightenment accusation, the pope nonetheless admits of the need for a renewed understanding of erotic love and the restoration of the "true grandeur" of *erōs*, which, "disciplined" and "purified," must form an integral part of Christian conceptions of what human and divine love truly is.

9. Ibid., note 7.

What exactly constitutes the unity of love as it appears in creation and salvation history? First of all (and quite contrary to a long tradition of interpretations), such unity here is approached from the side of *erōs*, which is already present at creation, in the image of the first man, Adam, who—having realized his solitude—rejoices over the fact of receiving a woman "helper" to whom he is attracted by the natural fascination of love. The Genesis story conveys the recognition that man is incomplete without entering into a loving communion with a companion who complements him and with whom a reciprocal love-exchange can be realized in a life-long economy of a ceaselessly given and received gift of life. The image of man is contrasted with a new image of God, who—according to the witness of Old Testament prophets—loves the human being, and especially his chosen people, with erotically passionate love in the manner of a bridegroom who faithfully never abandons his beloved spouse. Such a passionately committed love receives unexpected completion in the image of Christ, the second Adam, whose greatest sign of love, his body given up for all in the Eucharist, becomes a supreme means of "erotic" union with the Triune God; a kind of "sacramental mysticism" where erotic and agapaic love merge in an indissoluble manner and where God's descending love conjoins human, ascending desire in the tangible flesh of the incarnate *Logos*, who appears for us as nourishing Love. What comes to the fore from this concise narrative of creation and salvation history is the remarkable fact that the encyclical places the ultimate reason for the unity of love in God's divine love, which is seen as being both erotic and agapaic: "God loves, and his love may certainly be called *erōs*, yet it is also totally *agapē*."[10] It is in God that the unity of love is established, whose "love-story" with us reveals both God's passionate *erōs* and divine, unfailing *agapē*.

If the unity of love is grounded in God's indivisible single love for us, what distinguishes the dimension of divine *erōs* from the dimension of divine *agapē*? Is there a difference between these two aspects within God's unified, archetypal love? The encyclical does not reflect directly on this question. However, what is apparently implied is a difference between the passionate responsive and jealous love of a lover, one that imposes itself on him as a passion, and the gratuitous, forgiving, and noble love of someone who "loved us first." So is it passion that makes divine *erōs* differ from divine *agapē*? It seems so, and while one may hear in this context an echo of the old distinction between bodily passion and spiritual love, one is at the same time impressed by the noteworthy fact that love otherwise associated with bodily passion, that is, desire and passionate longing, is attributed here to

10. Ibid., note 9.

God without reservation or reluctance, drawing on a distinguished trend in the theological tradition that is palpable in Dionysios the Areopagite and appears even in Aquinas, even if it does not finally determine his theology of love.[11] Remarkably, the concept of love in the encyclical avoids an overly voluntaristic/rational interpretation by emphasizing also the feeling aspect of love, which is seen as engaging the whole of what we are: the intellect, the will, and the sentiments in an all-embracing act. The sentiments accompanying love are taken seriously and human feelings are not undervalued or scorned as superfluous elements that disturb the intellectual act of the will. There is no suggestion of an obligation to love one's neighbor through indifference to subjective emotions. Rather, the motive power of right human love is highlighted: "God does not demand of us a feeling which we ourselves are incapable of producing. He loves us, he makes us see and experience his love, and since he has 'loved us first,' love can blossom as a response within us. . . . Contact with the visible manifestations of God's love can awaken within us a feeling of joy born of the experience of being loved."[12] This is the experience lying at the root of human love that evokes both *erōs*—a passionate longing for the divine lover—and *agapē*—joyful and charitable action for the good of one's neighbors in the manner of the twofold ways of divine love. While the encyclical points to God as the ultimate source of the essential unity of love, it does not reflect on the basis of such unity or the assumed common element that is present in both divine *erōs* and in divine *agapē*. What makes

---

11. The encyclical refers to Dionysius the Areopagite's *The Divine Names*, 4.2-14: PG 3, 709-13. Dionysius here argues for the legitimacy of calling God equally "Yearning" (that is, *erōs*) and "Love" (*agapē*) because also Scripture employs this term for God's love: "Let us not therefore, shrink from this title of 'Yearning,' nor be perturbed and affrighted by aught that any man say about it. For methinks the Sacred Writers regard the titles 'Love' and 'Yearning' as of one meaning; but preferred, when speaking of Yearning in a heavenly sense, to qualify it with the word 'real' because of the inconvenient pre-notion of such men. For whereas the title of 'Real Yearning' is employed not merely by ourselves but even by the Scriptures, mankind (not grasping the unity intended when Yearning is ascribed to God) fell by their own propensity into, the notion of a partial, physical and divided quality, which is not true Yearning but a vain image of Real Yearning, or rather a lapse therefrom. . . . To those who listen aright to Holy Scripture, the word 'Love' is used by the Sacred Writers in Divine Revelation with the same meaning as the word 'Yearning.'" A footnote of the editor added to this paragraph gives the following explanation: "The word ἔρως is sometimes used concerning God to stimulate our minds by its unexpectedness and so to make us penetrate beyond the word to the mystery hinted at by it. On the other hand, ἀγάπη or ἔρως and ἀγάπησις is sometimes used concerning human relationships to prevent any degrading associations from entering in." Rolt, *Dionysius the Areopagite*, 104-5. Aquinas quotes Dionysius in his own account of love to the effect that "some holy men have held that love [*amor*] means something more Godlike than dilection [*dilectio*] does." *ST* IaIIae.26.3.

12. Benedict XVI, *Deus Caritas Est*, note 17.

them both manifestations of the one indivisible generic divine love? Or is there no generic love at all, but only intermediation across the two poles of desiring passion for the beloved and "intellectual" gratuitous *agapē*? And, eventually, what distinguishes divine *Logos* from divine *Erōs-Agapē*? How is it possible that "this universal principle of creation—the *Logos*, primordial reason—is at the same time a lover with all the passion of a true love" and that, consequently, "*Erōs* is thus supremely ennobled, yet at the same time it is so purified as to become one with *agapē*"?[13] These questions are elicited by the pope's reflection, but they remain unanswered within the context of the encyclical. We have to look elsewhere in order to find indications that can guide our inquiry.

Exegetical Arguments for the Unity of Love

On examining Scripture, and especially the Old Testament, one finds a rich implicit knowledge of the human experience of love. It is not only passages concerned directly with love that contain such intimate knowledge, but also oblique statements and indirect hints in various contexts which disclose a keen Old Testament awareness of this all-pervasive human experience. As István Jelenits notes, love in Scripture is portrayed as a multifarious reality appearing in various forms and according to different degrees that mutually illuminate one another and yet are non-interchangeable.[14] None of the senses associated with this rich concept is negligible and even the most profane employment of the term proves indispensable for a proper understanding of what love truly is. Besides interpersonal love, the Old Testament knows of the fundamental human experience of being fond of impersonal things, such as, for example, love of tasty food. With a striking realism, Isaac is reported to be fond of wild game when, on his deathbed, he asks his older son Esau: "Prepare me the kind of tasty food I like and bring it to me to eat, so that I may give you my blessing before I die" (Gen 27:4), and, put in a different manner in the same story: "Bring me some game and prepare me some tasty food to eat . . ." (Gen 27:7). This seemingly insignificant episode is not without importance for a proper understanding of the essential unity of love. In the simple everyday fact of Isaac's loving wild game one

---

13. Ibid., note 10.

14. See István Jelenits, "Jegyzetek a szeretetről" [Notes on Love], in Jelenits and Tomcsányi, *Tanulmányok a vallás és a lélektan határterületeiről* [Studies From the Margins of Religion and Psychology], 57–75. What emerges from Jelenits's account is an implicit plea for the re-integration of a sensible emotional element into a wholesome interpretation of biblical love.

can grasp a remarkable element of the nature of love: joy, pleasure, enjoyment as inseparable concomitants of the act of loving, which seem to be a general characteristics of every type of love, be it love between friends or family members, between man and woman, and the human being and God. Although the Old Testament speaks directly about love relatively rarely and with considerable emotional reserve, characteristic of a patriarchal society dominated by men, it is, however, consistent in portraying God as showing constant and profound love towards the people of Israel and in making one feel the elementary and moving power of human love. Love in the Old Testament is present with a potent invisible force, though it is often unnamed.

Such a diffuse concept of love, then, receives palpable expression in the person of Jesus Christ, whose gospel may be summed up in a nutshell as "God loves us." While Jesus announces the Father's all-encompassing and all-forgiving love, his entire ministry is the paradigm of such love, a supreme fulfillment not only of the Law but also of all previous intimations of the redeeming reality of love. Jelenits at this point draws our attention to the significant fact that while there is only indirect indication of the emotional depth of Jesus's love in the Synoptics and while, even in John's Gospel, Jesus speaks about his love for the disciples only towards the end of his ministry, on approaching his death (John 15:13), what one reads between the lines is evidence of the integrity of his love as it appears to our common understanding in the everyday sense of the word. That is to say, it includes an openness towards the other, sympathetic attention, real emotional involvement and joy over the one lost and found sheep. In one word, Jesus loves people in the same way we experience true love in our everyday life: with deep emotion, from his heart, and with reasonable deliberation. In a similar manner, the love Jesus asks from his followers does not primarily consist of selfless heroic deeds or purely volitional intellectual benevolence. Instead, it is love that is truly worthy of its name and is inseparable from affection and profound sentiment. Jelenits's interesting claim is that while all these aspects of Jesus's love are merely implied by the New Testament but never explicitly stated, the subsequent Christian tradition can be seen as the gradual unpacking of the emotional richness of such love in the light of the accumulating and deepening experience of natural human love in the course of the later centuries, and especially in mystical literature.[15] Therefore, Christian

---

15. Jelenits here refers to Jean Leclercq's study (*L'amour vu par les moines au XII siècle*), which from an examination of the love experience of Saint Bernard and Cistercian monks concludes that their concept of divine love was deepened by their experience of mature human love. These monks entered the order at a more mature age, some of them widowed, and most of them had firsthand experiences of the state of being in love. Jelenits, "Jegyzetek a szeretetről," ibid., 72.

love must be essentially conceived as wholesomely uniting an essential emotional element with intellectual insight and volitional determination: the Christian is able to love everyone because his or her heart has been enlarged by Jesus, just as the heart of the apostle Paul was enlarged, and so he was able to love those who were alien to him by birth. On this vision, love is not a heroic deliberation in an effort to overlook what is repulsive or evil; it is rather affectionate concern, even for the sinner or one's enemy, whose inner being is only known to God.

Ceslas Spicq, author of a monumental classic study of the semantic richness and theological significance of *agapē* in the New Testament, likewise stresses unity rather than discontinuity between human and divine love.[16] He takes issue with exegetical interpretations that argue for the completely unparalleled and unique character of *agapē* over against other types of love. While his detailed analytic study traces the wide gamut of shades of meaning associated with agapaic Christian love in the writings of the New Testament, pinpointing the distinctive features of such divinely inspired "love in the sense of charity," it nonetheless contests the opinion of those exegetes who would like to sever any ties with common Hellenistic ideas of various senses of love. Spicq famously lists the four classic terms that denote major senses of love in the Greek language.[17] The first, *storgē* (*stergō*), is instinctive attraction, an innate feeling towards one's parents, child, siblings, or even spouse and may also include sympathy for friends and compatriots. The second, *erōs* (*eraō*), does not occur in the New Testament. In the sense of covetousness, unreasoning passion, a strong appetite for sexual pleasure, which in Greek literature is said to bring endless suffering and disaster; it is not surprisingly absent from the specific New Testament conception of love. The third term, *philia* (*phileō*), denoting friendship, is an elaborate concept worked out by Greek philosophers, especially Aristotle. It implies affection, attachment and sympathy, a reciprocal bond between persons of the same standing. As Spicq notes, the reality expressed by *philia* at times comes very close to what is covered by *agapē*, without, however, being capable of expressing a love between God and humans or love for one's enemies, which is an essential element of *agapē*. The fourth type of love is *agapē* (*agapaō*). The etymology of the word is obscure, but Spicq opts for an interpretation that traces the root back to *aga*, meaning "very" and *age*, meaning "admiration,

---

16. See Spicq, *Agapè dans le Nouveau Testament*; and also Spicq, "ἀγάπη, agapē, love," in Spicq, *Theological Lexicon of the New Testament*, 8–22.

17. Spicq, "ἀγάπη, agapē, love," 9–14. A renowned and brilliant modern interpretation of the four senses of love is given by Lewis, *The Four Loves*. Lewis likewise argues for the essential continuity of these forms of love, all of which is present in each of the major forms.

astonishment." The first usages of the term are connected with the experience of the surprise of the host who receives a stranger. The verbal form *agapaō* has the ordinary meaning of "to be happy or satisfied," and so, as Spicq points out, the contentment implied by the meaning of this verb is in a sharp contrast with the distress accompanying the covetous desire of *erōs*. The love expressed by *agapē* is the most rational kind of love implying preference for someone, valuing or holding someone in high esteem. It involves admiration and respect for the other. It is not so much a hidden feeling as the outward demonstration of goodwill and charitable deeds. Unlike *philia*, *agapē* links persons of various standing and reaches across various social groups. In this sense, it is disinterested, generous, and reveals thoughtfulness and concern. It is because of the universality and complexity that *agapē* expresses that the term is applied to God's love towards the world. Human *agapē* is awakened by such a gratuitous and generous love and is expressed in gratitude, welcome, and acceptance with regard to God's prevenient love. The contentment associated with the ordinary experience of loving (*agapaō*) becomes, in the Christian usage, a reference to the experience of joyful love coming from heaven, which offers an enjoyable foretaste of eternal blessedness.

Before one gets the impression that Christian, divinely-rooted *agapē* is incompatible, in Spicq's view, with the larger reality expressed by *erōs*, one must recognize the fact that—although the negative sense of *erōs* (as covetous sexual desire and destructive irrational passion) does not enter New Testament reflection on love—the distinctive reality expressed by the notion of erotic love is by no means alien, in Spicq's account, to scriptural thought. This is at least what one infers from passing comments contained in Spicq's study. So, for example, he makes a remark to the effect that *eraō* is used by the Septuagint much more often than *phileō* (268 times versus thirty) with an affective sense that "determined that of the New Testament."[18] We also find mention of the fact that Hellenistic Greek or Septuagint authors did not suppose a sharp dichotomy between *erōs* and *agapē*, using the verb *agapaō* often for the love between a lover and his mistress.[19] Thus, erotic love is present in the biblical understanding of love expressed by various terms and means. In several passages Spicq argues for the essential continuity of common experiences of human love and also for the fundamental likeness between God's love for us and our love for God.

Where does he find the common element that unites human and divine love? Contrary to Jean-Luc Marion's option, who, as we have seen,

---

18. Spicq, "ἀγάπη, agapē, love," 11, note 18.
19. Spicq, *Agapè dans le Nouveau Testament*, 352, note 2.

attempts to subsume every type of love (*agapē* included) under the one indivisible concept of erotic love, Spicq argues for the archetypal nature of divine *agapē*, which, especially in the Johannine writings, is seen as founding every human love.[20] It is in God's unique and unified love that humans participate when they love in all the senses of the word. In the same way that God loves Godself and all humans, God's children love God and their neighbor, be they brothers or enemies. Christians, who participate in God's love, love with the same accents as God does in his affection towards us and Godself. It is therefore with such divine love that the Christian loves in every sense of the word. This idea, as we shall see, is at first sight diametrically opposed to Marion's recent claim that God loves "in the same way as we do": "God practices the logic of the erotic reduction as we do, with us, according to the same rite and following the same rhythm as us . . . ."[21] Do we have here two fundamental options directed to explain the unity of love: one starting from below (Marion), and another starting from above (the option practically of the entire theological tradition)? What are the consequences of choosing one or the other? Do they issue in two contrasting concepts of love? How do they handle the twofold question of unity that has emerged from our survey: the unity of different types of love and the unity of the intellectual and the emotional element in love? Before we attempt to seek an answer to these questions, we turn to some medieval accounts in order to gain insight into traditional ways of handling the issue and because the influence of medieval controversies, as we shall see, can be felt even up to the present. The unity of love is a classical issue of medieval theories, which seem to propose two diametrically opposed models of what love essentially is. We take Pierre Rousselot as our guide for medieval reflections on love. In his insightful essay *The Problem of Love in the Middle Ages*, Rousselot examined both the basis of the typical medieval claim for the essential unity between self-love and love of God and also a curious medieval dichotomy between two basic types of theories concerning love: one that he described as the Greco-Thomist physical conception and another that he identified as the ecstatic conception of love.[22] We shall read Rousselot's narrative from

20. Ibid., 328., note 1.

21. Marion, *The Erotic Phenomenon*, 222. I deliberately omitted here the end of the statement, which makes Marion's claim interestingly converge with Spicq's idea. We shall come back to this later when we consider Marion's account. The full sentence reads as follows: "God practices the logic of the erotic reduction as we do, with us, according to the same rite and following the same rhythm as us, to the point where we can even ask ourselves if we do not learn it from him, and no one else. God loves in the same way as we do."

22. Rousselot, *The Problem of Love in the Middle Ages*. The fact that Rousselot's doctoral dissertation was translated into English almost a hundred years after its

our own distinctive perspective, that is, in the light of the question concerning the emotionality of love.

Unity and Ruptures in Medieval Theories of Love

The problem of love that Rousselot examines concerns the relationship between love of self and the love of God, issuing in the question whether the two kinds of love are irreducible to one another or can be reduced to a common principle—a major issue in medieval reflections on love. What Rousselot pinpoints in a careful analysis of twelfth- and thirteenth-century medieval theories and miscellaneous reflections on love (amply demonstrated by quotations from various authors) is the presence of two, in his view, diametrically opposed conceptions: one that posits seamless continuity between self-love and love of neighbor and God on the basis of the metaphysical idea that all beings universally and naturally crave for the good according to their inbuilt appetite or desire as created beings (the Greco-Thomist conception), and another that sees a complete discontinuity between these two forms of love on account of an implicit understanding of personhood as a self-sufficient independent entity over against other persons and God (the ecstatic conception). What interests us here is not so much a solution to the problem of the connection between self-love and the love of God as the assumptions in which medieval solutions are couched. Namely, what is of interest at this point in Rousselot's account is what I see as an emerging conflict between a metaphysical spiritual understanding of love and a new "phenomenology" of love that unwittingly aims to reintegrate the emotional, bodily, passion-like aspect into the discourse on love. I employ the word, "unwittingly," because, at the same time, it does not contest the metaphysical frame of the primacy of intellectual attraction toward the good. What comes to the fore from an attentive reading of Rousselot's survey is the interesting fact that while, on the surface, that is, on the theoretical level of reflection, both conceptions of love (the Greco-Thomist physical conception and the ecstatic conception) work with the same assumed fundamental distinction between intellectual and sensible love and regard the latter as a subordinate reflection of the true essence of love, which is invariably argued to be spiritual, implicitly, and perhaps even largely in an unreflected manner, proponents of the ecstatic conception take erotic bodily love as a basic paradigm for their understanding of the essence of love. The body and sensible emotionality, which had so consistently been

---

completion is telling proof of the originality of its vision and its long-term significance. It is certainly also sign of a recently renewed interest in the "problem" of love.

left out from an intellectualistic theological concept of love, in a fascinating manner make their way back into the ecstatic conception, even if only as ways of expression, as metaphors applied to spiritual love. Nonetheless, as metaphors, they become a point of reference and in this manner overturn or at least considerably modify the perspective of a too one-sided intellectuality concerning the nature of spiritual love.

So what does Rousselot tell us about the differences between the two medieval conceptions of love? His preference ostensibly goes to the Greco-Thomist physical conception, which he sees as a metaphysically well-founded and coherent theory, in contrast to the ecstatic conception, which he describes as being less an articulate system than fragmentary intuitions lacking theoretical elaborations, which, therefore, occasionally run into logical inconsistencies when it comes to accounting for their ultimate philosophical ground. While the former is formulated as an explicit theory, the latter can be found in texts of various standing, such as sermons, meditations, confessions, and lyrical passages often lacking the appropriate conceptual means that would allow for a coherent articulation. What we have here is, then, not two kinds of theoretical arguments. The two conceptions are not on an equal footing and, as Rousselot observes, they even cross-fertilize one another, or at least may run parallel, even in the writings of one single author.[23] The ecstatic conception can be present in Greco-Thomist discourse as an undercurrent that counterbalances what I would term a phenomenologically thin understanding of natural universal love. Despite one's expectations to the contrary, the term "physical" in the case of the first conception does not refer to sensible corporeal love, since, as Rousselot notably explains, "even the most resolute advocates of this way of thinking regard sensible love [*l'amour sensible*] merely as a reflection, a feeble image of spiritual love."[24] "Physical" is used here in the sense of "natural" to signify the natural inclination of beings towards their own good, an idea that goes back to Aristotle's metaphysics and that is taken up and is further elaborated by Aquinas. Hence, the name Greco-Thomist conception is used to label this idea of love. Love is understood here in terms of a universal metaphysical desire or appetition that strives towards the good; a common feature of all beings and an innate tendency of every human being, who is seen as naturally tending towards God, the ultimate good. Within this scheme, the love of God and the love of self are not two conflicting propensities, just manifestations of the same indivisible appetite for the good. Consequently,

23. A prime example is, as we shall see, St. Bernard who, while adhering to the Greco-Thomist physical conception, is also a prominent proponent of the ecstatic idea. Hugh of St. Victor likewise belongs to both ways of thinking according to Rousselot.

24. Rousselot, *The Problem of Love*, 78.

the love of God is the basis for all other senses of love and the love of self is regarded as but a form of the love of God. Love, in Augustine's wake, is understood as the natural weight of the soul which draws it towards its ultimate resting place in the goodness of God.

Such a unitary conception of love is backed by three metaphysical assumptions concerning a transcendental understanding of unity: first, the theory of the whole and the part; second, the theory of the universal appetite for God; and, third, the theory of the coincidence of the spiritual good with the good itself. According to the theory of the whole and the part, human love is nothing else than participation in the all-encompassing and foundational divine love that every being possesses through the fact of its creation. That is why self-love does not work against the love of God; on the contrary, it is part of the love tending towards the Creator; every human being is viewed here as a member of a larger unity or whole. On the second principle, as we have seen, the universal craving of all things towards God is emphasized as a consequence of a natural desire to procure their own good. In the third place, the principle of the coincidence of the spiritual good with the good itself allows for a meaningful idea of sacrifice within the unitary Greco-Thomist conception of love on account of the fact that the ultimate good is seen in the intellectual possession of God, which is identified with final beatitude. Sensual goods are subordinated to the true good found on the spiritual plane. Hence, lower sensual goods can be meaningfully sacrificed for the sake of a greater spiritual happiness. What interests us in this threefold principle of unity is the omnipresent assumption—manifest in Rousselot's account—that the true good, true love, and true enjoyment belong to the soul alone, even at the expense of the sensible part, that is, the body, although the body may share in the spiritual bliss of the soul and the enjoyment of the ultimate beatitude. Rousselot himself seems to be holding to this underlying idea, taking it for granted without any difficulty as a necessary building block of the Thomist doctrine to which he readily subscribes. His implicit anthropology does not question Aquinas's claim that the soul contains the human itself in a truer sense and a more intimate manner than the body.[25] This common medieval assumption occurs in various forms in Rousselot's survey. And although he notes an inverse movement in St. Bernard, he nonetheless takes it as an equally valid instance

---

25. Aquinas (whom Rousselot quotes) contends: "Since there is in the human a twofold nature, namely, the intellectual that is more primary, and the sensitive that is less; those people truly love themselves who love themselves for the good of reason. But those people who love themselves for the good of sensuality which is contrary to the good of reason, more hate themselves than love themselves." Aquinas, *De caritate*, 12.6. Quoted in Rousselot, *The Problem of Love*, 102, note 29.

of the Greco-Thomist unitary conception of love. The passage quoted by Rousselot is the following:

> *Since* we are carnal and born *of concupiscence of the flesh*, it is necessary that our cupidity or love begin with the flesh; *if this is arranged in the right order*, this (love) advancing by its stages, led on by grace, will finally be brought to perfection in the spirit. For what is spiritual is not first, but what is animal, then what is spiritual.[26]

His comment on this passage is made to the effect that St. Bernard's statement demonstrates an obvious adherence to the Greco-Thomist idea of the complete continuity of self-love and the love of God, which Bernard radicalizes by placing a "narrow self-love, a perverted self-love, one that characterizes sinful nature" at the starting point.[27] The fact that corporeal love is here taken as the epitome of love does not seem to capture Rousselot's attention. He simply sees in it a radical version of the Greco-Thomist conception of love.

Nevertheless, St. Bernard is recognized as a proponent of both conceptions of love at the same time, whence arise what Rousselot regards as logical inconsistencies in his thought. What are, then, the characteristics of the ecstatic conception of love? Its dominant underlying principle—tacitly assumed rather than openly articulated—is the predominance of the idea of person over the idea of nature. Love is conceived on this view as ecstatic because it is viewed as reaching from one person to another; it is realized between two independent individuals, against any natural inclination, as a free act of self-abandonment for the sake of the beloved. As Rousselot points out, the ecstatic conception works with a metaphysically deficient notion of personhood inasmuch as "personness" is conceived to be completely independent of God, without participation in the divine being or the acknowledgment of the essential dependence of the creature on the Creator. The idea of natural participation on account of the creation (occupying pride of place in the physical Greco-Thomist conception) is replaced by the idea of free donation between two equal pre-existing partners who are not united intrinsically by any bond of nature. Therefore, the ecstatic conception is dualistic in the first place, since proponents of this view argue for the impossibility of real love without two distinct partners. Self-love within this scheme becomes meaningless or at least imperfect and hardly illuminating

---

26. St. Bernard, *De Diligendo Deo*, 15.39. Quoted ibid., 146. In another passage St. Bernard states: "Charity will never exist . . . without cupidity . . . but it orders cupidity." *De Diligendo Deo*, 15.38. Quoted ibid., 147.

27. Ibid., 145. Original emphases.

concerning the real nature of love. Rousselot quotes passages from various authors to the effect that charity is famously regarded as both a bond and a gift between two individuals, metaphors that in Augustine's wake emphasize the mutuality and the bilateral nature of love.[28] Gregory the Great, for example, argues that "[i]t is not possible to have a charity [sic] between fewer than two. For strictly speaking no one is said to have charity for oneself; rather charity becomes possible when love tends toward someone else".[29] William of Auvergne likewise holds: "For it is not fitting that one should be said to love oneself; for all love is a relation and exercises itself in relation to another."[30] And Richard of St. Victor makes this idea an express axiom of his trinitarian theology where the three persons are deduced by an exclusive reliance on such a dualistic conception of love: the perfection of love calls for a duality of terms between the Father and the Son and also the objectified personification of the love between them, the Holy Spirit. The argument exploits the idea that because perfect love cannot exist in just one person, therefore the Trinity of persons is necessary. Trinitarian love is reciprocal since it presupposes a mutual exchange of love between the persons and, in this manner, it also presupposes a plurality of persons. Richard of St. Victor writes: "No one is properly said to have charity on the basis of one's own private and particular love of oneself. And so it is necessary that love tend toward another for it to be charity. Therefore, where a plurality of persons is lacking, charity cannot exist at all."[31]

A second characteristic of ecstatic love, according to Rousselot, is its violent nature, as reflected in the writings of the proponents of this conception through powerful metaphoric expression, rather than discursive argumentation. Love is often described as a destructive power, an annihilating force contrary to natural movements, victorious attraction towards the other where one eventually loses one's soul. The fervor of love wounds the soul and makes it languish; love is languor and even paradoxical death. An intriguing feature of these poetic utterances is the fact that the metaphoric language of the violence of love is equally applied to God's love,

---

28. As Rousselot points out, Augustine applies both metaphors to trinitarian love. One finds the metaphor of the bond of love, for example, in his *De Trinitate*, 8.10.14 and the idea of gift is used in his theology of the Holy Spirit in *De Trinitate*, 15.19.

29. Gregory the Great, *In Evang.*, Hom. 17.1. Quoted ibid., 155.

30. William of Auvergne, *De Trinitate*, 21. Quoted ibid., 157. Elsewhere William explains: "Now it seems extraordinary and difficult to ascertain whether someone loves oneself, or even if it is possible to love oneself. For love is a bond and a ligature, but how is it possible for there to be a bond of the same thing with itself or a ligature?" *De Virtutibus*, 9. See ibid., 157., note 86.

31. Richard of St. Victor, *De Trinitate*, 3.2. Quoted ibid., 165.

which is also described in terms of a conquering and wounding affection, a violent ecstasy towards creation and man. Rousselot furnishes ample fascinating evidence from various authors, demonstrating the peculiar suggestiveness whereby this idea is expounded in poetic utterances. St. Bernard, for instance, speaks in terms of a love that "triumphs over God" and, in praising the power of love, he exclaims in the following words: "Therefore you, charity, have great power. You alone were able to draw God from heaven to the earthly regions. O how strong is your bond by which even God could be bound, and when bound as a human burst the bonds of sin!"[32] In his treatise on the degrees of charity, Richard of St. Victor likewise cries out with joy: "O insuperable virtue of charity, which indeed conquered the insuperable Himself; and Him to whom all are subject, you in some way subjected to all, when God, overcome by love, humbled Himself, taking the form of a servant . . . ."[33] Gilbert, abbot of Hoyland (the continuator of the commentary of St. Bernard on the Song of Songs), speaks in the following highly passionate manner even about God's divine love: "Sharp and effective and truly violent is that affection, good Jesus, which moves and wins your affection! Strong and violent is the force of charity that reaches and penetrates the very affections of God and like an arrow transfixes one's vital organs. What wonder if the kingdom of heaven suffers violence? The Lord Himself bears the wound of violent love."[34] As is clear from this last example, and as Rousselot himself admits, the idea of the violence of love can find ample supply in scriptural and patristic texts. It is not by chance either that texts praising the sweeping force of love can be found in commentaries on the Song of Songs. But what is of even greater importance for us is the fact that the idea of a love that makes even God ecstatically reach out of Himself appears also in Aquinas's thought, despite his adherence to the physical unitary conception of love. In a footnote, Rousselot remarks that Aquinas speaks about creation in clearly ecstatic terms, "[b]ut his restriction immediately follows"—Rousselot is quick to add.[35] Nevertheless Aquinas writes that in the act of creation: "[God] is brought outside of himself . . . and in a certain way is pulled and brought down from excellence . . . to the point that He is present in all things through the effect of His goodness according to a kind of ecstasy."[36] This passage is a clear indication of the fact that the two conceptions of

---

32. St. Bernard, *De Laude Caritatis*. Quoted ibid., 172.
33. Richard of St. Victor, *Tractatus de Gradibus Caritatis*, 1. Quoted ibid., 173.
34. Gilbert of Hoyland, *Sermones in Cantica*, 30.2. Quoted ibid., 174.
35. Ibid., 170., note 94.
36. Aquinas, *In Div. Nom.*, 4.1.10. Quoted ibid., 170., note 94.

love are not isolated from one another, but may intertwine in the thought of one single author, just as we saw in the case of St. Bernard.

A third feature of the ecstatic vision of love is its irrationality. It is universally characterized as unreasonable, careless, disordered, and blind. It is widely seen as conquering everything in the soul and subjugating even "our chief part," that is, the intellect. The madness of love overwhelmingly triumphs over every rational reason, leaving no space for cold consideration. Love is also egalitarian in its effect on all persons. Unlike the Thomist conception, which presupposes a fundamental dissimilarity between those who love one another, the ecstatic conception stresses equality as an effect brought about by the uniting force of love, which suppresses dissimilarity in "making the lovers one" in a loving union.

The fourth, and last, attribute of ecstatic love identified by Rousselot is its being the final end, namely, beatitude itself and the ultimate possession of the supreme Good. Love in this sense is transcendent and it carries with itself its own justification; it has primacy over every spiritual good, it is the towering virtue and the most eminent gift alone worthy of God. For example, Gilbert of Hoyland's eulogy of the unique status of love runs in the following manner: "Charity is the summit as charity is the foundation . . . . Love cannot be satisfied with itself and yet it can find nourishment only in itself; it is food sweet enough for itself. Love wants nothing more than to love. What will a human give in exchange for love?"[37] Love is regarded here as being self-explanatory, an ultimate self-sufficient principle of human and divine existence.

An interesting development of this last characteristic is detected by Rousselot in William of Thierry's account (in the wake of Gregory the Great), which formally identifies love and understanding, quite contrary to the consistent separation of these two notions in the Thomist doctrine, where love and understanding are viewed as being formally irreducible to one another. William of Thierry holds that love itself is understanding since love is a sense faculty, as it were, whereby we feel the divine; love (appetite) and knowledge (understanding) converge in a special affectionate knowledge of God. There is within the Triune God such an affectionate knowledge in a perfect form: the mutual knowledge of the Father and the Son is identical to their common love (that is, their common will) who is the Holy Spirit. The reason for such an identity is the simplicity of the divine essence, where knowledge comes forth from love. Perfect affectionate knowledge is then infused into humans by the Holy Spirit and so imperfect

---

37. Gilbert of Hoyland, *Sermones in Cantica*, 19.1.2. Quoted ibid., 198–99.

affectionate knowledge, as an imitation of the divine archetype, is imparted to us. Therefore, we are aware that true knowledge originates in love.

The conclusion Rousselot draws on the basis of the careful analysis of medieval texts does not concern the reason for the emergence of two opposing conceptions of love. He simply wants to document and conceptualize what he recognizes as a pivotal distinction, namely, the existence of two underlying medieval directions of thought concerning the understanding of the essential characteristics of love and, first and foremost, related to the problem of the continuity between love of self and the love of God. The two pinpointed directions are viewed by him as interconnected or at least often running side by side, despite the logical inconsistencies resulting from such a parallelism. Rousselot is fascinated by the curious fact that "these two opposite conclusions were derived from a unique principle, that of the unconditional primacy of love."[38] While the physical (Greco-Thomist) conception of love is capable of arguing in a neat philosophical manner for an essential continuity between all kinds of love by making the universal metaphysical longing (appetite) for the good the basic principle of every type of love and therefore placing the love of God at the root of self-love, the ecstatic conception, in a philosophically confused manner, severs the link between self-love and other types of altruistic love and places an essential duality at the heart of a proper understanding of love. Rousselot's great achievement is the admirable fact that, despite the fragmentary, conceptually inarticulate and philosophically shabby manner in which the ecstatic idea is developed, he nonetheless recognizes its vital importance and does not deny it citizenship among stimulating theories of love. His description of the ecstatic theory offers an invaluable means to capture an emerging countermovement that aims to correct the one-sided intellectualism of Greco-Thomist thought. Besides theoretical treatises, he takes medieval poetic utterances, sermons, and meditations as equally serious articulations, and he is not reluctant to read them attentively in order to understand their implicit truth claims. Last but not least, he is aware that, through the ecstatic conception, some profound intuitions are voiced (often in a metaphorical manner), ones that otherwise would not have been able to make their way into medieval conceptual thought. However, Rousselot stops at the phase of providing an ingenious diagnosis and making illuminating observations concerning the physiognomy of the ecstatic vision. His analysis does not go deeper to search for the causes underlying such a vision.

So what shall we make of Rousselot's insightful distinction? Why is it important for our inquiry? Alan Vincelette, the English translator of

38. Ibid., 234.

Rousselot's study, has suggested that one could take the ecstatic conception as standing for selfless and self-sacrificing, agapaic love since it can be described in very similar terms as "the free bestowal of one's personal self to another in disassociation from or opposition to one's wants and desires."[39] In such a love one no longer considers his own interests but regards solely the good of the beloved and so sacrifice is a natural element of *agapē*. In exercising this type of love, one may act in opposition to the innate tendencies of self-love; one is pulled out of oneself toward the other in a kind of ecstasy. As Vincelette argues, for Rousselot, there is no place for natural self-love within such a scheme. I would suggest, however, that one should set things in a completely different perspective and—without trying to contrast selfless ecstatic *agapē* and egotistic *erōs*—recognize in Rousselot's description of the ecstatic conception of love the incursion of the neglected aspect of love as a passion, as an emotion bound up with the body, as an experience essentially sensible and erotic, in a word, as truly human embodied love. In my view, what makes an incursion here on the metaphysical theory is a new tentative phenomenology of love that aims to supply the missing dimension in view of a wholesome understanding of love. Sensing the insufficiency of the assumed primacy of intellectual metaphysical attraction toward the good as the ultimate principle of love, it cautiously toys with the idea of taking embodied love as a paradigm for all types of love. So much so that—with a daring realism—the ecstatic vision understands God's love in the same emotional terms as human love; it speaks of God's ecstasy towards the world and his wounding passion for humans. Through the ecstatic conception the emotional aspect of love is recuperated in the Ricoeurian sense; it is the emotionality of the heart or the *thymos* which mediates between the vital and the spiritual. It is for this reason that these utterances are mostly metaphorical since they need to transpose experiences from the vital plane to the spiritual plane. What is needed is mediation between the elemental experience of sensible love and the ideal of spiritual love. This is evident from Vincelette's unease with regard to medieval metaphors of love. He makes a passing remark to the effect that one cannot decide "whether such statements about love being wounding or conquering are intended metaphorically or literally and hence whether these authors truly consider love as harmful to the lover," since "many of these authors readily speak of the joy and sweetness that is found in love elsewhere."[40] I think that by viewing literal and metaphorical statements as true alternatives one is asking

---

39. Alan Vincelette, "Translator's Introduction," in Rousselot, *The Problem of Love*, 14.

40. Ibid., 15, note 6.

the wrong question because what is at stake here is the expression of the "literal" spiritual meaning of sensible embodied love by way of metaphor. In other words, one can witness the re-entry of passion as a Ricoeurian mediation between the two, theoretically sundered, forms of love: sensible and spiritual. Love as an emotion is used here to interpret intellectual love, quite contrary to what is otherwise acknowledged as a legitimate procedure on the theoretical plane of argumentation. In other words, emotion and the body plead for a rightful share in a proper understanding of love, both human and divine. Could it be the case that a natural craving for the good or the intellectual enjoyment of the divine do not in themselves capture the rich fullness of the experience of love?

The Twofold Nature of Love in Aquinas

In fact, we do not do justice to Aquinas if we presuppose a complete dissociation in his works between spiritual and sensible affectivity or intellectual and sensible love since, while keeping these two aspects consistently apart, he also establishes connections between them. Such an attempt at unity despite a fundamental dichotomy can best be observed in his theory of love, which cuts across the domain of inanimate beings, animals, humans, angels, and God and which equally concerns human sensible and intellectual nature and also the divinely inspired grace of charity, elicited and received as a transcendental gift. It is beyond the purpose of our survey to elaborate on all aspects of Aquinas's complex account of love and charity. What is of interest here are but a handful of issues concerning the emotionality of Thomistic love and the role of the body in the act of loving. What makes our inquiry especially difficult is the extensive nature of Aquinas's reflections on this theme, which he treats repeatedly in various works and at different stages of his career. We shall rely here on three essential treatments: the reflections on love and charity in the *Commentary on the Sentences of Peter Lombard* (an early work written between 1252–56), which shows the young master's brilliant skills in handling the issue; the classical and most neatly and didactically organized treatment of the *Summa Theologica* (1266–73); and a third, partly parallel inquiry in the *Disputed Questions* entitled *On Charity* (1269–72), written for a proficient public and containing more complexity and detail at a greater depth.[41] These reflections on love complement one another on several important points. They also contain, to a large extent,

---

41. 1) *On Love and Charity*; 2) parts of *The Summa Theologica*: love as a passion (IaIIae.26–28), charity as a theological virtue (IIaIIae.23–27), God's love (Ia.20); 3) *On Charity*.

parallel discussions, and in certain cases, developments with respect to earlier elaborations. Obviously, the three major treatments are not exhaustive since love is also discussed by Aquinas in other contexts, such as, for example, with regard to trinitarian theology. The immensity of the material shows the extreme difficulty one must face in trying to come to terms with the exact shape of the Thomistic doctrine of love. What interests us here, however, is essentially the main thrust of his general argument and those major anthropological (and theological) assumptions that can be adequately outlined on the basis of these three accounts. What follows is my own attempt at gathering various scattered statements into a kind of synthesis grouped around some key issues relevant for our inquiry.

As has clearly emerged from the discussion of Aquinas's theory of the passions and also from his theology of the image, his anthropology is based on a crucial distinction between what is sensible and what is intellectual. It is the intellectual part that contains the image of God. The sensible part is secondary and—in being closely connected to the body—may only participate in its privileged status by receiving a reflection of its glory which reverberates also to the lower parts. This very same idea is repeated with respect to the doctrine of love, where Aquinas refers to this underlying dichotomy as a fundamental feature of the human situation that determines a proper understanding of what true self-love is: "Since there is in man a twofold nature, viz. the intellectual which is primary, and the sensitive which is lesser; he truly loves himself who loves himself for the good of reason."[42] Elsewhere, speaking about the special love of charity between man and God, Aquinas repeats the same distinction in a slightly different form, stating that "man's life is twofold" since, on the one hand, "[t]here is his outward life in respect of his sensitive and corporeal nature," and on the other, there is "man's spiritual life in respect of his mind."[43] What ensues for Aquinas from this basic difference is the fact that charity, that is, fellowship with God, is connected solely to the intellectual part or the mind, while the corporeal sensible part is excluded from fellowship or communication with God. In a passing statement we also encounter the similar idea that what makes one human comes from the soul and not from the body; therefore, "although man consists of soul and body, he has his specific being from the soul, not from the body . . . ."[44] This has important consequences for the way our likeness to God is realized in the act of charity, which again follows from our intellectual nature. While all

---

42. Aquinas, *On Charity*, 12.6.
43. Aquinas, *ST* IIaIIae.23.1.
44. Aquinas, *On Love and Charity*, 4.49.1.1.1.

created beings bear a certain likeness to God, the creator, by the very fact of their existence and their essential goodness as creatures, a further cause of similitude is added to this basic likeness in the case of humans through the possession of the intellect. And since the seat of charity is to be found in our intellect, Aquinas concludes that "in the act of charity God is more expressly perceived as in a closer likeness."[45] In a similar manner, ultimate beatitude, when charity will come to its perfection, likewise consists, first and foremost, in an act of the intellect and is accompanied by the intellectual delight resulting from the coming to rest of the will in a beatifying vision of God.[46] The list of examples could be continued. Nevertheless, what comes to the fore is the notable fact that the distinction between our intellectual nature and the sensible bodily part, and the idea of their unequal share in our relationship with God, is a constant element of Aquinas's thought and is also present with equal importance in his theory of love and charity.

Despite the assumed enduring rift or geological fault (to take Ricoeur's expression) in the human constitution between the sensible and the intellectual, Aquinas's theory of love is on the whole unitary, as Rousselot rightly perceives. And we may add that it is precisely the special case of love that seems to offer Aquinas a fundamental and traditionally founded metaphysical principle of unity. Love as a natural craving for the good is viewed as running across the entire gamut of creation as an ultimate metaphysical cogency. Moreover, it is not only characteristic of the inanimate world or the vegetal soul of humans, but is present in all of the soul's parts: in the sensitive and the intellectual appetite as well. This is what Aquinas calls "natural love." This universal attraction of the entire creation toward "what is suitable them according to their nature" is nothing other than a universal attraction of all existing things toward their Author, that is, God. Such a universal natural love permeates every level of existence and unifies all in one common tendency toward their originating centre in God. It is an unconscious craving, an unreflected natural movement. Aquinas likens it to the movement whereby a heavy body, by reason of its weight, tends toward the centre. It is against this background of natural love that Aquinas draws the contours of sensitive and intellectual love, both of which have the common characteristic of being related to apprehension, even if not necessarily rational apprehension, as in the case of animals. Natural love is thus contrasted with love in living beings and especially with human sensitive

---

45. Aquinas, *On Charity*, I.8.
46. Aquinas, *On Love and Charity*, 4.49.1.1.2.

and intellectual love. All these types of love (the intellectual, the animal, and the natural) belong to love in a general sense in Aquinas's account.[47]

Love, in the proper sense, for Aquinas, is first and foremost a passion connected to the sensitive part of the soul and in this manner to the body. In a wider extended sense it is also applied to rational love residing in the will. In fact, we find Aquinas struggling with the equivocity of the term and the various significations commonly assigned to the word love throughout his inquiry. Language does not seem to be capable of covering the distinctions he seeks to make between different types of love, and which is set against a larger scheme of unity. In an early treatment of this problem, Aquinas makes a remarkable observation that helps us detect the way he conceives what we may describe as the twofold nature of love. Here he admits that the names of the passions (properly found in the sensitive appetite) can be transferred to the intellectual appetite:

> It should be said that love is a certain resting of appetite, as was said above. Hence, just as appetite is found in the sensitive and intellectual parts of the soul, so too is love. Now, while things that pertain to the sensitive appetite get transferred to the intellectual appetite (such as the names of the passions), what is proper to the intellectual appetite is not applicable to the sensitive appetite (such as the term will). And thus love is found in each appetite. As found in the sensitive appetite, it is called "love" properly, for this implies a passion. As found in the intellectual part, it is called "rational love," for this includes the element of choice, which pertains to the intellectual appetite. Nevertheless, though the term "love" gets transferred from the lower part to the higher, the term "rational love" never gets transferred from the higher part to the lower.[48]

This we can readily take as telling proof of the fact that there are two sets of passions in the Thomistic scheme: sensitive and intellectual, in other words, passions proper and "pseudopassions" (in Peter King's term). This passage also contains the important recognition that the paradigm of love, at least on the level of linguistic expression and, therefore, concepts, is bodily passion, notwithstanding the Thomasian insistence on the primacy of intellectual love with regard to our relation to God and neighbor. In examining

---

47. To the objection that love cannot be the cause of everything the lover does because love is a passion, but man does not do everything from passion, Aquinas responds in the following manner: "This objection takes love as a passion existing in the sensitive appetite. But here we are speaking of love in a general sense, inasmuch as it includes intellectual, rational, animal, and natural love." *ST* IaIIae.28.6.

48. Aquinas, *On Love and Charity*, 3.27.2.1.

various expressions for love (friendship, dilection, and charity), Aquinas likewise seems to conclude that they, "in a way," refer to the same thing, namely, that they denote different aspects of the concept of love. In other words, these terms add certain qualifications to the basic unitary notion of love: friendship denotes a habit, dilection implies choice made beforehand (*electio*), and charity implies a certain perfection of love. Love is then the general umbrella term that serves as a point of reference for various specific significations, both linguistically and conceptually. And it is at this point that Aquinas makes the oft-quoted statement that "love [*amor*] is more Godlike [*divinius*] than dilection [*dilectio*]."[49] In an intriguing fashion, he applies in this passage the attributes of love as a passion proper (arising in the sensitive appetite) to the love whereby God attracts the human heart.

The aspect of passion in love is declared in this manner to be an essential element of the love between man and God, transferring indeed an attribute of sensible love onto intellectual charity. God imposes the attraction of passion as it were on the human being; God's love is passively "suffered," rather than rationally chosen through intellectual dilection (we remember that Aquinas sees the element of reasonable choice as an essential feature of dilection). God's divine love imposes itself on the human heart just as the irresistible human passion of erotic love is experienced as an outside force and attraction stronger than any rational consideration. One should always keep in view the interesting fact that Aquinas assumes an underlying unity to our experience of love; he consistently refers to various kinds of love as types of the one indivisible idea of love. That is to say, the love of concupiscence, the love of friendship, or the love of charity must be regarded as manifestations of the same type and not as three distinct loves.[50]

---

49. Aquinas writes: "The reason why some held that, even when applied to the will itself, the word 'love' signifies something more Godlike than 'dilection,' was because love denotes a passion, especially in so far as it is in the sensitive appetite; whereas dilection presupposes the judgment of reason. But it is possible for man to tend to God by love, being as it were passively drawn by Him, more than he can possibly be drawn thereto by his reason, which pertains to the nature of dilection, as stated above. And consequently love is more Godlike than dilection." *ST* IaIIae.26.3. It is quoted, for example, by Yves-Jean Harder to the effect that *erōs* is here declared to be superior to *agapē* (in Dionysios the Areopagite's wake), since it is seen as representing a strong attraction by God which man passively undergoes and which is stronger than the motives one can intellectually conceive for loving God. See Yves-Jean Harder, "Amour," in Lacoste, *Dictionnaire Critique de Théologie*, 37.

50. To the objection that concupiscence (that is, love of the good one wishes oneself or another) and friendship (love of someone whom one wishes the good) are two distinct things because concupiscence is a passion and friendship is a habit, therefore "habit cannot be a member of a division of passions," Aquinas replies that such a separation does not hold: "Love is not divided into friendship and concupiscence, but into

All in all, one may distinguish three levels of love in Aquinas's scheme: love as a passion on the sensible bodily level of existence; intellectual rational or spiritual love, which is regarded quite independently of the body; and supernaturally elicited charity, as a special case of love, which is God's gift for humans and is received as a grace, which elicits and perfects natural human love. Charity exists exclusively in the intellectual part, that is, the image-like nature of man. These three levels of love are in turn couched in a twofold affectivity: sensible corporeal and intellectual spiritual. Ostensibly, Aquinas has difficulties in keeping the three levels of love consistently apart. His treatments cannot escape the equivocation inherent in the term love either, and so one feels a constant oscillation between the two notions of love as a passion proper and intellectual love. It is noteworthy that intellectual love does not receive in Aquinas a separate treatment of its own but is dealt with either in the section concerning love as a passion or under the rubric of supernatural charity. Such a permanent shift between levels, on the one hand, reinforces Aquinas's insistence on the unity of love as a general craving for the good. At the same time, it also questions the validity of the lines of division along which the one single reality of love is eked out. And indeed, the discussion of love as a body-bound passion is indissolubly intertwined with talk about spiritual love, even to the point of equivocation where one no longer is able to distinguish the two distinct realities within the flow of Aquinas's argumentation. In fact, if passages concerning the "spirituality" of sensible passion were removed, what would be left is but perplexing fragments that do not add up to a coherent vision concerning the nature of sensual love. Love appears here as a passion spiritualized through and through. In a similar manner, elaborations on spiritual charity contain constant reference to observations made with regard to the passion of love.

Consequently, there is no easy answer to the question concerning the difference between love proper as a passion and spiritual intellectual love. Certainly, Aquinas's formal answer addresses the difference regarding their locality in the human soul: love as a passion is a movement of the sensible appetite, while intellectual love belongs to the intellectual appetite, that is, the will. Sensible love therefore is of the body, whereas intellectual love is of the (virtually disembodied) mind. Love as a passion is directed to sensible objects and intellectual love has spiritual objects. However, apart from such a formal difference hinging on the body, the actual phenomenology of the two loves seems in most part to be identical, also due to the fact that, in Aquinas's unitive vision of the relationship of body and soul, they are

---

love of friendship, and love of concupiscence. For a friend is, properly speaking, one to whom we wish good: while we are said to desire, what we wish for ourselves." *ST* IaIIae.26.4.

viewed as intimately linked and even contemporaneous: what occurs in the senses, also affects the mind. Passionate love is in some way simultaneously also intellectual, although the reverse does not necessarily hold. Moreover, both seem to have the same emotional character irrespective of whether the body is involved or left out. Intellectual love is accompanied by what we may term as "intellectual" emotionality: the feelings of joy, delight and deep affection, spiritual pleasure and enjoyment. The entire panoply of passionate emotionality is transposed by Aquinas to intellectual love. About the love that is in God, he writes: "Love therefore and joy and delight are passions; in so far as they denote acts of the intellective appetite, they are not passions. It is in this latter sense that they are in God."[51] Translated into our modern terminology, this statement can be taken to the effect that love and joy are spiritual "emotions" in God, without, however, the bodily change implied by the effect of real passions.

In another passage the positive emotions accompanying the act of intellectual charity are stressed: "the act of charity is especially enjoyable and especially inclines one to remain in charity, and through it everything we do or suffer is rendered pleasing."[52] Remarkably, throughout Aquinas's writings, one finds ample evidence of the idea of the twofold emotionality of love. The notion of God's love implies the notion of charity distinguished by Aquinas from everyday human love, either passionate or intellectual. Charity is a special kind of intellectual love; it is a kind of friendship with God, which presupposes communication (in the sense of sharing one's life with the other) between the human being and God. Since God communicates His happiness to us, His love for us and our love for him is a kind of friendship. Charity belongs solely to the spiritual part of the soul, that is, the intellect or the mind and it has God as its ultimate object. Just as the passion of love is accompanied by joy, charity too engenders joy: "spiritual joy, which is about God, is caused by charity."[53]

Aquinas defines love in a proper sense as willing the good.[54] Love in a general sense is a tendency toward the good through an unconscious craving, however, love in the primary sense is conscious: it is either willing the good of oneself, or the good of another. Charity then is the highest form of goodwill and friendship whereby one loves oneself or another with a view to everlasting happiness, wishing oneself or someone else God's goodness and the ultimate beatitude. Charity is participation in the love whereby God

---

51. Ibid., Ia.20.1.
52. Aquinas, *On Charity*, 1.22.
53. Aquinas, *ST* IIaIIae.28.1.
54. See, for example, Aquinas, *On Charity*, 7.61.

loves us and Himself, the object of charity is the perfect good, charity is the highest form of friendship with God. Although Aquinas defines love as wishing the good of someone, to the question whether charity is identical with goodwill, he replies with a noteworthy caveat, insisting that there is an important difference between merely wishing well to another and actually loving someone. The noteworthy fact is that such a pivotal difference seems to lie precisely in the emotional aspect of love on both the sensitive and the intellectual plane. As Aquinas explains, while love as a passion is not identical with goodwill on account of the fact that it implies "impetuosity or desire" and an "eager inclination," intellectual love cannot be conceived as simple goodwill either since it requires a "certain union of affections," that is, a distinguishing emotional element.[55] Thus, it is union of the affections or desire for the beloved, which makes simple goodwill charity or love.

And here we touch upon a salient point, since the difference that the union of affections makes with respect to love is crucial for a proper understanding of Aquinas's theory of love. In fact, this insistence on the emotional involvement necessary for true love is often overlooked in later appropriations of the Thomistic scheme or is at least attenuated by a one-sided emphasis on Aquinas's qualification, made for the special cases of loving even those with whom one does not have any real rapport, or the extreme case of loving one's enemy. For indeed, in these special cases, Aquinas, led by an admirable realism, does not insist on the absolute necessity of affection otherwise characteristic, in his view, of wholesome charity. The reason for this lies in our spatial and temporal limitation as creatures, "because no man is capable of having all men in mind in such a way that he would actually love each one in a particular way, nor is there any one capable of doing good or helping each and every one in a particular way."[56] Therefore, on account of such a human limitation, we are not expected to love those who are not related to us in any manner with a love that implies a union of affections. Yet, even in such cases—when those loved are far away and completely un-

---

55. "Goodwill properly speaking is that act of the will whereby we wish well to another. Now this act of the will differs from actual love, considered not only as being in the sensitive appetite but also being in the intellective appetite or the will. For the love which is in the sensitive appetite is a passion.... [T]he difference between goodwill and the love which is a passion [is] that goodwill does not imply impetuosity or desire, that is to say, has not an eager inclination, because it is by the sole judgment of his reason that one man wishes another well.... But the love, which is in the sensitive appetite, also differs from goodwill, because it denotes a certain union of affections between the lover and the beloved.... On the other hand, goodwill is a simple act of the will, whereby we wish a person well, even without presupposing the aforesaid union of the affections with him." *ST* IIaIIae.27.2.

56. Aquinas, *On Charity*, 8.70.

known to us—the affection by which we love our actual neighbors must in some way extend to those we do not know or meet: "We are bound, however, by the affection and the carrying out of the works of charity, by which we love all our neighbors and pray for them, not to exclude even those who are not joined to us by any special bond, as for instance those who live in India or Ethiopia."[57] And while one is not bound to love one's enemy with the special affection of love with which one loves a friend, such a heroic attitude is nonetheless possible, according to Aquinas, if one loves one's enemy for the sake of God in an act of perfect charity originating in God's love.[58]

All in all, love without an affectionate bond is an exception rather than a general rule in Aquinas, the paradigm of true love being the union of affections and not vice versa. Due to a curious shift in emphases, Aquinas's wise concession has increasingly been interpreted as an insistence on the secondary or even superfluous nature of the emotional element in loving, which can be added or removed without any serious damage done to the quality of true charity. Feelings came to be regarded as unimportant or at least optional concomitants of love that, however, do not influence its profundity or genuineness in any serious manner. Because Aquinas assigns charity and intellectual love to the intellectual appetite, in other words, the will, love has mistakenly been thought to lack an emotional aspect in itself, having just occasional contacts with the realm of feelings. The curious reality of "pseudopassion" or intellectual emotionality detectable throughout in Aquinas's account has been thus ignored, together with the pivotal distinction between simple goodwill and the real love of charity. The idea that love is not a matter of feelings, but an intellectual decision of the will whereby we want the good of others, no matter what we feel towards them, has been

---

57. Ibid., 8.70.

58. Ibid. Aquinas explains the obligation to love even one's enemy also in the *Summa Theologica*, where he distinguishes between three ways of loving. First, "to love our enemies as such"—this would be perverse, he notes. Second, to love them in general, with the love one loves one's neighbors in general—in this sense one should love enemies too and pray for them and assist them in case of urgency. Third, to love them with love specially directed to them, "that we should have special movement of love towards our enemies"—this is not required, since one need not love enemies individually (it would be impossible to love every individual man with a special movement of love). However, for God's sake, as the perfection of charity—which is not commanded, just counseled—one may love enemies on account of one's intense love for God: "For since man loves his neighbor, out of charity, for God's sake, the more he loves God, the more does he put enmities aside and show love towards his neighbor: thus if we loved a certain man very much, we would love his children, though they were unfriendly towards us." Aquinas here clearly takes the profound love for God as a paradigm for loving even one's enemies and does not appeal to a simple rational decision as the cause of such love. See *ST* IIaIIae.25.8–9.

perpetuated practically unquestioned up to the present day and is inherent in various formulations and contexts. For example, Alexander Willwoll, apparently inspired by the Thomistic stance and yet interpreting it through a modern anti-sentimentalist filter cast in the language of the time, represents such a dissociative view in his definition of love:

> Love is the value-affirming and the value-creating primordial power of the willing spirit. Considered essentially and experientially, love is an attitude of the will. ... Frequently but not necessarily love overflows into the realm of feelings and is reinforced by them, but it is not just a feeling of pleasure or some other kind of "higher feeling." Thus, for example, there can be a will-act affirming the supreme value of the other person (e.g. God) and this act of the will can persist even while one's feelings follow another scale of values.[59]

What we have here is a curious schizophrenic separation of one's will from one's feelings, the vision of a strange emotionless voluntaristic love that has no bearing on one's affective disposition and can operate in complete separation of what one feels. But is such a coldly rationalistic and emotionally thin notion of love reconcilable with Aquinas's original intention as it appears in his various treatments of love? Can the case when one loves God by sheer willpower and yet without any affection be regarded as a prime example of the Christian love of charity in the manner promulgated by Aquinas? And last but not least, is such a view faithful to our everyday experience of love or a biblical vision? Curiously, on defining emotion, the very same author takes up a markedly different stance, insisting that emotion arises from "the close unity of the spiritual and the sensual in our human experience.... Emotion influences the entire personal, social, ethical and religious experience of values."[60] If emotion is determinative for value-formation, which in turn is seen as an essential element of love, then can one meaningfully imagine a rational love of God, for example, which is not undergirded by emotion? Or, to put it in another way, if one's feelings "follow another scale of values" can one's love for God be wholesome? Is not simple goodwill confounded here with true love? Is there not a fatal dichotomy posited between will and emotion, one which ultimately sunders the unity of the soul, a dichotomy Aquinas never intended to create? Nevertheless, his implicit and largely inarticulate vision of the "emotional" aspect of intellectual love has left later interpreters conceptually unequipped to handle

---

59. Alexander Willwoll, "Love," in Brugger and Baker, *Philosophical Dictionary*, 233–34.

60. Willwoll, "Emotion," ibid., 108.

the affectivity of love in an adequate manner, giving the impression that it is ultimately insignificant for a proper understanding of truly Christian love.

What role does Aquinas assign to the body in the act of charity? Obviously, the body has a central role in the experience of love as a passion where it is considered as the material element of passion without which no passion would be conceivable; yet does it enter in any manner into the love of charity? Aquinas takes an interesting stance concerning the body. Since charity is portrayed by him as belonging to the intellectual part of man and being of a purely intellectual nature, its subject being the rational mind, one would expect the complete exclusion of the body from the purview of charity. Charity, as a special case of love, the highest form of intellectual friendship with God, does not seem to have any reference to our sensible bodily nature. Moreover, as Aquinas contends, charity extends only to things with a capacity for everlasting life. Everlasting life is only imparted to beings who hold the likeness of image, yet not to those having merely likeness by way of trace.[61] The body, as has been seen, has likeness by way of trace, according to Aquinas, since it is only the intellectual mind that is the seat of the image, and, on this logic, the body should have no share in charity. However, such logic would also imply that the body as trace cannot share in the glory of the resurrection and this Aquinas is obviously not willing to concede. The body is an essential element of resurrected everlasting life, participating in the glory of the resurrected soul, which redounds to the body, making it share the joy of ultimate beatitude. So what is the role of the body with regard to charity?

Aquinas holds the—to the modern reader—curious view that the body is one of the four distinguished objects one must love with the love of charity, the four objects being: oneself, the body, the neighbor, and God. Aquinas owes the fourfold classification to Augustine, whose authority he readily accepts and whose idea he further elaborates.[62] One may also be struck by the fact that oneself and the body are taken here as two distinct realities. However, such a dissociation is a direct consequence of Aquinas's separation of the intellectual nature and the bodily sensitive nature of man. "Oneself" in this scheme means loving one's rational nature over against one's sensitive part, as it clearly emerges from Aquinas's explanation concerning the rectitude of self-love questioned by opponents: "Those who love

---

61. "Likeness by way of trace does not confer the capacity for everlasting life, whereas the likeness of image does." See *ST* IIaIIae.25.3.

62. Aquinas writes: "Augustine says (*De Doctr. Christ.* 1.23): 'There are four things to be loved; one which is above us,' namely God, 'another, which is ourselves, a third which is nigh to us,' namely our neighbor, 'and a fourth which is beneath us,' namely our own body." *ST* IIaIIae.25.12.

themselves are to be blamed, in so far as they love themselves as regards their sensitive nature, which they humor. This is not to love oneself truly according to one's rational nature, so as to desire for oneself the good things which pertain to the perfection of reason: and in this way chiefly it is through charity that man loves himself."[63] The body, in this scheme, has an ambiguous position: it is viewed as belonging to the person and yet it is distinguished from him at the same time. The body is indispensable for life since we act through the body, but it does not constitute our true being, our innermost humanity as images of God. Nonetheless, Aquinas argues for the essential goodness of the body over against a Manichean dualism and the Manichean contempt for bodiliness. He insists that the body is fundamentally good "in respect of its nature" and it is only the effects of sin and corruption—due to punishment subsequent to the fall—that are detestable. Therefore, our bodies must be loved with the love of charity. And, although the body does not belong to our intellectual nature and is unable to share in the friendship with God or the fellowship of everlasting happiness, it nonetheless deserves the love of charity on account of the fact that the happiness in which the soul participates "overflows" also to the body with whose help one is capable of doing works that can lead to such beatitude. If one loves oneself in a manner distinct from one's own body, the question naturally follows whether the reason for loving the body of one's neighbor differs from the one for loving his soul. Aquinas's answer to this baffling question appeals to the essential unity of the human person, which, cast in our modern terms, appears as a complex of distinct entities only to one's inner consciousness. However, body and soul form an outwardly indissoluble unity where the body of one's neighbor must not be viewed as a separate object of love.[64]

By way of conclusion we may say that love in Aquinas is emotional even in its intellectual mode. This oft-overlooked aspect of charity and natural intellectual love is paramount for a proper understanding of the nature of Thomistic love. The emotional aspect of love, nevertheless, is assumed rather than openly stated or conceptually elaborated by Aquinas. The curious doubling of perspectives is at times perplexing and the difference between embodied and spiritual emotionality stays ultimately unclear. The chief cause of such obscurity lies in Aquinas's ambivalent view of the body, which is only half-included in his theory of love.[65] For, on the one hand, the

---

63. Ibid., IIaIIae.25.4.

64. "Man loves his neighbor, both as to his soul and as to his body, by reason of a certain fellowship of happiness. Wherefore, on the part of his neighbor, there is only one reason for loving him; and our neighbor's body is not reckoned as a special object of love." Ibid., IIaIIae.25.12.

65. As Lottie H. Kendzierski, the translator of Aquinas's *De Caritate* has pointed

body is seen as indissolubly linked to the soul with which it forms one unity. In this sense, bodily passion has a repercussion in the soul and affects the rational mind. Aquinas also concedes that an understanding of body-linked love is transferred to intellectual love and that the same terms that describe love as a passion are also employed to describe spiritual love. Moreover, the body is an ally in the accomplishment of acts of charity whereby one loves one's neighbors and is even partaker in everlasting life, sharing in the resurrection. Yet, on the other hand, the body is evidently not on an equal footing with the spiritual rational mind, which alone is capable of loving God with the special love of friendship and communion and which alone represents God's image in the human person. The body does not enter intellectual love and is not necessary for spiritual feeling and, although it is an object of charity with which one must revere one's ally in the accomplishment of virtue, does not share in the charity with which one loves God. Is love embodied or disembodied in Aquinas? It is very hard to tell. One registers here an essential ambiguity that at the end of the day cannot be dissolved. Aquinas's half-embodied love haunts many of the later accounts and it has repercussions on the entire shape of theologies of love. Without the body the emotionality of spiritual feelings becomes hardly arguable and conceptually vague. Love is turned into a disembodied act of the will set in complete opposition with emotion and lacking the mediation of the heart. Can one conceive a complete reversal of perspectives, one that takes bodily erotic love as the paradigm of every type of love in a radically unitary fashion?

---

out, according to Aquinas, the perfection of charity is not possible in this life. The reason for this being several impediments, among which Aquinas mentions "the infirmity of this life, and the burden of the body." As Kendzierski notes, the expression "burden of the body" as an impediment to the perfection of charity is a curious one in a framework where Aquinas argues for the importance of loving oneself and one's body through a love of charity. Without wanting to resolve the contradiction, Kendzierski suggests that Thomas here most probably follows Augustine who "is, for St. Thomas, the authority on theological matters" and whose works display a "penetrating and exhaustive emphasis on charity." See Lottie H. Kendzierski, "Introduction," in Aquinas, *On Charity*, 13., note 38.

6

Between Embodiment and Spirituality

> O how I love you
> who, made to speak
> both, the wily solitude which weaves its plots
> in the deepest caverns of the heart
> and the universe.
>
> —Attila József, "Ode"[1]

Passion and Passivity according to Jean-Luc Marion

In an essay written in 1994, which, however, remained unpublished until 2002, Marion addresses the issue of the separation of the virtue of charity from the human passion of love, or more precisely, what he sees as the philosophically imposed division between love as a passion of the soul and intellectual love.[2] His stance towards the issue of love here is more theologi-

---

1. Attila József (1905–32), "Ode," in Kabdebo, *Attila József, Poems and Fragments*, 71. Thomas Kabdebo's translation.

2. Jean-Luc Marion, "What Love Knows," in Marion, *Prolegomena to Charity*, 153–69.

cal than philosophical; what he attempts in this essay could be described as a theological prolegomenon to his later phenomenological treatment of love in *The Erotic Phenomenon* (2003).[3] The focus of his attention is the greatest of the theological virtues, charity, which, Marion claims, has remained "profoundly misunderstood by modern Christianity." What is the reason for such a misinterpretation? Interestingly, in Marion's analysis of charity one finds already, even if in an embryonic manner, all the major themes and central insights of his later phenomenological treatment of erotic love. On his view, love (and therefore charity) has been fatally misunderstood both as a passion and as an intellectual craving for the good, since neither traditional aspect allows for an understanding that would do justice to the true otherness of the other, the real alterity of the beloved one. Love, taken as a passion, in the Cartesian sense of "a perception provoked by the body that affects the soul," in Marion's view, runs into the circularity of solipsism and a closed-off subjectivity: it turns out to be ultimately nothing other than a perception from one's body, in one's soul and toward one's soul. Due to the lack of a real external end, there is no meaningful way out of such a circular subjective movement. Moreover, among all passions, love is the most exposed to the danger of solipsistic circularity, once it is understood in Descartes's wake as a passion "which consists in considering oneself as forming a part of a whole, of which the beloved furnishes the other part."[4] As Marion contends, no matter what variations one conceives within love as a structure of the part and the whole—whether one is seen as constituting the greater part of the whole, as in the case of love of commodities ("love of the bottle, of a woman taken by force, or of hoarded money"), or one is viewed as the lesser part, as in the case of the love for God or spouse or children—the same underlying pattern emerges: the other over against the *ego* is construed in terms of an object irrespective of the fact of whether it is inanimate or a living person or even God. All these loves are indeed similar, as Descartes implies, because all of them issue from the same act of the will of the loving subject who, in all cases, does nothing other than unify himself to an object. In such a perspective, one loves nothing that differs from him. For, on the one hand, love as a circular subjective passion is incapable of conferring real knowledge of the other, and, on the other hand, love as a unitive act of the will is ultimately irrational, because it is a

---

3. Derek J. Morrow suggests that one can trace a clear trajectory of Marion's thought of love articulated in three stages: "first the theological prolegomenon (*Prolegomena to Charity*) prepared by the phenomenological prolegomenon (*Being Given*), which then in turn prepared the properly phenomenological treatment (*Le phénomène érotique*)." Morrow, "The Love 'Without Being,' Part Two," 507.

4. Marion, "What Love Knows," 156.

passion, turning towards any kind of object without real knowledge or rational consideration. Love, understood as a passion and seen through such a lens, is unable to deliver the other as other precisely because it can make no room for the other within a closed system of subject-object dichotomy and a circular epistemological movement starting from the willing subject and incorporating an external object into its subjectivity.

If love, traditionally understood as a passion, proves to be too aporetic to be a helpful aid in thinking the phenomenon of true charity, its counterpart, traditionally labeled as intellectual or rational love (of God), is a no less problematic notion. Marion goes as far as to argue that it is a profoundly contradictory concept since it cannot meaningfully reconcile the sphere of knowing and the sphere of affection or will. While it is claimed to consist in union with a rational object within the horizon of representation and of understanding in the manner of a fundamental craving for the sovereign good, it is not very clear in what way such a rational knowledge is capable of effectuating the union of love. Here, once again, the otherness of love and the otherness of the one beloved are compromised for representation is unable to accede to something other than itself or even to another person. Consequently, the idea of intellectual love does not allow for serious talk of love.

If the dichotomy between love as a passion and intellectual, rational love leads to an impasse and prevents fruitful thought concerning love, could one find a more suitable dichotomy instead, one more faithful to the otherness of love over against knowledge? Marion is convinced that all traditionally conceived dichotomies (the one between *erōs* and *agapē*, the one between self-respect and self-love, or between self-respect and disinterested love) invariably lead to the same impasse and are useless for a meaningful discourse on love. What is needed is the re-unification of different types of love and the joining of love and charity, without repeating the traditional distinctions that have proved to be entirely futile. Over against what he sees as an unwholesome distinction between knowledge and love, Marion announces a new agenda directed towards thinking love itself as knowledge—knowledge that alone is capable of knowing the other as such.

How does love know? Or, in Marion's words, which apparently contain a playful and covert allusion to the Thomistic concept of love as willing the good to the other, one may ask: "What exactly is meant here by willing with a good will to recognize the flesh of the other?"[5] According to Marion, love does not know through an objectifying gaze. Love's knowledge is different from the rational representation of the other to a transcendental subject; love knows

---

5. Ibid., 163.

in an entirely different way. It is at this point that the pivotal role of the body enters Marion's reflection. More accurately, what enters the picture is not the objectifiable body but the lived experience of the non-objectifiable flesh, as this has been explored and conceptualized by Michel Henry, to whom Marion is admittedly indebted on this theme. In the essay, "What Love Knows," Marion does not elaborate his own distinctive concept of flesh in great detail (he will do that in the phenomenological analyses of *The Erotic Phenomenon*). However, some important features are outlined already at this earlier stage of inquiry. He registers the presence of a curiously abstract eroticism in contemporary culture where "we love by sight," just as we know, in an objectifying and disembodied manner; without real bodily involvement, that is, without letting ourselves be affected by the other person. Genuine eroticism, on the contrary, does not love the same way as one knows; it loves truly through the flesh; it is embodied or, more precisely, is enfleshed. All this is possible because one's body emerges as a phenomenon distinct from the world of objects on account of its capability to feel not only other objects, but feel itself feeling: "it feels aware of itself, experiences itself, and affects itself first of all."[6] The body in its status of flesh is, on the one hand, truly affected by the other, and, on the other hand, also returns such affection to the one loved, giving flesh to the other. Marion does not elaborate here on this issue, which he will only resume in *The Erotic Phenomenon*. What he does, however, in this earlier treatment is to reflect on the erotic aspect of (theological) charity, which he sees as analogous to the movement of the erotic flesh. This idea is more assumed than openly stated at this stage. Nevertheless, Marion thinks in terms of his major key notions, the gaze, the icon, and distance, and contends that the essential feature of charity must be seen in its kenotic function, for it alone opens the space where the other can appear as other in the manner of creation where God opens to the world and makes space for what is "unlike" God. Just as God presents creation with existence by withdrawal, so, too, charity makes space for the other by accepting his counter-gaze, which resists objectification and affects one with a true otherness coming from elsewhere. Marion insists that all forms of love display one and the same logic, which hinges on a crucial decision: one either accepts the other's gaze or refuses it, and "there is no other decision for such a determination" because all forms of love, "[f]riendship, the most carnal or the most sentimental love and the most brutal desire, just like the most disinterested benevolence and the most perfect charity, play out only according to this singular game."[7] It is the same idea of

---

6. Marion refers here to Michel Henry's *L'essence de la manifestation* and *Phénoménologie matérielle*. See ibid., 161, note 6.

7. Ibid., 166.

the underlying unity of logic inherent in every form of love that Marion will take up in his phenomenology of erotic love, together with the idea that love offers knowledge beyond rational knowledge, that is to say, that it represents a "greater rationality." In this manner, Marion's agenda is twofold. On the one hand, he aims to develop a renewed and unified concept of love based on the body; on the other hand, he seeks to couch such a concept in a renewed understanding of the relationship between love and knowledge. Let us focus first on the former issue, the phenomenology of embodied love.

If love is neither an irrational passion nor a rational union with the divine good, what is it then? We hope to find an answer in Marion's *The Erotic Phenomenon*, which offers a brilliant phenomenological account of bodily erotic love. Commentators on Marion's account unanimously note that what one has here is a real *tour de force* of the phenomenological method, one that gives a brilliant and forceful conceptualization of what has so far rarely been captured in philosophical discourse, namely, sexual love. Marion has truly broken the silence prevailing over this theme and has integrated into serious reflection a long-neglected segment of formative human experience.[8] His book recapitulates and further develops all of the major themes of his overall project (e.g., the idea of saturated phenomena and especially the face and the flesh, a critique of metaphysics and the development of an alternative rationality, a radical understanding of the gift and donation) and, as he himself confesses, it crowns a long process of reflection that started back in 1977 with *The Idol and Distance*. Marion in fact sees his entire career in retrospect, and in the light of this new book, as being in some way devoted to the development of this theme, even if only in an indirect manner: "All the books I have published since then [1977] bear the mark, explicit or hidden, of this concern"—he maintains in the preface to *The Erotic Phenomenon*.[9]

"What is love?," however, is not the question Marion asks in his phenomenological analysis of erotic love. In fact, faithful to his overall philosophical project, he explicitly argues for the inadequacy of approaching love

---

8. Thomas Finnegan, for example, thinks that Marion's *The Erotic Phenomenon* is "a fine example of how the phenomenological approach can articulate meaningful and perceptive descriptions of phenomena that in the hands of reductive materialists are reduced to utilitarian and chemical calculations." Finnegan, Review of *The Erotic Phenomenon*, 59. Paul J. Griffiths too acknowledges the exceptional mastery of Marion's analyses: "He is a master of that method [the phenomenological], and the result is an analysis of erotic love of unparalleled precision and depth. The depiction he gives of the erotic phenomenon is fundamentally convincing, and readers will find their own loves illuminated and questioned. All that is rare and valuable." Griffiths, Review of *The Erotic Phenomenon*, 26.

9. Marion, *The Erotic Phenomenon*, 10.

from a metaphysical essentialistic perspective; instead, he proceeds in a counter-Cartesian manner where the *ego* is not constituted by the certainty of thinking but receives assurance from a certainty of loving. Marion aims to liberate love from the derivative status of feelings, which Descartes had relegated to an accidental function of the thinking subject in his famous dictum: "I am a thinking thing, that is to say one which doubts, which affirms, which denies, which understands few things, which is ignorant of many, which wills, which does not will, which imagines, too, and which even feels."[10] For Marion, on the contrary, loving is not a secondary modality of the human being with respect to thinking, but is his most original mode of existing, that which defines him much more aptly than cogitation by rational thought. By asking the question of what love is, one regards love from a metaphysical stance governed by a language that accesses things in terms of rational logic and an intellectual objectivity. Marion's concern is to show that love follows an entirely different logic, only visible from within its own mode of operation and concealed from an objectifying rational gaze.

The right question, therefore, to ask with regard to love concerns not its reality as an object of thought but its mode of operation as an autonomous modality of knowing, one that is not subordinate to the power of rational thought. What one must do is to free the concept of love from metaphysical assumptions and see it as it is and in its pure phenomenality. Therefore, the right question concerning love is the one of "how love loves?" Within the economy of love (which is at the same time one of "radical gift" in Marion's scheme), one becomes a "radical lover" by leaving an economy of reciprocity and entering an economy of prevenient love. Marion's lover speaks in the first-person singular as someone involved in, and affected by, love. Self-involvement is a prerequisite for approaching this most originary phenomenon and so discourse concerning love must necessarily be auto-implicative. The would-be lover proceeds by an amorous monologue, asking a series of questions of which "Does anyone out there love me?" is the first. Marion is convinced that the idea of self-love is a conceptual absurdity and that a self-sufficient subject is capable of doing nothing other than hate itself. Taking issue with a long tradition of making self-love a natural paradigm of the love of others, Marion maintains that self-hatred is more originary than love of self, because love requires a real other who alone can deliver one to oneself and which a single subject can never adequately simulate. Moreover, since all others who could give love to someone are in the same situation of needing love from out there, a better question, according to Marion, would

10. Marion refers to Adam and Tannery, *Oeuvres de Descartes* VII, 34, lines 18–21: "*Ego sum res cogitans, id est dubitans, affirmans, negans, pauca intelligens, multa ignorans, volens, nolens, imaginans quoque et sentiens.*" Ibid., 6–7.

be, "Can I love first?" This alone gives assurance of one's act of true loving and leaves the inappropriate sphere of the economy of reciprocity. It is only then—after taking the risk of loving first—that one can ask about reciprocity. This issues in the third question, "Do you love me?" These are then the major questions that guide Marion's meditations on erotic love. These questions do not remain unanswered. They receive a response from the loved one: "Here I am," "Come," "You loved me first." In this sense the monologue is turned into a rudimentary dialogue "in between" two lovers that, however, is narrated from the perspective of just one of them.

I have deliberately stripped my brief survey of the major questions put into the mouth of the lover by Marion, of the complex anti-Cartesian claims in which they are couched and that mark an alternative way of establishing certainty (in Marion's terms, "assurance") other than the way followed by the thinking subject. What interests us here is Marion's understanding of passivity and the significance of the flesh for a renewed concept of "one-way" love, which is invariably erotic, even in its agapaic mode.

In order to answer the question "How love loves?" one must first seek a response to a preliminary question, namely, "How does one become a lover?" It seems that, in Marion's framework, the lover is distinguished from the thinker by his total self-involvement in the loving act. The lover becomes visible only within the "erotic reduction," which is governed by the radicality of the non-reciprocal gift and a non-objectifying stance. On the one hand, to become a lover, one needs to do nothing other than decide by one's free will to love in advance; on the other hand, the lover is distinguished and individualized by his essential passivity. These are the two pivotal claims upon which Marion's reflection rests. In attempting to reconcile the two seemingly contradictory statements, he develops his own distinctive notion of "passion," one which is not characterized as an irrational movement coming from an elsewhere to the consciousness of the lover, but one that arises consequent to a decision affecting the totality of one's inner life. If, as in common experience, falling in love, as an event, or being in love, as a state, impose themselves on someone by powerful force, how can one maintain the coherence of the claim that to start loving depends entirely on the lover or that it is the lover who decides to love in advance and without reciprocity? As Marion contends: "I have the sovereign freedom to make myself a lover—to make myself amorous. I become amorous simply because I want to, without any constraint, according to my sole, naked desire."[11] Marion apparently has recourse to the ancient Stoic idea (or one of its later appropriations) of "first movement" or "pre-emotion," insisting

---

11. Ibid., 93.

that the experience of involuntary emotion does not yet mean becoming amorous. One becomes loving only at the point where one consents to such an involuntary emotion, when one ratifies it. All this boils down to the ancient Stoic claim that involuntary motions of the soul are not yet emotions. The latter only come about as a consequence of the conscious assent of the mind.[12] This idea then enables Marion to establish love as an auto-affection in a phenomenological manner: one who is amorous is conscious of his state as loving; his love is capable of reflecting upon itself. Distantly echoing Aquinas (and also Augustine whose authority Aquinas acknowledges on this matter), Marion envisages the lover as a person who "loves loving" and whose conscious experience of "loving to love" can therefore be a matter of decision.[13] The lover who decides to love loving does so according to his sovereign will and no one else can interfere in such a decision: "My being in love with her does not depend on her, but rather on me, alone. And that is enough."[14]

However, and it is at this point that the traditional passion-aspect of love seems to enter the picture, the "assented" decision to love loving affects one deeply in one's inner being. It does not arise as a subjective emotion "that would be individual and prereflexive," but invades one as an "affective tonality that is powerful, deep and durable, and which, little by little or quite brutally, will contaminate the totality of my inner life: not only my emotional but also my intellectual life, not only my conscious but also my unconscious life."[15] Such a lasting and all-pervasive affective tonality is termed a lived experience of consciousness in the language of phenomenology. Marion insists that love, that is, the affective tonality of loving to love is not an emotion; neither is it a passion or a delirium; rather, it is a lived experience unrestricted to one's subjectivity because it "indissolubly involves the other as its intentional reference."[16] With this move, the stage is set for the other to enter the one-way radical economy of love.

In what way can the other affect the lover without being reduced to a function of the lover's subjective consciousness? Marion here restates

12. See Knuuttila, *Emotions*, 64–66.

13. In the *Summa Theologica*, Aquinas addresses the question "Whether we should love charity out of charity?" and in his reply he relies on Augustine's claim that "He that loves his neighbor, must in consequence, love love itself." (Augustine, *The Trinity*, 8.8.12). According to Aquinas, love is capable of reflecting on itself "by reason of its own species" since it is "a spontaneous movement of the lover to the beloved, wherefore from the moment a man loves, he loves himself to love." See *ST* IIaIIae.25.2.

14. Marion, *The Erotic Phenomenon*, 93.

15. Ibid., 95.

16. Ibid., 95.

his earlier observations concerning the "face" ("le visage," in apparent conversation with Levinas), which represents real alterity by offering the counter-intentionality of a gaze to the one looking at it. The face brings an unpredictable signification that imposes itself from without as a real exteriority and demands a respectful distance. Due to such genuine exteriority and non-reducable distance, the phenomenon of the other keeps its distinct alterity and offers the gift of signification, which, however is unconstitutable by the lover and therefore is truly exterior to him.[17] The encounter of the lover and the loved one constitutes what Marion calls (in the manner of his other "saturated phenomena") a "crossed phenomenon," one where the two distinct intuitions of the lovers are fixed by a single signification. In phenomenological terms, what is established between the two lovers, that is, through the joint experience of their erotic love for one another, is a unique phenomenon described by Marion as "the play of a crossed exchange of significations."[18] Or, in a less technical jargon that captures the experience of sexual union in a forceful manner, Marion describes the crossed phenomenon of the union of the lovers in terms of an interplay of distance and communion reflected in their reciprocal gazes: "We commune, but within the distance of our two fleshes. They cross, through the same erotic reduction, in a unique amorous phenomenon—each appearing in the other without ever intermingling. The crossing of our flesh in our suspended gazes renders our common soul finally apparent—at least to us, the lovers."[19]

What is crucial for Marion's understanding of the crossed phenomenon of erotic love is the fact that it comes about under the phenomenon of the flesh through which, in a covert biblical allusion, the lover becomes flesh of the loved one's flesh: "I become flesh in her flesh, flesh *of* her flesh."[20] What is at stake here is a reconsidered understanding of passivity and a specific concept of flesh as distinguished from "body." Or rather, there is a threefold distinction between body, flesh, and eroticized flesh. The body, an

17. Derek J. Morrow convincingly argues that Marion's concept of distance draws in many respects on Hans Urs von Balthasar's concept of distance within a trinitarian perspective. See Morrow, "The Love 'Without Being,' Part One," 281–98; and Morrow, "The Love 'Without Being,' Part Two," 493–511.

18. Marion writes: "The two *egos* are accomplished as lovers, and mutually allow their respective phenomena to appear, not of course according to an imaginary fusional logic—by exchanging or sharing a common intuition—which would abolish the distance between them, but by assuring one another reciprocally of a signification come from elsewhere—by lending themselves to the play of a crossed exchange of significations—thus firmly consecrating the distance within them." *The Erotic Phenomenon*, 105.

19. Ibid., 127.

20. Ibid., 119.

object among objects in its physicality among things, receives the status of flesh by virtue of the fact that it feels what is around it; it is affected by what is at hand. Moreover, not only does it feel outside objects, but it also feels itself feeling, giving rise in this manner to the experience of one's feeling oneself feeling the world around. The crucial question is, however, how can one feel the flesh of the other? What happens when the flesh that feels itself feeling experiences the impact of another flesh? How does one distinguish between feeling a body and feeling a flesh? While bodies resist the feeling touch of the flesh by their rigidity and impenetrability, the flesh does not display such resistance. On the contrary, it withdraws under the impact of another flesh, making room in this manner for the other to "enter" it "by not resisting, by withdrawing, by allowing itself to be stripped of its impenetrability, by suffering being penetrated."[21] It is within the space yielded by another flesh that one is given one's own flesh as in a "radicalized incarnation." The body, which proved to be flesh, is here turned into eroticized flesh within the sphere of the erotic reduction and in the experience of erotic bodily love.[22] The two lovers, feeling at the same time one another through the flesh, feeling themselves feeling and also feeling themselves being felt by the other, mutually make room for one another and accomplish the reciprocal eroticization of one another's flesh.

And here we come upon Marion's reconsidered concept of passivity. In accordance with the characteristics of the eroticized flesh, which actively receives itself through the acceptance of another flesh, the lover's passivity differs from passivity in the world of objects: "For my passivity as a lover evidently has nothing in common with the inertia of the nonreactive mineral that feels nothing; nor even with the passivity of the animate, which only reacts to programmed arousals, because it poorly feels."[23] The passivity of the lover develops in conjunction with his activity and is no longer opposed to activity. What one has here is at the same time the double activity and double passivity of the lovers. Passivity, as active non-resistance to the flesh of the other, goes hand in hand with activity, which is the result of the acceptance of the non-resistance of the other. Marion argues that within the erotic reduction, where passivity is bound up with the phenomenon of the flesh, the rules construed by metaphysics do not apply; activity of a flesh here does not occur to the detriment of the other's activity, "but through

21. Ibid., 118.

22. Marion holds that when one leaves the sphere of eroticization, one's eroticized flesh does not turn into a body but keeps the status of a lover's flesh by virtue of one's decision to remain a lover. Therefore, "[t]he gap between flesh and eroticized flesh repeats the gap between the flesh and the body." Ibid., 136.

23. Ibid., 112.

their double passivity." This is because "the growth of one is made as the passivity of the other provokes it; and the passivity of the one is deepened as the augmentation of the other allows."[24] In sum, passivity, for Marion, signifies the impact the other exerts upon the lover whereby both the other and oneself are received in a passively active acceptance. In this way, the sharp divide between passivity and activity is blurred. Passivity no longer means one's undergoing the impact of an outside force, but is aided by a concomitant active attachment to a passive and therefore affectable state.

It is on account of such originary passivity that one experiences finitude. Finitude, as Marion argues, does not concern the flesh as such, but appears in the eroticized flesh which eroticizes itself, under the impact of another flesh, on its own initiative and without one's will. Within such auto-eroticization, one's passivity is at once active reception of the impact of the other and is passive non-resistance to an outside force. Finitude is then erotic finitude whereby one discovers himself finite because one experiences one's flesh acting on its own accord by virtue of the fact that it is affected by another flesh. Marion compares the finitude disclosed by the erotic phenomenon to the metaphysical concept of finitude and concludes that erotic finitude is primary to a simply derived finitude in one's faculties, going much deeper and reaching as far as the inner core of the lover. While metaphysical finitude is assigned to the sensible aspect of knowing and regards sense knowledge as passive and receptive over against intellectual knowledge, which is active, the finitude disclosed through the eroticized flesh does not concern just one of the faculties, but determines the root of one's entire being. Such finitude is conditioned by another flesh, another person, who in this sense precedes one and defines one from an elsewhere to one's interiority.

The Spirituality of Enfleshed Love

Obviously, Marion's account of the encounter of two fleshes is far from being materialistic or physicalist. He approaches the erotic phenomenon from what we may term a spiritual perspective where bodily *erōs* is never simply seen as striving for the fulfillment of sexual desire. What is at stake here is not simple biological facts, but their philosophical significance for our self-understanding as "loving animals," as creatures distinguished from the rest of living beings and the inanimate world by our sole capacity to love. The radical immanence of the flesh is shown here to reveal an unexpected transcendence; nothing here is simply instinctively vital or insensitively

24. Ibid, 119.

automatic. The passive finitude of the eroticized flesh becomes a site of revelation where one's spiritual glory shines forth. At the peak of enjoyment the beloved is, as it were, transfigured. Marion even speaks in terms of a "glorified body" that resembles Christ's resurrected body.[25] The "accomplished transcendence" of the loved one makes her entire flesh become a face that reflects transcendental glory. In this manner, the erotic crossing of the fleshes becomes the site *par excellence* of the disclosure of one's most intimate spirituality. Bodily sexual love is portrayed here with irresistible mastery as genuinely human and even transcendentally mystical. However, the idea of mystical union, already marks a further step towards the "spirituality" of erotic love.

Marion's logic of one-way erotic love demands that it not be restricted to the specific circumstances of sexual union but be extended to every kind of loving relationship, such as the one between parents and children, love between friends, and even love between humans and God. How is it possible? How can the situation of the erotic crossing of the fleshes be transposed onto the plane of non-sexual love? Can it keep its most pivotal characteristics outside sexual union? What is the common feature of sexual and non-sexual (and yet erotic) love? Were the crossing of eroticized fleshes a pure matter of physical contact, that is, a matter of touching, there would be no way out of such a tangible encounter. However, and this is the pivotal move Marion makes, erotic union is preceded, accompanied, and followed by the verbal affirmation of the union of fleshes, namely, erotic speech. Marion makes speech the pivot that mediates between sexual and non-sexual love. Speech performs a function analogous with the flesh: just as the flesh of the lover—which gives flesh to another through the reception of her flesh in his own—speech too is capable of eroticizing and giving flesh to another through verbal activity. The difference between them lies in the manner in which contact is realized. While the two fleshes actually touch one another through physical contact, words likewise touch the loved one in a different way. Words affect her and move her deeply within, effectuating the same accomplishment of the (non-sexual) eroticization of her flesh. In order to understand Marion's analogy between fleshly eroticization and the verbal giving of the flesh, one must first consider what role he assigns to speech on the primary, sexual level of love.

Speech within the erotic reduction is first and foremost non-descriptive or non-enunciative. As Marion contends, the experience of sexual

---

25. "Look at the Risen Christ (and not always only the cadaver of the Crucified) on the Isenheim altarpiece, whose face, except for the eyes, whitens and almost disappears in the glory that submerges his flesh—thenceforward definitively living, irresistible for having known *not* to resist anything, even the worst death." See ibid, 127.

union is an "erased phenomenon"; it leaves no trace and ultimately presents nothing to verbalize: "Of eroticization, this erased phenomenon, one can say nothing, even to oneself, even from lover to lover. The words are lacking."[26] Notwithstanding the lack of communicable content, the lovers do not stay silent, but speak a language that does not predicate, state, or demonstrate anything. The only function of speech within the context of the erotic reduction, according to Marion, is to stimulate arousal, that is, the arousal of oneself and also of the other in order to give flesh to one another. Accordingly, speech here is non-deictic and non-predicative, but is performative, namely, it accomplishes what it describes. Marion goes so far as to draw an analogy between the sacramental use of language and the words of love-making, stating that "the lover makes love by saying it *ex opere operato*, without regard for his capacities or even for his intentions."[27] One's loving is realized, then, through one's amorous words. If the words of love have no specific content, what do they convey? Marion posits a sharp separation between the sphere of love and the everyday sphere of our relation to the world by insisting that the lovers' words are freed of every obligation to make statements concerning the world—their only aim being the provocation of the eroticization of the other. Consequently, the vocabulary of making love consists of "marginal, eccentric or even senseless words," that is, the obscene, the puerile, and the words of excess. These three lexicons are likened to the three stages of mystical speech: the affirmative (obscenity), the negative (puerility), and the hyperbolic mode (the words expressing the excess of union, such as, "Come!" "Here I am!" "Again!").[28] All three are indispensable for erotic speech and therefore it is not only the obscene and the childish but also "the language of the spiritual union of man with God" which together constitute the performative function of the words of love-making.

All this conceded, nonetheless the question of the transition from the sphere of fleshly love to the sphere of non-sexual love remains. What is the exact point of transition in Marion's scheme? In order to generalize the import of the specific experience of sexual union, Marion needs to unleash it from that limited experience and argue for a structural likeness between the sexual mode of giving flesh to someone and the non-sexual way of love. He does this by introducing another distinction (in addition to the one between

---

26. Ibid, 144.

27. Ibid, 147.

28. Marion suggests that the speech expressing excess can be seen as in common with mystical theology, just as the exclamation "Come!" is "to the letter, the final word of the Book of Revelation and thus of mystical theology, which is rooted there." Ibid, 149.

the body, the flesh, and the eroticized flesh) between eroticization as such (that is, in general) and the specific automatic eroticization of the flesh. By relegating automatic eroticization to the domain of sexuality alone, the stage is set for the appearance of the free (because not sexually stimulated and therefore not automatic) eroticization of the other, which, in this case, is done through speech alone, without physical (erotic) contact. What is such speech like? Such speech, like the loving flesh, is capable of bridging the ineradicable distance between the lovers. For, as Marion explains, the distance remains, notwithstanding the close physical contact of crossed fleshes, and so it is not the juxtaposition of physical bodies that matters. Making love to someone, taken in the original broader sense, means showing that one is in love with someone. Such showing is also done by words. It is on these grounds that Marion envisages the free and non-sexual eroticization of one's flesh by way of speech alone: "just, as it is not enough to enter into contact to make love, in order to make love I do not always, or first of all, or necessarily, need to enter into contact with the other; I can just as well give her her flesh, and thus have her experience my non-resistance (and reciprocally), by speaking to her. I make love *first* by speaking."[29]

What is the difference between the words of sexual love-making and the ones of non-sexual eroticization? Disappointingly, Marion does not elaborate on this point in any useful detail. The function he assigns to such an amorous language is nothing more than a restatement of what had been established with regard to the words uttered during fleshly communion. The lovers speak of nothing, stating nothing concerning the world or even themselves. Non-referential speech here has but one function: it is intended to touch and affect the other and through such metaphorical touching, give her flesh. One registers a certain hesitation in Marion's argument that, on the one hand, refers back to the idea of the non-deictic and non-predicative function of speech employed during fleshly love-making ("speech which . . . says nothing of nothing, predicates no predicate or substratum"), and, on the other, allows for a certain predicative content regarding the other and what is between them ("afterward, my speech will no longer speak to the other only of herself, but little by little, of the interval between the other and me, of what is between us [*l'entre-nous*], of this non-thing, unreal and invisible, wherein we stay with one another, live and breathe").[30] Then, in a hastily made and cursorily outlined transition, such speech is extended to all kinds of non-sexual loves, such as, friendship, the love between child and parent, and the love of man for God. This idea is taken up at the end of

29. Ibid, 181–82.
30. Ibid., 182.

the book when friendship is said to represent a "shorter way" to the erotic reduction whereby free eroticization of the flesh is accomplished through speech, without, however, climactic enjoyment.[31] Nevertheless we are not provided any further indication concerning the content of such amicable speech. Provided that one subscribes to Marion's idea of eroticizing language, one question, however, remains: What is meant here by touching without contact and what exactly is touched?

If amorous speech touches, moves, and affects the other without physical contact, what do the lover's words touch? How can one give flesh to the other through speech alone? One may recognize the experience Marion appeals to, that is, the idea of eroticizing speech, as genuinely authentic: loving words are known indeed to affect one, invigorating one's entire being, making of a languishing body enlivened and loving flesh. Through such love-conveying speech, one's innermost being is affected, the very centre of one's human nature in his heart of hearts. Is not making love to someone through speech intended to arouse one's feelings, to appeal to one's emotions, to win one's lasting affection? Does not a declaration of love include playing upon one's heartstrings? Is not the lover's oath safeguarded by the sincerity of his feelings towards the loved one? Does not talk concerning what is between the lovers [Marion's *l'entre nous*] consist in the articulation of sentiments, and an attentive shared listening to the passionate voice of one's heart? Is not love after all a passion, an emotion, a feeling of the heart?

In the endeavor to establish love as an alternative, greater rationality and a non-derivative mode of human existence, Marion seems to have overlooked the important phenomenon of the true emotionality of love. By briefly classifying it as an affective tonality and a phenomenologically-understood, lived experience of consciousness, however, he does not do justice to the traditional passion-aspect of love. Despite his brilliant analyses of a reconsidered experience of passivity, the dynamic emotional dimension of love is suppressed. What one is given here is a curiously passionless portrayal of the phenomenon of erotic love, one that faithfully captures sense perception and physical feeling and is also insightful concerning the way

31. "[W]hat exactly does the erotic phenomenon lack in friendship? Contrary to idle appearances, friendship does not lack the eroticization of the flesh, and it does not remain at the abstraction of the oath; in friendship, too, I can receive my flesh from the friend, who gives it to me without having it, as lover; the friend also embraces me and holds me (but also the mother and the child, the father and the son, etc.). Here it is simply that the eroticization of the flesh does not go so far as climactic enjoyment, and thus is not exposed to suspension. Neither is there any ambiguity to fear in such an eroticization of the flesh without climax: I already know that eroticization can remain free, or put another way, that the flesh can allow itself to be eroticized without the immediate touch of another flesh, through speech alone." See ibid., 220.

love knows, yet one that is without emotion beyond the sensation of affected flesh. In my view, the ultimately unbridgeable gap between physical contact and verbal love-making in Marion's account is symptomatic of a deeper insufficiency, which I would describe as a lack of mediation between the vital and the spiritual of which (in a Ricoeurian manner) the eminent zone would be the heart, that is, the realm of human affectivity. The emotions, which arise in the body and through the body, are nonetheless "spiritual"; they are born from the impact made by words and affect one's thought in turn. Therefore, it is the median zone of the heart where one's free eroticization through the words of the lover is eminently accomplished. In this median region, what comes by way of the flesh is spiritualized and what is received through words is turned into fleshly emotion. Apart from being playfully obscene, childish, or mystical, the speech of the lovers conveys emotions: a sense of tenderness and attraction, attachment and delight—they inform about the lovable sweetness of the loved one and the joy over his delightful presence. Love does speak and what it says is not merely nonpredicative; love does not simply use words to say nothing. On the contrary, the words of love are performative, that is, are capable of making what they say, because they do have reference to a "substratum," they do demonstrate, predicate, and state something concerning the world and the lovers, they do have a referential content, which is expressed in terms of feeling (and yet not independent of thought).

Without such mediation, the distinction between the flesh and the freely eroticized flesh ultimately is threatened with total separation. For if one can equally effectively give flesh to another through words, it is not very clear any longer in what sense flesh must be understood here. If there is no physical contact involved, the flesh given to the other can only be conceived metaphorically. But then, is the flesh needed after all? Could one not conceive the giving of flesh in entirely spiritual terms, in the traditional manner of the intellectual love between friends or the one between man and God? Marion's univocal, one-way concept of love on this point fails to provide a sufficient basis for unification, and so his account is practically unequipped for the danger of implicitly repeating the traditional division between bodily and spiritual love.[32] Moreover, his concept of love is one-

---

32. Werner G. Jeanrond, for example, registers the danger of an unwholesome dichotomy between flesh and body in Marion's account. See Werner G. Jeanrond, "Love Enlightened: The Promises and Ambiguities of Love," in Boeve et al., *Faith in the Enlightenment?*, 269–91, and also in Jeanrond, *A Theology of Love*, 155–61. John Milbank also thinks that Marion maintains a dangerous gap between body and flesh: "in keeping with the thought of Michel Henry, Marion insists on a strict dualism between the body and the flesh—a Cartesianism no longer of extension versus thought, but of exterior versus interior matter." John Milbank, "The Gift and the Mirror: On the Philosophy of

sidedly voluntaristic without, however, leaving space for the otherness of feelings or the surprising experience of exteriorly motivated emotion. The lover who falls in love according to his sovereign will and without any constraint, loving no matter whether the loved one is lovable, strangely seems to ignore the enjoyable and pleasing bliss of love. His impassive and heroic good will "to recognize the flesh of the other" can hardly be conceived without giving not only flesh but also a rejoicing heart to the other. In an effort to establish love as liberated from the traditionally derivative modality of feeling, Marion has entirely stripped it of emotionality, turning it into a kind of counter-rationality that knows but does not feel and hardly says anything. Certainly, as has been observed by several commentators, what phenomenology lacks is the hermeneutical element. This is why, within the context of the phenomenological method, one is ultimately unable to discern what love wants to say.[33] However, without such hermeneutics, one is likewise unable to account for the different degrees of one-way erotic love. Without a metaphorical extension of the concrete experience of the flesh, one cannot conceive of the unity of one-way erotic love either, and the phenomenon of the erotic crossing of fleshes stays oddly irrelevant for non-sexual "spiritual" forms of love.

And here we might bring Ricoeur into the conversation again. In an essay entitled "Love and Justice," Ricoeur, like Marion, contrasts what we may term the rationality of love and the rationality of justice, highlighting, in his own distinctive style, their essential disproportionality.[34] Steering a middle course between the two extremes of exaggerated exaltation and unthinking sentimentality, he suggests that one should listen to what love says in a language shaped by the biblical tradition, where love's discourse displays a certain strangeness or oddness. Strangeness results from the fact that love uses the poetic language of praise (just as in 1 Cor 13) and an odd poetic form of the imperative ("Love me!"—in the commandment of love). These two types of discourses of love create the third way of love as a feeling, and it is on account of his description of the feeling aspect of love that one may find Ricoeur illuminating.

Love," in Hart, *Counter-Experiences*, 266.

33. As Stuart Jesson remarks, "Marion has always insisted, against his critics, that his work remains true to phenomenology and as such conforms to its rule of describing appearances in their own terms, without reference to prior categories or assumptions. This commitment leads to an obvious conundrum: how do we discern what love 'wants to say' from among the great diversity of phenomena that may bear its name?" Stuart Jesson, Review *The Erotic Phenomenon*, 116.

34. Paul Ricoeur, "Love and Justice," in Jeanrond and Rike, *Radical Pluralism and Truth*, 187–202.

What he suggests is that the injunction "Love me!" launches a series of related emotions such as pleasure versus pain, satisfaction versus discontent, rejoicing versus distress, beatitude versus melancholy. Moreover, love not only engenders a wide variety of feelings "like some vast field of gravitation"; it also organizes these feelings according to an "ascending and descending spiral," that is, from the most carnal up to the most spiritual affects. Ricoeur holds that such feelings appear also on the linguistic plane and they become manifest in an extensive field of analogies among all of the affective modes of love, by mutually signifying one another. The various affective modes are connected by analogy and accompanied by the linguistic process of metaphorization whereby erotic love is capable of signifying more than itself. The fact that feelings themselves are analogically connected and that metaphor repeats this analogical process on the linguistic plane (by signifying more than itself), according to Ricoeur, point to the same phenomenon he names "the substantive tropology of love," that is, on the one hand, the real analogy between the feelings associated with *erōs* and the ones surrounding *agapē*, and, on the other, "the power of *erōs* to signify *agapē* and to put it into words."[35]

Apparently, what we have here is Ricoeur's own distinctive idea of the unity of love, which unfortunately remains only cursorily developed in the essay. Nevertheless the gist of his argument can be clearly inferred even on the basis of these brief remarks: both as a phenomenon and as a concomitant linguistic content, love is an essentially continuous experience by virtue of the fact that its various forms and stages are analogous to one another. All forms of love signify more than what they actually realize and, through such a surplus of significations, they are mutually interconnected, both semantically and experientially. This is why bodily *erōs* is capable of signifying more than itself and becomes a powerful means to express spiritual agapaic love as something different and yet inherently analogous to it. Ricoeur's account does not contradict Marion's concept of one-way love; however, it can be seen as supplying the missing hermeneutic element through the missing dimension of the mediating zone of feeling. Within the ascending and descending spiral of interconnected feelings of love, the body—and love expressed through the flesh—does not become superfluous for more spiritual stages because it serves as the *princeps analogatum*, as the basis and root of a vast field of analogies anchored in the phenomenon of erotic sexual love. Significations deployed by spiritual forms of love in turn provide an interpretative frame for a deeper understanding of the meaning of fleshly *erōs*. Love in this sense is not properly conceived as "univocal" (as

---

35. Ibid., 193.

Marion suggests) it is, rather, analogical in a Ricoeurian fashion. It is the analogical sameness of all modes of love that safeguards love's "univocity," that is, a basic continuity within all that is subsumed under the name of love.

In fact, Marion himself seems to appeal to the theological concept of analogy in insisting that God, who is named with the very name love, loves the same way as we do.[36] Similitude here is contrasted with a greater dissimilitude, which, however, does not consist in a different way of doing the same thing, but rather in doing the same by bringing it to infinite perfection. Marion ends his book on the (much-criticized) note that God is the first and therefore the paradigmatic lover: "God precedes us and transcends us, but first and above all in the fact that he loves us infinitely better than we love, and than we love him. God surpasses us as the best lover."[37] Whether this move from the human erotic phenomenon to God's love is justified, belongs to the difficult debate over the competence and frontiers of the phenomenological method. What is important for us here is the simple fact that the "univocity" of love becomes sheer equivocity if mediation and analogy are left out of the picture. Marion's brilliantly described, fleshly love is endangered by irredeemable autism without the mediating and analogical function of the heart. Yet, one must face here a further question: Can the heart be grasped at all phenomenologically? And what would be the place of feeling in a phenomenology of the erotic phenomenon?

These issues, to my knowledge, have not been addressed by Marion's critics and interpreters. However, one finds oblique statements and passing remarks that may be seen as accumulating evidence to the effect that the feeling aspect of love—due to an initial decision—is suppressed in Marion's approach. In the light of the foregoing, one may find several signs of such suppression. First, one registers Marion's insistence that love is neither an irrational passion nor a subjective emotion, but an affective tonality consequent upon a conscious decision of the will that builds up as a lived experience of consciousness, consisting of the affective tonality directed to loving to love. Such an affective tonality "contaminates" (a telling expression!) one's entire inner life: the emotions and the intellect as well, both the conscious and the unconscious sphere of the human person. While the idea that love rules over one's feelings and thoughts seems to highlight its traditional passion-like aspect, the equal insistence that loving depends on the sole decision of the lover and has nothing to do with involuntary affective

36. "God practices the logic of the erotic reduction as we do, with us, according to the same rite and following the same rhythm as us, to the point where we can even ask ourselves if we do not learn it from him, and no one else.... Except for an infinite difference. When God loves..., he simply loves infinitely better than do we." Ibid., 222.

37. Ibid., 222.

movements coming from a real exterior source turns love into a Stoically passionless emotion subsisting entirely in the intellectual/volitional mode. Second, Marion's renewed conception of passivity as active attachment to a passive and affectable state where the sharp contrast between passive and active is blurred, nonetheless does not do real justice to the traditional passion-aspect of love either, reducing the phenomenon of loving to a state of auto-affection and degrading the other as a simple function of the lover's lived experience of consciousness.[38] Third, Marion's *entre-nous*, the in-between of the lovers, expressed primarily through speech, lacks the dimension of feeling altogether and therefore also lacks real mediation between the lovers and between the flesh and the "spirit," between the vital and the spiritual. One has the impression that Marion only liberates love from the derivative mode of feeling at the price of cancelling love's feeling-aspect and making it meet the standards of impassive rationality.

However, should feeling have a place at all in a phenomenology of the erotic phenomenon? It seems to belong among the disputed questions of recent discussion. According to Claude Romano, there is nothing surprising in the fact that Marion's account of the erotic phenomenon lacks reference to the psychological categories of feeling, emotion, or drive.[39] Such an omission has to do with Marion's insistence that one take the claim concerning the unity of the erotic phenomenon seriously. It is because he intends to render love visible as a single and undivided phenomenon that Marion does not break it down to feelings, emotions, or desire. Despite the lack of vocabulary denoting "desire," "instinct," or "sexual drive," the corresponding phenomena are present and minutely described in his analyses. While one wonders whether the feeling aspect of love is present in any graspable manner in Marion's description of the erotic phenomenon, one also notes the interesting fact that Romano sees no contradiction between the idea that the emotionality of love is inherently represented and the observation that, for Marion, "love is a phenomenon that is rational through and through," that is, as Romano insists, in this account "[l]ove comes under the *logos*,

---

38. John Milbank's criticism is made along the same lines in that he insists that the idea of "double passivity" insufficiently captures what goes on in between the lovers: "if he [the loved one] cannot ontologically appear without contaminating his alterity, then, after all, my *ego* must take the lead in auto-affectively affirming his presence. . . . The latter notion [double passivity] is supposed to exceed the contrast of active and passive, but this could only be the case if my will, in the shape of its actions, were truly *influenced* by the actions of the other, in which case I would have to take account of their manifest forms." John Milbank, "The Gift and the Mirror: On the Philosophy of Love," in Hart, *Counter-Experiences*, 303.

39. Claude Romano, "'Love' in Its Concept: Jean-Luc Marion's *The Erotic Phenomenon*," in Hart, *Counter-Experiences*, 319–35.

not the passions."⁴⁰ In fact, it is the latter statement, namely, that love here is subsumed under the concept of rationality and that its passion-aspect is lost sight of, which adequately describes, in my view, Marion's procedure.

By contrast, John Milbank is less sympathetic towards Marion's rationalism, which he sees as a natural outcome of a too radically pursued phenomenology.[41] Were Marion's phenomenology complemented by an ontological consideration of the relationship between being and love, or love and knowledge, the contradictions inherent to his hesitation between a radically unilateral and a reciprocal view of love could be resolved. In Milbank's view, Marion's love without being is haunted by metaphysics in that it cannot meaningfully avoid the ontological mediating function of love as connected to being and knowledge. To remedy what he sees as Marion's insufficient phenomenology, Milbank presents the outlines of an ontology of love that is meant to "complete and modify" the phenomenology of love from an admittedly theological perspective. Such a modification is threefold. First, it explores the relationship between Being and love, arguing for their continuous overlap and yet their ultimate non-coincidence: Being as truth always remains distinct from Being as love, and yet they are interconnected to such an extent that one cannot be thought without the other. Next, a metaphysical modification of phenomenology is capable of demonstrating the analogical character of love as opposed to univocity. The third aspect of modification concerns the non-ontological status of evil and therefore self-hatred, which, however, falsely appear as an originary phenomenon in Marion's approach. What is of interest for our inquiry is the second way of metaphysical modification, where love is argued to be essentially analogical.

While Claude Romano, in defending Marion's option for a completely univocal concept of love, suggests that the apparently irreconcilable variety of love is best understood here as having a "single center with multiple contradictions," or as having the contradiction directly "fixed within the heart of love,"[42] Milbank—although agreeing with Marion's insistence on the essential continuity of various manifestations of love as species of a *genus*—rejects the idea of univocity. In his view, love is an analogical concept and it is the principle of analogy that provides its ultimate continuity. Unlike Marion, Milbank does not exclude, for example, love of things from an analogical concept of love because, on the level of analogy, our experience of dealing with things is illuminating for the nature of interhuman love. This can best be understood in terms of a logic of the gift, which appears also in

---

40. Ibid., 327.
41. Milbank, "The Gift and the Mirror," 253–317.
42. Romano, "Love in Its Concept," 323.

our experience of caring for things and receiving their benefits similar to the love-exchange of interpersonal relationships. In this manner, all loves, human and divine likewise can be imagined along the lines of an ascending analogical chain starting from the world of things and going upwards towards God, whose love one can only describe in terms of an analogy with human love of things and persons. For Milbank, there is nothing wrong with such a broad analogical concept of love, which is alone faithful to the vast richness of this phenomenon.

However, there is a more eminent manner by means of which love must be seen as analogical on the metaphysical level of being. If one conceives of being as ultimate harmony between differentiation and oneness, then love can be seen as *desire* for such harmony. That is to say, desire for the "blending of the same and the different" is viewed as forming the essence of love. Milbank suggests that love embodies analogy itself. Consequently there can be no univocal concept of love since it appears to us as the "very source and power of blending." Moreover, love and knowledge converge in the analogical process, since knowledge aims to recognize and judge the blending of love, while love aids analogical knowledge through such blending. Such an ontological view of love allows for conceptualizing Marion's deficient *entre-nous*, the in-between of the lovers, in terms of mediation between two loves that creates a shared microcosm of thoughts, feelings and an entire shared world, a shared affinity. Within such a shared microculture there is no need to restrict discourse to non-constative performative utterances, since everything one speaks about within the shared force field of love—that is, things and events in the "outside" world—contribute to the mediation of love itself. Clearly, Milbank's analogical concept of love is more accommodating towards the feeling-aspect of love, which may be viewed as being part of love's analogical mediating function, much in the same way as Ricoeur sees love as a series of mutually mediating feelings along a descending and ascending spiral. If love, viewed as in itself analogy, not only mediates between the two lovers, but also creates a mediatory zone of sharing, then such mediation cannot be conceived entirely in cognitive terms, but is equally one of feeling. Moreover, love within the individual may also be recognized as a power and source of blending with respect to knowledge and emotion, vitality, and spirituality.

Original Innocence and Original Love according to John Paul II

If God loves the same way as we do, according to Marion, John Paul II argues precisely for the reverse: we, as unique beings created in the image of God, love the same way as God does. While these two tenets seemingly deliver the same final conclusion, namely, that human and divine love ultimately converge in the vanishing point between immanence and transcendence, their respective logic is antithetical and so leads to two widely different visions of embodied human existence under the regime of love. One could describe the two approaches as love-from-below (Marion's way), on the one hand, and love-from-above (John Paul II's stance), on the other. In what follows, I wish to demonstrate that John Paul II's theological perspective on embodied conjugal love—as expounded in his catechetical lectures (1979–84)—in many respects appears as a theological counterpart to Marion's reflections, despite the obviously sharp differences in their basic assumptions and procedures, which, nonetheless, do not obscure some highly significant points of contact, even to the point that they may be seen as in some way complementing one another.[43] Love conceived in a philosophical manner, and love captured within a theological framework, show a structural likeness and also a basic dissimilarity; philosophy and theology enter into an intriguing conversation concerning the nature of embodied love. What is necessary here is to read John Paul's "theology of the body" for what it really is, i.e., not simply as a plea for the re-integration of the body into the image of God, or the re-insertion of the long-neglected theme of our embodied nature into theological discourse, or a papal admonition concerning sexual ethics, but as an insightfully renewed theology of love that takes embodied conjugal love as the pivot on which the Christian understanding of love may turn. What we have here is the same "erotic phenomenon," now described, however, in more hermeneutic terms and expounded in a manner faithful to the patristic tradition, which eminently takes inspiration from an exegesis of scriptural texts.

The place to begin is with a preliminary comparison between the genre of Marion's book and John Paul II's reflections. As John Milbank has suggested, no matter how rigorously Marion's *The Erotic Phenomenon* follows the procedure of phenomenological analysis, avoiding the incursion of metaphysical assumptions—and also despite Marion's deliberate dismissal of literature as a philosophically useful source of knowledge concerning love—it inevitably employs the method of narrative to tell the "story" of

---

43. John Paul II, *Man and Woman He Created Them: A Theology of the Body.*

phenomenologically unfolding lived experiences of consciousness (*vécus*) to describe love between the lovers.[44] This is so because a strict phenomenology of love can only deliver an unstable oscillation between the two poles of self and other, without, however, being equipped to employ any further interpretative frame. No wonder, then, that Marion's "philosophical novel" (in Milbank's insightful term) provides a kind of meta-narrative of love that sets events in time as a sequence of the "necessary moments of love" and gives, as Milbank explains, "a kind of Mallarméan 'final novel' about love—a novel so accurate and revelatory that all subsequent novels would be mere illustrative novelettes, struck with the vanity of unnecessarily multiplied pedagogy or diversion."[45] Marion's account, then, is not simply one more love-story, but intends to reveal the way love appears in different microhistories, occurrences, and plots—an endeavor that, in Milbank's view, is doomed to ultimate failure, since a universal metahistory of love will never be able to do real justice to the singular and the particular arriving in an unforeseeable manner through time.

By contrast, John Paul II's account of love unfolds as a traditional biblical commentary in the patristic sense. It takes already existing Scripture narratives and, through a careful and attentive exegesis, much in the manner of literary criticism, it continues the thinking that was started in the narrative mode. His analytical reflections proceed step by step, taking into consideration the particularities and singularities furnished by the texts. His understanding deepens together with a deeper consciousness of the analyzed texts and the perceived connections between them. His modern biblical commentary, which is, however, not exegesis in the strict scientific sense of the term, issues in a novel theological anthropological vision full of valuable insight and a wealth of detail. What are the narratives examined by the pope? From among the wide variety of texts commented upon in the catecheses, we shall only consider those strictly connected to his theology of love. First, he takes the two creation accounts (in Gen 1–2) and approaches them indirectly, seen through the lens of Christ's teaching about the unity and indissolubility of marriage (Matt 19:8; Mark 10:6–9), which appeals to

---

44. Milbank, "The Gift and the Mirror," 304. In the introductory section to *The Erotic Phenomenon*, Marion writes of poetry and fiction: "Poetry can tell me about the experience I have not known to articulate, and thus liberate me from my erotic aphasia—but will never make me understand love conceptually. The novel succeeds in breaking the autism of my amorous crises because it reinscribes them in a sociable, plural, and public narrativity—but it does not explain what really and truly happens to me." Marion, *The Erotic Phenomenon*, 1.

45. Milbank, "The Gift and the Mirror," 304.

the "beginning," the original order of creation.[46] In this manner, the beginning of human history, starting at the creation of the first human couple, is approached from a christological perspective and the two texts (the Old Testament narrative and the New Testament story) are brought together in a mutually illuminating interplay. The next two texts analyzed together consider the origin of the deficient love of sexual concupiscence (Gen 3 versus Jesus's words concerning adultery in Matt 5:27 in the light of the injunction of the "purity of heart" in Matt 5:8). The third important text for our inquiry is the pope's commentary on the Song of Songs, which is one of the key sections of the catecheses, continuing a long tradition of commentaries on this exceptional biblical poem. Going against the grain of traditional allegorical interpretations, and in harmony with what modern exegetical research suggests, John Paul II regards this unique song as a particularly forceful poetic expression of human love on its own level and in its specificity, without any necessary allegorical overtones or inherent reference to disincarnate intellectual love.[47]

It is the perspective of the creation and the fall in the book of Genesis, seen through Christ's words concerning the "beginning" as God's original intention, which provides the framework for the pope's reflection on the significance of the body for conjugal love. This modern version of a Genesis commentary and image-theology in the service of a modern and, in the pope's words, "adequate theological anthropology" at once refers back to the best of patristic thought and, at the same time, pinpoints new directions for a theology of embodied love. It appeals to human self-understanding and the primary human experience of bodiliness and love. In a manner advocated by Marion, it seeks to do justice to the immanent phenomenality of the passion of love without first imposing on it an interpretation through the Passion.[48] Instead of setting the discussion against the immediate background of the redemptive love of Christ, we are led back to the prototypical Garden of Eden where the first man becomes conscious of his unique status within creation and awakens for the first time to an experience of love. John Paul II's Adam can be compared to Marion's "lover" in that they both appear

---

46. Jesus says to the Pharisees who ask him about the possibility of divorce: "Moses permitted you to divorce your wives because your hearts were hard. But it was not this way from the beginning" (Matt 19:8).

47. John Paul II refers to this section as "the crowning of what I have explained." John Paul II, *Man and Woman He Created Them*, 549.

48. Recall that Marion dismisses theological accounts of love on the grounds that although theology knows what love is all about, "it knows it too well ever to avoid imposing upon me an interpretation that comes so directly through the Passion that it annuls my passions—without taking the time to render justice to their phenomenality, or to give a meaning to their immanence." Marion, *The Erotic Phenomenon*, 1.

as solitary protagonists on a stage empty of other humans and so both of them experience solitude, that is, longing for love, in Marion's phrase, "from out there." There is but one small yet crucial difference: while Marion's stage is devoid of any scenery provided by the surrounding ambience, brooding as a second Hamlet over the vanity or worth of loving, the first man of the Genesis account is staged on a scene that reflects the enchanting beauty of the created world, with full awareness of the Creator behind the scenes. We are with Adam in the original state of innocence; this is the state where human reflection on love must necessarily start.

While Marion's analysis of the erotic phenomenon seems to obliterate the traditional distinction between an ideal (original) state and the state of present fallenness, blurring thereby also the important difference between created finitude and later adventitious fallenness, John Paul II makes the distinction the pivot of his own theological account of the theological counterpart of erotic love.[49] Faithful to a long series of meditations within the theological tradition, the pope gives pride of place to the essential distinction between an order originally intended by the Creator and another order under the regime of sin, which, however, is also one re-shaped by redemption and destined to eschatological fulfillment. He does this in order to work out a proper theological anthropology of embodied erotic love. It might be useful at this point to recall Ricoeur's understanding of what he terms "the imagination of innocence." Ricoeur sees the task of philosophical anthropology in the imaginative restoration of the primordial grandeur of human existence through the imagination of innocence, and the construal of a contrastive background against which deviation and the inordinate can be interpreted. Such an imaginative construal of the primordially ideal beyond the present state allows one to understand the possible that is inherent in the actual, and also provides a frame of reference where the idea of digression or deficiency reveals its significance. We remember that Ricoeur keeps the primordially innocent and the fallen in a complex unity of intermediation whereby the primordial is mediated through the fallen and the fallen is understood in reference to an ideal state from which it has fallen. For him, these two states are not so much stages of a temporal sequence as coincident aspects of the one indivisible reality of the human condition: the ideally possible grasped through the actual, and the actual viewed over against the ideally possible.[50]

---

49. On the obliteration of the distinction see Griffiths, Review of *The Erotic Phenomenon*, 26; and Milbank, "The Gift and the Mirror," 308–9.

50. Ricoeur, *Fallible Man*, 203–24.

In a similar fashion, John Paul II speaks in terms of a stance of "historical *a posteriori*," that is, the state of "historical man" after the fall, which, however, can only be adequately interpreted in the light of a more original state, the state of original innocence or original justice where "man's theological prehistory" is revealed.[51] In other words, the "beginning" of the original meaning of human embodied love can only be understood through a contrast between the experiences of guilt, sinfulness, and shame and a sinless state where the true significance of the crucial triad: love, gift, and the body come to the fore. One needs to reconstruct the original meaning of the goodness of the human constitution on the basis of a fallen and at once redemptively re-created state foreshadowed in the Genesis account. Like Ricoeur, John Paul II too emphasizes the foundational character of such original experiences irrespective of the fact of whether they are seen as belonging to a prehistoric moment or are viewed rather as timelessly present in every age. The Genesis text seems to suggest that the original human constitution is characterized by the "spiritualization" of man and so differs from the subsequent fallen disposition, one that is familiar for historical man. John Paul II explains: "It is a different measure of 'spiritualization' that implies another composition of inner forces in man himself, another body-soul relation, as it were, other inner proportions between sensitivity, spirituality, and affectivity, that is, another degree of inner sensibility for the gifts of the Holy Spirit."[52] What, then, is an original awareness of our humanity like? Through a careful and perceptive reading of the second creation account, the pope delineates the threefold experience of the first human being as witnessed to by the text: original solitude, original unity, and original nakedness. In a remarkable anthropological procedure from below, the construal of the threefold human experience precedes the theological reflection on the significance of the divine creating act, although it is not entirely separated from considerations concerning creation.

Like Marion's "lover," the first man in Eden is aware of his solitude. But unlike Marion's "lover," man in the state of original happiness—that is, in a state of undisturbed relationship with God—does not in the first place seek love "from out there." Instead, he reflects on the significance of such fundamental solitude, which is prompted for him through a consciousness of his body. The act of reflection, before a love-engagement, nevertheless joins the two solitary thinking subjects in the philosophical super-novel and the commentary on the biblical creation narrative. According to the commentary, it

---

51. One finds scattered statements concerning these two states throughout the work. A more discursive argument is given in the section "The Mystery of Original Innocence," in John Paul II, *Man and Woman He Created Them*, 191–204.

52. John Paul II, *Man and Woman He Created Them*, 198–99.

is through an awareness of his body that the first biblical man comes to an understanding of his unique position in the world. For, on the one hand, his body links him to the rest of bodies in creation and makes him conscious of his belonging to the visible world; yet, on the other hand, his body also sets him apart from all other bodies by virtue of the fact that it alone differs from them significantly. Unlike the rest of bodies, his human body permits him to carry out specifically human activity, which, as prompted by the text, consists in a capacity to cultivate the earth and transform it according to his own needs. While biblical man comes to self-consciousness and an awareness of his relation to the rest of the world by means of the body, Marion's lonely self-hating subject sees the body (which is not the flesh yet!) as a gloomy reminder of man's continuity with the world of objects and natural bodies on which he reflects from a rather disembodied stance. Biblical man is alone, and his unique and lonely body teaches him a second lesson.

The next feature of original human experience is revealed by the appearance of the biblical other, the human helper, the woman companion, who is portrayed as a person partaking of the same indivisible humanity on account of the fact that she shares in the same human nature by being flesh of the man's flesh. This is an aspect of what John Paul II calls the experience of original unity. Beyond a common human nature that is realized through embodied existence, the other aspect of unity is related to the duality of sexual difference. Unity and duality in this manner both witness to a fundamental sense of complementarity or correspondence between man and woman. John Paul II suggests the existence of a parallel between the words of appreciation of the first man on seeing the newly created woman ("The man said, 'This is now bone of my bones and flesh of my flesh; she shall be called 'woman,' for she was taken out of man.'" Gen 1:25), and the fascination of the bridegroom at the sight of the bride in the Song of Songs. He detects the presence of deep emotion in the creation narrative, the emotion of the woman and man in one another's presence. Besides such a visible unity in duality, the narrative refers to an even deeper unity with the words, "and the two will be one flesh" (Gen 2:24). On the pope's commentary, the biblical formulation refers to the union expressed and realized in the sexual act whereby the body, as an intermediary, is a constitutive element of the union of the spouses. Unity is realized through the body and the incarnate and loving communion of persons is the real expression of their image character. This is why human sexuality must be seen as transcending the level of bodiliness or mere instinct in becoming the expression of "an ever-new surpassing of the limit of man's solitude, which lies within the makeup of his body and determines its original meaning."[53] With the idea of bodily union, the concept of erotic love is inserted into the discussion where love is viewed, unlike in Marion's account, from the perspective of reciprocity. This is the crucial moment when, in Marion's phrase, "the lover appears." Yet the two different lovers make their appearance at diametrically opposed moments. John Paul II's lover appears when he experiences a counter-look, when his love is requited, when his deep emotion is aroused by a responding sentiment. Although he seems to be loving first, his love immediately meets another love and is reassured by a corresponding affection. Quite to the contrary, Marion's lover appears when he deliberately suspends reciprocity and decides to love without requiring to be loved.[54] He loves first without assurance and by blinding himself in order to see exclusively with the eyes of love. It is only by virtue of the "anticipation to love first" that he "sees her as lovable and unique." While the biblical lover is moved by a delightful primordial passion, under the powerful impact of fascination, the philosophical lover coldly resists any outside influence that would weaken his heroic position as an unconditional lover. The biblical lover is awakened in a world ruled by original love, whereas the other lover is surrounded by a sea of original hatred, which he seeks heroically to overcome. Before we proceed to the pope's account of original love, the third anthropological aspect needs to be examined.

The third aspect of man's original experience is nakedness without shame. This experience is recorded in the biblical narrative in a lapidary statement: "Now both were naked, the man and his wife, but they did not feel shame" (Gen 2:25). John Paul II suggests that the original meaning of nakedness can be reconstructed through the secondary experience of shame, that is, fear in the presence of another "I," which is at the same time fear for one's own identity threatened by the other. Through shame one expresses the need for affirmation and acceptance by the other and for the recognition of one's values from outside. Shame creates both distance between two persons and also a common basis for reciprocal advance in an effort to overcome such distance in loving communion. It is against such a background experience of shame that one is capable of construing the experience of original nakedness without shame as the true non-existence of shame and not a simple lack of shame (as in the case of children, for

---

53. John Paul II, *Man and Woman He Created Them*, 167.

54. Marion writes: "When does the lover appear? Precisely when, during the encounter, I suspend reciprocity, and no longer economize, engaging myself without guarantee of assurance. The lover appears when one of the actors in the exchange no longer poses prior conditions, and loves without requiring to be loved, and thus, in the figure of the gift, abolishes economy." Marion, *The Erotic Phenomenon*, 78.

example) nor shamelessness (as an atypical state). The original non-presence of shame is characterized by a positive experience of one's body, which, as a sign of man's discontinuity with the rest of bodies, interiorly bears the image of God and exteriorly is marked by the features of femininity or masculinity. There is no inner break here between the spiritual and the sensible, just as there is no rupture between the humanity and the sexuality of the person. It is a situation where one sees the other both through the eyes of the body and through an interior gaze. Within such a fullness and simplicity of vision, the body is a totally transparent intermediary that allows man and woman to establish a true communion of persons.

For Marion, the gaze is only able to see the body—a physical object on a par with all other objects in the world, an objectified thing among other things and in continuity with the animal world—but never the personal flesh as it is experienced under the erotic reduction within the erotic union. The loving flesh of the other can only be felt and so the "feeling of the feeling of the other" is the only way to phenomenalize the other outside the dead world of objects or medical nudity. It is within the union of fleshes that the nudity of the physical body vanishes and the lovers do not experience shame. Marion describes the state after the union of the lovers in a covert biblical allusion: "Henceforward, we recognize that we are naked—not because we have committed the erotic reduction, but, on the contrary, because we have ceased to perform it."[55] He speaks in terms of a paradoxical nudity that covers the flesh; the uniform "garment of skin" masks the flesh and makes all bodies look alike. Shame is caused here by the recognition that one's body belongs to the physical world where it "usurps the flesh in us": "We cover our bodies in order to hide from ourselves and from others the disappearance of our flesh, in order to mask the shame of belonging once again to the order of bodies according to the natural attitude."[56] It is as if the erotic reduction in Marion's vision were an eminent site where the ideal can be construed through the actual; as if the erotic union of lovers allowed for an ephemeral insight into the ultimate dignity of our humanity and the innocent state of nakedness without shame.

Having laid the anthropological foundations of a theology of erotic love, John Paul II revisits the same human experiences of solitude, unity, and nakedness, this time, however, in theological terms, from within the perspective of creation. The overall hermeneutics he employs to describe the theological situation of the first human couple is one of the gift as a

---

55. Ibid., 136. On the concept of nudity see 115–16; 136.
56. Ibid., 136.

witness to original Love.[57] Gift introduces a new dimension in the interpretation of the original experiences of man and in his self-understanding, referring his existence to the Creator and an original donation. The pope's construal of the dimension of gift is threefold.

First, creation is seen as a fundamental and "radical" gift, an act of originary giving whereby existing things come into being from nothing. John Paul II even speaks in terms of a "radical, irrevocable, total gift of God."[58] And, although the creation account does not employ the word "love" to characterize the motive of such giving, the goodness of creation is nonetheless affirmed. Goodness and love ultimately converge since only love gives rise to the good. The radical gift of creation, therefore, bears witness to God as Love.

Second, gift does not only appear in general or impersonal terms on the level of creation, but is also manifest to man in a specific manner. Appealing to the traditional (trinitarian) notion of gift as expressing relation, that is, the triad of one who gives, one who receives, and the relation established between them, the pope applies the analogy to the relation between the visible world and man. The world appears as gift because man, made in the image of God, is able to interpret it as gift, since the act of divine giving assumes meaning only in relation to someone who has awareness of such giving. On the one hand, man is aware of his having received the world as gift; on the other, the creation account seems to imply the idea that the world too receives man as gift, as someone who rules and cultivates the earth as God's caretaker.

The third aspect of the dimension of gift is detected on the level of personal existence in the relation between man and woman. Their erotic love-relationship, realized through the union of their bodies and expressing their reciprocal love for one another, repeats God's creating gesture which gives the world as gift springing from Love. What is given through the body in sexual union is a true gift of self and since the body is witness to the fundamental gift of creation rooted in Love, it becomes a sign of that original creative donation in the reciprocal exchange of gift of selves. What we have here is John Paul II's pivotal triad of love, gift, and the body which intertwine in a complex way. One may take gift as the mediating term between love and the body. Gift originates in love; it springs from an original Love, which gives radically and unconditionally in a divinely sovereign manner. Gift thus refers to the Creator. The body in turn is recognized as having a two-way relation to love through donation. On the one hand, it is a visible

---

57. See esp. 180–223 in John Paul II, *Man and Woman He Created Them*.
58. Ibid., 122.

gift of divine creating Love, and, on the other, through its capacity to express love to the other person, it becomes gift doubly: it assumes a secondary gift character in addition to being a primary gift by virtue of creation. The body received as gift and given to the other as a sign and also an effective means of gift of self bears witness to the Love from which it originates. Its gift character reaches completion when the primary donation is supplemented by a secondary free giving in the conjugal act. Original Love maintains the cycle of gift-exchange and gives gift and body their ultimate signification.

It is in the state of innocence (as described by the Genesis account of the events before the fall) that the undisturbed connection between love, gift, and the body comes to the fore. On John Paul II's commentary, the state of original innocence is primarily a state of happiness rooted in love where man recognizes himself as gift emerging from love and where he himself is initiator of genuine human love towards the woman. Unlike Marion's love, which is sustained by a radically unilateral gift of giving flesh to someone—which then is crossed by an equally unilateral counter-gift—John Paul II's love is an essentially reciprocal gift of self, a mutual exchange in an at once fleshly and spiritual communion. The biblical lover repeats the radical (and unilateral) gift of the Creator in a nonidentical manner, through donation, which is a simultaneous reception of the other.[59] The spiritual is grasped here through a "phenomenology" of bodily union; reciprocal giving appears as realized coincidentally on the level of the body and on the spiritual plane. In very concrete terms, the pope speaks of a "reciprocal interpenetration of giving and accepting the gift" where "giving and accepting the gift interpenetrate in such a way that the very act of giving becomes acceptance, and acceptance transforms itself into giving."[60] All this happens through a "reciprocal experience of the body," which, as a primordial sacrament, signifies more than mere materiality in expressing through the visible what is invisible: the spiritual and the divine. The body speaks the language of love; this is what John Paul II calls the "spousal" meaning or attribute of the body. Belonging to the natural order, the body is source of fruitfulness and procreation; however, belonging to the dimension of divine giving, it is also expressive of a different order, the order of divine love. In its capability to express love, the body becomes the sign and the effective means of the realization of gift of self in the manner of original divine donation. Human erotic love is, as it were, participation in the divine Love, which sustains

---

59. On the idea of the crossing of two unilateral gifts without actual reciprocity and the notion of nonidentical repetition of a gift see Milbank, "Can a Gift Be Given?" 119–61. It is also treated in Milbank, "The Gift and the Mirror," esp. 292–300.

60. John Paul II, *Man and Woman He Created Them*, 196–97.

the process of giving and gives meaning to gift and body.[61] This is how the meaning of the "reciprocal disinterested gift" is reconstructed by John Paul II with meticulous care and through an attentive reading of the Genesis text. His argument proceeds in concentric circles rather than in a linear fashion, as his understanding grows by repeated considerations of the same basic issues presented in the text.

The reconstructed experience of original innocence is reached through postlapsarian experience and the two are carefully distinguished throughout the commentary. What has changed after the fall? John Paul II characterizes sin as an event of doubt cast on the original gift of love and the consequent gift of the created world and the understanding of the essence of one's humanity. It is the deepest meaning of gift that becomes obscured and the link between love and gift is broken. When love is no longer viewed as an unconditional motive of gift, gift itself disintegrates into mere ambiguity and becomes hopelessly dim. In the pope's words, formulated in response to the biblical expressions, when "man turns his back on God-Love, on the 'Father,'" he at the same time detaches himself from what "'comes from the Father': in this way, what is left in him is 'what comes from the world.'"[62] When the gift dimension of the body becomes vague, the certainty of the "image of God" expressed in the body is also lost and man loses with it a special sense of his humanity visible in the body. The body ceases to be a clear sign of man's distinctive humanity over against the rest of bodies and its material and animal character overshadows the fact of its participation—through its image-character—in the original Gift. Man feels himself irredeemably subject to mechanisms characterizing natural animal bodies and his awareness of the body as a visible sign of transcendence is dulled. This has important consequences for the human constitution or the inner proportions of the human disposition. In strikingly Ricoeurian terms and yet to the contrary effect, John Paul II speaks of a "certain constitutive fracture" or "breakup" in the interior of the human person whereby the original spiritual and somatic unity is lost and the somatic is experienced

---

61. The idea of the body as a primordial sacrament figures centrally in the pope's commentary, especially in Part 2 "The Sacrament," 465–615. Love, gift, and body interrelate in the pope's thinking: "The reality of the gift and of the act of giving, which is sketched in the first chapters of Genesis as the constitutive content of the mystery of creation, confirms that the irradiation of Love is an integral part of this same mystery. Only love creates the good, and in the end it alone can be perceived in all its dimensions and its contours in created things and, above all, in man. Its presence is the final result, as it were, of the hermeneutics of the gift we are carrying out here. Original happiness, the beatifying 'beginning' of man, whom God created 'male and female,' the spousal meaning of the body in its original nakedness: all of this expresses rootedness in Love." Ibid., 190.

62. Ibid., 237.

as threatening the spiritual through interior imbalance.[63] The appearance of shame is clearly symptomatic of such an interior breakup. An anthropological interpretation of the experience of shame is complemented here with a theological understanding. Shame is precisely fear of the other and of oneself, that is, fear of the lack of acceptance and affirmation from an outside source, due to a loss of the sense of participation in the Gift and a freely donating Love. Because the original grateful acceptance of the body as a visible sign of man's transcendence and an equally blissful sign of man's belonging to the world is obscured by the fact of man's doubting the gift and an his alienation from Love, shame appears as an existential projection of such disturbance, both in the relation with God and in interpersonal relationships. Through shame the original meaning of nakedness is changed. The body is no longer experienced as a transparent component of reciprocal giving or a clear expression of the person. No longer being a reassuring sign of the image of God, its spousal meaning is likewise flawed and its power to express love through reciprocal self-giving becomes defective. The reciprocity of mutual giving through the body is threatened and the communion of persons arising from the reciprocal gifts is liable to failure and multiple imperfections.

Is this not a too grim picture of the human predicament? We do not do justice to John Paul II's account if we overlook the essentially positive stance of his vision. Fallen human experience is used here to establish a contrast that allows one to reconstruct what he sees as God's original plan for human love, the general theme of his inquiry. What we have done here is to gather scattered statements to form a summary account of the postlapsarian state that is inserted in an overall positive framework in the commentary. The Genesis creation narrative can be seen as providing the lineaments of the pope's hermeneutic vision of human erotic love, where, however, things are assumed rather than discursively stated. And although the pope's insightful reading exploits every elliptical hint provided in the text, a real sense of the nature of human erotic love needs to be gathered from elsewhere.[64] This is why it is

---

63. Recall that Ricoeur detects a certain disproportion or rift in human nature as such, and as a neutral characteristic prior to sinfulness. For Ricoeur there is breach, rupture, or rift within fallible human nature, which, however, is not yet fallen or sinful. See *Fallible Man*, 32.

64. John Paul II gives a vivid account of the Genesis story. For example, in commenting on the dialogue between fallen man and God ("But the Lord God called to the man, 'Where are you?' He answered, 'I heard you in the garden, and I was afraid because I was naked; so I hid.' And he said, 'Who told you that you were naked? Have you eaten from the tree that I commanded you not to eat from?'" Gen 3: 9–11.), John Paul II notes: "The precision of this dialogue is overwhelming; the precision of the whole account is overwhelming. It shows the surface of man's emotions in living the events, in such a way that, at the same time, it reveals their depth." John Paul II, *Man and Woman He Created*

through a reading of the Song of Songs that flesh is put on the laconic statements of the creation account. The commentary on the Song of Songs admittedly contains the crowning of John Paul II's vision of erotic love, approached from the perspective of Genesis.

Erotic Love Seen through the Prism of the Heart

Comparing the two approaches, John Paul II observes that while the Genesis account records events in a concise manner by narrative means, the Song of Songs captures the experience of loving union by way of a poetic dialogue or a duet between the bride and the bridegroom.[65] What we have here is not short statements, but a full dialogue where the words of the lovers intertwine and complete one another as if in a duet of two distinct and yet harmonious voices. We are now, in his words, "in the vestibule" of erotic union where speech and conversation establish the atmosphere of that union and where the fascination and admiration expressed in Genesis reappears as a recurring theme in a yet more forceful fashion. Such reciprocal fascination at the delightful presence and radiant beauty of the other determines the entire poem, setting a peacefully affectionate tone from the beginning to the end. It is in the vestibule of blissful *entre-nous* that the "language of the body" expressed without words is interpreted and translated into the "language of the heart." Such language of the body corresponds to the meaning conveyed in the situation of original nakedness without shame; it is a continuation of the primeval experience, the prototypical beginning of wordless bodily speech. The communion of persons and reciprocal closeness is established through an intimate exchange of words occasioned by the sight and closeness of bodies and their influence exerted on the heart.

Interestingly, John Paul II's analysis is determined by a key concept, the heart, which is contrasted with the body throughout the commentary. The parallel drawn between the "language" of the body and the "language" of the heart runs across the entire catecheses and is also central to the comments made on the Song of Songs. In the pope's hermeneutic framework, the body communicates a meaning comprehensible only for the heart. The wordless speech of the body is put into words as the amorous language of the heart. The experience of beauty and the consequent pleasure, the experience of the intimate closeness of bodies and their reciprocal giving is seen, as it were, through a prism, a focal point where these experiences assume existential meaning for

---

Them, 239.

65. See the commentary on the Song of Songs ibid., 548–92.

the person. John Paul II speaks in terms of the "prism of the human heart": "The words, movements, and gestures of the spouses, their whole behavior, correspond to the inner movement of their hearts. It is only through the prism of this movement that one can understand the 'language of the body.'"[66] Body and heart are not set in opposition, however, but are held together in a tensile unity: their respective languages are seen as cross-interpreting one another, forming an irreplaceable bilingualism where one is understood through the other in a reciprocal movement of constant cross-referencing. The measure of the heart is applied to the body and the measure of the spousal meaning of the body imposes itself on the heart: it is through such intermediation that erotic love is adequately interpreted.

Yet, what exactly is meant here by the concept "heart"? John Paul II's commentary supplies no definition or discursive conceptual elaboration. All one can do is rely on scattered remarks and some concise formulations concerning the function of this symbolic organ with regard to the human experience of erotic love. What becomes clear on a closer look is the fact that the heart is taken here in a genuinely biblical sense as the dimension *par excellence* of man's interiority. The biblical perspective can clearly be recognized also from the fact that the heart is nowhere opposed, in post-Enlightenment fashion, to the intellect or human rationality, and nowhere does it signify a site of mere emotionality or irrational passion. Recall that in biblical thought the heart, as a key metaphor and the product of biblical synthetic thinking, denotes the centre, as it were, of the consciously living person. It is the site where one encounters one's interiority: feelings, emotions, conscience, reason and decisions, memory and knowledge, perception and judgment. It is at once the inner dimension of relationality, the inner core of the person that is turned towards fellow humans and also to God. With the notion of the heart is associated the idea of profundity and essential openness. As a unified centre of the human being, it is the focal point where life activities converge and where one makes sense of the outer world and one's inner experiences. It is the heart that is seen as praying within the human person as the deepest expression of one's innermost self.

John Paul II obviously appeals to such a biblical sense of the heart, calling it, in various expressions, a "dimension of the inner man," "man's innermost being," or "the interior" of the person. His implicit understanding of the notion is apparently enriched through an interpretation of Christ's words concerning the purity of heart in the Sermon on the Mount, and concerning marital faithfulness over against lustful and adulterous covetousness

---

66. Ibid., 552.

(Matt 5:27–28).[67] It is such an enriched notion he works with in the analysis of the Song of Songs. What he registers as a deeper sense of Christ's words concerning the purity of heart is a pivotal shift of the meaning of adultery from the body to the heart. As he notes, in Christ's teaching, the body is in no way accused as the cause of adultery; it is obviously the heart that must bear the blame as the site of decision, conscious attitude, and consented passion. This is so because the meaning of bodily action becomes clear through the interpretative prism of the heart. There is a two-way relationship between the meaning of the body and the meaning crystallized in the heart: "The 'meaning' of the body is not something merely conceptual. . . . [It] is at the same time what shapes the attitude: it is the way of living the body. It is the measure that the inner man—that is, the heart, to which Christ appeals in the Sermon on the Mount—applies to the human body with regard to its masculinity or femininity (and thus with regard to its sexuality)."[68] Moreover, beyond the interpretative function of the heart, John Paul II assigns to it an interesting individualizing function, one that defines the person as unique and irreplaceable: ". . . Christ appeals precisely to the human 'heart,' which cannot be the subject of any generalization. With the category of 'heart,' everyone is identified in a singular manner, even more than by name; he is reached in that which determines him in a unique and unrepeatable way; he is defined in his humanity 'from within.'"[69] The heart as man's innermost core is, then, for the pope an interpretative and deeply personal reality that holds together spiritual and sensual significations in a truly unique fashion.

Such a remodeled biblical concept of the heart allows for an interpretative moment in the wordless speech of bodily love. An anthropology of the body, supplemented by an anthropology of the heart, makes the *entre nous* of the spouses conceptually visible in all its dimensions of sensual pleasure, aesthetic fascination, emotional intensity, and intimate knowledge. The bifocal and tensile unity of body and heart is capable of intimating a sense of communion, the reciprocal closeness of the spouses, which, however, is more than the merely physical proximity of bodies. It is as if Marion's distance between the fleshes of the lovers were traversed by John Paul II's biblical hermeneutic of an interpretative process moving back and forth between the body and the heart, between the sensual and the spiritual, without, however, in any manner prioritizing the spiritual aspect of love.

---

67. See especially the first part of chapter 2 "Christ Appeals to the Human Heart," ibid., 225–314.

68. Ibid., 255.

69. Ibid., 266.

What comes through the senses is turned into deep affection and true sentiment in the heart, and a growing awareness of reciprocal communion in the innermost core of the spouses receives sensual expression through their bodily intimacy and the consequent unitive act. The commentary on the Song of Songs admittedly remains in the vestibule, stopping at the threshold of the inner chamber where bodily union takes place. And in this respect Marion's account is complementary to the pope's theological vision of erotic love, providing a forceful phenomenological expression of the process of fleshly eroticization. And yet the language of the body interpreted through the prism of the heart tells almost everything that can be told here, since, as Marion himself contends, the experience of sexual union in itself presents nothing to verbalize or phenomenalize; it leaves no trace or interpretable content. It is eroticization through words, the giving of flesh to the other by loving concern, that gives bodily union its love character so to speak. Nevertheless Marion's brilliant systematic conceptualization of erotic love is absent from John Paul II's commentary, written, as it is, in the literary critical mode, which evolves through a repeated encounter of biblical texts and therefore is formulated in a less coherent manner. It simply prolongs, as it were, the thinking that was started in the narrative or poetic mode and so it is secondary with regard to the primary articulation of the biblical texts.

In the final resort, John Paul II's conclusion is equally one of Marion's; both of them recognize that the "language of the body" or fleshly eroticization has its limits since "[l]ove shows itself greater than what the 'body' is able to express."[70] Or, as the Song of Songs puts it with unparal-

---

70. Ibid., 586. Marion too must take account of the fact that one continues loving even after the disintegration of the flesh, the death of the loved one. His moving reflections in the part "Concerning the Third Party, and Its Arrival" first explore the way the child, a third flesh born of the lover's united fleshes, guarantees a kind of immanent eschatology for the lovers, and, after the departure of the child, at the final *Adieu* of the lovers, real eschatological anticipation maintains the lover's unfailing love for the loved one. Marion's prose assumes poetic heights: "The anticipatory resolution thus results in the eschatological anticipation—as lover, I must, we must, love as if the next instant decided, in the final instance, everything. To love requires loving without being able or willing to wait any longer to love perfectly, definitively and forever. . . . The dawn and the evening make one single twilight—the time to love does not last and is played out in an instant, a fragment, a single beat—only one heartbeat, the smallest gap, the *articulum*, separates us from eternity. We love one another *in articulo vitae*, or in other words *in articulo mortis*; death frightens the lover no more than the finish line terrorizes the runner: rather, he fears not reaching it quickly enough. . . . This initial flight toward the definitive is called the farewell, the *adieu*. The lovers accomplish their oath in the *adieu*—in the passage unto God [*à Dieu*], whom they summon as their final witness, their first witness, the one who never leaves and never lies. For the first time, they say 'adieu' to one another: next year in Jerusalem—next time in God. Thinking unto God [*penser à Dieu*] can be done, erotically, in this 'adieu.'" Marion, *The Erotic*

leled acuity, "love is strong as death" (Song 8:6). John Paul II speaks in terms of a contest between love and bodily death. The inner dynamism of *erōs* points beyond itself; the restless desire it contains calls for fulfillment beyond death, the painful recognition of the impossibility to possess another entirely and forever shows the insufficiency of immanent love. The horizon of human love, which is "strong as death," is closed down by death and yet, in the biblical vision, another horizon is opened, one expressed by the apostle Paul's words, "Love will never end" (1 Cor 13:8). This is what John Paul II calls a "further truth" of love, one that can be described, in his view, as the agapaic perspective of love. Here we touch upon his "theory" of the unity of love *in nuce*, which is conceived in a truly biblical fashion. While a distinction is made between *erōs* and *agapē*, the entire problematic is set in a scriptural perspective and so is reconfigured as two dimensions of the same undivided phenomenon of love. Love "strong as death" and love "that will never end" are not opposed along the lines of erotic egotism and disinterested benevolence, nor is the body regarded here as a lesser modality of existence compared to spiritual modalities. Love "that will never end" is a full continuation of love "strong as death"; it fulfils human love in an unexpected fashion, it supplements what the (earthly) body is not able to express. What we have here is not the academic dichotomy between two irreconcilable types of love. It is rather a forceful expression of the biblical realism: while the body has limitations and in its present form is doomed to death and decay, love—arising in the body and expressed through the body—is mysteriously stronger than bodily death. Love "that will never end," in the pope's account, invites one to another communion, a communion fuller than the bodily union of the spouses. And, at the end of the day, is this not precisely what Marion's insightful phenomenology seems to suggest? Love in this manner is truly one and indivisible; it is inextricably tied to the body and is erotic in the wider sense of coming through the senses, the emotions and the reasonable judgment of the heart and reaching desirously toward another "flesh." However, it is not limited to the body, but—due to an irresistible inner dynamism—it ever seeks expansion and growth beyond existence in the perishable garment of skin. Love—seen from our limited inner worldly perspective—restlessly oscillates between embodiment and spirituality, having no other mediator than the at once judicious and emotional prism of the heart.

Phenomenon, 211–12.

7

Gathering the Threads

The Theological Contours of Human Emotionality

> No one can love by sheer willpower.
> —Fr. Roger of Taizé, *His Love Is a Fire*

What are the theological contours of human emotionality? This has been the guiding question throughout my inquiry. Does theological reflection furnish any graspable points of orientation concerning the significance of the emotions and affectivity besides the clearly formulated tenets it provides concerning the theological role of the intellect? In order to find an appropriate answer, I first had to delineate the context within which the issue can be adequately treated in a theological manner. The cultural historical claim that there is a rupture, a dissociation, between intellect and sensibility, reason and emotion, seems to articulate a deep-seated experience of our humanity that boils down to the perennial problem of the unity and the simultaneous diversity of the human constitution. The human being experiences himself as a composite of two diverse worlds, one of matter and another traditionally called spirit, and the two are never felt to form a seamless unity. Awareness of such a rupture seems to belong to common human knowledge concerning ourselves and so it forms part of the anthropological quest directed to explore the philosophical contours of our humanity. Paul Ricoeur's philosophical anthropology has proved to be a rich dialogue partner for theology in this respect. Ricoeur, who likewise registers a basic disproportion in the human constitution, interprets it as an essential feature of our humanity, a neutral and non-harmful given arising from the fact that the finite and the infinite merge in the human horizon and determine every level of human existence: the vital and the spiritual alike. Ricoeur's neither monist nor dualist anthropology builds on the key concept of mediation whereby multiple cracks in the human constitution are mediated through a median zone, namely, affectivity. Affectivity is the synthesizing or mediating function itself, which mediates by paradoxically rearticulating and interiorizing the rifts it aims to overcome. What comes to the fore in this manner is the inner polarity of mediation itself that at once overcomes and perpetuates the inner fragility of man. Affectivity is epitomized by the Ricoeurian heart, the dynamic site where the sensibly vital and the spiritually intellectual intertwine. The heart comprises an initial polarity, a divergence of affective tension that is set between the finite and the infinite—the finite, which also characterizes the spiritual, and the infinite, which is also present in the sensible. Man moves between two fundamental tendencies, which are by no means seen as tearing him apart; rather, his whole self is viewed as being made up of multiple mediations whereby the sensible reverberates in the spiritual and the spiritual resounds in the sensible. A fundamental unity, attained through complex mediation, underlies the apparent duality of spirit and matter and the pivot of such a unity is the heart, the site where extremities meet and are paradoxically reconciled in a conflictual tension.

Ricoeur's complex account has proved to be illuminating for theological anthropology because it supplies a positive vision of the dichotomy between the vital and the spiritual and because it also works out a conceptual framework in which mediation overcoming the dichotomy can be thought. Affectivity as a specifically human property has pride of place within such mediation, both in its orientation towards finite vital pleasure and as directed towards spiritual, infinite happiness. It is specifically human in all dimensions because it does not bifurcate squarely along the lines of finite vitality (common with the animal world) and infinite spirituality (specifically human); rather, it displays the infinity of vital desire as a uniquely human characteristic, pointing towards the "spiritual" even in the sensible. The concept of the heart—understood as the place of an unstable balance, a site of restless quest and endless pursuit where the self is constituted at the intersection of the vital and the spiritual—is a valuable clue, not only for philosophical discussion where it has long been neglected as an interpretative tool for the understanding of what constitutes the centre of our humanity, but also for theological anthropology, which has only recently re-discovered the significance of a scripturally-based vision of the innermost core of the human person symbolized by the synthetic biblical concept of the heart. Such a synthetic approach is necessitated by the long conceptual separation between emotionality and rationality where rationality has been awarded primacy over what was seen as body-bound, and therefore earthly, emotionality.

Ricoeur's overall framework, the question of human fallibility or fragility, and his quest to determine the site where evil may enter into an essentially non-sinful, neutrally constituted human state, reminds theology of its traditional discourse concerning a pre-fallen ideal state and a consequent state of fallenness. Christian reflection upon the human condition has traditionally been carried out with reference to creation and the eminent place of such discourse has been the creation accounts of the book of Genesis. The context offered by a long history of interpretations crystallizes around the issue of human likeness to God and, in this manner, the main elements of a possible framework for a discussion of the theological contours of human emotionality are also pinpointed. If the human being is created in the image of God—as the biblical evidence obviously claims—then the human constitution must be considered in the context of such likeness and in reference to God. And, first and foremost, the consequences of the human image-character need further consideration.

There is, however, one traditional obstacle to the analysis of our entire humanity in the light of the image: the place of the image has conventionally been situated exclusively in the human intellect, and the body—together with bodily grounded emotionality—has been relegated to a position of at best second-order likeness. Does our affective dimension enter into the picture of likeness in any important manner? In order to answer this question, I have revisited patristic thought on the issue of the place of the image within man. A re-reading of a wide gamut of patristic texts and the corresponding interpretations of patristic scholars reveal the presence of a healthy diversity of approaches and views within the patristic period. Despite the vast richness, one can nevertheless discern a major tendency to localize the image within the intellect, the highest part of the immortal and incorporeal soul. This, however, does not mean that the body would be completely dismissed as irrelevant for the present and the future of man in his relation to God. What one registers from a close reading of patristic texts is the presence within patristic literature of a sustained effort to make room for the body in the theology of the image. While these authors formally profess the tenet of the spiritual nature of the image, intimately linked to the soul, they seek at the same time to attenuate the theoretical import of this claim by implicitly extending the benefits of the image even to the body on theological grounds. One can observe two major trends among the attempts directed at the inclusion of the bodily and the sensible into a theology of the image. One option is to reconcile the division of body and soul by establishing their stable unity in the operation of God's Spirit, who is seen as giving life to both the body and the soul in a divinely imparted unity. This is a minority option, however, and it is linked to early (and, for fear of anthropomorphism, later discarded) views that do not draw a clear borderline between the image-bearing intellect and the rest of the human person, but place the image within the whole of man. The majority of accounts follow the other option of making room for the body in the image by subordinating the body to the soul and arguing in this manner for its participation in the soul's image character.

The normative and, for later developments, determinative anthropology of Thomas Aquinas likewise works with a distinction between the intellect and the body, situating the image squarely within the intellectual soul and allowing for "likeness by trace" for the body, that is, lower-level likeness that is characteristic of the entire gamut of existing things on account of their createdness. For Aquinas, it is without any doubt the human intellect, the site of knowing and understanding, that distinguishes man from other living beings on earth and therefore makes him "near to God in likeness."

A long history of interpretations receives a new direction in John Paul II's catecheses on the significance of conjugal love as both bodily and spiritual union. John Paul II here works out the implications of a long-drawn-out process by including the body in the image-character of the human person. He at the same time breaks away from the old scheme of the intellect versus body dichotomy and makes the biblically understood heart the centre of what is "spiritual" in man, while, however, not setting the heart over against the body, but making it the body's spiritual dimension. The pope's reflections mark a momentous development also on account of the fact that he returns to the traditional framework of the Genesis account, seen, however, through a christological lens. On his reading of the Genesis texts, the body is an archaic sacrament that renders visible the invisible spiritual nature of the human being and so is also a sign of human transcendence. Far from being the obvious common factor with the animal world, the human body is the distinctive marker of human difference from the rest of visible bodies.

This interesting current move in image-theology necessitates a closer look at the traditional place of human emotionality with regard to the image. Such an analysis is all the more important because ancient philosophy is hesitant and divided on the issue of the place of the emotions within the human constitution. One equally finds arguments for their belonging to the soul or their siding with the body. Patristic authors are apparently aware of philosophers' hesitation and they seek to find their own distinctive way amidst the uncertainties. Their views concerning human emotionality are part of a larger discourse that addresses the issue of the primordial state of innocence prior to the fall and the characteristics of postlapsarian existence, and that also reflects on the final completion of what started at the creation, the eschatological fulfillment of final beatitude. The state of innocence is generally conceived as one without the harmful effects of emotions and although there is no consensus on the issue of whether the first man had an earthly or rather a spiritual body, the detachment (*apatheia*) attributed to the ideal prefallen state is by no author conceived as implying the lack of spiritual happiness or spiritual love and joy. One can register the evolution of an interesting bifurcation whereby bodily passions are distinguished from spiritual affectivity, and the birth of another pivotal distinction between, on the one hand, negative and harmful emotions and, on the other, wholesome passions associated with love. While bodily passions and negative emotions (such as fear, pain, and distress) are denied to the ideal unfallen human constitution, spiritual passions and positive emotions are seen as perfectly compatible with the state of original happiness and also with the state of final beatitude. Within such a framework, the philosophical idea of detachment is reconfigured around the Christian ideal of love. Authors like Augustine argue against the pagan philosophical ideal of a completely emotionless state on the grounds that Christian existence is unthinkable without the centrality of love which is equally present in the blissful state of original innocence and will also be an indispensable part of the everlasting joy of the blessed. The Christian version of detachment is perfectly compatible with the presence of good emotions rooted in love and is never considered as a completely emotionless state.

The undisturbed positivity of love-related emotions is marred by the fall. With original sin, fear, suffering, and pain enter the picture and determine postlapsarian human affectivity. The initial harmony between the body and the soul, the intellect and the emotions, is broken and an inner discord appears; a ruinous disharmony occurs at the core of the person. The intellect no longer obeys God and such rebellion causes the infirmity of the mind, which has repercussions over the entire human constitution. The weakened intellect is no longer able to discern with perfect clarity the good of the person and the things necessary for eternal life. Consequently it loses full control over the lower parts of the soul and over the body. The passions—freed from the controlling power of the intellect—tend to incline towards immediate satisfaction and the good easily available, and do not keep man's supernatural goal in view. Even though affectivity is thought to be capricious and at times a hindrance to reason's judgment, it is not taken to task for man's sinful state in the first place, because in the hierarchic order of the parts of the human constitution the emotional part is subordinated to the intellect. The passions have only second-order responsibility in the disorder subsequent to the fall.

What emerges from an analysis of theologies of the prelapsarian state and the fall are three significant interrelated points. First, the Christian understanding of human emotionality works with an implicit distinction between bodily and spiritual emotions that results in a curious doubling of perspectives and a constant oscillation and even equivocation between discourse on first-order, bodily rooted emotions and second-order, spiritual-intellectual affectivity, although the paradigm for spiritual emotions seems to be invariably our bodily emotionality. Second, the dichotomy between sensible and spiritual passions is cut across by another distinction between negative emotions (seen as non-foundational for ideal humanity) and good passions (regarded as indispensable both for the state of original innocence and the state of final beatitude). The third point is related to the latter idea of the non-equal status of negative and positive emotionality. Human affectivity is seen as crystallizing around the root-passion of love, which shapes spiritual emotions and governs affectivity associated with the intellect. Love in its spiritual mode is part of the image of God in man and so it is an essential component of human likeness to God. Therefore, the best entrance to a theological examination of human affectivity is offered through a theology of love. Love is not simply taken as a passion or a spiritual affection on an equal footing with other passions, but has a special status in Christian discourse about affective experiences; love is a category of its own that gradually absorbs talk about detachment and serves as an organizing principle, giving coherence to piecemeal accounts of emotionality. The refined theological anthropology and the related Christology of Thomas Aquinas has proved to be highly illuminating for a better understanding of these three pivotal issues. Aquinas first elaborates an anthropological framework where the passions are considered at unparalleled length and in extraordinary depth, and where human emotionality (and even passions like anger) is given a positive treatment. The passions are an indispensable part of our humanity and a helpful aid in the attainment of virtue. His Christology interestingly shows the ambiguity resulting from the implicit distinction between negative and positive passions: although Christ experienced suffering and pain just like us, the negativity of passion as a kind of emotional disorder was absent from Christ's soul. Christ is claimed to have had propassions, that is, passions that—unlike our common emotions—always follow reason's command. Sensibility and reason were in a perfect harmony in the human nature of Christ. Finally, Aquinas's theology of love is elaborated along the lines of a twofold perspective: the passion of love and spiritual love are distinguished, however, spiritual love does not receive a treatment of its own in Aquinas, but is discussed either under the rubric of love in general (as a passion) or is subsumed under the topic of supernatural charity, a God-infused virtuous capacity to enter into fellowship with God. What is missing from such an account is mediation between spiritual and body-based emotionality.

And it is at this point that the biblical notion of the heart, as the centre of the human person and the innermost core of every human life activity, assumes paramount importance. A rich concept of the heart—contrasted with a traditionally thin notion that makes the heart an exclusive site of religious affectivity over against reason—offers the conceptual means whereby one may think the missing mediatory zone between the sensible and the spiritual or the emotional and the intellectual. Understood in this manner, the heart may even take over the traditional function of *noūs*, the intellectual part of the soul which has traditionally been regarded as the seat of the image of God and the distinctively human in man. On a more holistic approach, what is distinctively human is not so much the abstracted intellect as the symbolic heart, the seat of complex mediaton between rationality, emotionality, and will and the site of relationality with regard to fellow humans and God. Such a rich concept of the heart is indispensable for a renewed understanding of love that aims to break away from the centuries-old alleged antinomy between vital-sensible (egotistic) *erōs* and spiritual-intellectual (selfless) *agapē*.

While love has been discovered as an organizing principle that unifies and governs theological discourse concerning affectivity, it has also been detected to bifurcate along the same lines that affectivity did. Love is either a passion linked up with the body or is an intellectual affection connected to the will. In other words, while love has traditionally been recognized as an analogous concept, comprising a wide range of phenomena and appearing on every level of the created world (including even the craving for the good, in the case of inanimate objects, as a metaphysical principle in the Thomistic scheme), the continuity between various forms of love is interrupted in the affective dimension by the assumed dichotomy between sensible passion and intellectual affection. Such an inherited dichotomy without conceptual mediation threatens the otherwise rightly claimed unity of love and also leads to distortions, such as a purely voluntaristic concept of love that is allegedly independent of emotional involvement. While actual Thomism does reckon with an emotional dimension also in the case of intellectual love—although it remains largely inarticulate on the precise mode of such emotionality and its difference from sensible affectivity—later appropriations of the Thomistic framework tend to overlook this pivotal dimension and make of love a pure act of goodwill perpetuating in this manner—and despite their original intention—the traditional dichotomy.

Might such a traditional dichotomy be overcome if one reversed the conventional hierarchy between bodily erotic and intellectual agapaic love and made erotic love between man and woman the fundamental paradigm of all kinds of loves? Can the unity of love be safeguarded by recuperating the (erotic) body for philosophical/theological inquiry? I have registered a growing tendency in recent treatments of love to emphasize the essential unity of the "phenomenon" of love, and to posit a fundamental continuity between all its manifestations. Does the inclusion of the body make a revolutionary difference in recent theories of love? Interestingly, what has emerged from a contrastive survey of Jean-Luc Marion's philosophical attempt to phenomenalize love as a one-way process hinging upon the body (in his term "the flesh") and John Paul II's theological account of embodied spousal love, is the curious fact that a simple reversal of views does not automatically resolve the problem of the bifurcation of love. While, on the one hand, Marion's reflections convincingly show the uniquely human nature of erotic love and its spiritual dimension, on the other hand, his account is less equipped to demonstrate the significance of the "flesh" in non-sexual types of loves. It is as if the bifurcation, which is suppressed by a strong insistence on the one-way nature of invariably erotic love, made its way back to such a one-way concept by the backdoor of a distinction between two modalities of "flesh": one sexually eroticized (therefore automatic and vital), and another freely eroticized (therefore spiritual). The mediation between the two modes of bodily and spiritual *erōs* is not adequately worked out in Marion's framework and so the transition from the sphere of fleshly love to the sphere of non-sexual love remains problematic. Moreover, another residue of the traditional bifurcation between sensible and intellectual love can be detected as determining Marion's treatment of erotic love. Just as misinterpreted conceptions of intellectual love downplay the emotional dimension, Marion's love likewise suppresses emotionality and, while the feeling aspect of love is overlooked, the volitional element is over-emphasized. In an effort to liberate love from the traditionally derivative modality of passion, Marion divests it of affectivity and turns it into a kind of counter-rationality that offers more comprehensive knowledge than reason but does not evoke a host of deep feelings and positive sentiments. Feeling as mediation between the vital and the spiritual is lacking in this crypto-dualistic scheme.

Conversely, John Paul II's theological reversal—although it differs in many respects from Marion's rigorous phenomenology—is more accommodating towards mediation and the feeling dimension of love. While his account is articulated in terms of an explicit bipolar tension between the body and the heart, at the same time it avoids dangerous bifurcation by making the heart the median zone where the vital is transformed into the spiritual and the spiritual is turned into vital. Erotic bodily love is interpreted here through the prism of the heart, which allows for an interpretative element in the pope's understanding of love. Moreover, the heart is not opposed here to reason, but is seen in a truly biblical manner as the centre of all human life-activities where rationality and emotionality correlate in one simultaneous movement. What we have here is a bipolar conception of love that moves between embodiment and spirituality, but that is not divided into two separate domains. The essential unity of love is safeguarded despite the preservation of the traditional distinction between sensible and spiritual emotionality. While these two accounts of erotic love (Marion's and John Paul II's) make a strong case for the absurdity of disembodied intellectual love, they also implicitly argue for the impossibility of unspiritual bodily love. A univocal one-way concept of love cannot be thought without multiple mediations between the finite and the infinite, the sensible and the spiritual, human love and divine charity, between the love that is strong as death and the love that will never end. The theological contours of human emotionality are drawn by love understood precisely in this manner and under the impact of a tender eternal Love.

Bibliography

Aquinas, Thomas. *In librum beati Dionysii De divinis nominibus expositio.* Edited by Ceslas Pera. Torino: Marietti, 1950.

———. *On Charity.* Translated by Lottie H. Kendzierski. Milwaukee, WI: Marquette University Press, 1960.

———. *On Love and Charity: Readings from the "Commentary on the Sentences of Peter Lombard."* Translated by Peter A. Kwasniewski, Thomas Bolin, and Joseph Bolin. Washington, DC: Catholic University of America Press, 2008.

———. *Summa Theologica.* Translated by Fathers of the English Dominican Province. 2nd ed., 1920. Online: http://www.op.org/summa/summa-Iq93.html.

Aristotle. *The Nichomachean Ethics.* Edited by Lesley Brown and translated by David Ross. Oxford: Oxford University Press, 2009.

Augustine of Hippo. *City of God.* In *St. Augustine's City of God and Christian Doctrine.* A Select Library of the Nicene and Post-Nicene Fathers of the Christian Church 2. Edited by Philip Schaff, translated by Marcus Dods, 6–952. Online: http://www.ccel.org/ccel/schaff/npnf102.iv.html.

———. *Eighty-Three Different Questions.* The Fathers of the Church: A New Translation 70. Edited by Roy J. Deferrari and translated by David L. Mosher. Washington, DC: Catholic University of America Press, 2010.

———. *On Genesis: A Refutation of the Manichees, Unfinished Literal Commentary on Genesis, The Literal Meaning of Genesis.* In *The Works of Saint Augustine. A Translation for the 21st Century. On Genesis.* I/13. Edited by John E. Rotelle and translated by Edmund Hill. Hyde Park, NY: New City, 2002.

———. *On the Soul and Its Origin.* In *Anti-Pelagian Writings.* A Select Library of the Nicene and Post-Nicene Fathers of the Christian Church 5. Edited by Philip Schaff, translated by Peter Holmes, 605–706. Online: http://www.ccel.org/ccel/schaff/npnf105.html.

———. *The Trinity.* Translated by Stephen McKenna. Washington, DC: The Catholic University of America Press, 1963.

Augustinus, Aurelius. *A Szentháromságról* [On the Trinity]. Ókeresztény Írók 10. Translated by Ferenc Gál. Budapest: Szent István Társulat, 1985.

Azouvi, François. "Homo Duplex." *Gesnerus* 42 (1985) 229–44.

Balthasar, Hans Urs von. *The Glory of the Lord: A Theological Aesthetics 3: Studies in Theological Styles: Lay Styles.* Translated by Andrew Louth et al. San Francisco: Ignatius, 1986.

———. *Cosmic Liturgy: The Universe According to Maximus the Confessor*. Translated by Brian E. Daley. San Francisco: Ignatius, 2003.

———. *Epilogue*. Translated by Edward T. Oakes. San Francisco: Ignatius, 2004.

———. *Love Alone: The Way of Revelation*. Translator not named. New York: Herder & Herder, 1969.

———. *Theo-Drama: Theological Dramatic Theory 4: The Action*. Translated by Graham Harrison. San Francisco: Ignatius, 1994.

Beinert, Wolfgang, ed. *Lexikon der Katolischen Dogmatik*. Freiburg im Bresgau: Herder, 1987.

Benedict, XVI. Encyclical Letter *Deus Caritas Est*. Vatican: Libreria Editrice Vaticana, 2005.

Bernard, Charles. *Théologie Affective*. Paris: Cerf, 1984.

Bernard, of Clairvaux. *De Diligendo Deo*. Patrologia Latina 182. Edited by Jacques-Paul Migne, 973–100. Paris: Garnier, 1844–55.

———. *De Laude Caritatis*. Patrologia Latina 184. Edited by Jacques-Paul Migne, 583–635. Paris: Garnier, 1844–55.

———. *Sermones in Cantica, 59*. Patrologia Latina 183. Edited by Jacques-Paul Migne, 785–1198. Paris: Garnier, 1844–55.

Blanc, Élie. *Dictionnaire de Philosophie Ancienne, Moderne et Contemporaine*. Paris: Lethielleux, 1906.

Boeve, Lieven et al. eds. *Faith in the Enlightenment? The Critique of the Enlightenment Revisited*. Amsterdam: Rodopi, 2006.

Brady, Bernard V. *Christian Love*. Washington, DC: Georgetown University Press, 2003.

Brambilla, Franco Giulio. *Antropologia teologica*. Brescia: Queriniana, 2005.

Brümmer, Vincent. *The Model of Love: A Study in Philosophical Theology*. Cambridge: Cambridge University Press, 1993.

Brugger, Walter, and Kenneth Baker, eds. *Philosophical Dictionary*. Spokane, WA: Gonzaga University Press, 1972.

Burghardt, Walter J. *The Image of God in Man according to Cyril of Alexandria*. Woodstock, MD: Woodstock College Press, 1957.

Canto-Sperber, Monique, ed. *Dictionnaire d'ethique et de la philosophie morale*. Paris: Presses Universitaires de France, 1996.

Caputo, John D. Review of *The Erotic Phenomenon*, by Jean-Luc Marion. *Ethics* 118 (2007) 164–68.

Catechism of the Catholic Church. London: Chapman, 1999.

D'Arcy, M. C. *The Mind and Heart of Love—Lion and Unicorn: A Study of Eros and Agape*. London: Faber and Faber, 1954.

De Rougemont, Denis. *Love in the Western World*. Translated by Montgomery Belgion. Princeton, NJ: Princeton University Press, 1983.

Descartes's Philosophical Writings. Translated by Norman Kemp Smith. London: Macmillan, 1952.

Dionysius, the Areopagite. *On the Divine Names and the Mystical Theology*. Edited by Clarence Edwin Rolt. London: SPCK, 1920. Online: http://www.ccel.org/ccel/rolt/dionysius.html.

Dixon, Thomas. "Theology, Anti-Theology and Atheology: From Christian Passions to Secular Emotions." *Modern Theology* 15:3 (1999) 297–330.

Dodds, Michael J. "Thomas Aquinas, Human Suffering, and the Unchanging God of Love." *Theological Studies* 52 (1991) 330–44.

Eliot, Thomas Stearns. *Essays Ancient and Modern*. London: Faber and Faber, 1936.
———. *On Poetry and Poets*. 1957. Reprint. London: Faber and Faber, 1971.
———. *The Varieties of Metaphysical Poetry*. Edited by Ronald Schuchard. London: Faber and Faber, 1993.
Feiner, Johannes, and Magnus Löhrer, eds. *Die Heilsgeschichte vor Christus*. Mysterium Salutis: Grundriss Heilsgeschichtlicher Dogmatik 2. Köln: Benziger, 1967.
Finnegan, Thomas. Review of *The Erotic Phenomenon*, by Jean-Luc Marion. *Praxis* 1:2 (2008) 59–61.
Fitzgerald, Allan D, ed. *Augustine through the Ages: An Encyclopedia*. Grand Rapids: Eerdmans, 1999.
Frijda, Nico. *The Emotions*. Cambridge: Cambridge University Press, 1986.
Gallagher, Michael Paul. "Truth and Trust: Pierangelo Sequeri's Theology of Faith." *Irish Theological Quarterly* 73 (2008) 3–31.
Gavrilyuk, Paul L. *The Suffering of the Impassible God: The Dialectics of Patristic Thought*. Oxford: Oxford University Press, 2004.
Gilbert, of Hoyland. *Sermones in Cantica*. Patrologia Latina 184. Edited by Jacques-Paul Migne, 155–59. Paris: Garnier, 1844–55.
Goldie, Peter. *The Emotions: A Philosophical Exploration*. Oxford: Oxford University Press, 2000.
Gondreau, Paul. *The Passions of Christ's Soul in the Theology of St. Thomas Aquinas*. Münster: Aschendorf, 2002.
Gregory, of Nyssa. *Against Eunomius*. In *Gregory of Nyssa. Dogmatic Treatises Select Writings and Letters*. A Select Library of the Nicene and Post-Nicene Fathers of the Christian Church. Second series 5. Edited by Philip Schaff, 52–395. Online: http:/www.ccel.org/ccel/schaff/npnf205.html.
———. *On the Making of Man*. In *Gregory of Nyssa. Dogmatic Treatises, Select Writings and Letters*. A Select Library of the Nicene and Post-Nicene Fathers of the Christian Church. Second series 5. Edited by Philip Schaff, 606–72. Online: http://www.ccel.org/ccel/schaff/npnf205.x.ii.ii.xvii.html.
———. *On the Soul and the Resurrection*. In *Gregory of Nyssa. Dogmatic Treatises, Select Writings and Letters*. A Select Library of the Nicene and Post-Nicene Fathers of the Christian Church. Second series 5. Edited by Philip Schaff, 673–742. Online: http://www.ccel.org/ccel/schaff/npnf205.x.ii.ii.xvii.html.
Gregory, the Great. *Homiliarum in Evangelia. Homilia 17*. Patrologia Latina 76. Edited by Jacques-Paul Migne, 1138–49. Paris: Garnier, 1844–55.
Griffiths, Paul J. Review of *The Erotic Phenomenon*, by Jean-Luc Marion. *Commonweal* 134.5 (2007) 24–26.
Griffiths, Paul J., and Reinhard Hütter, eds. *Reason and the Reasons of Faith*. London: T. & T. Clark, 2005.
Hahn, Lewis Edwin, ed. *The Philosophy of Paul Ricoeur*. La Salle, IL: Open Court, 1995.
Hamman, Adalbert G. *L'Homme, Image de Dieu: Essai d'une anthropologie chrétienne dans l'Église des cinq premiers siècles*. Paris, Desclée, 1987.
Hart, Kevin, ed. *Counter-Experiences: Reading Jean-Luc Marion*. Notre Dame, IN: University of Notre Dame Press, 2007.
Henry, Michel. *L'essence de la manifestation*. 1963. Reprint. Paris: Presses Universitaires de France, 1990.
———. *Phénoménologie matérielle*. Paris: Presses Universitaires de France, 1990.

Irenaeus, of Lyon. *Against the Heresies*. In *The Apostolic Fathers with Justin Martyr and Irenaeus*. A Select Library of the Nicene and Post-Nicene Fathers of the Christian Church 1. Edited by Philip Schaff, 513–954. Online: http://www.ccel.org/ccel/schaff/anf01.html.
Jeanrond, Werner G. *A Theology of Love*. London: T. & T. Clark, 2010.
Jeanrond, Werner G., and Jennifer L. Rike, eds. *Radical Pluralism and Truth, David Tracy and the Hermeneutics of Religion*. New York: Crossroad, 1991.
Jelenits, István, and Teodóra Tomcsányi, eds. *Tanulmányok a vallás és a lélektan határterületeiről* [Studies from the Margins of Religion and Psychology]. Pécs, Hungary: Szeretetszolgálat, 1988.
Jesson, Stuart. Review of *The Erotic Phenomenon*, by Jean-Luc Marion. *International Journal of Systematic Theology* 10:1 (2008) 114–18.
John of Damascus. *Exposition of the Orthodox Faith*. In *Hilary of Poitiers, John of Damascus*. A Select Library of the Nicene and Post-Nicene Fathers of the Christian Church. Second Series 9. Edited by Philip Schaff and translated by Stewart. D. F. Salmond, 541–781. Online: http://www.ccel.org/ccel/schaff/npnf209.i.html.
John Paul II. *Letter to Families*. Città del Vaticano: Libreria Editrice Vaticana, 1994.
———. *Man and Woman He Created Them: A Theology of the Body*. Translated by Michael Waldstein. Boston: Pauline Books and Media, 2006.
———. *The Dignity of Women: Apostolic Letter of the Supreme Pontiff John Paul II on the Dignity and Vocation of Women on the Occasion of the Marian Year*. Dublin: Veritas, 1988.
———. The Splendor of Truth Shines: Encyclical Letter *Veritatis Splendor*. Città del Vaticano: Libreria Editrice Vaticana, 1993.
Kabdebo, Thomas, ed. *Attila József, Poems and Fragments*. Budapest: Argumentum, 1999.
Kant, Immanuel. *Critique of Pure Reason*. Translated by Norman Kemp Smith. New York: St. Martins, 1961.
Kerr, Fergus, ed. *Contemplating Aquinas: On the Varieties of Interpretation*. London: SCM, 2003.
Knuuttila, Simo. *Emotions in Ancient and Medieval Philosophy*. Oxford: Clarendon, 2004.
Lacoste, Jean-Yves, ed. *Dictionnaire Critique de Théologie*. Paris: Presses Universitaires de France/Quadrige, 2002.
Lactantius. *A Treatise on the Anger of God*. In *Fathers of the Third and Fourth Centuries: Lactantius, Venantius, Asterius, Victorinus, Dionysius, Apostolic Teaching and Constitutions, Homily, and Liturgies*. A Select Library of the Nicene and Post-Nicene Fathers of the Christian Church 7. Edited by Philip Schaff, 259–80. Online: http://www.ccel.org/ccel/schaff/anf07.html.
———. *Divine Institutes*. In *Fathers of the Third and Fourth Centuries: Lactantius, Venantius, Asterius, Victorinus, Dionysius, Apostolic Teaching and Constitutions, Homily, and Liturgies*. A Select Library of the Nicene and Post-Nicene Fathers of the Christian Church 7. Edited by Philip Schaff, 10–393. Online: http://www.ccel.org/ccel/schaff/anf07.html.
Leclercq, Jean. *L'amour vu par les moines au XII siècle*. Paris: Cerf, 1983.
Lemmens, Willem, and Walter Van Herck, eds. *Religious Emotions: Some Philosophical Explorations*. Newcastle, UK: Cambridge Scholars Publishing, 2008.
Letter of John Paul II to Women. Città del Vaticano: Libreria Editrice Vaticana, 1995.

Lewis, C. S. *The Four Loves*. San Diego: Harcourt Brace, 1960.
Lindberg, Carter. *A Brief History through Western Christianity*. Oxford: Blackwell, 2008.
Lobb, Edward. *T. S. Eliot and the Romantic Critical Tradition*. London: Routlegde and Kegan Paul, 1981.
Lombardo, Nicholas E. *The Logic of Desire: Aquinas on Emotion*. Washington, DC: The Catholic University of America Press, 2011.
MacDonald, Scott, and Eleonore Stump, eds. *Aquinas's Moral Theory: Essays in Honor of Norman Kretzman*. Ithaca, NY: Cornell University Press, 1999.
Manstead, Antony S. R. et al. eds. *Feelings and Emotions: The Amsterdam Symposium*. Cambridge: Cambridge University Press, 2004.
Marion, Jean-Luc. *Prolegomena to Charity*. Translated by Stephen E. Lewis. New York: Fordham University Press, 2002.
———. *The Erotic Phenomenon*. Translated by Stephen E. Lewis. Chicago: The University of Chicago Press, 2007.
Michon, Hélène. *L'Ordre du Coeur: Philosophie, Théologie et Mystique dans les Pensées de Pascal*. Paris: Honoré Champion, 1996.
Milbank, John. "Can a Gift Be Given? Prolegomena to a Future Trinitarian Metaphysic." *Modern Theology* 11 (1995) 119–61.
Mondin, Battista. *Dizionario enciclopedico del pensiero di San Tommaso D'Aquino*. Bologna: Studio Domenicano, 2000.
Morrow, Derek J. "The Love 'Without Being' That Opens (to) Distance, Part One: Exploring the Givenness of the Erotic Phenomenon With J-L. Marion." *The Heythrop Journal* 46:3 (2005) 281–98.
———. "The Love 'Without Being' That Opens (to) Distance, Part Two: From the Icon of Distance to the Distance of the Icon in Marion's Phenomenology of Love." *The Heythrop Journal* 46:4 (2005) 493–511.
Nemesius of Emesa. *On the Nature of Man*. Translated Texts for Historians 49. Edited by Mary Whitby et al., translated by Philip J. Van der Eijk. Liverpool: Liverpool University Press, 2008.
Nemes-Nagy, Ágnes. *51 Poems*. Translated by Peter Zollman. Budapest: Maecenas, 2007.
Nygren, Anders. *Agape and Eros*. Translated by Philip S. Watson. New York: Harper and Row, 1969.
O'Donovan, Oliver. *The Problem of Self-Love in St. Augustine*. New Haven, CT: Yale University Press, 1980.
O'Reilly, Kevin. *Aesthetic Perception: A Thomistic Perspective*. Dublin: Four Courts, 2007.
Oeuvres de Descartes. Edited by Charles Adam and Paul Tannery. Paris: Vrin, 1996.
Ottlik, Géza. *A Hungarian Quartet: Four Hungarian Short Novels*. Translated by John Bátki. Budapest: Corvina, 1991.
Pannenberg, Wolfhart. *What is Man? Contemporary Anthropology in Theological Perspective*. Translated by Duane A. Priebe. Philadelphia: Fortress, 1974.
Pascal, Blaise. *Thoughts*. Translated by W. F. Trotter. New York: Collier & Son, 1909. Online: http://etext.virginia.edu/toc/modeng/public/PasThou.html.
Pasqua, Hervé. *Blaise Pascal: Penseur de la Grace*. Paris: Téqui, 2000.
Pieper, Josef. *Faith, Hope, Love*. San Francisco, California: Ignatius, 1997.
Preminger, Alex, and Terry F. V. Brogan, eds. *The New Princeton Encyclopedia of Poetry and Poetics*. Princeton: Princeton University Press, 1993.

Pugmire, David. *Rediscovering Emotion*. Edinburgh: Edinburgh University Press, 1998.
Puskás, Attila. *A teremtés teológiája* [Theology of the Creation]. Budapest: Szent István Társulat, 2006.
Rad, Gerhard von. *Old Testament Theology. The Theology of Israel's Historical Traditions* 1. Edinburgh: Oliver and Boyd, 1973.
Reagan, Charles E., and David Stewart, eds. *The Philosophy of Paul Ricoeur: An Anthology of His Work*. Boston: Beacon, 1978.
Reagan, Charles E., ed. *Studies in the Philosophy of Paul Ricoeur*. Athens, OH: Ohio University Press, 1979.
Richard, of St. Victor. *Tractatus de Gradibus Caritatis*. Patrologia Latina 196. Edited by Jacques-Paul Migne, 1195–1224. Paris: Garnier, 1844–55.
———. *De Trinitate*. Patrologia Latina 196. Edited by Jacques-Paul Migne, 887–994. Paris: Garnier, 1844–55.
Ricoeur, Paul. *The Course of Recognition*. Translated by David Pellauer. Cambridge: Harvard University Press, 2005.
———. *Fallible Man*. New York: Fordham University Press, 1986.
———. *Freedom and Nature: The Voluntary and the Involuntary*. Translated by Erazim V. Kohák. Evanston, IL: Northwestern University Press, 1966.
———. "The Metaphorical Process as Cognition, Imagination, and Feeling." *Critical Inquiry* 5:1 (1978) 143–59.
———. *Oneself as Another*. Translated by Kathleen Blamey. Chicago: University of Chicago Press, 1992.
———. *Philosophie de la volonté*. 1: *Le volontaire et l'involontaire*. Paris: Aubier, 1949.
———. *The Symbolism of Evil*. Translated by Emerson Buchanan. New York: Harper and Row, 1967.
Rousselot, Pierre. *The Problem of Love in the Middle Ages*. Translated by Alan Vincelette. Milwaukee, WI: Marquette University Press, 2001.
Schnelle, Udo. *Neutestamentliche Anthropologie*. Neukirchen/Vluyn: Neukirchener Verlag, 1991.
Schoot, Henk J. M., ed. *Tibi Soli Peccavi: Thomas Aquinas on Guilt and Forgiveness*. Leuven: Peeters, 1996.
Schreiner, Josef. *Theologie des Alten Testaments*. Würzburg: Echter, 1995.
Sellier, Philippe. *Pascal et Saint Augustin*. Paris: Librairie Armand Colin, 1970.
Shults, F. LeRon. *Reforming Theological Anthropology*. Grand Rapids: Eerdmans, 2003.
Smith, J. Warren. *Passion and Paradise: Human and Divine Emotion in the Thought of Gregory of Nyssa*. New York: Crossroad, 2004.
Smitheram, Verner. "Man, Mediation and Conflict in Ricoeur's *Fallible Man*." *Philosophy Today* 25:4 (1981) 357–69.
Spicq, Ceslas. *Agapè dans le Nouveau Testament: analyse des textes*. Paris: Gabalda, 1958–59.
———. *Theological Lexicon of the New Testament* 1. Translated and edited by James D. Ernest. Peabody, MA: Hendrickson, 1994.
Stiver, Dan R. *Theology After Ricoeur: New Directions in Hermeneutical Theology*. Louisville, KY: Westminster John Knox, 2001.
Stump, Eleonore. *Wandering in Darkness*. Oxford: Clarendon, 2010.
Tertullian. *Against Marcion*. In *The Apostolic Fathers with Justin Martyr and Irenaeus. A Select Library of the Nicene and Post-Nicene Fathers of the Christian Church* 3.

Edited by Philip Schaff, 271–474. Online: http://www.ccel.org/ccel/schaff/anf03.html.

———. *On the Resurrection of the Flesh*. In *The Apostolic Fathers with Justin Martyr and Irenaeus*. A Select Library of the Nicene and Post-Nicene Fathers of the Christian Church 3. Edited by Philip Schaff, 545–94. Online: http://www.ccel.org/ccel/schaff/anf03.html.

Thunberg, Lars. *Microcosm and Mediator: The Theological Anthropology of Maximus the Confessor*. La Salle, IL: Open Court, 1995.

Viller, Marcel, and Ferdinand Cavallera, eds. *Dictionnaire de Spiritualité: ascetique et mystique, doctrine et histoire*. Paris: Beauchesne, 1983.

Wainwright, William J. *Reason and the Heart: A Prolegomenon to a Critique of Passional Reason*. Ithaca, NY: Cornell University Press, 1995.

West, Christopher. *Theology of the Body Explained: A Commentary on John Paul II's "Gospel of the Body."* Leominster, UK: Gracewing, 2003.

Westermann, Claus. *Genesis. Kapitel 1–3*. Berlin: EVA, 1985.

William, of St. Thierry. *Expositio super Cantica*. Patrologia Latina 180. Edited by Jacques-Paul Migne. 473–546. Paris: Garnier, 1844–55.

———. *Speculum Fidei*. Patrologia Latina 159. Edited by Jacques-Paul Migne. 365–98. Paris: Garnier, 1844–55.

Wolff, Hans Walter. *Anthropology of the Old Testament*. London: SCM, 1974.

Wynands, Sandra. Review of *The Erotic Phenomenon*, by Jean-Luc Marion. *Christianity and Literature* 57:1 (2007) 142–46.

Zalta, Edward N, ed. *The Stanford Encyclopedia of Philosophy*. Online: http://plato.stanford.edu/.

Subject Index

Adam, 74–75, 77, 84, 102, 106, 109, 110, 114, 120, 163, 216–17
affectivity, 11, 15, 55, 68, 100, 115, 122, 143–55, 156, 218, ancient Greek theories, 123–28, duality, 33–53, of God 134–43, and the heart in John Paul II, 227–39, logic of, x–xiv, of love in Marion, 206–13, in the original state, 101–14, patristic theories, 129–33, Ricoeur's account, 44–60; sensible and intellectual, 170–91, theological account, 14–20, Thomas Aquinas's account, 114–22
affectus, 132
agapē. *See* love.
Albert, the Great, 116
anger, 102, 103, 111, 122, 126, 127, 146, 153, 236, in God, 135–37, 140–43
anthropology, theological, xi, xii, 7, 57, 156, 172, 180, 216, 217, 228, biblical a. of the image, 68–76, and the Fall, 101–14, of the heart, 143–55, 232–39, John Paul II's a. of the image, 93–100, Pascal's philosophical a., 26–29, 115, 133, patristic a. of the image, 76–90, and philosophical a. 60–67, Ricoeur's philosophical a., 21–26, 30–53, Thomas Aquinas's a. of the image, 90–93
apatheia. *See* impassibility.
apathēs. 79, 129. *See also* impassibility.

Aquinas, Thomas. *See* Thomas Aquinas.
Aristotle 30, 38, 45, 48, 101, 116, 124, 125, 126, 167
Athanasius, of Alexandria 82–83, 88
Augustine, of Hippo, ix, 88, 91, 92, 94, 128, 130, 132, 145, 148, 160, 172, 174, 189, 191, 199, 235, and Aquinas, 112–16, on feeling in God, 137–39, and image theology, 85–86, and Pascal, 6–9, 29, 61, on passions in the original state, 108–11

Balthasar, Hans Urs von, 10, 18, 19, 87, on God's anger, 141–43
Benedict, XVI, 161, 162
Bernard, of Clairvaux, 17, 166, and physical and ecstatic conceptions of love, 171–76
body, xiii, 11, 23, 27, 28, 29, 35, 37, 56, 58, 71, 74, 75, 95, 132, 133, 137, 138, 140, 141, 151, 155, 161, 163, 170, 172, 173, 178, 229, 230, 238, and ancient emotion theories, 124–26, and anthropology, 64–67, and charity in Aquinas, 189–91, and christology in Thomas Aquinas, 116–22, and concupiscence, 110–13, and emotionality, 233–39, and erotic love in Marion, 192–213, as flesh in Marion, 200–202, 203–8, and the image in John Paul II, 93–100, and the image

in Thomas Aquinas, 90–93, John Paul II's theology of, 214–26, language of, 227–30, and the original state in patristic thought, 101–11, and the original state in Thomas Aquinas, 112–14, and patristic image theology, 76–90, and sensual passions, 144–48, 179–85

Cappadocian fathers, 106
Christ, Jesus, 66, 77, 78, 81, 82, 83, 88, 89, 94, 107, 108, 127, 135, 140, 141, 142, 146, 163, 166, 189, 203, 161, 216, 228, 236, and affectivity, 114–22, as God's image, 73–76
Cicero, Marcus Tullius, 128
Clement, of Alexandria, 80, 81, 88, 131
concupiscence, 50, 110–14, 173, love of c. in Aquinas, 183–84, 216
Cyril, of Alexandria, 89, 242

demut, 72. *See also* image of God.
Descartes, René, 30, 31, 34, 53, 54, 193, 197
desire, 168, 184, 186, 190, 195, 198, 202, 211, 213, 230, 232, and Greco-Thomist concept of love, 170–73
Dionysius, the Areopagite, 164
disproportion, of the human person, 1, 7, 225, in Pascal, 27–29, in Ricoeur, 23–26, 30–53, 56, 225, 232
duality, of human existence, 10, 34, 35, 37, 64, 65, 100, 154, 161, 219, 232, of affectivity, 40–51, of body and flesh, 207, Gnostic dualism, 76, of love, 174–79, Manichean dualism, 190, Platonic dualism, 89, substance dualism, 22, 25

Eliot, Thomas Stearns, 3, 4, 5, 12
emotionality. *See* affectivity.
emotions, 48, 52, 149, 152, corporeal and intellectual, 179–91, in erōs and agapē, 163–79, 231–39, and God, 134–43, good and bad, 102–14, 128–33, 146–47, 235–36, in John Paul II's account, 214–30, in Marion's account, 192–231, passions of Christ's soul, 114–22, propassion, 122, 127, pseudopassions, 147–48, and reason, 1–20, Ricoeur's theory, 49–60, and theology, ix–xiv, 231–39
Enlightenment, x, 13, 14, 16, 17, 83, 141, 149, 151, 162, 207, 227
epithumia, 43, 44, 51, 106
erotic reduction, 160, 169, 198–213, 221
erōs. *See* love.
evil, 21, 22, 23, 24, 25, 29, 30, 32, 33, 39, 45, 47, 54, 59, 62, 105, 107, 109, 112, 114, 116, 120, 128, 130, 135, 136, 141, 148, 153, 167, 212, 233,
ex opere operato, 97, 204

faith, x, 1, 63, 66, 74, 76, 91, 148, 150, 160, 207, and agapē, 161–65, in Pascal, 9–12, 18, 28, and reason, 12–17, 56–60
Fall, 23, 25, 30–34, 40, 41, 47, 58, 110, 233
finitude, Marion's account, 202–3, 217, Ricoeur's account, 21, 22, 23, 25, 33–40, 44–51, 154,
flesh. *See* body.

Genesis, 32, 41, 68, 94, 102, 109, 111, 163, 233, 234, and the image of God, 68–77, and John Paul II's account, 214–26, and patristic accounts, 76–90
gift, 12, 13, 15, 17, 63, 66, 72, 78, 79, 82, 84, 87, 89, 96, 97, 107, 113, 135, 162, 163, 174, 176, 179, 184, 196, 207, 211, 212, 215, 217, 218, hermeneutics of, 221–26, nonidentical repetition of, 223, radical g., 197–202, 220, reciprocal g., 223, 225, unilateral g., 223

Gilbert, of Hoyland, 175, 176
Gregory, of Nyssa, 27, 83–85, 88, 95, 102–5, 107, 144, 145
Gregory, the Great 141, 174, 176

happiness xii, 26, 55, 115, 116, 145, 154, 155, 161, 172, 185, 190, 218, 235, Ricoeur's account, 37–40, 44–53, 232–33, in the state of original innocence, 109–14, 223–25
heart, iv, x–xiv, 14, 15, 19, 26, 29, 70, 97, 98, 101, 143–55, 166, 167, 177, 178, 183, 191, 231–39, John Paul II's account, 226–30, Marion's account, 160, 192, 206–8, 210, 212, 216, Pascal's account, 5–12, Ricoeur's account, 40–60
Henry, Michel, 64, 195, 207
hermeneutics, 22, 23, 24, 25, 95, 208, 221, 224
homoiōsis, 129, 130. See also image, of God.
Hugh, of St. Victor, 171

icon, 195
image, of God, xii, xiii, 14, 57, 60, 64, 67, 122, 140, 143, 156, 160, 163, 164, 233–37 in the Bible, 68–75, and emotionality, 101–14, 131–33, in John Paul II, 93–100, 214, 216–26, and likeness in patristic thought, 76–90, in Thomas Aquinas, 91–93, 180–91
imago Dei. 66, 67, 68, 76, 86, 101. See also image, of God.
immutability. See impassibility.
impassibility, of God, xiii, 134–43, human, 119, 106–7, 108–11, 111–14, 121, 122–33, 146, 156, 235
intellectual appetite, 117, 181–91
intellectus, 9, 11, 138. See also reason.
Irenaeus, of Lyon, 76–78, 79, 81, 87, 89, 94

Jerome, Saint, 121, 127

John Paul II, theology of the body, 93–100, 214–30, 234
John, of Damascus, 116
John, of the Cross, 93

Kant, Immanuel, 30, 35, 38, 47, 56, 93

Lactantius, 132–33, 136–37, 141–42
likeness, of God. See image, of God.
love, 11, 15, 16, 17, 93, and Christian account of affectivity, x–xiv, 231–39, and Christ's affectivity, 120–22, divine, 60, 90, 134–43, 210, erōs and agapē, 161–65, 165–70, and human impassibility, 122–33, Marion's univocal concept, 158–61, 192–202, and patristic image theology, 102–14, philia, 46, 167–68, and reason, 14, 18, 19–20, sensible and intellectual/spiritual, 44–53, 145–55, 156–58, 170–79, 179–91, 202–13, and theology of the body, 95–100, 214–26, 226–30

Manicheans, 85
Marion, Jean-Luc, 64, 158–61, 169, 192–213, 214, 215, 216, 220, 221, 229, 238
Maximus, the Confessor, 86–87, 88, 98, 106–7, 130, 144, 145
mediation, xii, xiii, 18, 65, 66, 85, 88, 207, and the body, 96–100, between the fallen and the primordial, 32–34, between finitude and infinitude, 34–40, and the heart, 40–60, 154, 231–39, and love, 178–79, 190–91, 208–9, 210–213, between the sensible and the intelligible, 29–32, 107, 146, 148, 207
mens, 85–86. See also reason.
Milbank, John, 134, 135, 136, 141, 207, 211, 212–13, 214, 215, 217, 223,

Nemesius, of Emesa, 116

noūs, 75, 79–90, 151, 158, 237. *See also* reason.
Nygren, Anders, 160

Origen, of Alexandria, 81–82, 85, 87, 88, 104, 109, 127, 129, 131
original innocence, state of, xiii, 156, 235, 236, John Paul II's account, 214–26, and patristic thought, 101–14, 131–33, 134–36, 144–45, Thomas Aquinas's account, 120, 111–14

Pascal, Blaise, 1, 5–12, 26–29, 30
passions. *See* emotions.
passio, 118. *See also* emotions.
pathē, 81, 108, 128. *See also* emotions.
Paul, Saint, 49, 74, 92, 167
Pesch, Otto Hermann, xiii, 63
Peter, Lombard, 91, 119, 179
phenomenology, 15, 22–25, 170, 178, 184, 196–202, 202–13, 215, 223, 230, 238
philia. *See* love.
Philo, of Alexandria, 79–80, 81, 83
Pieper, Josef, 160
Plato, 14, 30, 43–49, 79, 80, 101, 123–26
pleasure, xii, 130, 153, 154, 155, 159, 166, 167, 185, 188, 209, 226, 228, 232, and finitude, 44–53, and the original state, 105–14, 144–45, in Plato and Aristotle, 124–26
Plotinus, 129
Posidonius, 83

Rad, Gerhard von, 69, 70, 71, 72
Rahner, Karl, 62
ratio, 8, 9, 12, 13, 15. *See also* reason.
reason, 63, 157, 164, 172, and affectivity, ix–xiv, 1–5, 12–17, 18–20, 134–43, 179–91, 210, 231–39, and ancient emotion theories, 122–31, and biblical image theology, 68–76, and dissociation in Ricoeur, 21–26, 30, 34–37, 38, 39–53, 54–56, 60, and the heart, 5–12, 143–55, 160, 226–30, and human disproportion in Pascal, 26–29, and John Paul II's theology of the body, 93–100, logos, 165, and patristic image theology, 76–90, 101–14, and Thomistic image theology, 90–93, 114–22
relationality, 65–67, 72, 76, 153, 227, 237
Richard, of St. Victor, 174, 175
Ricoeur, Paul, 21–26, 29–60, 62, 64, 155, 208, 209, 213, 217–18, 225, 232
Romantic movement, 149
Rousselot, Pierre, 160, 169–79, 181

Scheler, Max, 64, 93
selem, 72. *See also* image of God.
sensibility, dissociation of, 3–5, 12. *See also* affectivity.
sensitive appetite, 116–19, 121, 140, 157, 182–87
Solomon, Robert C., 53–56
Song of Songs, 94, 132, 175, 216, 219, 226–30
soul, 17, 27, 30, 33, 34, 42, 52, 55, 64, 65, 66, 75, 138, 140, 141, 161, 172, 174, 176, 192, 193, 199, 200, 218, and the emotions, 101–14, 122–33, 144–55, faculties of, 8–11, 43–44, 180–91, and the image of God, 77–100, 233–39, passions of Christ's s., xi, 115–22
Stoicism, 108, 109, 119, 122, 124, 126–30

Tertullian, 78–79, 81, 87, 94
Thomas Aquinas, xi, xiii, 9, 11, 17, 47, 48, 50, 108, 110, 124, 134, 148, 150, 164, 171, 172, 175–76, 199, 236–38, and Christology, 114–22, 127–28, on God's impassibility, 139–41, and image theology, 90–93, 94, 95, 234, on love, 179–91, on the original state, 111–14, 130, 145–47
Thomism, 237

thumos, 43–53, 54, 58, 60. *See also* heart.
trace, of God, 92–93, 94, 137, 189, 234
Trinity, ix, 66–67, 82, 85, 90–91, 97, 137, 142, 172

vestigium, 92. *See also* trace.

will, 10, 11, 16, 29, 30, 71, 78, 83, 128, 237, and the emotions, 147–55, and the Fall, 104–14, 145–46, God's, 137, 140–41, goodwill, 157, and love, 164, 182–91, 193–202, 208, 210, 211, Ricoeur's philosophy of, 21–26, 34–40, 54–56, in Thomas Aquinas, 115–18, 121
William, of Auvergne, 174
William, of St. Thierry, 176
Wolff, Hans Walter, 71–72, 101, 152, 153
Wolfhart, Pannenberg, 62

www.ingramcontent.com/pod-product-compliance
Lightning Source LLC
Chambersburg PA
CBHW030823230426
43667CB00008B/1350